THE CONDITIONS FOR ADMISSION

THE CONDITIONS
FOR ADMISSION

*Access, Equity, and the Social Contract
of Public Universities*

JOHN AUBREY DOUGLASS

STANFORD UNIVERSITY PRESS

Stanford, California

2007

Printed in the United States of America on acid-free,
archival-quality paper

Library of Congress Cataloging-in-Publication Data

Douglass, John Aubrey.
    The conditions for admission : access, equity, and
the social contract of public universities / John Aubrey
Douglass.
        p.   cm.
    Includes bibliographical references and index.
    ISBN 978-0-8047-5558-0 (cloth : alk. paper)—
ISBN 978-0-8047-5559-7 (pbk. : alk. paper)
        1. Public universities and colleges—United States—
Admission.   2. Educational equalization—United States.
I. Title.   II. Title: Access, equity, and the social contract
of public universities.

LB2351.2.D68 2007
378.1'610973—dc22
                                            2006100234

Typeset by Newgen in 10.5/13 Bembo

To my inspiring daughters,
Claire and Aubrey,
and my beloved Jill

CONTENTS

Figures

Why most states chose to create public universities in the mid-1800s and, in essence, to reject a model of private institutions solely fulfilling the higher education needs of the United States marks a profound shift in the course of the nation's development. It is a choice that relatively few historians have broached in much detail. Yet the character of our contemporary public universities and, arguably, much of the nation's economic growth and its relatively high rates of socioeconomic mobility relate directly to this powerful movement.

The route to mass higher education in the United States came through the progressive attempts of state governments to create public universities, buttressed and prodded at key moments by federal funding aid and influence. Although it began slowly, no other nation embarked with such enthusiasm on a model of widely accessible higher education. A remarkable aspect of this early push to establish public universities was the relatively low initial demand. The actual number of Americans enrolling in some form of higher education would remain small well into the twentieth century. Government and public university leaders ventured to nurture and encourage this demand; the charters of these institutions and their subsequent admissions policies sought wide participation among America's population—although with many ugly caveats—that formed a *social contract* that grew more expansive and more complex over time.

Research for this book began as I was completing another on how California developed its pioneering higher education system, *The California Idea and American Higher Education* (Stanford University Press, 2000). More than midway through that effort, I was asked by the University of California's academic senate to develop a series of policy briefs on the development of admissions policy at the university focused on the question of authority for "setting the conditions of admission": the faculty, the university's board of regents, or the administration. This request came just after the board of regents decided in 1995 to effectively end affirmative action and, more specifically, the use of race and ethnicity as factors in admission, hiring, and contracting. These reports helped support ideas for alternative approaches to admissions and successfully advocated a greater faculty role in setting not only admissions standards but in overseeing the actual process of admissions—a revival of the senate's historical responsibilities.

As I delved into the university's early efforts to set the conditions for admissions and to broaden participation in California higher education, and assessed the highly charged political environment surrounding university admissions, I sensed there was an important need to tell a tale central to the American experience; my hope was also to enlighten contemporary policymakers and the public on the historical purpose of public universities.

Archival resources form the basis of most of the early chapters in this book, including extensive use of the University of California's main archives located at the Bancroft Library on the Berkeley campus, the records of the University of California board of regents located in the University of California Office of the President in Oakland, the records of the university's academic senate, the California State Library, and the California State Archives in Sacramento. I also made trips to the archives of a number of major universities, including Pennsylvania State University and the University of Michigan, and I made use of a growing body of digital resources that include original charters and other documents related to the University of Virginia, the City University of New York, MIT, the University of Wisconsin, and other institutions.

The work of previous historians also greatly informed and shaped my analysis, particularly Harold S. Wechsler's *The Qualified Student* (1977) and Marcia Graham Synnott's *The Half Open Door* (1979). These and other important works reflected to some degree a fascination with the admissions policies at Ivy League and similar selective private institutions. But there is a dearth of analysis regarding the unique history and mission of public universities and a general lack of understanding regarding the complex and very different political world in which they must operate. As I argue in later chapters of this book, and while reserving an important role for the nation's collection of private colleges and universities, the future of America's democratic experiment and its global economic competitiveness are tied directly to the future vitality of its public universities.

Over the course of my research, I interviewed or discussed admissions policy and the role of public universities with a number of higher education leaders, most whom reviewed various chapters or related articles, including Clark Kerr, David Gardner, Albert Bowker, Jack Peltason, Michael Ire Heyman, Karl Pister, Robert Berdahl, and Richard Atkinson (all were, at one time, a University of California chancellor or president of the system), David Ward, and Katharine C. Lyall. Various colleagues read portions of the manuscript and offered their criticisms and constructive comments as well. They include Marian Gade, who offered many important critiques and corrections, Pat Hayashi, C. Judson King, Philo Hutchinson, Bruce Leslie, Todd Greenspan, and Pamela Burdman. John R. Thelin, in particular, provided me with perhaps the most beneficial overall review of the evolving manuscript.

I was also influenced by discussions and written works by a host of colleagues, including Martin Trow, Tom Kane, William G. Tierney, Warren Fox, Bruce Hamlett, Bruce Johnstone, Norton Grubb, Philip Altbach, Brian Pusser, Robert Shireman, Sheldon Rothblatt, Arnie Lieman, Daniel Simmons, Keith Widaman, Duncan Mellichamp, Steven Brint, Margaret Miller, Roger Geiger, Calvin Moore, Richard Flacks, Rudy Alverez, and Dennis Galligani. Particularly in reference to the last two chapters related to higher education policy among competitor nations, I gained the input of a number of non-American scholars, including David Palfreyman and Ted Tapper at the Oxford Centre for Studies in Higher Education, Sarah Guri-Rosenblit, Guy Neave, Michael Shattock, Gareth Perry, Clark Brundin, Roger Brown, Celia M. Whitchurch, Marijk van der Wende, and Christine Musselin. Final work on the manuscript occurred while I was a visiting professor at Science Po, and discussion with faculty and graduates there and with colleagues at the OECD on the path of reform in the European Union helped fashion additional observations in these final chapters.

Kate Wahl and others at Stanford University Press provided much needed guidance and an enthusiasm for the topic and content of the resulting book. My thanks to Andy Sieverman for his assistance in the final production of the manuscript.

Finally, it appears a cliché but it is an irrefutable truth that family and friends make all the difference in a large and time-consuming venture. My deepest of thanks and indebtedness to my wife, Jill Shinkle, who patiently and critically read numerous reiterations of chapters; a smile for my two daughters, Claire and Aubrey, who watched as I toiled in my home office through a number of ups and downs. I also have been informed by friends and acquaintances with children who, captured by the modern competition to get their child into the right college or university, regularly conversed about the dynamics of admissions practices at selective institutions.

Attesting to the primacy of higher education in the postmodern world, many students in the United States, and increasingly throughout the world, are intensely vying for a place at a brand-name college and university. For public universities in the business of, essentially, dispersing a highly sought public good, this means increased scrutiny and political pressure. How these essential institutions have made these choices, and how they may do it in the future, is the subject of this book.

John Aubrey Douglass
Center for Studies in Higher Education
University of California—Berkeley
November 2006

THE CONDITIONS FOR ADMISSION

Part I

Building a Public University and Creating the Social Contract

Chapter 1

The Public University Movement and California

Among the universities of America there is none which has sprung up by itself like Bologna or Paris or El Azhar or Oxford, none founded by an Emperor like Prague, or by a Pope like Glasgow. All have been the creatures of private munificence or denominational zeal or State action. Their history is short indeed compared with that of the universities of Europe. Yet it is full of interest, for it shows a steady growth, it records many experiments, it gives valuable data for comparing the educational results of diverse systems.

—Lord James Bryce, *The American Commonwealth*, 1891

Now comes the turn of this new "Empire State." California, queen of the Pacific, is to speak from her golden throne, and decree the future of her University.

—Daniel Coit Gilman, inaugural address as the second the president of the University of California, 1872

In 1872, three years after the completion of the transcontinental railroad, Daniel Coit Gilman boarded a train in New Haven, Connecticut. It was the start of a journey that lasted just over a week, a dramatic new chapter in the opening of the American West. Gilman, a geographer, historian, and well-known member of the nation's emerging scientific community, was leaving Yale's Sheffield Scientific School to become the second president of the University of California, a new land-grant university chartered in 1868. There were a number of reasons he exchanged the prestige of Yale for California. One was the relatively low status Yale faculty gave to the sciences and to practical training—a common feature of most private colleges and the smattering of private institutions that called themselves universities. Yale would eventually change in this regard, but it was slow in doing so, and Gilman was impatient. Another reason was more personal: His wife had recently died, leaving him to raise two young daughters, the younger of whom had become ill.

California offered a milder climate and a new setting, far from the memories of New Haven. But perhaps the most compelling reason for his journey to California was the opportunity to shape one of the nation's new state universities. The University of California was to be a modern public university, serving the broad needs of society, embracing literature *and* the

3

sciences and professions, and as Gilman observed, it "would be open to all" and not simply to a privileged social class.

On November 8, 1872, Gilman arrived at ten in the morning at the Oakland train station. There was no time for a period of rest at a local hotel. There to greet him was a large crowd that included members of the university's board of regents, faculty, prominent members of California society, and local politicians. A group of university cadets, nearly all the current male students of the California's sole land-grant university, helped form a procession.[1] Gilman was to be formally inaugurated as the new university president that very day. With no suitable hall yet built on the new campus located in the Berkeley hills, the procession ended not at the university, but at Oakland's Congregational Church. California's state university was a devoutly nonsectarian institution but not a godless one.

Less than two hours after arriving in Oakland, Gilman approached the podium to give his inaugural speech. He had never been to California; indeed, he had never been west of the Mississippi. Gilman was forty-one and, as described in one local San Francisco newspaper, "an active, energetic apostle of the new and progressive school of education."[2] Looking out on his audience, Gilman noted the important progress made by the nation's major higher education institutions, including Yale, Harvard, and Princeton. In short, they were becoming universities that reflected both European and evolving American norms.

Yet the nascent public university movement in the United States was distinct, something quite different from the private institutions that dominated the Northeast and much of the American Midwest. It was a new and bold experiment that captured the interest of an emerging generation of academic leaders such as Gilman. These were not traditional colleges that embraced reluctantly the Enlightenment and its progeny, the physical sciences, engineering, and agricultural sciences. The founders and constituents of public universities were not the small and largely sectarian cohort who populated the governance boards, occupied the presidencies of the institutions, hired like-minded faculty, and welcomed largely a limited cadre of socially and religiously acceptable students—the typical behavior of most private colleges and the small group of institutions such as Yale.

The purpose of public universities was more grand and populist, and more complex: Their assignment was to meet the social and economic needs of the states that chartered them, to open their doors to a broad swath of society, and to build departments and programs that both taught a classical curriculum and promoted scientific inquiry intended to develop and support local economies. Public universities were also an essential part of a larger cause; they were to help build a state system of public education, stretching from the local primary school to the university, and thereby fundamentally reshape social and economic opportunity. Honoring these ideals and considering the practical problems of making them a reality, Gilman told his receptive audience, "It is not the University of Berlin, or of New Haven" that was to be built, nor was it to be "the University of Oakland, or San Francisco, it is the University of the State which created it." And in that effort, he stated, "it must be adapted to its people, to their public and private schools, to their peculiar geographic position, to their undeveloped resources. It is not the foundation of an ecclesiastical body, or of private individuals. It is of the people and for the people—not in any low or unworthy sense, but in the highest and noblest relation to their intellectual and moral well-being."[3]

Gilman's vision was not a unique one. The state legislature and people of California expected as much. In the midst of forging their own public universities, lawmakers and presidents in other states had recently made similar statements of a broad social mandate, invoking egalitarian promises. In the early stages of the public university movement, the 1816 charter for Indiana's state university, for instance, called for a university open to all who graduated from "township schools" and "equally open to all." At the University of Michigan, President James Burrill Angell famously stated in his 1879 inaugural speech that Michigan's public university was established to provide "an uncommon education for the common man." Andrew White, the founding president of Cornell, exclaimed that in the development of state universities lay "the educational hope of the South and West." While reserving an important role for private institutions, Stanford's first president, David Starr Jordan, stated that the public university was the "coming glory of democracy," the "most wonderful thing in educational development since Alfred found Oxford and Charlemagne Paris."[4] A few decades after Gilman's speech, the University of Wisconsin's president insisted that public universities formed part of the "soul of the state." The "state owns the university; and every citizen feels himself to be a stockholder in that ownership."[5] It was incumbent on public universities to help build educational opportunity, to open its doors to the people, and essentially, to push the demand for a higher education and supply it.

As Gilman also noted in his inaugural speech, a university was not merely a high school, a college, an academy of science, or an industrial school. Some element of each might be part of a university, but a university must be more, much more. Gilman defined the university as a comprehensive institution intended "for the promotion and diffusion of knowledge." At the time of his inaugural speech, the University of California was a single campus with only two buildings nestled in Strawberry Canyon in the Berkeley hills. Some 182 students were enrolled, including thirty-nine women; the university had only thirteen faculty members.

Today, the University of California is a vast enterprise, serving a state with the largest population in the United States and with an economy that ranks among the top eight largest in the world. With ten campuses and more than 210,000 students, the University of California has become the largest research university system in the nation and arguably the most prestigious. California's land-grant university is also one of the nation's most selective institutions in its admissions standards and has often been at the center of heated national debates over who deserves access to a limited and highly sought educational good.

This book provides an historical study of the admission policies and practices of public universities in the United States, linking their evolving "social contract" with contemporary debates over affirmative action, standardized tests, changing definitions of merit, the influences of privatization and globalization, and the very purpose and future of these important institutions. At their founding, public universities devised a *social contract* that included the profoundly progressive idea that any citizen who met a prescribed set of largely academic conditions would gain entrance to their state university—a sharp contrast to most private institutions that, throughout most of their history, proactively used sectarian and racial, and sometimes social caste, criteria to exclude groups. Further, public universities sought to proactively mitigate barriers to access. How that social contract was formed, how it grew and has changed, its successes and failures, and the accompanying political battles, both past and present, over its meaning is the subject of the following chapters.

Throughout much of the narrative, a case study of the University of California provides an illuminating window for exploring the historical and contemporary role of sectarianism, geographic representation, economic background, social standing, gender, and race in the evolving admissions policies of America's public *and* private universities. Within its 1868 state charter, California's state university was charged with the responsibility of "setting the conditions for admission." How the University of California went about the important business of determining access is a complex social and political history, marked by the ideal of achieving broad access with the difficulties of constructing actual admissions policies. In telling this story, one objective is to bring the original purposes of a major public university more clearly into view. The intent is to give context for contemporary debates and perhaps to arm academic leaders, lawmakers, and the public with a stronger sense of the broad social purposes of America's groundbreaking grand tradition of public universities.

As chronicled in the following pages, the question of who should or should not have access to a widely perceived and increasingly sought public good is not new, but it has changed in its intensity, in the stakes for individuals, and in its role in creating a more equitable and prosperous society. In the postmodern and globalizing economy, access to higher education continues to grow mightily as a determinant of socioeconomic mobility and global competitiveness. Within a highly stratified network of public and private higher education institutions in the United States, demand for access to the most prestigious colleges and universities is now mind-bogglingly competitive; moreover, it will escalate to greater heights as the population grows and the value of a higher education for the individual and for regional and national economic competitiveness becomes even more essential.

At the same time, there are relatively new and troubling signs of a weakened resolve in the United States to support the historic purposes of public universities. These institutions are seeking other financial resources and, really for the first time, threatening to shift their allegiances. Under these circumstances, the social contract is undergoing a metamorphosis that may not be advantageous to socioeconomic mobility and the nation's long-term economic competitiveness in a globalizing economy. There are deliberate and substantial efforts by other competitor nations to surpass America's higher education access and degree completion rates. It is not clear that the United States, as a first mover in creating both mass higher education and a progressive and high-quality network of public universities, will retain its historic higher education advantage. Now is a good time to assess the success of the social contract and to ponder the future of America's public university movement and, in turn, the nation's democratic experiment.

Identifying the Social Contract

To a degree perhaps unmatched by any other single institution in our society or by any other nation in the world, America's public universities were conceived, funded, and developed as tools of socioeconomic engineering—an observation that is perhaps uncomfortable for those who view markets and the rugged individual as the hallmark of the nation's development. These institutions were to benefit the individual not as a goal unto themselves but as a means to shape a more progressive and productive society. In that cause, they were to open their doors to the farmer and laborer, as well as the more well to do—to all that demonstrated academic and civic talent. They were to be devoid of sectarian and political influence in choosing students, to serve communities in all corners of a given state, and to offer a practical, as well as classical, curriculum, with special emphasis on the professions of agriculture, the mechanical arts, mining, military science, civil engineering, law, medicine, and commerce.

These principles were articulated in the early debates on education's role in America's evolving republic and in the charters of the first wave of public universities. If America was to be the most educated, the most democratic, the most inventive, and the most prosperous country in the world, it would need broadly accessible schools *and* a set of public universities. Indeed, the two institutions were deemed inseparable by many of America's earliest political leaders, part of an emerging comprehensive system of education that would make the United States an enlightened leader among the nations of the world. This grand vision, of course, met the hard realities of an American society torn by racial strife and economic hardship. Yet through the common school movement and the push by states, often with the help of the federal government, to create great public universities, the ideal remained. Broad and equitable access to a quality education, and the role of government to make that happen, is an integral part of the nation's political culture.

In building higher education systems, states made progress at different rates. Over time, however, their actions and those of academic leaders collectively grew to include five core and interrelated responsibilities that helped define and give meaning to the *social contract* of public universities. Each influenced the admissions practices of public universities, and each emerged in one form or another largely by the early twentieth century. Each has undergone marginal forms of redefinition as public universities and society have changed over time.

1. Public universities have been duty bound to primarily serve the constituents of the state that have chartered, funded, and regulated their establishment and development—a conceptual starting point that has frayed marginally with the increased influence of federal funding and now, more recently, the forces of globalization.

2. Public universities have a responsibility to operate as components and partners of a much larger public education system that includes public schools and, over time, an emerging network of complementary public ter-

tiary institutions; indeed, historically, public universities have had special responsibilities to help nurture these other institutions.

3. Public universities must encourage participation in higher education by setting clear admissions criteria (or conditions) that, if met, offer access to any citizen regardless, in theory, of socioeconomic background; as an ancillary, public universities should proactively mitigate barriers to access and seek a student body that reflects in some measure the broad spectrum of society, including lower income and disadvantaged groups.

4. Public universities must provide academic and professional programs relevant to individuals and society and to local, state, and increasingly in modern times, national and international economies.

5. Public universities, in concert with other public higher education institutions, must grow in some form in their enrollment capacity and academic programs as the population of a state grows and changes.

An equally important factor for understanding the distinct social contract of America's public universities is the political and economic environment that continually shapes it—a reality quite distinct from that of private universities. Admissions policy in public universities has many sources of influence and authority: the institution's faculty and administration, its lay governing board, state lawmakers and the legislative process, federal initiatives and the executive orders of presidents, increasingly the courts, special interest groups, and more generally, the influence of public opinion. The interplay of these forces is complex, changing over time and not always in a linear fashion, often influenced by economic troubles, social upheaval, competing demands, political divisions, and regional cultural peculiarities.

Still, the development of this social contract, replicated in one form or another in all states of the union, proved relatively uniform in its breadth and content and was a remarkable success. The establishment and development of public universities changed the course of the nation. Scholars are just beginning to assess fully the impact universities and educational attainment have had on society.[6] What we do know is that without America's public universities, the nation's economic development would have been significantly different. The paths for socioeconomic mobility would have been much more limited. Public universities influenced profoundly the nation's agricultural productivity, championed the field of civil engineering, populated small and large businesses with their graduates, and proved a core source for much of America's eventual technological prowess. Indeed, although it is important to note the significant role of private colleges and universities, the arrival and evolution of America's public university arguably proved an essential component in America's emergence as a democratic society and as an economic and technological behemoth.

Why states chose to create public universities and, in essence, to reject a model of private institutions as the primary source for fulfilling their higher education needs marks a profound shift in the course of the nation's history. The reasons are complex and vary by region of the United States. But the simple explanation is that the initial wave of private institutions, while valuable, could not meet the broad needs of individual states intent on expanding access. In mid-nineteenth century America, the loyalty and curriculum of most private institutions remained devoted to the needs of the sectarian communities that sustained them.

By the 1860s, most state governments established and supported one or more universities as alternatives to private institutions. In this venture, they sought to create supply before there was any clear understanding of the demand for higher education. Two years before the passage of the Agricultural College Land Act of 1862 by Congress, private colleges dominated higher education in the United States. Of an estimated 246 small colleges and so-called universities founded by that year, only seventeen were state institutions. The number of students who enrolled in some form of higher education was miniscule in relation to the total population.

One hundred years later, in 1960, nearly 70% of all postsecondary students in the United States were enrolled in a vast network of public universities and colleges, and 30% of all eighteen- to twenty-four-year-old Americans were in college. By 2000, some 75% of all students in higher education were in public institutions—a percentage that will likely grow in the coming decades—and participation rates among this traditional college-age cohort increased to nearly 38%, with the enrollment of high school graduates at around 58%. Today, public universities grant nearly 70% of all bachelor's degrees and some 70% of all degrees in science and technical fields. They produce most of the nation's engineers, doctors, teachers, and lawyers.[7] Further, most students are enrolled in multicampus public institutions. In 1971, about 40% of all American higher education students were in such multicampus systems. In 2000, three out of four undergraduate students in the United States were enrolled in one of some fifty public multicampus systems dispersed among thirty-eight states.[8]

CALIFORNIA'S TALE

In its organization and mission, each public university reflects in some measure the larger political and cultural environment of its particular state. At first, California's land-grant university was much like other public universities; in its youth, it started out with grand designs but soon struggled with finances, political support, and the difficulties of cultivating student demand in an era when higher education was not a prescribed route to a prosperous livelihood. But over time, California did invest substantial taxpayer funds to support its state university, enrollment demand grew dramatically, and programs emerged that met local social and economic needs. California's state university, as Gilman had hoped, did indeed "become worthy of the state." In that path from a rather small to a rather huge educational venture, the University of California attained a number of unique features that distinguish it from the pantheon of public universities and colleges in the United States. Each had important implications for admissions policy.

For one, in 1879, California's land-grant university gained an unusual level of autonomy when it became a "public trust" under a major revision to the state's constitution. Because of a much larger and tumultuous political debate in California about the rights of citizens and the organization of government, the university's governing board gained the ability to manage the institution as nearly a fourth branch of government, subject legally only to fiduciary regulations of state government. Only five other public universities have a similar status in their state constitutions. For the University of California, this legal status did not isolate the institution from the power and influence of lawmakers and the state's political milieu, but it did create a substantial buffer—including the authority to set admission standards.

Another important and related peculiarity is the development of California's pioneering and highly differentiated public higher education system by the early part of the twentieth century—what I have called *the California idea* in an earlier book. California created the nation's first coherent public higher education system through two major innovations. First, and in part because of the advocacy of University of California officials, beginning in 1907, California was the first state to develop and fund a network of public junior colleges. Other institutions, including and most famously the University of Chicago, experimented with the notion of the junior college; California was the first state to create a legal framework and public funding mechanism to make it a key component in its emerging higher education system. California also pioneered the Associate of Arts degree, which by 1910 guaranteed a student could transfer to the University of California at the junior year.

The junior college did not obviate the need for the University of California to also grow. To avoid the rise of competitors, the University of California established new campuses, beginning with the establishment of what became UCLA in 1919, and in so doing, it became the first truly multicampus university system in the United States. Many rapidly growing states established new universities and colleges; yet up to that time, they were separate public institutions. The board of regents and academic leaders at the University of California sought a different path. They created and retained a "one-university" model. This development has continued to have important implications for admissions policy.

Today, although not all of the undergraduate campuses are equal in academic reputation or in the breadth of programs they offer, each shares a common mission as comprehensive research universities, with common academic personnel policies, common criteria for their respective claim on state funding, and as noted, common policies for determining eligibility at the undergraduate level. Under the one-university model, any student who met the university's published admissions criteria was guaranteed a place in the university, and until the 1980s, students would be accommodated almost always at the campus of their choice. Most other state university systems were formed after World War II by combining different existing universities, often with different missions and different admissions criteria.

The University of California's unusual level of autonomy, the advent of the community college and a set of regional institutions (what became the California State University) linked with the university through matriculation agreements, and the one-university model allowed the institution to retain a unique role in California. It remained the state's primary research institution and, within the state's evolving public higher education system, retained exclusive authority to grant professional and doctorate degrees (until very recently); it provided the rationale for the university to maintain relatively high admissions standards and indeed to raise them marginally at important junctures—a policy built on the shoulders of the other two public higher education segments. Today, California's state university is among some 10% of the nation's four-year higher education institutions, both public and private, that are highly selective—not as selective as Harvard or Stanford, but nearly so.[9]

These peculiarities noted, the University of California has confronted many of the same challenges faced by other major public universities in the United States. Public universities, in California and elsewhere, have long struggled with the match between their obligations to meet growing demand for access with resource questions. As demand has grown for access, public universities engaged in debates over merit and, more specifically, the proper criteria for selecting among well-qualified students. Perhaps most evident in recent decades, public universities are increasingly subject to public attention and criticism regarding who they do or do not admit. Stakeholders, and the courts, are intervening or attempting to intervene in a realm of institutional policymaking that was at one time largely internal to public universities. This is not necessarily a bad phenomenon unto itself, but it raises questions regarding the proper autonomy of public universities to determine their entrance requirements, admissions practices, and the composition of their student bodies.

The University and Democracy

A distinct element of the contemporary network of higher education in the United States is the diversity of institutional types, including the mix of public and private colleges and universities. The path to this diverse system lay in the dominance in the early 1800s of a great number of semiprivate and private denominational colleges, many originally funded with public funds but with no clear responsibility to the state governments that chartered them. In no small part, the later emergence of a distinct set of public universities, including the University of California, was a reaction to the initial investment in these sectarian institutions. Particularly in new states in the expansive West, private colleges, although useful and important, seemed incapable of or simply not interested in serving the broader needs of society; they were often exclusionary and faithful not to the larger wants of the public but to the constituency that gave them life.

The United States was largely a God-loving nation and home to a growing variety of ethnic and religious communities. Religious tolerance *and* the ideal of separation of Church and State made America a unique nation. Though heavily influenced by Protestant culture, government and public institutions, whether federal, state, or local, were never to adopt or overtly support any single religion or religious organization. For these reasons, sectarianism in the 1800s was increasingly viewed as a divisive force in the effort to establish and develop public institutions, including schools and universities. As younger states attempted to mitigate conflicts between competing ethnic and religious communities, the answer was not to bring secularism to sectarian institutions but to create new secular public institutions intimately linked with revolutionary ideas on human abilities.

America included only a small number of colleges in 1779 with the emergence of the first Continental Congress. Grand ideas met the realities of a nation just getting on its feet. State governments were rarely able to think expansively about promoting education. The sparse collection of academies and colleges had their roots in royal charters and local community interests. Under the imported rules of England's Parliament, colonial governments usually offered only one charter within their respective borders.

Chartering was commonly used as a mercantile tool. In the case of the colonial college, chartering established an acceptable monopoly where one sanctioned institution acted as the sole (or nearly so) provider of degrees and social status. Chartering often included formal and paid roles for colonial officers on governing boards and meager financial subsidies from local taxation. Unlike their English counterparts, the colonial colleges varied in their denominational affiliation, reflecting an increasingly diverse aggregation of ethnic and religious groups in America. The colleges operated initially without a body of learned men central to their European counterparts. Instead, they relied largely on each new crop of graduates to create a core of teachers. In all, eight colonial colleges were established. These colleges formed the first attempt in America's adventure in building a unique network of colleges and, eventually, universities—semiprivate institutions with public sanction but with more of the character of private than public institutions.[10] The colonial colleges trained the clergy and increasingly the laity of a denomination and reinforced the local class structure. They found their curricular model in standard classical courses offered in Europe and particularly England. Out of these colleges came a number of the nation's most captivating leaders; many embraced the ideals of higher education but also complained of the staid condition of the colonial colleges in the aftermath of the American Revolution. They did not entirely reject these institutions or a breed of new private institutions that emerged and struggled for financial existence in the decades after 1776. Their role in society was valued. But these institutions were not enough.

Each successive expansion westward caused political and community leaders in the frontier territories and in new states to profess the dawning of a new democratic experiment. Once again, plenty of arable land and the lack of a set social and economic hierarchy offered the necessary seeds for socioeconomic mobility and egalitarianism. But these new states also were desperate for public institutions that could bind their communities and promote their affluence. The prospect of great public universities educating the young and promoting the economy of a state, inducing culture, and creating democratic leaders grew in its allure as states struggled to establish themselves. The notion of the "state college" tied to the wants of an agrarian world had other characteristics. At one level, it was a staunch rejection of perceived eastern elitism. On another level, the proliferation of state universities reflected status anxiety and the desire to avoid a brain drain of talent to more established states. Among advocates of statehood, public education, and the state university specifically, would mitigate the roughness and lawlessness of the frontier. There were great expectations for these institutions, though they were barely established, their resources were meager, and the nature of the academy itself was deeply traditional and conservative.

In the discourse that swirled around the creation of new institutions, three major and interrelated tensions became evident. The first was the proper curricular balance between practical education and classical studies. The second focused on the appropriate autonomy of institutions intended to serve the public interest in a society often wracked by sectarian and class conflict. And the third centered on the degree to which these public institutions should be selective in their admissions and representative of the state's population.

On the Edge of the Frontier

California gained 150,000 acres under the Morrill Act passed by Congress and signed by President Lincoln in 1862. The land could be sold or leased. In March 1866, the state passed the first of two Organic Acts, just in time to meet the required federal deadline to submit a plan. This 1866 charter called for the creation of a public polytechnic, primarily to serve agricultural and industrial interests. Two years later, however, Henry Durant convinced Governor Frederick Low that California should expand the purpose of the proposed land-grant institution into a university. Part of a contingent of Yale men who came to California during the Gold Rush, Durant in 1852 helped establish the small and financially struggling College of California in Oakland with an affiliation with the Congregational church. Durant, along with other cofounders of the college, dreamed that they might eventually create a university modeled on Yale. It could be focused on a classical curriculum with room for emerging applied and scientific fields. Durant offered the College of California and all its buildings and land to the state to help create a secular University of California. By combining private and public resources, he argued, California could create a new public university that would be "something more than a polytechnic."[11]

In March 1868, the legislature passed a second Organic Act. The state accepted the land in Oakland and a site in the hills overlooking the bay from the College of California—what would become Berkeley. It stated the formal absorption of the college's small number of liberal arts-oriented faculty and students, set out the governance and organization of the academic departments, *and* provided statements regarding the purpose of the new state university. A lengthy document written in large part by Durant, Samuel Willey (acting president of the College of California), and Assemblyman John Dwinelle, this charter offers an example of the ethos of a new era in university building. It was shaped by the spirit and demands of the Morrill Act and by the experiences in other states. Pre-Morrill Act state constitutional and statutory provisions for public universities and colleges, such as for Michigan, tended to be rather short statements, focused almost exclusively on the rudimentary particulars of the organization and governance of the institution. California's charter offered a much broader outline of the university's charge, including the appropriate composition of its leaders and the parameters for selecting and admitting students.

A remarkable level of consensus had formed in the United States on the value of the lay governing board, conditioned in part by the process of chartering and by the ideals of a formal tie to civic concerns. California's 1868 Organic Act created a board of regents with responsibility to manage the fiscal affairs of the university, yet subject to legislative mandates. Membership and appointment to the board followed similar practices in other states. Ex officio members would include "His Excellency the Governor," who also acted as the chair of the board, the lieutenant governor, the speaker of the California State assembly, the superintendent of public instruction (a constitutionally elected officer), and the presidents of the state agricultural society and the mechanic's institute of the city and county of San Francisco—the state's largest population center. With the advice and consent of the state senate (the second house in the state's bicameral legislature), eight members would be appointed by the governor. Eight additional appointed members would be selected by the new board to create a total membership of twenty-two.

To ensure a high level of autonomy and knowledge within the board on the particulars of the university's affairs, the sixteen appointed members would serve sixteen-year staggered appointments. In this way, no one governor and his party would gain sway over the board, it was thought. California's charter also "expressly" provided "that no sectarian, political, or partisan test shall ever be allowed or exercised in the appointment of Regents, or in the election of professors, teachers, or other officers of the University." [12] It is not clear how such a standard could be met in such an innately political process as appointing members. But the veracity of this issue in the minds of the authors and legislators gave motive for another provision: The 1868 legislation stated that at no time "shall the majority of the Board of Regents be of any one religious sect, or of no religious sect." [13]

Secular notions did not mean an exclusion of Christian standards of morality and civility. The objective was to service a diverse number of people from different denominational communities and a range of beliefs, with no one community in a position to dominate the operations and management of a public university. These concerns over equity were extended to the board's selection of officers of the institution (they could not come from only one secular group) and, most important for this discussion, to the admission of students.

Secularism and Geographic and Economic Representation

Within the university's founding charter, the regents were charged with the authority to regulate the selection of students within this framework and to "determine the moral and educational qualification of applicants for admission to the various courses of instruction." The autonomy of the board, and through them its president and the university's faculty, was clearly stated. In selecting students, a number of important stipulations were added, creating an initial set of principles that guided University of California admissions. Three of these principles were created in the original charter.

The first principle was a natural extension of the rule on the selection of regents. It should be free of undue influence: *The selection of students and granting of scholarships by the president should also be free of secular and political influence.* Similar statements could be found in the charters of other state universities, and this principle would often be cited in battles over university admissions in the 1990s. A second principle incorporated in the charter was the idea of *proportional representation and, specifically, by geographic region of the state.* It is the "duty of the Regents" to select students "according to population, to so apportion the representation of students, when necessary, that all portions of the State shall enjoy equal privilege therein."[14] The concept of geographic representation, also a bulwark of other state university charters of the era, ensured that the university served the entire state. It was also a clear statement that the university must not be simply a regional institution. There were already charges of its potential domination by the scions of San Francisco. Broad geographic representation, possibly in relation to population although never clearly defined, was not only democratic in spirit. It offered a sense of ownership, and access, to all Californians.

In some state universities, the idea of proportional representation was central and occasionally a dominating influence on admissions practices. State legislatures gave birth to these institutions, and it was not uncommon to demand proportional benefits; it was a matter of equity and, for many young public institutions, a matter of political necessity. Pennsylvania State University offers one example. Established in 1846 as an agricultural college, the campus became the state's land-grant institution devoted to the study of all phases of farming. In 1857, admissions were designed to accept a total of one hundred students that year, apportioned from each county of the state on the basis of its population. Students needed to be sixteen, of "good moral character," and with a recommendation from their county agricultural society. Tuition and room were set at $100, figured to be "about one third of the rate charged by most other colleges in the state."[15] Later, the institution's board would abolish tuition.

The University of California never established a similar model of formal apportionment. Geographic representation was, however, a consistent and important value in admissions that did not dissipate until the 1960s (a story we will return to in later chapters). Geographic representation and participation would also later create a rationale for the university's decision to establish new University of California campuses in the state, built around the concept of dividing the state into service areas.

A third principle reiterated the determination of broad access to a public university and reflected a consensus among a majority of state universities: *The university was to be free to all California residents to reduce economic barriers to access.* In these initial years, the principle of no direct costs for a student's education was extended to the barring of fees for the admissions process— for example, a fee for the process of taking an examination. A "free university" implied that public subsidies would be perpetually adequate for educating students. The proclamation that the university be "absolutely free" fit the hubris and excitement of the era. Other states made similar commitments. Eventually, the university would, it was hoped, be part of a larger and complete system of public education free to all state citizens. It was an incomplete thought. Most states, including California, struggled to establish truly free public schools. Legal argument persisted, in particular in the American Midwest and South, regarding the appropriateness of public taxation to support public education. Such arguments remained salient for those who opposed the idea of taxes as an unfair redistribution of wealth. Roads and law enforcement were acceptable forms of local taxation, but schooling other people's children in an era of agricultural labor and apprenticeship remained controversial.

The charters of many other post-Morrill Act state universities professed the hope of excluding tuition. Beyond the progressive ideal for a tuition-free public university, a major influence was the largess offered by the Morrill Act. It seemed a generous subsidy. In California and other states, legislators thought tuition might be avoided permanently. The federal act allowed for endowment income to be used only for the purchase of land and the operational costs for supporting a new or existing college or university that included a program in agriculture and mechanical arts. Yet many states quickly found difficulty in selling the land. The quality and market value varied tremendously, and the process of selling the land, usually under the authority of university boards, became steeped in charges of mismanagement and corruption.

At the same time, the cost of developing a new campus, or expanding existing public institutions, was not fully understood. And these costs grew as enrollment demand increased and the complexity of the institution and its required infrastructure, including libraries suitable for a research university, also grew. Most states slowly adopted measures to provide a steady flow of taxpayer funds for their state universities, first in the form of yearly appropriations and increasingly tied to a small percentage of state income derived from property taxes—before the era of state sales taxes and income taxes adopted largely in the 1930s. The initial commitments of state funds proved inadequate as well. In the 1880s, many state universities adopted modest tuition fees.

Although also suffering the maladies associated with poor financing, California's state university did not incorporate tuition for 120 years. In part, this was because of the stipulations in the Organic Act that the university be free for its citizens. Another reason was the difficulty of attracting students, rich or poor. Though simply making the institution tuition-free did not make enrolling in Berkeley affordable to all California citizens, it stood as both a meaningful and symbolic principle that economic barriers should not dissuade talented students from furthering their education and contributing to California society. In 1874, students on average attended sixteen hours of class per week. In part, this seemingly light workload was the result of the long commuting time of many students and their need to work. In these early years, many students needed three to four hours a day for commuting from their homes in Oakland and San Francisco. According to an early university publication, *The Berkeleyan*, approximately 50% of all enrolled students worked either at the university as largely groundskeepers or in San Francisco businesses and in private homes as helpers.[16] A "Free Employment Bureau" established in 1891 helped students find work in "typewriting, copying, tutoring, gardening, carpentering . . . to earn a part, or all of the funds to carry them through the year," noted the student paper *The Occident*.[17] In 1888, some 45% of the university's students lived in Oakland or San Francisco, either at home or in residences close to their jobs.

Before the board of regents, Professor and former President John LeConte in 1875 stated, "One of the best characteristics of the American college is the bringing together on terms of equality, free from artificial and conventional distinctions, [of] young men of different pecuniary conditions. The sons of the rich and the needy grow up side by side, and the honors which they receive from one another and from the Faculty are bestowed without any reference to the homes from which they come."[18] Access to higher education based on merit, not economic class, appealed to Californians as a commitment to democracy befitting a progressive society. Under the Organic Act, educational opportunity was defined not only in economic terms but also, as noted previously, by geographic representation so that all Californians, in theory, could have the opportunity to attend the state university.

All of these founding elements—nonsectarian and nonpolitical decision making, the tuition-free policy, and the mandate for geographic representation—became extremely important principles, not only guiding the development of the University of California but also influencing the development of a set of regional state teachers colleges and, as will be discussed later, acting as a catalyst for the creation of California's junior colleges. In one form or another, the ideals of access to and representation of all major sectors of California's population drove the state to create one of the nation's first coherent systems of public higher education.[19]

The Issue of Gender

At the dedication of the new Berkeley campus, the Reverend Horatio Stebbins proclaimed the new university as pivotal to "free Republican government," affirming the view that "the state is bound to furnish the citizens the means to discharging the duties imposed on him. If the state imposes duties that require intelligence, it is the office of the state to furnish the means of intelligence . . . it is for the dignity of the commonwealth." The Morrill Act, he concluded, enabled California to create a "complete system" of public education: "The University, then, is the last term in the ascending series of public schools."[20]

In these and similar pronouncements of egalitarian ideals, there were many caveats and gross contradictions, conveniently ignored. American society was not a place of equal rights or devoid of hurtful prejudice and discrimination. The same year that the university's board first met in late 1868, teams of Chinese immigrants toiled to help build the transcontinental railway, while denied any right to own property in California. With the onset of a depression in the early 1870s in California and the nation, race riots erupted, exacerbated by a growing population and growing unemployment. And women were not among the first class that enrolled at the University of California. Although there was no rule against their admission, there also was no statement that women might be freely admitted. In 1870, however, and over a year before the new campus opened on the Berkeley site, the board of regents first considered a proposal from the university's faculty senate to admit women. A year later, the board agreed, establishing a fourth principle in its evolving social contract: *The university should admit women on an equal basis with men.* At the time, the university enrolled forty male students in the buildings in Oakland—the former campus of the College of California. A year later, eight female students enrolled, joining a class that totaled ninety-three. When the university moved to its new buildings in 1873 in Strawberry Creek nestled in the Berkeley hills, the university enrolled a total of 191 students. Twenty-two were women. In its 1872 report on the status of the university, the board boasted of their progressive ideals.

A University organized upon a complete plan may be briefly defined to be an institution of learning in which everything is taught in science and learning which the student desires to learn. But most Universities are hampered with conditions and restrictions which limit their scope and impair their usefulness. They are generally so expensive as to be beyond the reach of youths of even moderate means. Young women are almost universally excluded; they are generally sectarian in their character; most of them are encumbered with monastic traditions of the middle ages; others impose conditions of admission which exclude large classes of students; and almost all require courses of instruction to be pursued, so that a student cannot learn that special thing which he wishes to learn without being compelled to study something else for which he has no inclination. The University of California has, happily, avoided all these evils. Its instruction is free, and its incidental expenses so low that a student can complete his four years course for less than it would cost him to leave California, spend a year at an Eastern University, and then return.[21]

The report also stated that the university was not only "open to both sexes," but its young women were also not "insulted" by the creation of a "Female Department." Women could "pursue the same curriculum of instruction as the other sex." Nor did it have any hint of sectarian character: "An institution fostered by the State cannot teach religion beyond the ethics which form the character of the honest, truthful, cultivated gentleman. It admits all youth of good character and proper age to its classes, and it permits any person to receive its instruction in any branch of study at any time when it is given in due course, whether he wishes to study anything else or not, and it furnishes University lectures, in which science is popularly and yet accurately treated, to a large class of the population of the State." In these pursuits, the regents, and the faculty, believed that the "young University of California is far in advance in most of these respects of all the Universities in the world." [22]

The exuberance of the university's faithful ignored significant barriers to access by women and the social mores that influenced their education once at Berkeley. The courses and majors women pursued sometimes fit personal choices. But women were subject to the pressures of male faculty and students who dominated the culture of the institution. Women tended to major in literature, in nursing, and in the university's program for training secondary teachers, but not exclusively.

Josephine Lindley was among the first women registered to attend the state university in 1871. She was twenty at the time and a native of Sacramento. She became one of the first editors of the student newspaper, *The University Echo*. "Every young lady should be fitted to *do* something in life," she wrote. "Men cry out against women's extravagance and trifling, yet they are the first to condemn the opening of paths to her; Her education will not necessarily prevent her from properly filling her sphere in domestic life. If she knows why fire burns, why bread rises, is it incompatible with her making fires or good bread? Women demand a broader education and a greater degree of usefulness. There are many positions suitable for them given to men, sometimes not as capable, simply because custom thinks it unlady-like for women to do anything but sew or teach when it becomes necessary for them to earn a livelihood." For Lindley and her cohorts, much was riding on California's advent in admitting women in relatively large numbers. "The new system of education is now being thoroughly tested in the United States. May it prove successful! The fate of young women's attempt in California to reach a higher, a more real education, depends upon this experiment." [23]

Ten years after opening the university to women, the number of women enrolled grew to sixty-two of a total undergraduate enrollment of 244. A decision in 1879 by the California Supreme Court extended the right of women to enroll in graduate programs at the university. The court ruled that an applicant for admission to the Hastings Law College "could not be rejected on the sole ground that she is female."[24] Between 1900 and 1930, women represented approximately 40% to 45% of all enrollments in the University of California, mostly in the university's teacher credential and nursing programs and in fields such as English and home economics. In 1920, the university included the largest enrollment of women of any college or university, public or private, in the nation. Graduate enrollment of women was also significant, although the definition and scope of graduate-level instruction have changed over time.

Comparatively, the University of California was a beacon of enlightenment. At the turn of the twentieth century, most eastern colleges and universities remained all male. Even such progressive universities as Michigan maintained quotas—arbitrary limits to keep female students often at around a magical 20% of all students. "It has been well said," wrote Lord Bryce in 1891, "that the position of which women hold in a country is, if not a complete test, yet one of the best tests of the progress it has made in civilization." In Bryce's opinion, and in comparison with his native Europe, America was a vital liberator, "evidence of the high level their civilization has reached." "Taking one thing with another," he wrote, "it is easier for women to find a career, to obtain remunerative work of an intellectual as of a commercial or mechanical kind, than any part of Europe. . . . In no other country have women borne so conspicuous a part in the promotion of moral and philanthropic causes."[25]

In contrast to most of Europe, women in America could own property and file for divorce in most states. A few states gave them the right to vote—all in the expansive West, starting with Wyoming in 1868 and Utah in 1870 but not in California until 1911. "Custom allows to women a greater measure of freedom in doing what they will and going where they please than they have in any European country, except, perhaps, in Russia."[26] By 1900, all state universities with the exception of the University of Virginia, the University of Georgia, and the University of Louisiana admitted women. Yet in the North Atlantic states, there were few opportunities for women beyond a small set of private women's colleges. Bryce was aware of these regional differences in education and social expectations. "If a lady enters some occupation," for instance, noted Bryce, "heretofore usually reserved for men, she is subject to much less censorious remark than would follow her in Europe, though in this matter the society of Eastern cities is hardly so liberal as that of the West."[27]

The restrictive admission policies at most private institutions led to separate institutions and arrangements. Vassar College (1861) and Smith College

(1871) were established with substantial endowments specifically to provide a collegiate education similar to Harvard and Yale. When Harvard did offer instruction for women, it was in the form of a separate college. "Harvard Annex" was established in 1879, later renamed the Society for the Collegiate Instruction of Women, and chartered as Radcliffe College by the commonwealth of Massachusetts in 1894. Yet it is important to note the first true experiments in coeducation occurred in the 1830s when two private institutions, Oberlin and then Antioch, both in Ohio, enrolled women. But even in the more adventuresome midwestern and western states, progress was slow and contested.

When the state university in Michigan and later Wisconsin opened their doors in the years leading up to the Civil War, there was no provision for the admission of women on any terms. Despite proposals entertained by the University of Michigan's board in the 1850s, university President Henry Tappan successfully voiced his stern opposition. He doubted the mental capabilities of women. Perhaps most important, he sincerely thought their presence at the Ann Arbor campus would distract from building a university with a national reputation. Hence, Tappan's worry related not simply to the effect of women on campus but to the wider public perception of the quality of the institution. Beyond the battles over denominational influence, Michigan's board also struggled with the issue of admitting women, making a decision in the affirmative only after passage of the Morrill Act.

A similar slow shift occurred in Wisconsin and with a similar story of consternation. Admitted as a state in 1848, Wisconsin soon incorporated and organized its university under a provision in the state constitution similar to Michigan's, including a decree that "no sectarian instruction shall be allowed in such university." No provision was made for enrolling women. However, the 1866 Organic Act passed by the Wisconsin legislature forced the reorganization of the university to meet the demands of the Morrill Act. It not only outlined a plan for new colleges on the Madison campus to include the "physical, and natural sciences, with their applications to the industrial arts." All departments and colleges of Wisconsin's state university would also be "open alike to male and female students."[28]

The shining light of equality did not come on with a burst. Though the University of Wisconsin was fifteen years old, it remained financially troubled in 1866, awaiting a hopeful wash of funds from federal land grants. Then with the prospect of an improved financial standing, the university's regents could not secure the services of a new president after the passage of the 1866 act. The reason, according to the regents, was the new policy regarding admissions, which explicitly stated that women could be admitted to all programs at the university. In their annual report, the regents noted that a number of candidates, including Paul R. Chadbourne of Williams College, refused their offers. It appeared "extremely difficult, if not impossible," explained the regents, "to secure the services of a thoroughly competent and experienced educational man at the head of the institution."[29] At the request of the board, the state legislature modified the relevant statute, stating that admission of women be conducted "under such regulations and restrictions as the Board of Regents may deem proper."[30] Chadbourne then agreed to assume the presidency.

What followed was his establishment of a separate female college by the summer of 1867. Women could attend lectures given in any department of the university, but the "recitations and other exercises are distinct from those in the other colleges." Chadbourne imagined a separate program for women, taught largely by women, and focused on music, drawing, and painting, and with separate graduations and other accoutrements thought protective for both female and male students. But beyond separate housing, his model soon gave way to inclusion of women in the normal courses of the university.

In the third decade of Penn State University's development as an agricultural college, its board of trustees and faculty voted in 1871 to open admissions "to both sexes without distinctions as to qualifications or privileges." An education of a "matron instead of a parlor ornament" was the board's objective. The next academic year, of 800 total students, six female students were enrolled. Several years later, Rebecca Hannah Ewing was the first of the female students to graduate.

Many state universities, particularly those devoted to agricultural education, required a period of farm labor as part of their training—an option debated but rejected at the University of California. Penn State exempted women from this requirement. Enrollment of women at first flowed but then ebbed. In 1879, Penn State counted forty-nine women; in 1904, it was a mere nineteen. Charles H. Brown, in his history of the university, blamed a curriculum oriented largely to farming. In part to attract women, in 1907 Penn State, like many other public universities did in that era, established a home economics program. This helped bring the number of women at Penn State up to seventy-six in 1913.[31]

In the same decade that Penn State and Wisconsin's state universities cautiously included women, the University of California's board of regents launched their own debate on admitting women. The final 1871 decision in California was decidedly more resolute. No other public university proceeded to enroll such a high percentage of women in their undergraduate program in the 1800s and into the first decades of the twentieth century.

Selectivity and the Qualified Student

Within the University of California, a fifth principle first emerged in the 1870s, becoming more pronounced as the university matured and with the development of other public institutions: *The university should be a selective institution.* In this regard, California was different from most state universities. Many land-grant institutions bowed to populist demands to keep admission standards low and to admit almost any student. At the same time, most institutions attempted to seek the ideal of a university. As demand grew, many students who perhaps were not ready for a university education failed their courses and dropped out. Attrition rates at most state universities were extremely high.

The University of California and a handful of other public universities took a different route. Three factors explain the University of California's particular path. The first related to the leadership of its second president, Daniel Coit Gilman. The second related to a historic political battle over the appropriate autonomy of the university. And the third factor related to the eventual emergence of alternatives to the university, namely, the junior college and a set of regional colleges. Each facilitated the interest and ability of university leaders to create a selective admission policy. As a result, today, the University of California, along with the Universities of Michigan, Wisconsin, and Virginia, is among the most selective public universities in the nation.

In his 1872 inaugural speech, Gilman outlined the essential features of the University of California's future maturation. But it was slow in coming. He instantly suffered resistance, not from the university community but from lawmakers and impatient and politically powerful farmers. Two years after coming to California, the state Grange charged that agricultural and mechanical arts programs were too slow in developing. Enrollments were small, and resources allocated to the university's new College of Agriculture were minimal. The Grange and other critics, including the Workingman's Party based largely in San Francisco, charged malfeasance in the management of federal lands allocated to the university's board of regents.

Gilman and the university faced numerous bills to focus the university's curriculum entirely on "practical instruction" or to change the composition of the board of regents to reflect the interests of the Grange. Gilman found that most of his energies no longer went to building a university but to defending its autonomy in legislative hearings and community gatherings. He resigned in 1875 and left California to become the first president of Johns Hopkins University. For "university fighting I have no training," he wrote in his letter of resignation; "in university work I delight." Within the confines of a private institution and with the support of a wealthy benefactor, Gilman quickly developed one of the first truly research-based universities in the United States.

The loss of Gilman and the legislative and political forays gave rise to a proposal at California's second state constitutional convention in 1879 for elevation of the university to the status of a "public trust." The new constitution included the public trust provision and was passed by California voters narrowly. As noted previously, the net effect of this change in the legal status of the University of California was enormous. It gave a defined level of autonomy for the board of regents, and the university president working with the faculty, to manage the university, including setting admissions criteria. The university would never be devoid of political influence, of course. But constitutional autonomy constricted the ways political and outside influence could shape university decisions. It reinforced the ability of the regents, while including the governor and a number of other ex officio members, to act as a buffer between the political and academic world. And there is very little doubt that, absent the constitutional change, the selective admissions policies pursued by the University of California over its history would have been impossible. Subject to legislative mandates, not only would the university's history be substantially altered, but California's entire public higher education system would have evolved differently.

For the regents and faculty of the University of California, autonomy formed a barrier against repeated demands to lower admissions standards. Although the regents hold the authority over all aspects of university management, they delegated the setting and implementation of admissions policies to the faculty early in the history of the university. The 1868 Organic Act establishing the state university not only provided for a lay board, but it also required the establishment of an academic senate "created for the purpose of conducting the general administration of the University." It consisted of all faculty and deans and was to be presided over by the university president.[32] The regents looked to the faculty to create admissions standards and to conduct the process of interviewing and selecting students.

Gilman had set out the ideals of the University of California as a selective institution. How to accomplish this? Simply setting high admissions standards made no sense in an era when there were few public high schools and, it was feared, limited demand for a university education. Shortly after the 1868 charter, the regents purchased a set of buildings in Oakland to establish a university preparatory department to recruit and properly prepare students for enrollment on the Berkeley campus. The state boasted only eight public high schools, four of which were not yet four years old, and a handful of private academies. In 1870, Oscar P. Fitzgerald, regent and California's state superintendent of public instruction, introduced a successful resolution to the board establishing "a fifth class or otherwise, which shall bring the different University schools into direct relation with the Grammar Schools of the State."[33] A debate soon emerged among faculty, however, with a majority insisting that a university should not be engaged in preparatory education; instead, the new state university needed to focus on building its own academic departments. Insistence among faculty led to the regents closing the school in August 1872.[34]

Enrollment growth at the Berkeley campus in the 1870s was slow, and some lawmakers questioned why state funding should continue. There was strong sentiment among many farmers and laborers that keeping their children in school past the common school simply delayed their apprenticeship on the farm and in factories. Others charged that funding the high school delayed the development of the common school, siphoning away much-needed funds, and ultimately, was a ploy to get farmers and laborers to pay for the schooling of a new privileged class that wanted to avoid the cost and inconvenience of sending their children to eastern boarding schools. As a result, the new constitution prohibited state funding of high schools. The result was a significant delay in the development of secondary education in California and a lack of qualified students for university enrollment.

Between 1879 and 1883, enrollment at the university dropped from 332 to 215. "As nearly as I can determine," observed the university's fourth president, William T. Reid, a graduate of Harvard and former principal of Boy's High School of San Francisco, "out of the fifty-two counties in the State but seven offer opportunities for preparation for the University at the public schools, and under the operation of the new Constitution the number of High Schools has already diminished by one. In other words, our boasted free University is free to those who can afford to pay for preparatory education, but practically cut off from those who are not able to incur the preliminary expense—the very persons whose education it is of especial interest to the State to secure."[35]

Reid joined the faculty in advocating that university admissions standards not be lowered to increase enrollments. Instead, two major reforms were advocated by the academic senate and endorsed by the regents along with an active campaign to promote the expansion of the public high school. First, the university established written examinations that could be taken by a prospective student outside the confines of the Berkeley campus.[36] The second reform encompassed the development of a system by which university faculty would accredit the curriculum of California's high schools and was modeled on the system first adopted in 1871 by the University of Michigan. In 1884, University of California faculty began accrediting secondary schools, setting standards for preparatory courses required for admission in areas such as algebra, geometry, and classical language. Accreditation offered a new method of admitting students. On the written recommendation of the principal, students who graduated from an accredited school would be admitted to the Berkeley campus.[37] Later, a principal's recommendation was not required.

Following the advent of accreditation, university faculty, President Reid, and his successors began their campaign to promote the high school. Faculty met with the growing number of local school boards, legislators, and local government officials; President Reid spoke before numerous community meetings urging the establishment of at least one high school in every county of the state.[38] Sacramento lawmakers passed a bill to provide greater flexibility for local government to institute taxes for high schools, largely helping the urban communities in and around San Francisco, Sacramento, and Los Angeles. But it would not be until 1903 that state funds, the largest source of funding for schools in an era when the state collected most property taxes, could be used to operate public secondary schools. In June 1884, five high schools applied for UC accreditation, and three were accepted; the following year, three more schools applied for and gained accreditation. University enrollment began to rise once again, increasing from 216 during the 1883–1884 academic year to 241 the following year and to 401 by 1889–1890.[39]

How wide the door should be open for California's students, however, was not entirely clear. The university proceeded under the theoretical concept that admissions standards should be calibrated in some form to indicate both preparedness and success at the university. As the institution entered the twentieth century, it improved considerably in the quality of its academic programs, while facing for the first time a significant increase in demand for access. For private institutions, rising demand offered an opportunity to become more selective. For public institutions, even one with constitutional autonomy, it created considerable public expectations to take all students deemed qualified.

In 1900, the University of California found itself at the edge of a rising tide of enrollment demand. Between 1890 and the turn of the century, the university grew to 2,906 students—an average of 222 additional students per year. In our contemporary world, these are relatively small numbers. But the idea of a campus reaching 20,000 or more students was unthinkable in the early 1900s. The university faced an issue familiar to contemporary higher education policymakers: a mismatch between enrollment demand and possible funding sources.

In 1899, when Benjamin Ide Wheeler, like Gilman some thirty years earlier, traveled across the country from the relative financial health of Cornell to become the new University of California president, he faced what he thought was a dire situation. Funding from the state was tied to property values and had nothing to do with workload. Philanthropic gifts were occasional, and the income from the original federal land grants was rapidly declining. In his first report to the governor, Wheeler complained that inadequate buildings and facilities along with increasing enrollments meant that "we are crowded out of house and home." Wheeler was appalled at the large classes and the number of courses that faculty taught, leaving little room for research and new notions of public service: "The situation here at present is, I sometimes think, pathetic, and sometimes ludicrous," he wrote, with "nothing comparable to it in the United States today." The trickle of demand had turned into what Wheeler described as an "avalanche."

Chapter 2

Building a Higher Education System and Broadening Access

We cannot accept the dictum of certain self-styled "prestige" institutions that a state university must be content to operate on a lower plan for a less gifted group of the population.
—Robert Gordon Sproul, University of California president, 1930

In the three decades after 1900, California's state university grew tremendously and not only in its enrollment. It grew in its administrative structure and in the quality and breadth of its academic programs; it gained significant new financial stability and grew decidedly in its real and perceived value to the state of California. The university became a central part of California's evolving cultural identity. It was a widely recognized wellspring of political reform leaders, a successful route for creating a more professional and expert society, a source of engineers and business acumen, a resource for attacking society's social ills—in short, an engine for shaping economic opportunity and prosperity.

In California and in many other key states, there was another outcome of the public university movement: an expanded public discourse on issues of postsecondary access and opportunity. How selective should a public university be? How could the notion of educational elitism survive in a society that professed egalitarian ideals? What other routes might there be to a higher education degree? This was a discourse found in few if any other parts of the world that, as in Europe, largely defined higher education as an elite function of a small cadre of universities.

In America, many state governments struggled with how to expand access to higher education—to essentially redefine higher education as a mass *and* elite function. The vast majority of states did not come to grips with how to structure their public higher education systems until well after

31

World War II by forming multicampus systems. California was different, creating the first coherent approach to mass higher education in the United States, one that retained the idea of a state university that was selective, yet linked through matriculation agreements to a growing network of new postsecondary institutions.

California's pioneering path was part and parcel of a larger American political reform movement in the first two decades of the twentieth century—the Progressive Era. California's progressives constituted a class of professionals and small business interests joined by philanthropists and activists, often women, bent on creating greater order and good in California society. Many of the Progressive movement's political leadership, including Governor Hiram Johnson and journalist Frank Norris, attended Berkeley. Most graduated from college. Many desired an improved environment for business. Others were more concerned with government corruption and issues of morality, and many obsessed about the wave of increased poverty linked to foreign immigration flowing into California's growing urban areas.

Most important for our story, California Progressives were convinced of the centrality of education as an ameliorating agent for society's social, moral, political, and economic ills—themes articulated in earlier eras but now adopted with a fervency unmatched in American history. Many in the reform movement worried about the fate of the country and embraced a nearly puritanical drive to reshape society in ways that were both self-serving and ultraistic. Expanding access to education and improving its organization and quality became broadly acceptable political goals. Increased educational opportunities would encourage socioeconomic mobility, facilitate the Americanization of the immigrant, and cultivate the "natural" development of community and business leaders. Progressives gained political power and passed legislation to extend education to include the kindergarten. And in California, they laid plans to build the University of California into a powerful and central source of research and training.

The university taught many of the state's new political leaders and generated new ideas that influenced political and institutional reforms. In turn, this created both strong political support for its continued mission and rising expectations regarding its future influence. The tumult of California society, and a romantic sense of California as the vanguard of a more democratic and meritocratic society, generated a sense of the historical moment. A great public university was an essential component in the reform movement. Here, noted one advocate of the university, the nation's "grave industrial and administrative problems will have to be worked out. And these problems can be solved only by highly trained and efficient intelligence."[1] The university would be a primary source of research and a highly educated cadre—an expanding version of Jefferson's "natural aristocracy." But there remained a glaring and seemingly competing need to expand postsecondary opportunities below the modern university—to complete the rungs of the educational ladder that now stretched from the kindergarten to the university.

The panacea of education became a popular clamor in California and throughout the nation. New initiatives created a new caste of professionally trained and accredited teachers and school administrators, the kindergarten became part of building a complete school system, and local schools were reorganized into "unified" districts with elected boards. New truancy laws reflected the primacy of education. It was not simply a student's right to go to school but a requirement. In most states, including California, school attendance was mandatory up to the age of sixteen, at least in law. To fund the enterprise, most states revised their tax systems. To promote the growth of public education, new funding policies were pioneered in New York and California, including formulaic assessments of student attendance (average daily attendance, or ADA) to ensure a relationship of adequate funding to teacher workload. New laws allowed for the issuing of state-backed bonds for capital construction.

In 1902 and in the early stages of these reforms in California, an archaic law placed in the 1879 state constitution barring state funding of public high schools was removed. Prior to 1902, only local communities with the financial means and initiative could fund the high school. In that era, state governments collected most property taxes and then redistributed them to local communities for schools. With the shift in state policy, new levels of government funding fueled a tremendous wave of construction and school enrollment. In a state that nearly doubled its population every decade, California's high school enrollment grew from 12,620 in 1900, to 39,650 in 1910, and to 140,352 in 1920. An influx of new citizens came to California from all over the world, but the largest numbers were from the Midwest. Migrants from these states highly valued public education. As a result, California was populated by a relatively new middle and professional class majority with aspirations that often included some form of postsecondary education for their children.

The University and the Junior Colleges

With the political and financial support of California Progressives and under the leadership of university President Benjamin Ide Wheeler (1899–1919), the University of California emerged as one of the leading research universities in the nation. Under Wheeler's aggressive leadership, the University of California grew in enrollment, reorganized much of its academic structure, and dramatically expanded its role in the life and economy of California. With the support of progressives, many of whom were alumni, the university gained for the first time a steady source of state funding that was no longer based on state property values but on actual enrollment workload—a new idea in the financing of public higher education.

Dramatic increases in state funding based largely on the advent of enrollment-based formulas, combined with the infusion of federal funds for agricultural research stations, allowed Wheeler and university faculty to establish and run the nation's largest agricultural extension program. Faculty and university staff offered courses to farmers and the general public throughout the state and a vast array of literature on everything from improved irrigation techniques and soil conditioning to the promotion of new hybrid plants. California's citrus industry, to cite one example, emerged with the development of orange tree hybrids grown in Riverside, one of several agricultural research stations. The birth of a thriving wine industry in the state depended on research and education developed by the university's branch college of agriculture located in Davis.

As the university's public service role grew, faculty worked with Wheeler to reorganize the university's curriculum, with important implications for admissions policy. On the recommendation of the academic senate and mirroring a nationwide effort of standardizing credit for courses, the university established the modern pattern of lower and upper division courses. Reflecting the norms of a vanguard of American universities, the senate also adopted uniform units per course (i.e., three hours of class time and one hour lab or study time equating to four units of course credit) that remain, remarkably, the standard today in the United States. Faculty set new requirements for degrees, and Wheeler established a graduate division to regulate graduate education and restructured the university's colleges and professional schools. By 1916, with nearly 7,000 students, Berkeley was the largest higher education institution in the nation and ranked as one of the top universities, a new rival to such institutions as Harvard, Yale, Cornell, Michigan, and Wisconsin. A 1906 study on "American men of science" by James McKeen Cattell ranked Berkeley as sixth in the nation in its collection of science faculty. Edwin E. Slosson's widely distributed *The Great American Universities*, published in 1910, stated that Berkeley was among the nation's top thirteen higher education institutions.[2]

The rise in the university's popularity and the tremendous increase in enrollment demand, however, created a vexing problem for university officials. With no other large public institutions providing postsecondary training in the state, many Californians insisted that the university lower admissions standards and grow even faster in enrollment. Stanford and a small collection of other private institutions helped meet a portion of this demand, as did the state's growing number of state normal schools, which offered teacher training at the elementary school level. There was also a new polytechnic at San Luis Obispo with a teacher training and agricultural extension mission. But none of these satisfied the insatiable appetite of a rising middle class for access to postsecondary training, particularly in areas such as Los Angeles, which boasted only a few small private colleges and a public normal school despite a booming population.

President Wheeler and Alexis Lange, professor and the new dean of the School of Education at Berkeley, along with others in the university, wanted to focus the university on its mission as a selective institution and a center for advanced training and research—an ideal supported by leaders in the progressive reform movement. At the same time, they valued and espoused the need to expand California's public education system to meet the changing economy and labor needs of the state. Both Wheeler and Lange advocated the development of relatively new institutions, including the kindergarten, the junior high school, and most importantly, the junior college.

Lange in particular was a key proponent of the junior college. It could satisfy enrollment demand and provide training for the mass of students coming out of high school. For those who would benefit from college and professional training, the local junior college could provide a new and critical route to the university. A public network of junior colleges, the first such system in the United States, would be extensions of the state's public high schools, perhaps later organized under separate districts with their own local governing board.[3] Specifically, the junior college would not only prove the salvation for the state university, explained Lange. It would "popularize" college training and represent a "normal development within a state school system in the making, which, in turn, is itself being shaped largely by factors and forces that are national and even world-wide in their scope."[4] These new colleges, he claimed, could eventually "secure for the nation the greatest efficiency for the greatest number."[5]

With Wheeler's ardent support and Lange's leadership, the academic senate developed new admissions policies to promote the junior college and to make the state normal schools more attractive to Californians. In 1905, the university established matriculation agreements with the state's collection of six normal schools, and a number of private colleges as well, to more readily admit students to the junior year at Berkeley.[6] Two years later, the university offered a defined "lower division" curriculum program leading to the nation's first "junior college certificate," which would become the Associate of Arts degree. Any student completing the requirements laid out by the university at one of the state's normal schools or at any junior college in California would be admitted at Berkeley.

The same year, the California legislature passed a bill authored by state Senator Anthony Caminetti and supported by Lange and other university officials allowing local school districts to establish junior college programs as extensions of their local high school. Similar to the state's high schools, junior colleges would be accredited by University of California faculty. The first junior college in California began operating in Fresno in 1910. Local school authorities in Fresno proceeded to give a broad interpretation of the junior college mission, embracing a vocational curriculum as an equal goal with university preparation.[7] Not only would the institution provide university-equivalent courses for "young people who cannot afford the time and expense of actual university attendance," explained *The California Weekly* in 1910, but it would also "provide practical courses in Agriculture, Manual and Domestic Arts, and other technical work." The vocational and technical aspects of the new junior college at Fresno were incorporated into subsequent institutions established in Santa Barbara and Hollywood in 1911 and in Los Angeles in 1912.[8]

By 1920, California boasted sixteen junior colleges, far more than any other state. Legislation also allowed for the formation of separate junior college districts by local community initiative, thereby separating them from the jurisdiction of local school boards. Until the 1960s, California established an average of nearly two new junior colleges, or as they were renamed in that decade, community colleges, each year. In 2006, California had 109 community colleges operating in seventy-two districts and enrolling over 2.5 million students. In 1920, California also placed all of the state's evolving normal schools under the state board of education and renamed them the state teachers colleges. Previously, each of California's normal schools boasted its own governing board, with no central authority to guide its overall development. Reflecting the demand for post-secondary education throughout the state, these four-year colleges grew in number and expanded their mission beyond offering teaching credentials at the elementary level; by 1935, legislation allowed them to grant liberal arts degrees and, by 1947, master's degrees.[9]

The development of the general framework of today's tripartite system of public higher education significantly expanded educational opportunity in California. Not only were there new junior colleges and new state teachers college campuses in Humboldt County and San Luis Obispo, but the University of California established a southern branch campus in Los Angeles in 1919, becoming the first multicampus university in the nation.[10]

The redefinition of the University of California into a multicampus system was reluctantly agreed upon by the regents and faculty and strongly opposed by many Berkeley alumni. Civic leaders in Los Angeles, however, insisted that only by opening a southern branch could the state university properly provide educational opportunity in southern California, where the population now exceeded that of the northern section of the state. The threat of a bill to establish a new and entirely independent state university in Los Angeles forced the regents to capitulate. As advocated by Los Angeles boosters, the university absorbed the state normal school located on Vermont Avenue—what later became UCLA. The annexation proved an important precedent for future university expansion; while the University of California served the entire state, it needed multiple campuses and research stations to serve distinct portions of California's population.

The University of California proceeded to experience a substantial jump in total enrollment. In 1900, a total of 2,660 students attended the Berkeley campus and the medical school in San Francisco; by 1920, with the addition of the southern branch in Los Angeles, enrollment climbed to nearly 14,000, a staggering 425% increase. By 1923, California's state university, already the largest university in the nation, enrolled more than 19,000 students at its northern and southern campuses.[11] Helping to expand access to the University of California during this period, in 1919 the university temporarily dropped the requirement for specific courses (the subject requirements, like English and chemistry).[12]

As noted previously, California's new tripartite structure of institutions, largely formed by 1920, created a comprehensive and coherent system of public higher education.[13] Each institution had a distinct role in the new system (what was termed a "differentiation of function"). They were formally linked through matriculation and accreditation agreements. This new system significantly expanded postsecondary educational opportunity, with the junior college quickly bearing much of the weight of expanding opportunity. In 1920, California ranked only eleventh among the states in total population, yet it was first in the total number of students in public higher education—an indicator of its high and growing reliance on public colleges and universities. California was always among the top five states

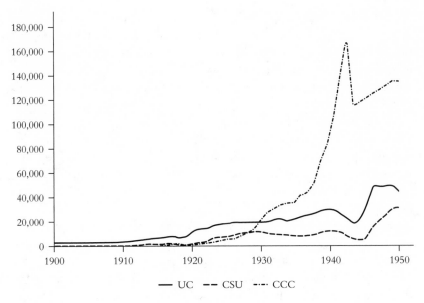

Figure 2.1. Enrollment growth in California public higher education: 1900–1950

SOURCE: John Aubrey Douglass, *The California Idea and American Higher Education.*

in the percentage of its eighteen- to twenty-one age cohort going to some form of postsecondary education. In 1920, some 10% of California's youth went to college, while the national average was 8%. In 1930, the college-going rate for this group was 16% in California, and the national average stood at close to 13%. By 1950, California's college-going rate was 35%, while the national average was close to 19.27%.

For California's land-grant university, the advantages of the tripartite system were tremendous. The university maintained its central and elevated role in graduate education and research, and the university was given license to continue its relatively high admissions standards—indeed, to raise them. Most states moved toward a horizontal organization of different and highly independent higher education institutions, but California's system, in large part built around its highly autonomous state university, was distinctly vertical. The other two "segments" of California's system proceeded to absorb the vast majority of postsecondary students in California, with what became the CSU system surpassing UC's enrollment by 1955 (see Figure 2.1). Although the University of California would maintain a market share of postsecondary enrollment relative to California's population, the junior colleges became the primary source for postsecondary education. No state relied so heavily on the two-year community college as the primary entry point to higher education—with implications discussed in later chapters.

Admission by Exception and a New Board of Admissions

Throughout the history of the University of California, the concept of "admissions by exception" offered an important alternative path to the university. But it was not well defined; rather, it was essentially an informal policy. In the immediate aftermath of World War I, the academic senate formalized and extended its use to a variety of populations. This included any student recommended by the Student Army Training Corps, veterans returning from World War I, students with exceptional talents in music and art, applicants from rural areas or from disadvantaged families, and students without the benefit of high schools with comprehensive and quality academic programs.

In 1923, the university also established a category of "special students" as a method for providing access to Californians "of mature age who have not had the opportunity to complete a satisfactory high school course but who, by reason of special attainments, may be prepared to undertake certain courses, though not as candidates for degrees." These students, however, could eventually meet the general requirements to then enter a formal degree program.[14] With these shifts came a gradual change in nomenclature. Students were either "regularly" admissible or could be admitted under the rules of admission by exception as "special action" students.

Most public and many private institutions in the United States incorporated exceptions to their regular admission requirements, although with varying degrees of magnitude. Many institutions offered "conditional" admission, requiring students to make up deficiencies, such as a required course. They could do so by either concurrently enrolling at another school or by taking special courses offered by the institution itself. At Columbia, a student could take up to one year to make up a deficiency and meanwhile be placed on probationary status. The use of exceptions grew nationwide in the early part of the twentieth century. One cause was the increasing number of requirements demanded by more selective institutions.[15] In 1910, Nicholas Murray Butler, the president of Columbia, justified the use of exceptions and conditions to avoid rejecting the worthy student. The university could not afford to deny admission to every "student who did not comply completely with the technical requirements, or whose conditions were not so slight as to be quite unimportant." It would lead to "serious educational injustice and grave wrong to many students." And without it, Columbia's admissions process would be "mechanical in character."[16]

The increasing scale of California's population, and the increased complexity of University of California admissions, including formal policies on special action and revisions to high school accreditation, required a new administrative structure—a story important for understanding the locus of authority over admissions. In 1920, as part of a larger reorganization of the senate that came in the aftermath of the regents delegating significant new powers to faculty, four standing senate committees related to admission were combined into one. In April of that year, the board of admissions replaced the committee on credentials, the committee on admissions, the committee on special students, and the committee on entrance examinations.[17] By 1939, the work of another senate committee created in the 1880s to accredit secondary schools and later junior colleges, the committee on schools, was also absorbed into this single committee, creating the board of admission and relations with schools (BOARS)—an entity of the academic senate that exists today.[18]

In turn, BOARS delegated certain powers to university administrators to implement aspects of the admission process, including the admission of students from accredited high schools and the administering of written examinations. For students that fit into these general categories, the university examiner, the recorder of faculties, and the dean of the undergraduate division could pass judgment on whom to admit on a temporary basis. But for other categories, such as exceptions and special students, BOARS maintained close control and made all decisions. The addition of the Los Angeles campus also added new administrative difficulties. Similar authority was granted to the assistant director of the southern branch and the registrar of the Los Angeles campus.[19]

From 1919 to 1960, the university maintained four major categories for accepting undergraduate students: graduates of an accredited California high school and with the principal's recommendation, acceptance by examination, acceptance by exception, and acceptance of junior college transfers with the AA degree to advanced standing. The only major change came in 1928 when subject-area requirements were reestablished.[20] At the same time, the university's board of admissions slowly elevated their admissions requirements as high schools altered their curricula to provide more vocational courses. Many principals became vocal critics of the University of California's role in accreditation. The university's use and publication of a ranking of high schools according to the academic performance of their graduates at the university, for one, caused significant consternation. The California High School Principals Association harshly criticized the university for being "arbitrary in its judgment of high school graduates." A proposal subsequently emerged in 1928 at the association's annual meeting in Long Beach to end university accreditation. Instead, a new agency composed of high school principals might instead grant accreditation. Another proposal asked the university to adopt standardized tests as a new method of evaluating freshman applicants. Many private institutions in the state, including Stanford, allowed students to take the examinations as one way to gain admittance.

University faculty, however, refused to give up their power of accreditation. For a period after 1903, the university's authority to accredit high schools did more than determine whether a student was eligible for admissions. It determined if a local school district could receive full state funding, such was the desire of Progressives to assure that high schools include a curriculum set to university entrance requirements. The link of accreditation with funding ended by the 1920s. The increasing professionalization of school administration and the growth in the size and complexity of California schools caused school administrators and many local school boards to seek more autonomy. Was the next stage simply to replace university accreditation? The threat of school officials accrediting themselves worried the university's academic senate. Faculty equated the proposal with an overall effort by some school officials to get the university to open its doors wider. "The University cannot afford to abandon its selective policy," stated Berkeley Professor Oliver M. Washburn. "Otherwise our enrollments would double and the state [would be] required to double our facilities for freshmen instruction at least."[21]

The senate's admissions committee also rejected the proposal to adopt standardized tests into the regular admissions process, which was an important decision not revisited until the late 1950s. Clarence Paschell, the university's examiner of schools, stated, "I have studied hundreds and even thousands of individual cases with high school principals, and it is my judgment that a high score in an intelligence test does not afford any guarantee as to successful work in college."[22] However, the senate did allow testing, and for the first time, the submission of test scores was approved as an alternative method for entrance for a small cohort of students, particularly students from out of state.

As noted, in 1928, the university reestablished the concept of subject areas that would be required by all students seeking regular admission to the

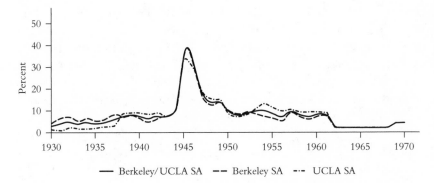

— Berkeley/UCLA SA   −− Berkeley SA   −·− UCLA SA

Figure 2.2.   Percentage of Berkeley and UCLA freshmen admitted as special action: 1930–1970

SOURCE: Board of Admissions and Relations with Schools, Representative Assembly Minutes, October 25, 1960; University of California Office of the President, Enrollment Reports.

university from an accredited high school.[23] By the late 1950s, the subject-area requirement for freshman applicants from accredited high schools included "a B average in the last three years, expressed in grade points, in a pattern of 10 high school academic subjects; one year in American history and civics, three in English, one in algebra, one in geometry, one in laboratory science, two in foreign language, and one additional in either mathematics, foreign language, or laboratory science."[24] Approximately 90% of the university's entering freshmen qualified for admission under this plan. The remaining 10% qualified under alternative plans, which included not only admission by exception but also possible admission if a student graduated in the top 10% of his or her high school class.

Beginning in the 1930s, special action admissions grew in importance as one means for the university to meets its social contract. Figure 2.2 illustrates the relative role of alternative admissions practices. For a period following World War II and at the height of the GI Bill, they comprised between 35% and 45% of all freshman admissions at Berkeley and UCLA. In 1947, at the peak of the flood of GI Bill students, some 50% of the university's total enrollment of 40,800 students were veterans. By the late 1950s, special action remained an important alternative path for admissions at Berkeley and UCLA. Not until the 1960s, and for reasons discussed later, was special action sharply curtailed as an alternative admissions route.

How Wide Should the Door Be?

As in California, a debate occurred in Minnesota regarding admissions to its state university during the first decades of the twentieth century. The University of Minnesota also enjoyed a significant level of autonomy due to a provision in the state constitution. And like most states outside the eastern seaboard, Minnesota relied on high school accreditation for both ensuring a college preparatory program throughout the state and for setting admissions standards. In the 1920s, university leaders in Minnesota debated the appropriate function of the admissions process and how wide the door should be.

Like the University of California, Minnesota's state university began a broad use of admissions by exception. President Lotus D. Coffman thought the didactic requirements set by the university regarding high school courses did not capture a large enough pool of potentially talented students. A relatively wide door was necessary to recognize the variety of aptitudes, sometimes latently discovered, of students and, most important, for developing civic and business leaders. But it could not be too wide, he argued; otherwise, the university would be overwhelmed. If it was to remain efficient in its purpose, it must necessarily be semi-elite. Finding the right balance and fitting it to a public university were difficult. In national meetings and in personal contacts and communications, presidents and officers of public universities discussed their similar problems and opportunities. Coffman came to the conclusion that, within the parameters of the university's admissions policies, all minimally qualified students should be admitted. Admissions policies should thus be calibrated, in theory, according to both proper preparation of students, their chances for success at the university, and their contribution to the academic milieu.[25] The key determinant for keeping the door open to a wide swath of talented students was consistent state funding for enrollment growth. Without it, the door would need to be partially closed.

Coffman took this argument to his state capital and was generally successful. Yet the predilection of most state universities was to accommodate as many students as possible. Minnesota arguably erred on the side of being too inclusive. In the 1920s, for example, attrition rates were extremely high, particularly following the freshman year. Freshmen constituted a lopsided 60% of the university's total enrollment.[26] The University of Washington experienced a similar phenomenon: Fewer than 50% of the entering freshmen matriculated to the junior year. Yet defenders of public institutions then, as now, also noted the often difficult economic background of their student clientele. Attrition rates related not only to academic preparation and aspirations. They correlated with a student's financial circumstances and a myriad of social factors.

There remains a natural tension regarding the elite concept of the university and the duty of a public institution to be, within reason, broadly accessible—a tension exposed repeatedly in interaction with state lawmakers, public school officials, university alumni, and the general public. The struggle of America's public universities to find a balance stood in sharp contrast to a cadre of increasingly selective private institutions. Beginning in earnest in the 1920s, a cohort of private colleges and universities faced a whirl of increasing enrollment demand. It was not the perceived duty of private institutions to keep pace with demand. Instead, it offered a great opportunity to enhance prestige. The race for numbers was over, remarked Frank Aydelotte, president of Swarthmore, in 1928. The "race for quality has begun. A few years ago our colleges and universities were competing for students, and great emphasis was laid upon 'healthy growth.' Now we are beginning to limit our numbers, to compete only for the best students, and to point with pride to the multitude that we turn away."[27] In an era of rising demand, institutions such as Yale, Princeton, and Harvard limited their enrollments to fewer than a thousand students.

With the innovation of the junior college and the slow yet steady emergence of California's state teachers colleges into regional four-year institutions, the University of California's new president, Robert Gordon Sproul, thought California's higher education system was a triumph of democratic and meritocratic values. It did not "force all to travel the same road" as in so many other state systems of higher education, few with anything approaching California's robust system. California was the innovator, providing "a number of highways of varying grades leading to many useful careers and open, every one of them, to all whose talents and desires make it seem probable that they may come thereby to a happy and successful life."[28]

Before the Commonwealth Club in San Francisco in 1930, Sproul explained that only through the invention of the tripartite system could the University of California remain focused its own mission: "The University is hard to enter—you will vouch for that and many a star athlete who is elsewhere today will confirm your statements."[29] But Sproul was well aware of inherent tensions in this marvelous system. In his inaugural address that same year, Sproul claimed the university occupied a proud "but not altogether comfortable position." A large crowd had gathered at the university's Greek Theater, an ode to the ancients built in 1903 with funds from university benefactor Phoebe Anderson Hearst. With his signature booming voice, Sproul noted a conundrum. On the one hand the university "is criticized for being too aristocratic." There were those, including a growing contingent of public school officials, who maintained that it set its standards "on an unreasonable plane; that it should admit every high school graduate." But this, he insisted, "would be a fatal blow to the quality of education by the state and to the careers and happiness of great numbers of young men and young women. Surely it is not aristocratic to insist that students who come to us should have such training as will make their success at the University probable. . . ." On the other hand, "we are criticized for being too democratic, for admitting and keeping too many, on the theory that the efficiency and value of a university are determined by its selective and eliminating process; that the fewer it admits and the more it weeds out, the better it is." [30]

For a time, the invention of the junior college reduced the pressure on the University of California to lower its admissions standards—to essentially make it more accessible. But the relief was temporary. The value of a higher education continued to increase, and with it came public demands for the university to be less selective. The social inequities of American society, made even more glaring with the onset of the Depression, added to the concept that the University of California needed to rethink its admissions practices. Admissions, traditionally thought the purview of the academic community, became the increasing concern of external constituents. In the 1930s, a relatively new debate began in earnest concerning which California citizens were gaining access to the public university of the state and which were being excluded. Geographic and economic representation and gender became more relevant in policy discussions. Added to this was a relatively new issue: the seeds of a debate over racial and ethnic representation.

Chapter 3

Inclusion, Exclusion, and the Issue of Race

When the University of California awards the medal to the senior having the highest scholastic average at today's commencement exercises, the recipient will not be present to receive it. He is an American-born Japanese and has been evacuated! A student in the college of chemistry and enrolled in a premedical course this semester, [Akio] Itano, who is 21, maintained a straight "A" average for four years at the university in Berkeley. He is a member of the Phi Kappa scholastic honor society; Sigma Xi, chemistry honor society, the university Y.M.C.A. cabinet and the student health committee. He was evacuated on April 22. As soon as the university authorities determine where he is, Itano will be sent his diploma—and his medal—by mail.

—*The Oakland Post-Enquirer*, May 13, 1942

In May 1988, the University of California's board of regents approved the following university policy: "Mindful of its mission as a public university, the University of California has an historic commitment to provide places within the University for all eligible applicants who are residents of California." In addition, the board stated, "The University seeks to enroll, on each campus, a student body that, beyond meeting the university's eligibility requirements, demonstrates high academic achievement or exceptional personal talent, and that encompasses the broad diversity of cultural, racial, geographic, and socio-economic backgrounds characteristic of California." This pronouncement of university policy reiterated many of the historic elements of the University of California's social contract. What was new was the explicit inclusion of cultural and racial diversity.

This chapter offers an analysis of the University of California's arduous path toward honoring this commitment and discusses differing approaches American universities and colleges took over time toward the issue of race in admissions. In tracing this history, one must take into account more than the biases of the academic community. Public institutions reflect and are affected by the cultural values and policies of the larger world. The fate of Akio Itano offers one rather extreme example, juxtaposing his academic success within the university with political events. In historically relative terms, the University of California was a progressive institution that offered opportunities since its inception for minority populations and international students to attend its campuses. However, Itano's academic credentials and his inclusion in campus organizations did not protect him from the larger political world. He achieved the highest scholastic honor given to an undergraduate, yet was evacuated to an internment camp before he could receive his award and his diploma, the tragic result of a growing fear of a Japanese invasion of the West Coast.

As in every corner of America, social and political issues related to race have played an extremely important role in the history of California. In the late 1840s, although separated physically by deserts and mountain ranges from an intensive political discourse between the northern and southern states, California was an important player in the national division over the future of the nation. Slavery was a major source of debate at California's first constitutional convention. "Free-soil" Republicans, mostly Yankees with abolitionist predilections and a majority of the convention delegates, argued with Democrats with southern sympathies that California should be a free-state, devoid of the morally bankrupt institution of slavery. Ultimately, the proposed constitution stated, "All men are by nature free and independent, and have certain inalienable rights," and "Neither slavery, nor involuntary servitude, unless for the punishment of crimes, shall ever be tolerated in this State."

The diversity of California's population, fueled by the rush of Argonauts in search of gold and a new life, fostered broad sentiments for the ideal, if not the reality, of tolerance and inclusion. "Under the peculiar circumstances in which California becomes a state," wrote the convention delegates in an open letter to all Californians, "with an unexampled increase of a population coming from every part of the world, speaking various languages, and imbued with different feelings and prejudices, no form of government, no system of laws, can be expected to meet with immediate and unanimous assent."[1] In the midst of the bitter debate over the issue of slavery, the convention preached harmony and advocated extending the rights of citizenship, particularly toward "natives of Old Spain, Californians who have voluntarily relinquished the rights of Mexicans to enjoy those of American citizens."[2] California's new constitution also incorporated relatively liberal views about the ownership of land by women and offered important guarantees of rights and privileges to the California families of Spanish and Mexican heritage.

Nonetheless, harsh policies of discrimination related to land ownership, labor, taxes, segregated schools, and suffrage followed, particularly in reaction to a large influx of Chinese labor for the building of the transcontinental railroad. The 1879 state constitution authorized cities and towns to segregate and even exclude Asians and other minorities from living within their borders. California was the first state to establish discriminatory zoning laws. Many local communities excluded Chinese children from public schools—a practice that continued despite a California court ruling in 1885 making it illegal. A number of cities proceeded to create separate schools. Following the 1906 earthquake, San Francisco rebuilt a public school for Chinese children and resolved to force Japanese children into the school as well. Chinese immigration came to a virtual halt after the passage of the federal Exclusion Act of 1882. Japanese immigration increased significantly around 1900 to replace the Chinese as a source of cheap labor. But increasingly, Japanese immigrants became the new focus of anger.

The school incident in San Francisco caused a national stir, with a formal protest by the Japanese government. California pursued a number of laws intended to restrict civil liberties, notably a bill that barred Japanese immigrants from holding legal title to land and restricted their rights to lease property. Many California Progressives shared the curse of racial and ethnic bigotry found in other American reform movements. While touting ideas of a participatory democracy and expanding civil liberties, they simultaneously rationalized the exclusion of minority populations from entering the mainstream of society. Progressive leader and California Governor Hiram Johnson, for example, joined with Chester Rowell, editor of the Fresno *Morning Republican* and a University of California regent, in advocating federal antialien legislation.

How did these glaring and overt policies of racial and ethnic discrimination influence university admissions and, more generally, the broad ideas of access to education envisioned by progressives? Answering this question accurately is difficult. The dynamics of admissions include not only the standards set by an institution and the process of admissions but the vitality of public schools and the socioeconomic conditions and biases of a larger society. The following offers a discussion of the general patterns of racial and ethnic exclusion *and* inclusion practiced by private and public colleges and universities, including the University of California. There are essentially different stories to tell, tied to institutional type, regional factors, changing societal norms, and the eventual influence of both federal legislation and legal decisions.

However, there are general themes that help illustrate the significant differences in the historical purposes and missions of public versus private colleges and universities in the United States. Rooted in their original charters as extensions of a democratic society, public institutions tended to set general academic criteria that, if met, guaranteed admissions, often irrespective of race or nationality. With the exception of the deep South, there were few overt university policies setting racial quotas, or for even knowing the race or nationality of the applicant—except through less overt knowledge of the demographic character of a student's high school and local community. Gender was a different matter, although most public institutions began to open their doors earlier and with more conviction than most private institutions. Public universities also provided various alternative routes for students to gain access, such as the special admissions process discussed in the previous chapter, with a focus on socioeconomic and geographic representation.

Private institutions varied greatly in their admissions practices, but many developed formal policies to exclude undesirable groups and to make sure they served their perceived constituents and biases—usually Protestant, predominantly male—and only reluctantly welcomed women, and then largely after World War II. Particularly among the nation's more prestigious private institutions, growing demand for admissions offered a means to exclude groups. Yet this is not to paint public universities as all enlightened beacons of egalitarian ideals. The caveats were often ugly. And although the structural approaches embraced by public versus private institutions by the turn of the twentieth century were divergent, there has been over time a general convergence as enrollment demand has increased and as institutions have attempted to broaden the racial and socioeconomic background of their students. The usage of criteria other than grades and the adoption of standardized testing by private institutions in the early twentieth century were, by and large, vehicles for excluding ethnic groups and women. Later in the history of higher education in the United States, holistic or "comprehensive" review of student applications and testing would shift in their intended purposes. The origins and evolution of these two approaches, the public versus private model, for setting the conditions for admission are important for our later discussion of contemporary admission objectives and practices.

Quotas, Testing, and Exclusions

In the years before the 1964 Civil Rights Act, overt policies of discrimination, or more commonly, the use of quotas, were prevalent in some state universities and many private institutions. Despite the charge to serve the people of Alabama, its state university remained devoted to segregation for

the vast majority of its history. In 1963, six years after a similar battle over
segregation and local schools in Little Rock, Arkansas, Alabama's governor,
George Wallace, famously chose to block a federal order to enroll qualified
African Americans in the state university. Like a number of southern states,
Alabama purposely created higher education institutions for African Americans under the ethos of separate but equal, reserving the University of
Alabama as a white-only institution. Limited opportunities meant that only
1.3% of the total black population graduated from college in 1940, com-
pared to 5.4% of the Euro-American population.[3]

Overt segregation and the barring of one or more racial groups, typically
African Americans, Jews, and other immigrant groups, were methods of
exclusion. A more common pattern, however, was the use of quotas, built
around a rationale of restricting the numbers of a specified group. As noted
in previous chapters, exclusion of women was common in most institutions
during the 1800s. Criticism and political pressure led many colleges and
universities to remove blatant restrictions and instead to use quotas. The
rush of Jewish and central Europeans to eastern cities such as New York,
and their academic success, caused great concern for both academic leaders
and their increasingly influential alumni, particularly within private universities and colleges. In the 1920s, Brown University imposed "limitations in
the enrollment of Jews and Negroes." New York University and Columbia,
in a city of immigrants, also set quotas on Jewish students.

Throughout the 1800s, Columbia's enrollment included mostly students
from the city of New York. Like public universities, the campus developed
close ties to local schools and agreements similar to accreditation to ensure
a steady flow of students. But opportunities afforded by growing enrollment demand and patronage resulted in efforts at a larger geographic draw
and higher level of selectivity. In 1910, Jewish and other immigrant students came to represent some 40% of the institution's enrollment, and this
was disturbing to the university's faculty and supporters. As described by
historian Marcia Graham Synnott, Columbia proceeded to determine ways
to quickly "cut its undergraduate Jewish enrollment in order to regain its
former status as an elite institution for native American sons of downtown
business and professional men."[4]

As part of that effort, Columbia required a formal application form with
information on a student's social and racial characteristics. For the first
time, admissions officers asked for photographs and personal interviews.
An added tool for both inclusion and exclusion was standardized tests. Columbia professor and psychologist Edward L. Thorndike's development and
advocacy of intelligence tests for determining "mental alertness" created an

assumed means to assess the general aptitude of students and their talents. Testing held the theoretical promise of calculating the abilities and knowledge of a student irrespective of social class, ethnicity, and attendance at an elite or common secondary school. But this is not how testing was often used. First introduced in 1919 as a replacement for earlier written examinations, the new admissions process required students to meet precollege course requirements, demonstrate their suitability for Columbia, and take Thorndike's test. These were the published requirements, although they were optional for some students, including children of alumni.

On another level, the test proved a deliberate tool for ethnic screening. A representative from Yale reviewed the success of Columbia's efforts and noted that Jewish enrollment dropped from 40% to 20% in a short period. A similar approach, he suggested, might be taken at Yale. "These tests," he explained, "by enabling the Board of Admissions to review again the records of all candidates, may in some cases be arbitrarily made to serve the end desired."[5] The test largely measured familiarity with American colloquialisms and customs. Most first-generation immigrants, including Jews, had difficulty in mustering relatively high scores. The cultural bias of the test was extreme.

The attractiveness of standard tests, as opposed to the traditional institutionally derived examinations, caused a number of private colleges and universities concentrated in northeastern states to cabal at the turn of the century. In 1906, this interest led to the establishment of the College Entrance Examination Board (CEEB). The CEEB first focused on creating a uniform written exam administered under the auspices of the board and for use by member institutions in reviewing applications. The use of CEEB tests gained significant momentum with the completion of studies that condemned a lack of rigor in the admissions practices of many private institutions.[6] By 1916, Yale, Princeton, and Harvard all agreed to use the exam. Increasingly, each of these institutions drew student applications from a wide number of states and actively sought a national market. The test would replace or in some instances complement their prior dependence on the uneven accreditation framework operated by public universities. By 1926, the CEEB converted from the written exam to a version of Thorndike's IQ test, creating the Scholastic Aptitude Test.

Columbia's example provided three cornerstones of admissions to selective private institutions that remain valid today: academic performance in high school, subjective review of a student's character and accomplishments, and a standardized test. The relatively new luxury of increasing demand and limited supply allowed for a more sophisticated shaping of their student bodies. These practices were in part developed to help limit specific groups for, as the president of Harvard, Lawrence Lowell, stated, "no college can admit unassimilables with impunity."[7] But they also were constructed to help diversify and strengthen the quality of the students coming to a campus, although within the constructs of a restricted idea of diversity. Many presidents of private colleges stated their desire to draw more students from different backgrounds and to conjure methods that would identify promising students. "It would be incompatible with all the conceptions of democracy," stated the president of Dartmouth, "to assume that the privilege of higher education should be restricted to any class defined by accident of birth or by the fortuitous circumstance of possession of wealth." Yet he also noted, the "opportunities of higher education ought to be restricted," with the objective of creating "an aristocracy of brains."[8]

Dartmouth College was the first to formally develop a plan to assist in the process of creating the "aristocracy of brains." The plan included seven criteria. Two of these related to academic ability: *exceptional scholarship*, which was deemed sufficient in itself for selection, and *high scholarship*, which was important but not sufficient in itself. The other five criteria included factors related to personal characteristics and circumstances. *Personal ratings* were one of these criteria, determined by admissions officers through interviews or recommendations made on behalf of the student and based on the secondary school activities of students, with evidence provided by the applicant. Added to this were values long espoused by public universities: the consideration of the *occupational and the geographic distribution* of students. Another factor was the *sequence of applications*, favoring early applicants. Finally, all "properly qualified" *sons of Dartmouth alumni* and faculty and officers of the colleges would be guaranteed admission—a formal policy nonexistent in public institutions, although later adopted on a limited scale by a few universities, usually with no formal policy sanction by its lay board.[9]

Dartmouth stated its intention to select the "entire" class on the basis of these qualifications. Other private institutions professed similar ideals. But there were significant nuances. Purposefully shaping the character of the student body further legitimated the active inclusion and exclusion of groups irrespective of academic qualifications. Dartmouth eventually set a limit of 3% on Jewish students entering the college. Previously, Yale set a quota of 10% to 12%. Princeton also set a figure of only 3%, rationalized as an approximation of the percentage of Jews in the United States. Between

1930 and 1940, Princeton enrolled on average only ten to twenty freshmen of Jewish background. Catholics, although considered by many more desirable than Jews, were also subject to restrictions. The University of Chicago set a similar quota beginning around 1932 under a proportional model of representation. The university "does not accept all students that apply," stated Chicago's admissions office. "It attempts to see that we have a representative student body" and so ventured to "keep the percentage of Jews at the University the same as the percentage of Jews in the city."[10]

Harvard was generally less restrictive and more liberal in its admission of students from different social and economic backgrounds. This was largely because of President Charles Elliot. Reflective of Harvard's cultural link with abolitionists, this venerable institution was one of the first to accept African Americans. However, Elliot's successor, Lawrence Lowell, was much more conservative. He became a prominent and vocal opponent of the surge in immigrants and their supposed detrimental influence on American society and on private universities and colleges like Harvard. Similar to other supporters of new and harsh immigration restrictions, Lowell distinguished between earlier and contemporary immigrants. America was a land of immigrants; some, however, were more equal than others. The first immigrants, including the Protestant majority and the first wave of Catholics, showed a proclivity for assimilation. The second wave, he thought, was tribal and resistant.

Lowell espoused the ideals of the Oxbridge model: the creation of a residential community, imposed by a requirement that most undergraduate students live in college residences. Where Elliot saw advantage to greater inclusion, Lowell favored some diversity in the socioeconomic background of white students but not much else. In 1914, he banned the small number of black students from living in freshman dorms, forcing them to live in segregated housing off campus.[11] Later, as the number of applications from Jewish students grew beginning in earnest by 1920, Harvard set a limit of 10% for these students.[12]

Quotas and exclusions in the admissions process were not limited to these major American universities. A study of private institutions in New York, commissioned in 1946 and sanctioned by the state legislature, investigated discrimination in higher education in the state. The resulting report showed a significant pattern: Sixteen institutions, a mix of Catholic, Protestant, and "nonsectarian" affiliated colleges, self-reported the use of quotas to exclude blacks, Jews, or other groups. Six restricted the number of blacks; twelve did the same for Jewish applications. Eleven limited the number of Protestants, presumably including the nine Catholic institutions reported in the study.[13] This raises the important point that private institutions often exist to serve a specific constituency. The existence of women's colleges is one example. Overt quotas and specific exclusions of groups, in some instances, fit into a legitimate form of discrimination, bolstering the diversity of institutional types.

But in the case of many institutions, such policies were manifestations of blatant prejudice. Through the 1940s, most students at Yale, Princeton, and Harvard came from well-heeled private schools—approximately 50% to 60% at Harvard and up to 90% at Princeton. Admissions policies at these and other private colleges and universities were consistently generous to the offspring of alumni and potential benefactors, constituting more than 20% of all admissions. Once at a campus, minority students often faced significant difficulties, whether they were Italian, Catholic, Jewish, or African American. Before World War II, in private and public institutions alike, the social life of most college and universities was structurally biased. This bias included the central role of social eating clubs, fraternity and sorority housing, and private societies—most famously at the privates like Princeton. Most private institutions still required chapel attendance as well, no matter what the student's religious affiliation. At Harvard, again generally more liberal, priority for housing was given according to the prestige of a student's private boarding school. Students were constantly reminded of the social pecking order and who was at the bottom.

There were internal efforts to tear at this private college paradigm. "If we are not to have a racial aristocracy, democracy must have a dwelling place within our colleges," remarked the president of Amherst College, Alexander Meiklejohn, in a 1921 speech. "We dare not shut our gate to our fellow citizens nor to their influence," he argued. "And if they do not come, we must go out and bring them in."[14] Meiklejohn's opinions, however, were not the norm, and his admonishments were largely ignored. A group of concerned alumni of Princeton in 1940 condemned the existing social order, arguing that it created "a racial intolerance almost worthy of Hitler, and wholly alien to any ideal of a university or even a college in a democracy."[15]

Some of the more progressive state governments embarked on their own efforts to address racial discrimination in public and private institutions and in businesses. In 1938, New York's revised state constitution prohibited discrimination on the bases of race, color, or religion.[16] City officials in New York proceeded to use this change in the constitution to pressure Columbia to end quotas. But the discriminatory practices of

these institutions generally stood strong, awaiting the civil rights awakening and the rise of a class of university reformers. The first significant
change came after World War II.

Breaking the Pattern: Federal and Legal Influences

The Equal Protection clause of the Fourteenth Amendment to the U.S.
Constitution provided the legal framework for extending educational
opportunities to minority populations, stipulating that "No State shall . . .
deny to any person within its jurisdiction the equal protection of the laws."
But the application of this commitment proved a tortuous path for America. In the 1890s, *Plessy v. Ferguson* interpreted the clause to mean that a
state was required to offer education to all citizens, not just to the Protestant Euro-American majority. But it also sanctioned segregation as a legal
means to extend this right. Not until *Brown v. Board of Education of Topeka*
in 1954 was this ruling overturned.

A significant influence on the admissions practices of American higher
education came as a result of the federal government's postwar agenda for
both promoting economic development and extending civil liberties. The
1944 GI Bill offered a national commitment to expand access to higher
education. This watershed in American history was followed two years later
by an aggressive and ultimately extremely influential report on the future
of American higher education. In 1946, President Truman appointed a
Commission on Higher Education. The "Zook Report," named after its
chairman, George F. Zook, benefited from the support of and research
conducted by the American Council for Education, the National Research
Council, and the Association of Land-Grant Colleges and Universities.

The GI Bill was primarily a mechanism for bolstering demand for higher
education. It provided vouchers to individuals who could then use these
funds to enroll in a college, university, or training program of their choice.
The commission focused primarily on the issue of supply. How could the
nation expand educational opportunity? The answer lay in expanding state
and federal resources for higher education, bolstering the development
of new institutions, particularly the community college, and exposing and
attacking the biases of existing institutions.

The immediate post–World War II years launched a new and significant
era in government activism, in part bolstered by the success in managing
and winning the war. Truman integrated the armed forces. Congress passed
legislation setting a goal of full employment. The GI Bill expanded access to higher education in part to help mitigate an anticipated economic

downturn and high levels of unemployment. Within this environment, the Commission on Higher Education completed its report, *Higher Education for America Democracy* (the first volume of a two-volume treatise under the title *Higher Education in America*). A broad agenda linked the nation's labor needs with issues of social and economic rights. This agenda included removing economic and racial barriers to higher education, increasing the number of junior colleges, and creating more opportunities for professional and graduate education. In seventeen states and the District of Columbia, noted its report, widespread segregation persisted in all phases of education, almost always sanctioned by state and local laws. This needed to end. "Although segregation may not legally mean discrimination as to the quality of the facilities, it usually does so in fact."[17] The report took aim at the use of quotas, which were in use primarily by private institutions.

In 1947, the year *Higher Education in America* was issued, the private sector of the higher education community enrolled about 50% of all students in the nation, although the publics were growing fast and by the end of the 1960s enrolled some 70% of all students. "At the college level a different form of discrimination is commonly practiced," noted the report. "Many colleges and universities, especially in their professional schools, maintain a selective quota system for admission, under which the chance to learn, and thereby to become more useful citizens, is denied to certain minorities, particularly to Negroes and Jews." The use of quotas, insisted the report, and similar discriminatory practices "is certainly un-American." Zook and his compatriots, including T. R. McConnell (a name to which we will return) used the nation's engagement in World War II and the cause of freedom as political tools. Quotas were, they stated, "European in origin and application, and we have lately witnessed on that continent the horrors to which, in its logical extension, it can lead. . . . The quota system cannot be justified on any grounds compatible with democratic principles."[18] The spirit of the statement was sound, if not the historical interpretation regarding the origin of quotas as strictly a European invention.

Under increasing criticism and with a replenishing of academic leaders influenced by the democratic impulses of the era, many institutions, including Yale, Princeton, and Harvard, had already begun to change their admissions policies during World War II. They began to remove overt quotas and eliminated questions of race, ethnicity, and religion in applications. The tremendous influx of GI Bill students at private institutions helped reframe the objective of admissions, broadening their idea of their role in society. The Zook Report clarified the shame of blatant discrimination by all colleges and universities and its costs for individuals and for the nation. America claimed a moral high ground as it fought communism and regimes that rejected Western ideas of civil liberties—at least those that were not allies. The Cold War forced higher education institutions and state governments to face in some measure the inequalities at home. The blatant discrimination of most private colleges and universities, and the segregated higher education systems in the South, came more clearly in view and under attack.

Famed Harvard economist John Kenneth Galbraith, who attended Berkeley as a graduate student, in 1975 noted the significant transition. Galbraith observed that Harvard had moved from a "slightly ludicrous aristocracy to a somewhat serious meritocracy."[19] Privilege and favor remained, although less so. In making this transition, Harvard and other selective private institutions raised their academic standards. They married these higher standards with the expanded use of supplemental criteria, both to maintain the traditional flow of students from elite American families and to include a greater variety of students from middle and lower income groups. This balanced framework became increasingly flexible and eventually extended to include greater racial, ethnic, and gender diversity.

Within private institutions, the supplemental criterion first used in an organized way at Dartmouth was, at first, a tool primarily for unwarranted discrimination. The criteria were often used to further the ingrained racial, ethnic, and socioeconomic biases. Eventually, however, as these institutions changed in character in reaction to initiatives such as the GI Bill, the use of supplemental factors in admissions became a great strength for more inclusive admissions policies. Three fundamental values articulated much earlier by leaders such as Charles Elliot and later by Harvard President James Bryant Conant finally took hold. First, a large number of private institutions recognized a duty to extend greater opportunities to potentially talented students from all walks of life. Second, a greater diversity of students created a more stimulating educational environment. And third, both of these previous values promised to produce more dynamic civic and economic leaders. These values combined to slowly reduce (but not eliminate) the aura of class privilege and promised to place these institutions more squarely in the life of the nation.

The Publics: The East Coast and the Example of CUNY

"In the 1920s and 1930s," remarked Historian David O. Levine, "American institutions of higher education engaged in egalitarian rhetoric, but their performance was a mockery of American ideals." When new types of students knocked on the door of colleges and universities, many institutions

embraced narrow notions of academic competence. And "when opportunity presented itself to select a heterogeneous and meritocratic elite,"
continues Levine, "America's best colleges chose openly the sons of native
stock, even if they were less qualified."[20] Yet it is important to again stress
the great diversity of American higher education. There are examples of
distinctly more progressive approaches to the issue of race and ethnicity,
although they are never far removed from the larger social mores and
biases of society.

Most public institutions approached the issue of admissions in a significantly different manner than selective private institution. They developed
and remained devoted to largely, but not exclusively, mechanical approaches
to determining the eligibility of a student. High school accreditation,
which in some form guaranteed geographic and social diversity, and the
submission of transcripts, devoid of supplemental materials, were the ticket
to most state universities. Many, first in the East Coast and then moving
slowly to the West, required standardized test scores as well. Before the
1960s, however, test scores were usually employed as a method to gauge
the academic quality of the entering class, not individual students. Rarely
were they used in public universities to determine a student's eligibility.

On the East Coast, where private institutions dominated and public institutions grew more slowly, minority students found their way increasingly
to public universities. The restrictive policies of Columbia, for example,
contrasted sharply to that of the City College of New York. Columbia's
discriminatory policies, and cost, pushed many of the best and brightest to
the city's public university.

Established in 1847, City College was one of the nation's first municipal colleges. It remained free to all local residents, increasingly devoted to
opening opportunities for the city's working and middle class students. To
a significant degree and for much of its history, the student population reflected the demographic composition of the city. But even at City College,
there was a period of restrictive admissions. Its secular charge and the desire
to build a complete public school system were the primary reasons that the
college initially prohibited enrollment of students from private and paro-
chial schools. With the end of this practice in the 1880s and reflecting demographic changes in the city particularly after 1890, significant numbers
of Jewish and Catholic students entered City College. By 1903, 75% of the
students were Jews from eastern Europe and Russia.[21]

Within the vast microcosm of New York City, the college grew in its
number of divisions and campuses and in its academic reputation. By the
1930s, there were undergraduate professional programs in business, educa-

tion, public administration, and science and technology, along with new campuses in Brooklyn, Queens, and the Bronx, including Hunter College, opened in 1928 as a women's college, although all programs of City College were open to women. Very much like California's statewide tripartite system of institutions and programs, City College evolved into a comprehensive system of institutions. Only in this case, the system served a single city and its immediate environs. It too relied largely on high school accreditation and a student's grades to determine admissions, but eventually, it also adopted standardized testing to create a "composite score."[22] In the 1950s, approximately the top 20% of the city's high school graduates were admitted to one or more campuses, each of which operated semiautonomously. When the state of New York consolidated and absorbed a number of public and private institutions to create the State University of New York shortly after World War II, City College was renamed City University of New York (CUNY) and remained a separate entity. It continues to operate as nearly the sole public provider of higher education in the city.[23]

CUNY proved a tremendous producer of talent, widely known for its academic rigor. Its selective policies and the aspirations of New York's immigrant pool of students made the university a major producer of academic and professional talent. But with the rise in demand for higher education, was CUNY too selective? Relative to other public universities, its admissions standards were not particularly high. But it operated without the benefit of a clear understanding of its responsibilities to the constituents of New York City and without a vibrant system of other postsecondary institutions that could justify its specialized mission. New York City included no community college programs, only a set of vocationally oriented high schools. By the mid- to late-1950s, however, in reaction to this perceived need, three community colleges were added to the municipal system, broadening access. But they grew slowly, failing to satisfy growing discontent. Initially, these three colleges enrolled small numbers of students—only 3% of the total enrollment in the multicampus City University.

Political pressure mounted in the 1960s to both significantly lower admissions standards and to increase enrollment. At first, the motivation of critics and city officials was to harness CUNY to more broadly meet local labor needs. A report to the city's board of education estimated that there was an immediate need for 25,000 additional college graduates and even more with some level of postsecondary education experience. A political movement began to make CUNY a more equitable and accessible provider of higher education. In the midst of rising numbers of public and private high school graduates, CUNY had relatively little enrollment growth.

Indeed, reflecting a disjuncture among public demands, city government, and internal academic management, CUNY increased admissions standards. The objective of university leaders was to hold enrollment numbers steady because of the lack of public funding. Meanwhile, New York was undergoing yet another significant change in the composition of its population. Although the city's total population was relatively constant, blacks and Puerto Ricans became more predominant components. Approximately 1 million blacks and Puerto Ricans migrated into the city, and an equivalent number of Euro-Americans moved to the suburbs or other locations. Yet City University's enrollment in the 1950s and into the early 1960s remained predominantly white.[24]

Appointed as the new chancellor of City University in 1963, Albert Bowker quickly determined two things. First, CUNY needed to alter its admissions practices to more generally reflect the population of the city. Second, City University needed additional resources to grow in enrollment. A year before his arrival, a master plan for CUNY argued that the path of increased selectivity was not "in keeping with the functions of a publicly supported university." At first, Bowker argued for increasing the university's target to about 25% of all city secondary graduates. In return, he asked the state of New York and the city to increase funding for both operating and capital costs. CUNY needed to revise its admissions policies and grow to remain relevant and, conversely, to avoid political disaster. Bowker raised the possibility of incorporating tuition if adequate funds could not be leveraged from public coffers, a politically unpalatable choice purposefully posed to lawmakers repeatedly by other leaders of public universities throughout the twentieth century.[25]

Racially charged politics in New York City, financial problems of a city approaching bankruptcy, and the suggestion of imposing tuition at City University created a powerful political powder keg. It finally blew in 1968 when 150 minority students "seized" one of the new campuses. Chancellor Bowker, notes historian Harold Wechsler, "concluded that CUNY could not remain an arena for racial confrontations." For the university to remain viable, Bowker pushed for a "100% Admission Plan" as the means to immediately gain significant minority inclusion. Graduates of the city's secondary schools could all go to CUNY, but not necessarily to the campus or program of their choice. The hope was to create a greater sense of differentiation within CUNY's array of institutions, including its nascent community colleges, thereby maintaining the excellence of some portion of the university. Through its admissions process, CUNY administrators proceeded to assign students to a specific academic program. It was a plan bound to fail. Constituent and government pressure and the university's muddled approach eventually caused City University to move toward an open admissions policy for all campuses and most programs.[26]

In 1970, CUNY's board guaranteed admission to one or more of the undergraduate four-year programs and not simply the community college divisions. "We have concluded that the City University should initiate an open admissions policy as quickly as practicable," stated the board. "Accordingly, we are directing the Chancellor of the University to immediately determine the feasibility of initiating this policy at The City University of New York for September 1970."[27]

In the midst of this transition in admissions policy, a 1969 statement by CUNY's academic senate outlined the general problems faced by public university systems, not just the system in New York City. "To a significant degree, the deficits of the black and Puerto Rican students are the result of inadequate preparation in the elementary and high schools," they stated. At the same time, "a private university is largely free to select students from the population of all American high schools and the most prestigious colleges do just that. The City University, however, is tied to one set of high schools; it is not free to sample the secondary schools." And if an institution like CUNY could not rely on traditional norms of collegiate preparation, "then any educational process based on the traditional premise is bound to be ineffective."[28]

The tumult led to a fundamentally altered admissions policy that did more than simply open the door as wide as it would go.[29] Borne of financial and political crisis and burdened by a lack of coherence (particularly the absence of a sufficiently robust community college network), the changes in admissions policy redefined the academic culture of the institution. It quickly moved from a university in most (but not all) of its parts with an elite function to largely a broad-based extension of the city's secondary schools. There were many benefits in rushing to this new paradigm, not the least of which was the rapid inclusion of minority students. But there were costs as well.

The Publics: The West Coast and the Example of UC

Like City University of New York, the University of California never adopted racial or ethnic exclusions or any formal quota policies. Early in their history, most public universities such as Michigan and Wisconsin incorporated quotas for women, but California's state university specifically avoided any such limits. And like CUNY, which provided access to the New York City's Jewish population, the University of California proved an important route for Asian Americans as well as Jews and other minority groups.

Yet over time, three factors influenced the flow of minority students to Berkeley and later to the other campuses of a burgeoning multicampus system. The first was the reality of segregation and cultural biases within the state's public school system. The second was the educational environment, including the value the university put on cultural diversity and the level of financial and social support given to minority students. And the third relates to potential biases of the admissions process. The following discusses each of these factors.

DEMOGRAPHIC CHANGE AND SEGREGATION

As in many other states, the components enforcing segregation changed over time in California from a legal choice afforded local communities to an indirect outcome of local laws and prejudices as legal rulings and government policies overturned overt policies. Adding to the complexity of this phenomenon were the differences in immigrant groups, their educational background and cultural norms, and the reactions and prejudices of the majority Euro-American population. Succeeding waves of different immigrant groups often precipitated different discriminatory policies. California provides a complex and contradictory mix of egregious segregation and discrimination and frequent progressive efforts at integration. This mix is illuminated in the state legislature's passage of a bill in the 1880s ending the legal exclusion of certain racial groups, African Americans, from attending local schools while allowing such discriminatory policies for others, specifically the Chinese and Japanese.

Attorney John W. Dwinelle, a University of California regent and coauthor of the university's 1868 charter, took the case of several black parents attempting unsuccessfully to enroll their children in schools reserved only for Euro-Americans. In 1874, he presented his argument to the California Supreme Court. Like *Brown v. the Board of Education* some seventy years later, Dwinelle stated that the school violated the Thirteenth and Fourteenth Amendments of the U.S. Constitution by denying admission of children to a public school nearest their home in San Francisco. Similar to *Plessy v. Ferguson* twenty-five years later, the court resolved that separate was equal. In instances where the "races are separated in the public schools," wrote Chief Justice William T. Wallace, "there is certainly to be found no violation of the constitutional rights of one race more than of the other, and we see none of either, for each, though separated from the others, is to be educated upon equal terms with that of the other, and both at the common public expense." But where there was no separate school provided by a community, "whether white or colored," then all students retained "an equal right to become pupils at any common school organized under the laws of the state."[30]

Six years after that ruling, the California legislature forbade segregation of African Americans (a relatively small population in the state) even if a community established a separate school, but they made no similar provision for Chinese and Japanese students. The efforts of San Francisco's school board to maintain a separate public school for Chinese children and then to include Korean and a growing Japanese student population in 1906 led to an international incident. The Chinese population in the state was declining, while the Japanese population was increasing. Both racial prejudice and the fear of economic competition, real and imagined, posed by Japanese farmers made them the new target of blatant discrimination.

Unlike China, which remained a weak international power, Japan was emerging as an industrial and military force, demonstrated by the outcome of the 1904–1905 Russo-Japanese War. When ninety-three Japanese students were told to enroll in the Chinese school, including twenty-two native-born second-generation Japanese Americans who were therefore U.S. citizens, the Japanese government protested and Washington reacted. President Theodore Roosevelt called the school board's plot a "wicked absurdity." He convinced the board to come to Washington. After a week of discussions with White House officials, the school board and the city, backed by prominent California politicians, agreed to repeal the segregation order. In return, the federal government offered to severely limit Japanese immigration.

In the midst of this controversy, California's educational organizations and a vast majority of leaders remained largely nonaligned. The California Teachers Association, then a professional association and distinctly not a union as it later would become, offered no stated position. California school superintendents turned down a resolution to support segregation at their 1906 convention but made no statement against it either. To their credit, however, University of California President Benjamin Ide Wheeler, President David Starr Jordan of Stanford University, and Ernest Carroll Moore, superintendent of schools in Los Angeles, offered a contrary view, appealing to America's ideals of inclusion. Wheeler spoke of the need for internationalism and tolerance and the importance of having foreign students at Berkeley. Jordan did the same for Stanford. Moore was a former faculty member at Berkeley, later becoming the driving force for creating what became UCLA. He claimed that students of Japanese ancestry were "a most helpful influence upon the other pupils" and criticized the action of the San Francisco school board: "As a California school man, I bitterly regret the action of the San Francisco school authorities. It was wholly unnecessary in my view and is, I am glad to say, not representative of public opinion in California." But Moore's assertion did not exactly jibe with the state's history.[31]

Beginning in the late 1800s, state and local government in California aggressively attempted to expand school attendance but not for all groups. California was one of the first states to enact a compulsory education law in 1874. By 1900, California launched a momentous effort to expand the number of elementary and secondary schools, experimented with the idea of the junior high school, and created a separate tax for expansion of the high school. Seven years later, 93% of California children between the ages of ten and fourteen attended school, a rate well above the national average. Attendance among native-born Euro-Americans stood at nearly 95%, and among blacks, it was 94%. But among Chinese, Japanese, and Native American groups, the percentages were much lower. In the critical ages of six through nine, these groups attained attendance figures of only 59.8%, 51.2%, and 49.1%, respectively.[32] Mexican Americans were a significant if small percentage of California's overall population. Their participation rates are difficult to assess because the U.S. Census at that time did not distinguish between Euro-Americans and Hispanics.

In discussing the issue of segregation and educational opportunities in California, it is important to have a general sense of the demographic mix of the state over time. The onslaught of the Gold Rush and later the recruitment of Chinese labor for constructing railroads resulted in a budding minority population by the 1870s. But the vast majority of subsequent migration was from America's eastern seaboard, from Europe, and by 1900, most prominently from midwestern states. Federal restrictions on Chinese immigration in 1882 and Japanese immigration in 1924 shaped the state's demographic trends. Not until World War II, with the influx of African Americans to war-industry jobs largely in Los Angeles and San Francisco and the first large-scale importation of Mexican farm labor, did California begin its current trajectory toward what is today the most ethnically diverse state in the nation. Census figures show that California's Euro-Americans represented approximately 85% to 90% of the population beginning in the mid-1880s, and this percentage didn't begin to decrease markedly until the 1960s. Yet there existed significant concentrations of minority groups, particularly in urban areas. Zoning laws adopted by many cities restricted housing for blacks, Asians, Latinos, and Jews. Even after cities were legally barred under a 1948 U.S. Supreme Court ruling from such provisions and from segregation shortly after World War II, these laws had a potent legacy.[33] There was, to a significant degree, a transition from de jure segregation (deliberate segregation) in many communities to de facto segregation (unintentional segregation, where separate schools were the result of established residential patterns).

In the 1950s and earlier, immigration and patterns of settlement correlated with the availability of jobs spawned a significant population of Mexican Americans in Los Angeles and in the small farming communities in the Central Valley. Asian Americans were concentrated largely in the Bay Area, with a scattering of Japanese farmers and small businesses throughout California. Particularly after World War II, African American communities clustered largely in the East Bay in areas such as Richmond and Oakland and in sections of Los Angeles. Attracted first by jobs in defense industries such as at the Kaiser shipyards, approximately 26% of Oakland's population was minorities in 1960, mostly African Americans. In Los Angeles, the total number of minorities was estimated at approximately 17%, including both African American and Mexican American communities that were distinctly separate physically from one another.

Segregation became a more significant factor as minority populations grew. By the 1960s and 1970s, despite efforts at desegregation in cities like Los Angeles, segregated communities led to more segregated schools. In 1970, some 80% of Hispanics lived in urban areas, largely in Los Angeles. It was the same for African Americans. In the Los Angeles school district, an estimated 23% of the district's children were Hispanic, and another 25% were black. Some 90% of the African American schoolchildren attended one of the 117 predominantly black schools. Approximately 75% of Latino and Mexican American schoolchildren attended one of the 100 schools that were predominantly populated by children of their own ethnicity—a higher percentage than in 1950. Some 80% of Euro-American children in the district went to nearly all-white schools.[34]

Influencing the educational opportunities for minority groups, from the public school to the University of California, were growing differences in funding for local schools. California's laws until the mid-1930s provided relatively equalized state funding for local schools. But shifts in tax laws during the Great Depression placed the burden largely on local property taxes to fund schools. Disparities in funding among school districts resulted in a constitutional amendment in 1945. The Fair Equalization Law created three types of state-funded aid: basic aid for all schools allocated on the basis of average daily attendance (ADA); an additional "equalization aid" per ADA for districts with property values, and hence property taxes, below a prescribed amount; and finally, "supplemental aid" for the very poorest districts. At that time, the state funded approximately half of all expenditures in local schools. But over time, rising property values, particularly among upper income communities, and declining state funding for schools on a per-pupil basis, later exacerbated by a series of tax revolts, contributed to growing disparities in funding and in the quality of local schools.

From about 1910 to 1960, California ranked among the top five states in spending per pupil. In the late 1960s, however, this ranking did not translate into equalized funding. A rich community such as Beverly Hills, which also benefited from parental philanthropy, spent $1,192 per student. Palo Alto, another extremely wealthy community in northern California, spent $984. But in Baldwin Park, a poor district in Los Angeles, they spent only $577. This fact led to an important California Supreme Court decision in 1971, *Serrano v. Priest*. In the largely Hispanic community of Baldwin Park, plaintiff John Serrano claimed that his son's education was inherently inferior in light of the vast differences in local school funding. The court agreed. California government, however, passed only minor laws to respond to the ruling with seemingly marginal effect. More important, any notion of reform and greater equity in the financing of public schools became even less likely with a taxpayer revolt against spiraling property taxes.

Voters approved Proposition 13 in 1976, placing a cap on property tax revenues and suddenly reducing monies available for all schools. In response, the state stepped in to provide greater funding and increase state regulatory powers, including a growing array of statewide mandates. The result was a reduction in the public coffers for schools in both rich and poor districts. The huge increase in California's immigrant population, particularly after the relaxation of federal laws in the early 1970s, changed the demographic mix of students and brought a surge of enrollment. For many of these new students, English was a second language. Special education programs grew in number and in their claim on resources, reflecting increasing rates of poverty and a substantially expanded notion of what exactly constitutes a learning disability. Today, the disparities are even greater among wealthy and poor districts. More generally, the overall funding per student in California tragically ranks near the bottom nationally.

Over time, de jour and de facto segregation, the disparities in the funding and the quality of public schools, and social and cultural division in

California influenced the flow of students to the University of California. At the same time, there were social forces and policies that helped open the university to minority populations, including the evolving notion that cultural and ethnic diversity had an important place in a public university.

THE EDUCATIONAL ENVIRONMENT
AND THE IDEA OF CULTURAL DIVERSITY

Cultural diversity has become a major focus of American higher education in our contemporary world for two primary reasons. The first is that universities, and in particular, public universities, have a responsibility to enroll a broad and representative spectrum of society. The second relates to the educational goals of universities: Advocates of affirmative action have argued for the concept that undergraduates should be exposed to different racial, ethnic, and economic backgrounds in the course of their academic and social experience at a university—that there is added value in cultural diversity among the student body, particularly in a globalizing world. Both concepts have roots in earlier debates on the role of public universities in society. At first, the value placed on cultural diversity had more to do with enrolling international students than native minority populations.

As early as the 1870s, University of California leaders began a discussion on the importance of enrolling international students from various parts of the world. The university's second president, Daniel Coit Gilman, was the first to articulate why this was of interest to the university and California. A great university needed to be cosmopolitan. Looking not toward Europe but to the vast markets of Asia, he thought both the enrollment of international students and the promotion of scholarly research on major international powers held numerous benefits. They would enlighten the academic community, provide a service for other nations and cultures, and promote commerce. California was a "new civilization of the Pacific Coast" and, as such, needed to foster and build on "the enlightenment of Asiatic nations . . . for it is obvious that California is not only granary, treasury, and mart for the American States which are growing up on this long coast, but it is the portal through which the Occident and Orient must exchange their products and their thoughts." China, Japan, Australia, and the "Islands of the Sea," he noted, "are the neighbors and the customers of the Golden State. Shall they not also look here for instruction in the arts and sciences, and for an example of a well-organized and well-educated community? The endowment of a professorship, which shall be devoted to the study of Chinese and Japanese, indicates an early recognition of this intimate relationship. We can not be too quick to prepare for the possible future which may open upon us."[35]

By the early part of the twentieth century, university officials claimed that California's state university enrolled the largest number of foreign students of any public university (a claim that is difficult to verify). University President Benjamin Ide Wheeler, like Gilman, saw the presence of these students and the development of academic programs with international components, such as commerce, as pivotal for the maturation of the campus. The relative isolation of California, even with the transcontinental railroad, made such programmatic efforts seemingly even more important. The educational background of many faculty at Berkeley also was an influence. Like many academic leaders, Wheeler, for instance, gained his graduate degree at a German university. Prior to coming to Berkeley from his position at Cornell, he proved an accomplished scholar in linguistics and the antiquities and a renowned internationalist. He helped to reestablish the Olympics while serving for a year as the chair of the American School for Classical Studies in Athens. The purpose of the Olympics was to promote not only athletic competition but also international understanding.

Taking the job of University of California president in 1899, Wheeler sought state and philanthropic contributions in part to fund international anthropological expeditions. Just prior to the San Francisco school board's efforts to rebuild the segregated "Oriental School," Wheeler argued, "A fixed prejudice is a case of arrested development. Like the petty village aversions, racial and social prejudices generally affect what is near at hand, what one sees and does not know. The man who has made up his mind that he dislikes Jews or Chinese or some other blood has introduced into his life a persistent source of narrowness, blindness, and poverty. He has raised a barrier between himself and the exceeding richness of human fellowship."[36]

A year after the incident in San Francisco, Wheeler purposely struck an apologetic note when he spoke to a gathering of the university's Japanese students on campus. A personal friend of President Roosevelt from his days at Cornell, he remained concerned about the sting of California's racist predilections. He insisted that the "Japanese and the people of the Pacific Coast must be good friends." The mutual location along the Pacific Ocean not only required it, but it was destiny. California and Japan, he continued, must trade together.

> They must know each other and commune frankly with each other, and the one must help the other where the other lacks. The instincts of the two peoples are in many regards different; their inheritance is

very different. But they are able, working together, to help each other greatly because one can bring to service what the other lacks. We Americans, and especially we Californians, admire very greatly the ready adaptability of the Japanese man to new conditions and strange tasks. We admire very greatly his capacity for organization, such as he showed in the medical department of his army during the recent war with Russia. We admire beyond all measure his devotion to his country and his Empire and his willingness to make personal sacrifice for the greater cause. We admire the delicate taste in form and color and action which the best of his people display. There is no finer taste in color and there is no finer courtesy of act than that which appears under the name and the auspices of Japan. May the two peoples always fairly understand each other.[37]

Internationalism was strongly rooted in the ideas of manifest destiny and the need to learn about, influence, and exploit new markets. Commerce was clearly a major objective, although, realistically, California's economy long remained focused on agriculture and domestic markets. But it was more than just that. There was an element of altruism and a sense that inclusiveness strengthened the university and society. The international predilections of University of California officials did not necessarily reflect the sentiments of state lawmakers or the university's governing board. In fact, the university's relatively high enrollment of foreign students caused a serious confrontation. The bitter and often violent anti-immigrant, and specifically, anti-Asian, sentiments of Californians gave rise to a period of internal evaluation of the merits of enrolling foreigners and, by implica-tion, non-Euro-Americans. California, like the rest of the nation, turned decidedly isolationist in the aftermath of the war in Europe. Within the context of significant state budget cuts and a dramatic rise in enrollment demand during a post–World War I recession, members of the board of re-gents voiced serious concern about the number of foreign and out-of-state students attending the university. The university, and essentially, California taxpayers, subsidized their education. But to what end? One option was to limit their numbers; another was to charge tuition.

Supported by the academic senate, Wheeler's successor, David P. Bar-rows, argued against imposing an additional fee. Within the social mores and political context of the post–World War I era in California, Barrows made a formal plea for cultural diversity among the university's student population. In his report to the university's regents, Barrows stated that Berkeley enrolled a total of 9,967 students. At least 1,151 of these were nonresidents, representing nearly 12% of Berkeley's students. Most came from other western states, Hawaii, the Philippines, China, and Japan. For the purpose of his report to the regents, Burrows had the university registrar tabulate the ethnic and racial composition of a significant part of the student body in 1921—the first such attempt in the university's history. Approximately 172 Asian students were residents of California, including sixty-six of Chinese ancestry, sixty-two Japanese, thirty-three Filipinos, and eleven Hindus.[38] Combining nonresident and resident, the Berkeley campus enrolled a minimum of 312 students from minority populations, or approximately 3% of all graduate and undergraduate enrollment. Although this may seem a statistically small percentage, it is significant when compared to the total minority population of the state, which in 1920 stood at approximately 8%.

The president cited no figures on the number of African Americans or Native Americans, perhaps in part because the report focused on foreign student populations. Berkeley did have a small number of African Americans in 1920. The total number of blacks in the state, however, was extremely small, representing less than 2% of California's population between 1880 and the late 1920s.

Of more importance than the actual numbers of Asian and Asian American students, and of nonresident students, was the conviction of Barrows and other university officials that the presence of these students was a positive influence on the academic culture of the university. The consternation over their enrollment, insisted Barrows, was misplaced. In most areas of university management, Barrows was inept, and his tenure, as a result, was short. The university was wracked by state budget cuts and had undergone a successful drive by faculty for more power over university affairs. In many areas, Barrows was extremely conservative. He served as the superintendent of schools in Manila before taking a professorship in political science at Berkeley and then the presidency. Barrows was convinced of America's destiny as a world power, with the markets of Asia its first major conquest. Ironically, his imperialistic tendency made him, in effect, a staunch defender of foreign students at the university. California, he stated before the regents, "must enjoy its due weight in the councils of the nation through superior character and education of its people and through their unification in common spirit." He continued:

> I think it could be shown that the state is economically benefited due to the increase in wealth and new tax-payers by the privileges of free education which it accords to potential citizens. As for the foreign-born

students: they are not very significant. They do not impose any special burdens. In some cases, notably the Chinese and the Russian students from Siberia, as well as certain students who are beginning to come from Latin American countries, I feel that the promised advantages to the commerce of California, as well as to our international relations, are considerable.

Barrows' counsel was successful in convincing the regents to continue admission of foreign students. Less than a decade later, Berkeley would enroll some 340 foreign students from forty-four countries. But accommodating these and all students flowing to Berkeley and to UCLA created a crucial housing problem. Until 1929, the University of California operated not a single dormitory. Instead, students rented from local communities or joined a growing number of fraternities and sororities whose principal attraction was a place to live near the campus. In 1874, the regents approved the construction of eight cottages for the use of students on university property. Each cottage accommodated ten persons. By 1900, there were forty-five social fraternities.[39] All operated relatively independently, with minimal oversight by university officials. Most if not all excluded minority groups. The city of Berkeley allowed for exclusionary clauses in rentals, as well as in property deeds—a common form of racial and ethnic discrimination pervasive until a state court ruling in 1947 made it illegal. In the area around the Berkeley campus, landlords and the city would not rent to African Americans and most other minority groups, including the sizable population of foreign students.

In part because of the difficulties in finding housing near the campus and its cost, as late as 1926 nearly half the male students at Berkeley lived in San Francisco and commuted across the bay to attend classes. One reason was the availability of jobs in the city. By one university estimate, 70% of male students engaged in some form of part-time employment—a figure similar to that of the 1880s.[40] However, the pattern for women was different. A survey completed in 1923 showed that of 3,217 female undergraduates attending Berkeley, a high percentage, some 43%, reported living at home or with friends and relatives in the East Bay. Another 16% lived in mostly "approved" boarding houses, and another 15% lived in social clubs. Only 5% resided in apartments. Some 10% of all women students lived across the bay in San Francisco.[41]

Most major American colleges and universities and all public higher education institutions at first relied largely on local communities to provide housing for students, unlike the English model, which insisted on

university-operated residences as a key component in building an academic community. In part, the decision for public institutions was an economic one: Resources were limited for capital construction, and institutions
devoted most funding to academic buildings and operations as they grew in
enrollment. A turning point came in the late 1920s, as both university officials and students identified the need for housing as critical for the welfare of
the institution and students alike. The biases of local landlords and increasing rental rates prompted two important projects, both funded by outside
sources. The first was a gift from Mrs. Mary McNear Bowles for the building of Bowles Hall, Berkeley's first university-operated dormitory, with
accommodations for 204 men. The second was an initiative to establish the
nation's second International House on the Berkeley campus.

The first International House came to fruition under the leadership
of Harry Edmonds, director of the YMCA in the city of New York. He
observed the racism and isolation experienced by foreign students attending Columbia. Edmonds then successfully asked John D. Rockefeller Jr. to
fund the construction and operation of a complex to house both foreign
and American students. Interaction would breed familiarity and eventually collegiality. The first International House opened in 1925. Edmonds
soon sought to establish another on the West Coast. Working with University of California President William W. Campbell and Vice President Robert Gordon Sproul, Edmonds agreed on Berkeley as the best possible location, in part because of its relatively large population of foreign students.
Proposed principally as a means to house international students, I-House
(as it became known) also offered housing to native African and Asian
American students. When first proposed and publicly discussed in 1927,
Berkeley residents and the city loudly noted their objections. The idea of
an interracial, coeducational residence in the nearly all-white neighborhoods that surrounded the Berkeley campus incited some 1,000 residents to
protest the proposal. Placement of I-House on campus property, however,
meant that the project was outside the jurisdiction of city zoning laws and
covenants.

I-House opened in 1930 and soon accommodated 530 undergraduate
and graduate students. It offered the only local housing available for African American students. It also offered dining facilities, in part because
most local restaurants refused to serve minorities. Other forms of housing
that accepted ethnic minorities followed, encouraged by university officials
and prompted by Berkeley students affiliated with the YMCA. In 1933,
students concerned with the availability of low-cost housing and the social

conditions of a nation in the midst of a severe economic depression created the first housing cooperative open to all races. It grew to house more than 500 students in five buildings in just six years, including one dormitory exclusively for women. A similar cooperative was established at the Los Angeles campus in 1935 and, like the one at Berkeley, required boarders to help maintain the facility.

The presence of foreign students and domestic minority groups, the context of the Great Depression, and the changing academic culture of a growing public university raised the social consciousness of at least a portion of the student body and faculty. But the discriminatory policies of local communities remained a significant problem as university enrollment continued to grow. In and around Berkeley, members of the African American community requested that the university make a more concerted effort to mitigate and fight discrimination by landlords. Black students at first welcomed the opportunity to take residence at I-House. But they soon viewed it as just another form of segregation because there were few other housing choices. In this environment, a group affiliated with the YWCA and concerned with race relations circulated a petition against discrimination in local boarding houses. Berkeley's student government, the Associated Students, followed this by establishing a list of approved boarding houses that did not discriminate on the basis of race. They also circulated a petition calling on students to boycott those that did not make its list. At least initially, university officials were reluctant to support these initiatives, perhaps in part because housing was a limited resource and because of a desire to reduce an already antagonistic relationship with the local community.

Not until World War II and its aftermath did the university's administration adopt the student government's list of approved accommodations and, in general, take a more active role in developing student housing. The first state-funded dormitory was built after the war. And not until July 17, 1959, did the regents, largely due to student activism, state that fraternities and sororities could not bar any student membership on the basis of race, religion, or national origin. At the behest of University of California President Clark Kerr (1958–1967), this policy was extended to all student organizations.

The value placed on cultural diversity and the improvement in the practical need to house and in some way support international and minority students contributed to a slow awakening. But it is difficult to assess the progress in enrolling and supporting minority students, in part because the university kept no data on a student's ethnic or racial background.

THE PROCESS OF ADMISSIONS AND SEEKING DATA

In the first decades of the University of California's existence, Euro-Americans, largely Protestants, remained the majority. But there were also students of Mexican Spanish heritage and, by the turn of the twentieth century, Asian students, both foreign nationals and domestic. The innovation of high school accreditation meant that, in effect, a student's race, ethnicity, and economic background were not clearly identified in the admission process itself and were not generally known until the student arrived at the institution. Yet there were potential biases in the process shaped by disparities in the quality of schools and, for instance, the predilection of high school principals who, up until 1960, had the authority to recommend students for university admission. University admissions policy was neither overtly biased against racial minorities, nor was it proactive in the way that geographic and economic representation was used in special action admissions.

The lack of data on the background of students arguably was well intentioned. Indeed, sensitive to public criticism in the 1920s that the University of California enrolled too many foreign and undesirable minority students, the board decreed by the early 1930s that no statistics be gathered related to the race of not only students but of faculty and staff as well. In invoking this rule, the university was unlike most private and some public universities where, beginning in the 1920s, students were often required to provide such information on their application.

However, a visual and unscientific scan of past student yearbooks at Berkeley offers a glimpse into the diversity of the student body over time. This visual scan indicates that, although African Americans and students of Mexican and Latin background were rare, Asian Americans appeared to overcome multiple societal obstacles and, over time, gained a more significant level of representation at Berkeley and UCLA. The university's census of 1920 indicated that about 3% of undergraduate students at Berkeley were of Asian American background; by 1936, they represented some 4%; in 1951, and after the peak of the GI Bill, their numbers increased to almost 8.5%. At the time, Asian Americans constituted approximately 3% of California's total population. In short, Asian Americans had became an "over"-represented minority in the university by 1950 and perhaps much earlier.[42]

With the political shifts of the late 1950s and 1960s toward greater recognition of racism in society, the lack of systematic gathering of race and ethnicity data by the university, and by the state school system in general, posed a problem. It was difficult to gauge the extent of the university's inclusion or exclusion of racial groups and impossible to monitor change. Federal and state government demands for data, however, forced the University of California and other public institutions (less so with privates) to eventually collect information on students and employees regarding their race and ethnicity. Under pressure from the NAACP, and as a supporter of the Civil Rights Movement, in 1963 Governor Edmund "Pat" Brown requested information on all university employees and students regarding their ethnic identity.

Brown, a self-professed "pragmatic liberal" and Democrat, worked with a state legislature to expand employment and educational opportunities for minorities. He viewed data gathering as one road to that goal. The Unruh Civil Rights Act and the Rumford Act, passed in 1959 and 1963, respectively, forbade discrimination in business and unfair housing policies and practices. Increasingly, lawmakers turned their attention to public higher education. But the university was reluctant to gather information on race. In considering Governor Brown's request, the University of California's academic senate noted, "Listing of minority group members by name is in conflict with university policy which is to ignore completely an individual's ethnic background in all decisions." A systematic survey, it was thought, "would be detrimental to the interests of the University and inconsistent with University policy toward minority groups."[43] Brown did not get the information he sought, and he had no legal recourse. University policy was not changed until the federal government passed the 1965 Higher Education Act. Among other initiatives, the act launched the development of a federal system for gathering data on higher education enrollments, facilities, and financing. Failure not to comply might mean losing federal funds for research and student aid. But this was not yet an annual demand for data. Not until the early 1970s, in the midst of a substantial demographic shift, did California begin gathering data on race and ethnicity on an annual basis. This delay in systematically gathering racial and ethnic data in California was mirrored throughout the nation.

Federal civil rights and higher education legislation of the 1960s, part of the Great Society programs, proved a powerful influence on university admissions. As we have seen, California's state university created an admissions policy framework in which factors such as economic, geographic, and "special circumstances" were thought adequate methods to include disadvantaged groups. They were essentially race-neutral approaches. There were few university efforts to reach and nurture the development of these students. That would soon change. In one of the first meetings on the issue of disadvantaged racial minorities, University of California President Clark Kerr met with the academic senate's academic council—the executive committee of the university's faculty senate. Several months after the 1963 Civil Rights Act, Kerr observed that the university "has provided equality of opportunity in the sphere of its influence, but perhaps has not actively searched for the means to increase opportunity for equality."[44]

Like the pressures seen in the example of CUNY, inequalities in California society, combined with a new national consciousness and the beginning of a dramatic demographic shift, altered the policy context. Like other public institutions, the University of California would seek more proactive policies to increase minority participation.

Part II

The Managerial University
and the Post–World War II Era

Chapter 4

The Master Plan, the SAT, and Managing Demand

The changes that take place in intellect and character are coming to be measured with the same general technique, and, we hope, with the same passion for clearness and precision, which has served the physical sciences for the last two hundred years.
> —Edward L. Thorndike, Teachers College,
> Columbia University, 1912[1]

Public institutions ordinarily admit all students above a minimum "floor," who meet stated basic entrance requirements. Private institutions often have both a "floor" and a selective process for choosing among applicants who meet minimum requirements. It may be that the state colleges and the University in particular will have to work out some such combination plan in order to select the best students from the forthcoming flood of applicants.
> —California Master Plan for Higher Education, 1960

During the two decades after 1950, American higher education nearly quadrupled in enrollment. Most state universities remained committed to selecting primarily students who graduated from high schools within their respective states and to grow, in some form, in enrollment to keep pace with the population. With projections of a fourfold increase in enrollment demand by the mid-1970s, in the late 1950s, University of California officials negotiated with other members of the state's higher education community and with Sacramento lawmakers on how to expand California's higher education system. The result was the famed 1960 California Master Plan for Higher Education. A "Master Plan Survey Team," a group with representatives from public and private higher education and chaired by Arthur Coons, president of Occidental College, negotiated the plan. The master plan is often portrayed as the product of a single mind: University of California President Clark Kerr. But this is only part of the story.

In the last 1950s, Kerr sought to preserve the university's position as the primary research and doctoral-granting public university in California and successfully pushed for a process for negotiations. The actual job of creating a shared vision was the assignment of the survey team, with Coons as an arbitrator between the main protagonists: the university and the state colleges. The state colleges wanted to extend their mission into doctoral programs and to receive state aid for research; the University of California opposed any such expansion and sought the preservation of the tripartite system. With pressure by Governor Pat Brown and leading legislators to end the conflict, the higher education community was forced to reach an agreement on issues such as segmental mission, enrollment planning, new campuses, and possible shifts in admissions pools. Cutting future costs emerged as one important goal. Projections showed that California State government could not fully fund the anticipated growth in enrollment demand in the coming two decades under existing admissions policies at both the University of California and state colleges.[2]

Under a proposal formulated by survey team member Glenn Dumke (president of San Francisco State), the university, the state colleges, and the state of California could benefit by raising admissions standards—essentially gaining a more selective student body. The main motivation was financial. To reduce costs, the University of California and the state colleges (what would become CSU) agreed to reduce their eligibility pools of high school graduates. The University of California would raise its admission standards with the purpose of lowering its pool of eligible freshmen from approximately its historical figure of the top 15% to the top 12.5% of public high school graduates. California State University raised its admissions standards and lowered its eligibility pool from approximately the top 50% to the top 33.3% of California's secondary school graduates. In turn, these revised targets would shift in the new term approximately 50,000 students to the junior colleges (what would be renamed the California Community Colleges) with lower operating costs and funding primarily from local property taxes.

The eligibility pool targets substantially modified the social contract of the University of California and the state colleges. The plan suggested the two institutions reduce access. How that was to be done would be a prerogative of university and state college officials. As Arthur Coons noted, over time both UC and the state colleges might need to adjust their admissions standards in light of "the forthcoming flood of applicants."[3] The revised admissions pools, it was thought, should not be carved in stone; they might need to be revised upward or downward, subject to financial resources and the labor needs of the state.

In negotiating the master plan, it was understood that the transfer function pioneered in California remained central to socioeconomic mobility in the state. To assure a place for all junior college transfers with a grade point average of 2.4 or better, the University of California promised to maintain a ratio of upper to lower division students of approximately 60:40. With a requirement for a grade point average of 2.0 for transfer students, the state college (what would become the California State University) also adopted the 60:40 ratio. Based on this matriculation policy, lawmakers agreed to provide state funds for the construction of community colleges. Previously, all capital funding came from local coffers. The master plan agreement also set a mere 2% limit on the number of students that could be admitted by exception at the freshman level as part of the effort to shift more students to the community colleges.[4]

Even with the reduction in the percentage of high school graduates eligible to enter the University of California, enrollment growth would be substantial. Between 1960 and 1975, student enrollment at the university was expected to grow from approximately 43,100 to 118,750 students, a 175% increase.[5] "No historical precedent exists for such a Herculean task in higher education," remarked an academic senate committee in its study on managing enrollment growth at UC. "Worldwide attention is now focused on the University of California to see how and if it can meet the challenge." Such growth, they concluded, required a reassessment of the university's "precious academic heritages" and to question "established traditions." How might this rapid growth, including the establishment of new campuses, affect the quality of the institution? For university faculty, this was a deep concern.[6]

In the years just after World War II, in addition to Berkley and UCLA and graduate programs at the medical campus in San Francisco, the University of California established three new "general" campuses to cope with enrollment growth. Santa Barbara was a state college and was absorbed by the university in 1944, becoming the third campus to offer a liberal arts program. Davis and Riverside were established in 1952 and 1954 as new general campuses. Previously, they served as agricultural research stations and offered extension programs. By the late 1950s, preliminary plans were made for three more campuses. The result was the establishment of UC San Diego in 1960 and campuses at Santa Cruz and Irvine by 1965. All eight general undergraduate campuses provided doctoral training, and each was designated as a research institution. The University of California remained "one university," with each undergraduate campus sharing the same academic mission and collectively devoted to accepting all "eligible" students.

In planning new campuses, California made an important assumption: There should be limits on the size of campus enrollments. Planning studies as early as 1948 indicated that there were no significant economies of scale achieved in either operating or capital costs by developing campuses with relatively large enrollments. It was assumed that a campus with more than 25,000 students would result in a significant decline in the educational experience of undergraduates and a breakdown in the sense of community among students and faculty.[7] This assertion essentially argued against a path taken by a number of other states where the public university eventually grew to 40,000 or more students—a size matched by no private institution. Enrollment limits offered a rationale for assessing the number of new campuses needed to meet projected enrollment demand. The master plan adopted these assumptions and set a goal of distributing campuses in underserved areas, essentially offering the prize of a new state-funded campus to competing communities and their representatives in Sacramento. State-funded campuses became widely recognized as a method for ensuring socioeconomic mobility for the individual student and as an important stimulus for regional economic growth.[8]

With the master plan deal struck in 1960, the University of California needed to raise its admissions standards to become even more selective. There was a range of options: UC could raise the required grade point average in selected preparatory courses, increase the required number of courses, adopt for the first time a minimal SAT score, or some combination of all three.

UC Considers Standardized Testing

In the late 1950s and extending into the 1960s, the University of California began a lengthy debate on the possible uses of standardized tests. Many of the same issues discussed by supporters and opponents of testing today were vetted in this era: the socioeconomic biases of tests, their predictive value of collegiate success, and most important, their proper use in the admissions process. Why did public universities adopt standardized testing? And how did their adoption influence the social contract of universities?

As a sorter of lives and proclivities, intelligence tests were born out of an American infatuation with the potential power of "scientific" methods to better organize and manage society. In the midst of industrialization, a flood of immigrants, and increasing demands for skilled and professional labor, scientism gained increasing sway as a source for not only technological innovations but also for managing society and attacking its real and perceived social ills. At first, much attention was focused on time and motion studies that found methods for making industrial workers more productive. This was soon followed by the idea that human intelligence could be scientifically measured. Intelligence tests might help identify the best potential workers, the best civil servants, the best military officers, and the best students.

As noted previously, the establishment of the College Entrance Examination Board (CEEB, or College Board) in 1906 created an administrative framework for a single written admissions examination. With the initial membership of Columbia, Harvard, and later, Yale and Princeton, CEEB examinations became the building block for a marginal expansion of access to middle class and occasionally working class students. It also was a decided tool for excluding "unassimilable" populations, in particular, Jews. In turn, the CEEB offered a vehicle for developing intelligence tests that would help in college and university admissions. The first test under the name SAT was administered on an experimental basis in 1926. Within largely private institutions, it slowly became an important component in the admissions process. The growing industry of testing later led to the establishment in 1948 of the Educational Testing Service (ETS) in Princeton, New Jersey, merging several competing testing agencies and launching a concerted effort to eventually test all high school graduates. Was ETS a public service or a business? That question remains today.

Much to the chagrin of ETS and its supporters, public universities, the fasted growing part of America's higher education system, proved reluctant to embrace the SAT. Public universities operate in a separate world. As discussed previously, their applicant pool was more defined and included, first and foremost, students who had graduated from a state's network of public high schools. Their time-proven admissions criteria focused on grades and on a system of assessing and encouraging quality within secondary schools. Public universities marginally practiced favoritism toward alumni and had, thus far, not engaged in large-scale fund-raising or catering to donors—an important link for private institutions in their admissions practices. As enrollment demand grew, the publics received a corresponding increase in state funds. Whereas private institutions sought only minor increases in enrollment, or simply stability, as a route toward greater selectivity and prestige, public institutions welcomed enrollment growth. It was their duty. It was also a means for increasing financing for academic programs and for widening their social, economic, and political influence.

Until the late 1950s, few public universities required the SAT or other available tests. Beginning in the 1930s and up to the 1960s, interest in the SAT by public institutions tended to focus on two rather narrow uses. Standardized tests were embraced as an alternative admission criterion for

out-of-state students and others who graduated from nonuniversity accredited high schools; by the 1950s, testing a sample group of students after
they enrolled in a university served as an occasional analytical tool for assessing their admission criteria.

By 1949, the vast majority of ETS clients remained along the eastern
seaboard, with the most significant use by the Ivy League and a select group
of other private colleges and universities. ETS opened a West Coast office
in Berkeley in 1947 with the ambition to get the University of California and other public and private colleges and universities in the region to
adopt the test. ETS President Henry Chauncey did persuade the University
of California to join the ETS board as an institutional member—the first
public university to join. Normally, usage of the SAT by an institution was
a prerequisite for membership. In the case of the University of California,
Chauncey made an exception in the hope of enticing the university into
the fold.[9] Chauncey aggressively marketed the tests to public universities
and was beginning to make inroads in Michigan, Texas, and Colorado.

Chauncey's strategy was not very successful in California and elsewhere,
at least initially. In 1951, for example, some 81,100 students took the SAT
in the United States. The vast majority of these students were located in
the greater New England area, where private institutions dominated. Ten
years later, the number taking the test nationally jumped to 805,000. Yet
the vast majority of test takers were still students from the Northeast, with
some growth in the South and to a lesser degree the Midwest. After a ten-
year campaign, few students in the western states took the test.[10] By 1959,
the SAT also had a rival: the American College Test (ACT), which was
marketed as a more subject-based test.

One ETS official noted why California was so reluctant to adopt the
test. The "big problem" was that "UC was already selective and really with
no need to adopt standardized tests."[11] At least until the late 1950s, faculty
and academic leaders largely thought they had a highly successful admissions process. And how did university officials assess this? It was largely by
the high rates of academic success of their students, both freshman admits
and transfer students. In 1955, an estimated 62% of students who entered
the Berkeley campus as freshmen completed their eighth semester and usually graduated. When including those who took a ninth semester, the rate
climbed to around 80%. Students often worked part time, and many took
more than four years. Considering these variables, "This is a good record,"
noted a university report, matched by few other selective institutions at
the time, public or private. Transfer students, who at that time represented

nearly 45% of enrollments at campuses such as Berkeley and UCLA, had similar graduation rates.[12] When accounting for transfers into UC and students who temporarily drop out of the university, a later study showed that some 73% of those entering UC gained a baccalaureate degree in a four-year period of actual enrollment.[13]

Nevertheless, by the late 1950s, a number of University of California faculty and administrators showed interest in the SAT and achievement tests, particularly for freshman entrants. Grade inflation within the state's secondary schools was viewed as a growing problem. There was a sense that perhaps too many students, particularly freshman entrants, were qualifying for university admission. The problem might grow, and the university would need new mechanisms to recalibrate their admissions requirements, particularly with the expected flood of students over the coming decades. Perhaps standardized testing could help manage future enrollment growth by altering admissions criteria? The SAT also represented a new gold standard for measuring the apparent academic aptitude of American students and in turn the prestige of an institution.

A state-sanctioned study on the future of California higher education completed in 1955 suggested that the university should "experiment extensively with aptitude and achievement examination in combination with high school scholastic records in admitting freshmen."[14] On the heels of this study, a University of California academic senate task force on admissions recommended the adoption of the SAT as a requirement for all entering students. Chaired by Richard W. Jennings, a professor of law at Berkeley's Boalt Hall, the group looked into a wide variety of issues related to how the university might manage enrollment growth. Jennings' task force argued that testing offered a method for processing a great mass of applications and for "equalizing the wide variations in grading standards among high schools and to provide a rank-order list, if limits are to be set on enrollments." The university should investigate how to adopt it.[15]

Yet the academic senate, and in particular, the senate's board of admissions and relations with schools (BOARS), with responsibility for admissions policy, rejected Jennings' recommendation. Not only did yearly assessments of the academic success of admitted students buttress the sense that the universities admissions practices were sound, but BOARS members had grave concerns regarding the validity of standardized tests in predicting the academic performance of university students.[16]

But the issue was not dead. At a meeting in May 1957, BOARS again discussed the possible adoption of the SAT as a method to "impose enrollment limitations." The SAT might be useful "if and when that became necessary," noted their board's chairman, UCLA Professor Charles Nixon. Nixon stated that discussions with high school principals resulted in no great opposition to the idea of the SAT. The university might then avoid raising its GPA requirements, a seemingly more politically worrisome prospect for school administrators.[17]

Under Nixon's leadership, BOARS outlined the possible use of standardized tests to university faculty, specifically the senate's university-wide legislative assembly, which would need to approve its adoption. Nixon did not argue for the test's immediate use in the admissions process. Rather, he and his fellow BOARS members thought it might become "a supplementary selective device" for determining UC eligibility "if one becomes necessary." In the interim, BOARS stated that, at a minimum, test scores could provide "information about the student which is necessary for proper [academic] counseling."[18]

Six months later, in early 1958, BOARS wanted to launch an experiment. Charles W. Jones, a professor of English at Berkeley, replaced Nixon as the chair of BOARS, and he and other board members met with ETS representatives. ETS offered to administer the test for free to prospective students. The university's new president, Clark Kerr, also urged a closer look at the SAT. Since 1953, when he was chancellor of the Berkeley campus, Kerr sat on the College Board as the university's representative. But he was cautious in his advocacy. The senate was the designated authority on admissions—a role that dated back to the 1880s, as discussed earlier. But with the ETS offer, he now argued for the advantages of at least requiring the test; at a minimum, it could be an analytical tool for assessing university admissions practices.

Jones and the board then approached the academic senate's legislative assembly and successfully argued that standardized tests be required of applicants for an experimental period of two years—not as a tool in the actual admissions process, but for analysis of its potential use. BOARS would then initiate a major study on the validity of such tests as a predictor of university success. Only after the results were known would the senate consider the use of testing for setting admissions requirements. Academic Senate Regulation 256 was subsequently adopted by the assembly in the spring of 1958. For the first time, with the entering class of fall 1960, students applying to the University of California were required to take the SAT or similar exams identified by BOARS.

In May 1958, BOARS met with representatives of ETS to discuss the first large-scale use of the SAT. Anxious to gain the university's business, ETS again agreed to administer the test at no cost to students. In late 1958,

TABLE 4.1
BOARS 1958 *study: Comparing high school and first-semester UC freshman GPAs*

	#	HS GPA	UC GPA	% UC Fresh Above 2.0 (C) Avg.
Berkeley Campus				
1936–1937	1,672	3.31	2.37	71%
1946–1947	1,927	3.32	2.32	73%
1956–1957	2,189	3.38	2.39	75%
Los Angeles Campus				
1936–1937	1,305	3.21	2.15	63%
1946–1947	1,227	3.36	2.27	72%
1956–1957	1,550	3.49	2.48	73%

NOTE: No veterans were included in 1946–1947 data.
SOURCE: University of California, Academic Senate Legislative Assembly, October 28, 1958.

BOARS also completed a major study on the validity of the university's existing admissions criteria, an unprecedented review looking at data extending back before World War II. In investigating the academic performance of students enrolled at Berkeley and UCLA, the study reiterated earlier findings: There was an extremely high correlation of student high school grade point average (GPA) with freshman performance at UC (see Table 4.1). Generally, students who achieved a B-plus average in their UC-required high school courses achieved a C-plus grade point average during their first year at the University of California.[19] Freshman grades, as opposed to grades during the entirety of the collegiate experience, provided the best tests of validity for two reasons. First, the freshman year represents the immediate transition from secondary school to a university curriculum. And second, as students progressed, their coursework would vary as they moved out of general education courses toward courses that would directly serve their major.

BOARS also analyzed the predictive value of students according to their admissions path—regular admissions or the various paths offered under "special action." As discussed in previous chapters, special action in one form or another dated back to the 1880s. This alternative path acknowledged the varying quality of the state's high schools and the need to account for the varied social and economic backgrounds of students as well as their talents, all of which were not always recognized in the more formulaic process of regular admissions. Between 1952 and 1956, for example, 13% of all students admitted to Berkeley were enrolled as special admissions students (see Table 4.2). BOARS observed that, generally, special admits achieved grades slightly below those of regular admits. Yet despite this difference, BOARS noted the general success of the university's existing admissions standards.[20]

TABLE 4.2

BOARS 1958 study: UC freshman admissions by status, high school, and UC Berkeley GPA

1952–56	% of Total UC Fresh Admissions	HS GPA	UC Berkeley GPA
Regular Admissions ("B" Avg. or above)			
In-state	83.8%	3.41	2.42
Out-of-state California residents	3.1%	3.42	2.51
Special Action			
Out-of-state nonresidents	1.2%	3.63	2.57
Highest 10% in class	1.6%	3.28	2.38
"A" or "B" grades in last three years	2.5%	3.51	2.34
Six "A" or "B" grades in last two years	1.0%	2.93	2.11
"Exceptions to the rules" policy	6.8%	2.95	2.08

SOURCE: University of California, Academic Senate Legislative Assembly, October 28, 1958.

The 1958 analysis also indicated that admissions standards related to junior college transfers were generally successful. Between 1952 and 1956, 33,804 students entered the university, with 18,439 (54%) entering as advanced-standing students, largely junior-year transfers (see Table 4.3). The robust nature of the transfer function was an essential component of the California higher education system. As a result of California's pioneering community college sector, no other public or private university in the nation included such a high percentage of transfer students. A similar analysis of transfer students at UC showed good academic performance and persistence rates.[21]

In the postwar period, for the first time, junior-year transfer students outnumbered entering freshmen at the university. This was a shift first bolstered by the returning GI cohort and sustained until the immediate post-1960 master plan years (see Figure 4.1 for data related to the two largest campuses, Berkeley and UCLA). The transfer function, first envisioned by faculty at the University of California, made California's higher education system unique, both in the high dependence on access through the junior college and in the number of students who then matriculated to a public four-year institution.

The 1958 analysis by BOARS bolstered confidence in the University of California's existing admissions process and in its heavy reliance on grades as a predictor of collegiate academic success. Yet BOARS and its chairman, Charles Jones, kept an open mind on the potential uses of standardized testing. BOARS and the university needed to await the gathering of the test data. This would not occur until the first cohort of entering students took the test in spring 1960 and then completed their freshman year in

TABLE 4.3
BOARS 1958 study: Comparison of junior college
transfers and regular and special action admits enrolled
at UC Berkeley and UCLA

1952–1956	UC GPA	2-Year Persistence
Regular/Special Action Admits	2.63	85.8%
Junior College Transfers		
Eligible at HS Graduation	2.45	80.4%
Ineligible at HS Graduation	2.07	65.2%

SOURCE: University of California, Academic Senate Legislative Assembly, October 28, 1958.

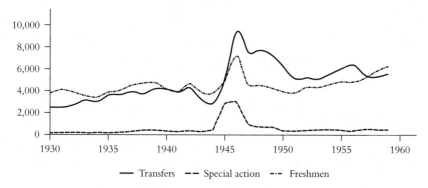

— Transfers − − Special action − · − Freshmen

Figure 4.1. Berkeley and UCLA admissions: Freshmen, advance standing (transfers), and special action students: 1930 –1960

SOURCE: Board of Admissions and Relations with Schools, Representative Assembly Minutes, October 25, 1960.

spring 1961. A firm decision on adopting or rejecting standardized tests as anything other than an alternative route for access the university, or as an analytical tool, was nearly two years away.

An Initial Rejection of the SAT and Achievement Tests

By early 1961, and in the wake of the adoption of California's Master Plan for Higher Education, BOARS initiated a series of meetings to determine how to reduce the University of California's high school admissions pool. The master plan suggested dropping special action, raising university admissions standards, and adopting standardized tests for that cause. Simply eliminating special admissions posed an administratively expedient remedy for pushing students to the community colleges. But there was considerable consternation within BOARS and the academic assembly regarding the possible impact on disadvantaged students.

During a two-day meeting of the board in December 1961, the costs and benefits of curtailing or ending special admissions were debated. Harold Reiber, a professor of chemistry at the Davis campus, stated his doubt about "the wisdom of eliminating alternate methods of admissions." Such action "might well bar the doors to the university to potentially good students whose high school records" were not what they might be simply "as a consequence of a bad start." [22] Yet the pressure for the university to reduce access in the aftermath of the master plan agreement led BOARS and the senate's legislative body to reduce special action from around 10% of all UC admissions to a mere 2%. But that would not be enough to meet a target of diverting some 50,000 students from the University of California and the state colleges toward the junior colleges over the next several years—many of whom would have been UC eligible otherwise.

At another BOARS meeting held in early 1962, raising the required grade point average or using the SAT to cull out students was discussed at length, this time with the benefit of perhaps the most extensive study up to that time in the nation on the predictive power of the SAT. Analysis of university test scores caused the board to reach a significant conclusion: "Extensive analysis of the data," BOARS Chairman Charles Jones stated, and "careful and lengthy deliberation of the Board, leave the Board wholly convinced that the Scholastic Aptitude Test scores add little or nothing to the precision with which the existing admissions requirements are predictive of success in the University." The board unanimously recommended ending the SAT requirement beginning with the class entering in the fall of 1962. Instead, BOARS sought to raise the GPA requirement in required courses. For the near term, the University of California had no plans to adopt the SAT. Supporting the conclusion of the board, the senate's representative assembly voted to repeal Senate Regulation 256. [23]

The finding of BOARS was a major blow to ETS. Yet the university's faculty did not close the door completely on standardized tests. The board promised to launch a similar investigation into the possible future use of CEEB's achievement tests, which purported to evaluate the knowledge level of students in specific academic subjects. These tests had been used in one form or another for admitting a small cohort of students from non-accredited high schools or from out of state.

A little over a year later, in 1963, at a meeting at Berkeley, BOARS sanctioned a study of achievement tests, requiring a cohort of entering university freshmen to take the test. Frank L. Kidner, a professor of political science at Berkeley and the new dean of education relations, led the effort. Yet with the results of the SAT study in, many members of the board remained skeptical. Brewster Smith, a professor of psychology at Berkeley, argued that high school students did not ordinarily take achievement tests and noted that it "might be a large hurdle for students in the lower socio-economic classes or for students from small remotely located high schools."[24]

One important context for the sustained interest in achievement tests related to a pending eligibility study by the California Coordinating Council for Higher Education. The coordinating council was an agency established by statute at the recommendation of the master plan to help with planning, to provide reports to the legislature and governor regarding California's higher education system, and to assess progress on the master plan's recommendations. In advance of the coordinating council's study, BOARS and university officials completed their own eligibility study. They found that the university was still drawing well above the top 12.5% of high school graduates—even after the introduction of additional course requirements. The coordinating council's report would likely come to the same conclusion (and they did). That would mean the university would need to take further action to raise, in some additional way, admissions standards.[25]

In February 1964, Kidner's staff issued their report regarding the potential use of achievement tests. BOARS had asked two questions: "Can achievement test scores be utilized for the placement of students in freshman courses?" and "Does the use of the achievement test scores materially improve the accuracy of the prediction of first-year grade-point averages in the academic colleges on each campus?" Edward W. Bowes, the director of admissions who reported to Kidner, was the main author of the study, and his conclusion echoed the findings of the previous analysis of the validity of the SAT. "The insistent question becomes, can any constructive use be made of the additional information which is supplied by the achievement scores?" His preliminary answer was that it probably couldn't. Achievement tests unto themselves, Bowes noted, proved of marginal value in predicting academic success, although they were of slightly better value than the SAT.[26] High school GPA remained the best indicator, Bowes stated. High school GPA explained 22% of the variance in university grades, and the achievement tests explained only 8%. He stated, however, that combining test scores and high school GPA appeared to offer a marginal improvement in predicting freshman grades, "though the superiority is admittedly slight." This conclusion warranted caution. Within the sample group, there were a number of cases where achievement test scores were actually inversely related to freshman grades. For example, in seven of the nine subject areas, the average test score for those who received a freshman grade of F was higher than those who received a D, and in four subject areas, their test scores were higher than those achieving a grade of C. "It would appear that it takes knowledge to earn an F grade," Bowes caustically stated.[27]

Yet Bowes made a prophetic observation. There were other potential reasons, beyond actual prediction of students' academic aptitude that might be considered. For one, it could be a somewhat arbitrary tool for reducing eligibility—less politically volatile than raising GPA requirements. This "added practical advantage" could reduce the complaints of students who came close to meeting the university's eligibility requirements but who were now denied admissions.[28] Bowes stated five potential uses for the achievement test: (1) admissions; (2) financial aid; (3) academic placement, in lieu of a battery of university placement and qualifying examinations given during the first week of a semester; (4) guidance counseling; and (5) academic planning.

Bowes urged caution in interpreting his results, and BOARS took him at his word. Although there were political advantages to using the SAT and achievement tests in regular admissions, the board concluded that was not good enough. Until there was a more concrete study that showed the predictive value of standardized tests—and ETS had no similar study to contradict the studies at the University of California's findings—then the issue could only be revisited at a later date.

The conclusions reached by BOARS contradicted the promotional efforts of the College Board and ETS. But the University of California also was running against the tide: Standardized tests were being widely adopted by American public universities. There is great irony in the story of this earlier conclusion by the university not to adopt standardized testing in its admissions practices. As the following chapter describes, the university would incrementally adopt standardized tests, first in 1968 for determining general university eligibility and later in the process of selection at campuses such as Berkeley. Beginning in 2001, the University of California launched a series of studies that mirror those conducted in the early 1960s, focused on the predictive value of the SAT. The result? Nearly the same conclusions—a story discussed in a later chapter of this book.

Chapter 5

Countervailing Forces: Standardized Testing and Affirmative Action

Irritated, disgusted, disappointed are all adjectives that convey my feelings at the present time toward the University of California. I cannot say that anyone else would have the same feelings or even be interested if the facts be known, but one tends to become more vocal when affected personally. My son-in-law graduated from the University of California at San Diego last June, 1975 with a 3.7 average. He had applied to the medical schools at the Los Angeles and San Francisco campuses. San Francisco never granted him an interview and the Los Angeles campus notified him that he was on the waiting list.
—Melvin Rush to Governor Edmund (Jerry) Brown, May 12, 1975

The University of California historically maintained admissions policies intended to be broadly inclusive, with variables such as income, geography, and inequities in collegiate preparation taken, to some degree, into account. Until the 1960s, however, the specific issue of enrolling "historically underrepresented minority groups" had not entered the lexicon of Californa policymakers. The 1960 California Master Plan for Higher Education, for instance, made no mention of racial or ethnic representation. The dominant concerns were disparities in the quality of local schools and obstacles to access and college preparedness related to poverty and economic class, which are long a part of America's political tradition.

In no small part, public support for mass higher education revolved around its promise to create a more egalitarian world. In the view of those who negotiated the master plan, the largest hindrances to access were economic and geographic factors. Inequities in society related to race were not fully recognized and, in the area of university enrollment, would presumably be transcended by the availability of low-cost and strategically placed public higher education institutions.

The Civil Rights Movement, antipoverty programs, inner-city riots, and the student unrest that marked the late 1960s altered the consciousness of the nation. The problems of race and poverty were now more fully exposed. The Cold War battle with communism also shaped national and local policies related to education and the lingering problems of racial discrimination. "The United States," notes John David Skrentny in his study of the affirmative-action movement, "was then competing with the Soviet Union for dominance in the ultimate struggle for modernity: attainment of the most just and advanced society possible."[1] Following the federal action to end racial segregation in Little Rock, Arkansas, and throughout the southern states, Secretary of State Dean Rusk in 1961 pronounced that the "biggest single burden that we carry on our backs in our foreign relations in the 1960s is the problem of racial discrimination here at home."[2]

The passage of the 1964 Civil Rights Act provided an important demarcation. More aggressive federal and state policies and initiatives sought color-blind remedies and programs intended to broadly support disadvantaged groups. These policies focused on equal opportunity in employment and housing and segregation in education. Within the national debate on civil rights, which included all segments of society suffering the plight of poverty, the dilemma of African Americans dominated political discourse. The pluralistic nature of American society offered innumerable cases of discrimination. But all appeared less tragic and consequential than the systematic violations of basic human rights wrought on African Americans—a condition inseparable from the legacy of slavery. Before the major demographic shifts of the 1970s, federal efforts to reduce racial discrimination in the 1960s focused largely on ameliorating the segregated experience of black Americans.

Two changes shaped the national debate regarding race and educational opportunity, with particular relevance to California. First, with the social upheaval of the late 1960s and the collapse of President Lyndon Johnson's antipoverty programs, the issues of racial discrimination became a primary focus of policymaking. Conversely, economic class simply declined in political salience. Second, dramatic demographic shifts bolstered by more liberal immigration policies increased the complexity of the social problems related to racial discrimination and poverty. It also contributed to the claim of racial and ethnic groups for remiloration.

The Politics of an Era

Affirmative action gained its initial political legitimacy because of long-term and rampant institutional and social discrimination against African Americans within American society. The rhetoric and political power of the Civil Rights Movement grew from the particular history of blacks, the vast majority of whom could trace their arrival in the United States to the slave trade of the 1700s and early 1800s. In the 1970s, new racial and immigrant groups began to embrace and use the language and strategies of affirmative action to serve their needs. As Hugh Graham noted in a study on the convergence of affirmative action and immigration policy, by the 1970s, coalition building among liberals broadened the scope of what constituted disadvantaged racial groups. Fueled by the arrival of 25 million immigrants, most from Latin America and Asia, the "political implications of these converging trends were enormous," notes Graham, yet "neither trend was foreseen or even sought by policymakers in the 1960s."[3]

With increasing political pressure to broaden access to all minority groups, by the early 1960s, the University of California embarked on a long-term effort first to develop color-blind policies and programs and later to seek more proactive efforts to promote more equitable access. But there were two emerging centers of power in the university with differing views on admissions policy. On the one hand, the interest and actions of the academic senate, as the representative body of the faculty, increasingly embraced a standardized understanding of academic merit, all but abandoning individualized assessments of student qualifications. As those responsible for setting the conditions of admissions, members of the senate sought greater efficiencies and mechanization in the admissions process to help manage the growing number of student applications. On the other hand, university administrators, led by succeeding presidents of the university and increasingly by campus chancellors, sought new methods and programs to expand access to primarily underrepresented minorities.

Arguably, the senate and many faculty sought refuge in the buffer offered by a growing cadre of administrators from the increasing political pressures placed on the institution by lawmakers and the public. The political firestorm that would soon envelop the University of California had its own peculiarities, with attacks coming from both the left and the right. The birth of the Free Speech Movement and its metamorphosis into large-scale student unrest helped fuel a profound conservative shift by state voters, symbolized by the victory of Republican upstart Ronald Reagan over liberal Democratic pragmatist Pat Brown in the California gubernatorial election of November 1966.

The long-brewing criticism of the university as a haven for communists and radicals grew in political salience. Reagan based much of his campaign against Brown on his plans to "clean up the mess in Berkeley." Once elected, Reagan promptly used his influence with more conservative members of the university's board of regents to fire Clark Kerr as president in 1967. For Reagan and a significant number of regents, Kerr was seen as too indecisive and forgiving of student protesters. He also appeared to detractors as overly protective of those vocal faculty members who were sympathetic to the student protests. For those on the left, Kerr was viewed as a caretaker and defender of what Mario Savio proclaimed as the corrupt "machine," an elite institution intractably tied to the predilections of an unjust society. In an age of political passion, symbolism trumped reality.

During his tenure as governor, Pat Brown viewed the university and all of public higher education in California as a great asset to be nurtured and protected. Reagan saw the university as an enemy and a political target, particularly during his first term. He sought to directly confront protesters and, in an unprecedented move, called in the National Guard to quell demonstrations in Berkeley and Isla Vista, the student community next to the university's Santa Barbara campus. Among his first actions as governor was a proposal to cut the University of California's budget by 10% and a request that the regents substantially raise student fees. Kerr had openly opposed both the cuts and instituting tuition.

In 1968, less than a year after Kerr's firing, economist Charles Hitch, Kerr's successor as president, spoke before the academic senate's assembly. Hitch stated that the university was doing relatively well internally in the recruitment of top faculty and in the quality of its research. But externally, "we are embattled and harassed . . . our position outside of the academic community has never been weaker." There was a "chasm" between the university and lawmakers and the public, and he thought there were three main causes. First, Hitch saw "bewilderment and outrage at the tactics of student activists, and a belief that they are aided and abetted by many faculty and condoned by weak and vacillating administrators." The seeming radicalization of the campuses was leading to a broad public perception that a "new generation is being deliberately indoctrinated in radical, violent, and revolutionary doctrines." Second, growing disillusionment with the faculty's apparent infatuation with research prompted widespread criticism. Third, the "escalating costs of higher education," observed Hitch, coupled with a growing taxpayer revolt, meant hard times for the university. "Many taxpayers and legislators are looking for good excuses and rationalizations not to raise taxes," Hitch concluded. Not only was Governor Reagan still pushing the adoption of tuition but also voters earlier had turned down a major bond act central for capital construction and enrollment expansion. "The irony," lamented Hitch, "is that never before has there been such a need for public support of universities—burgeoning enrollments, urban crisis—and even the minimal support is not there."[4]

A First Wave of Intervention: EOP and Special Action

The political milieu of the 1960s very much shaped the evolving effort by public universities to expand the racial and ethnic diversity of their student bodies. These institutions created new programs to prepare, recruit, and support disadvantaged students. Initially, these initiatives were based almost entirely in student-service programs functioning outside the regular admissions process. In 1964, a number of universities established Educational Opportunity Programs (EOPs). Dartmouth and Princeton gained funds from the Rockefeller Foundation for outreach efforts to local high schools. Clark Kerr participated in the deliberations at the foundation and conceived of a similar program for the University of California. He presented a proposal to the university's board of regents in early 1964.

Less than a year before that, the academic senate voted to end university accreditation of the state high schools. In the midst of Kerr's desire to reach out to disadvantaged students, there was a growing political and operational distance between the state's public schools and the university. The end of the University of California's accreditation of high schools was symbolic of this trend. The idea of university-run Educational Opportunity Programs was one way to refashion a relationship with California's schools within a new political environment. The concept was less interventionist, designed to help prepare and recruit individual low-income and minority students to the university. In 1964, Kerr asked the regents for the allocation of $100,000 in funds to finance the university's first Educational Opportunity Program on the Berkeley campus. The office of relations with schools would coordinate EOP as an administrative function, providing scholarships to students from selected low-income schools to attend summer programs at campuses such as Berkeley, introducing them to the university, and offering preparatory courses and guidance. These new "outreach" programs were intended to "start with the youngster not later than the eighth grade, before he has embarked upon a non-college course and before he is over-awed by impending cultural and financial barriers."[5]

EOP proved the first of a number of efforts to shape the university's potential pool of applicants to include more individuals deemed "disadvantaged." Berkeley was the first University of California campus to operate an EOP program. Soon, each campus of the University of California had similar programs intended to recruit, enroll, and retain students from low-income families coming primarily, but not exclusively, from minority backgrounds.[6]

By 1967, however, it became evident to university officials, and increasingly to lawmakers and a growing community demanding greater inclusion, that EOP and the university's special action admissions limit of 2% were not sufficient to expand enrollment of minority and disadvantaged groups. A study completed that year by California's Higher Education Coordinating Council offered the first-ever systematic data in California on the disparities in admissions related to ethnicity. Based on a sample of students from high schools throughout California, it was estimated that African Americans constituted 3.6% of public high school seniors yet only 1.2% of those who were UC eligible. Of the entire pool of UC-eligible African American students, only 17.6% planned to enroll at the University of California. Chicanos-Latinos had similar ratios. Some 8.7% of all high school seniors were Chicano-Latino, but only 3.3% were UC eligible, and within that small group, only 26% planned to enter the university.[7] This finding bolstered public criticism that the university was not doing enough. Within the university's administration, there was a conviction to seek new policy solutions.

In this tumultuous era of student protests over the Vietnam War and issues of racial equality, a fractured yet powerful student movement included demands for ethnic studies departments and more proactive efforts to increase minority enrollments. Externally, minority populations in urban areas of the state—in particular, African American communities in Los Angeles and the Bay Area—were growing in political clout, with representatives in the state capital insisting on action by the university's leadership. The rise of the militant Black Panthers in Oakland, while segregationist and marginal in number, offered a visible and threatening force in the political cauldron of racial politics.

University officials faced another problem. Once again, a state-sanctioned study showed that the University of California was accepting freshman applications well above the master plan target of 12.5% of the state's top high school graduates. The California Coordinating Council for Higher Education estimated that in 1967 the university was drawing from the top 14.6%. Despite post-master plan changes in admissions policies, the University of California was drawing from approximately the same high school pool as they had in the 1950s.[8] The surge in enrollments had already proved a huge challenge for the institution. There was a broad sense within the university community that the institution was absorbing enrollments "in excess of the numbers that can be effectively accommodated," noted one faculty senate report.[9] Once again, the senate's admissions committee, BOARS, considered either raising the GPA requirement of students or possibly requiring the SAT and incorporating it into assessing eligibility. The SAT might not be a good predictor of future academic achievement, but it was a tool for excluding students and, thereby, reducing enrollment demand.

In 1968, BOARS chose to slightly raise GPA requirements for regular admissions from 3.0 to 3.1 and proposed requiring the SAT or a similar test, like the ACT. Tests scores would be used for regular admissions but for a narrow purpose: to determine the eligibility of students with high school grade point averages between 3.00 and 3.09—those that just missed the required 3.1 threshold. Yet simply requiring the SAT of all freshman applicants would narrow the pool of eligible students. Many students would simply not take the required test, either out of ignorance or choice, with the most harmful effect on low-income and minority groups. BOARS showed concern with this problem but tended to favor increasing admissions standards to limit enrollment growth.[10]

The divergent impulses of faculty and administrators made policymaking both complex and contradictory. BOARS gained the approval of the senate's legislative assembly and sought the approval of the board of regents to require the SAT. President Charles Hitch and other university administrations worried about the assumed negative impact on minority enrollments and the reaction of lawmakers. Simultaneously, Hitch proposed to the regents the raising of special admissions from 2% to 4%—the alternative route for freshmen and transfer students. Increasing the number of students admitted under special action could act as a countervailing force to increasing GPA requirements and adopting the SAT. In his proposal to the regents, Hitch argued that the new 4% target would be pivotal for admitting more students "whose ethnic or economic background had disadvantaged them."[11]

In 1968, the regents approved both requiring the SAT and raising the special action admissions pool. Curiously, BOARS passed no formal judgment on the increase of the special action pool. It was Hitch's proposal. In a dereliction of its duty, the leadership of the academic senate was largely uninterested in any efforts outside of determining the requirements for regular admission process—a change that contrasted sharply with the actions of the senate only five years earlier.

In his campaign to expand access to disadvantaged groups, President Hitch also sought a more concerted use of special action by the eight undergraduate campuses. Before 1968, many campus chancellors and admissions officers used the alternative admission process sparingly. Averaged across the system, in 1967 only 1.86% of all freshman admissions entered the university under the special action program. There was also disproportional use among the campuses at the junior-year transfer level. The

UC-wide average was only 1.56%, with great variance within the system. For example, Berkeley admitted 2.44% as special action at the junior year, in excess of the 2% target, and Los Angeles admitted only 0.84% (a total of only fifty-four students).[12]

EOP and the expansion of special action to 4% constituted the first wave of efforts to increase access to the university within a California society at the cusp of a huge demographic transformation. The next major reform came in 1971. Reflecting the rise of a relatively new managerial structure, Hitch and other university leaders thought the growing discretionary power of the campus chancellors offered a route toward a more robust effort to enroll minority and disadvantaged students. The burden fell to the administrative leadership—those that confronted the increasingly problematic demonstrations and had to answer the university's increasingly vocal critics from both the right and left.

By 1970, Hitch and other university administrators wanted to create flexibility in the regular admissions process and to give campus administrators greater authority in making admissions decisions (once the purview of faculty), leaving the setting of UC eligibility criteria to the academic senate. As a result, beginning in 1971, the office of the president established new undergraduate admissions policies for implementation by campus chancellors that essentially reflected norms at many private institutions.[13] For the first time, a few of the university campuses were beginning to get more applications by UC-eligible students than they had space for, in particular, Berkeley, UCLA, and the relatively new and very popular Santa Cruz campus. With growing enrollment demand, it was understood that more campuses would need to eventually choose among UC-eligible students. At "campuses receiving applications in excess of the number required to achieve their enrollment quotas," stated Frank Kidner, the newly appointed vice president for educational relations, "50% of the number of applications to be retained and processed . . . shall be the most highly qualified based upon scholastic criteria." A campus would choose the remaining 50% of UC-eligible applicants, stated Kidner. This would require the

> exercise of judgment with respect to each individual application and should be based upon such criteria as academic interest, campus programs, hardship factors which prohibit or restrict an applicant from attending another campus, selective recruitment efforts, special achievements and awards, and similar considerations.[14]

Within this category, priority was given to intercampus transfer students, community college transfers with sufficient transferable courses, "veterans of the Vietnam crisis," students "who will experience unusual hardship as a result of redirection" to another UC campus, and California residents.[15] Curiously, the directive made no reference to race or ethnicity as a criterion. Battles over establishing ethnic studies programs, a highly charged political environment featuring student riots and undoubtedly the purview of an increasingly conservative governing board, caused Hitch and Kidner to state broad purposes such as "hardship factors." Yet the major intent was clearly to increase minority enrollments.

The immediate effect of the policy was minimal. Kidner's directive anticipated a future disjuncture between campus enrollment capacity and applications. University leaders realized and lamented that the most important method to expand minority enrollment lay outside of the doors of the university. African American and Chicano-Latino students had relatively low high school graduation rates. Of those that graduated, only a few were UC eligible. Here lies the crux of a long-term problem: While the university attempted to alter is admissions criteria, broad access to the university related more fundamentally to growing inadequacies in the schools, in the cultural predilections of different ethnic groups, and in the expanding disparities in society. How could the university take the nascent affirmative-action tools it and other public universities had developed and do more?

Access Versus Selectivity

The complex challenge of expanding access to disadvantaged students generated a relatively new and growing body of research. One general and broadly understood conclusion: Expanding access to higher education related not just to admissions practices but also to the complexities of a larger society. In the late 1960s, the U.S. Department of Education launched a major effort to collect data on higher education and began to fund research on questions related to educational opportunity. New entities such as the Carnegie Commission on Higher Education, established in 1967 under Clark Kerr's leadership, published studies and helped develop a community of scholars and analysts concerned with higher education issues.

Many national studies indicated that socioeconomic status was the prime determiner of college attendance. A 1968 examination of 10,000 high school graduates in the lowest 40% ability distribution, for example, showed that if a student's father was in a high-level occupation, there was a 57% chance the student would attend college. If the student's father was in a low-level occupation, the student's chance of attending college was reduced to 20%. Socioeconomic status was particularly important for women.

Other important variables included the average age of enrolled students and the increase in part-time students. Until the late 1960s, most educational planning efforts, including projections of financial aid needs and student support services, fixated on a traditional "college age" population of eighteen through the mid-twenties. Reinforcing the need for continual retraining of skills at a variety of age levels, the U.S. Department of Labor estimated that the average person soon would change careers three times in a lifetime. In the meantime, research continued to show that among enrolled students, persistence and attrition rates correlated clearly with socioeconomic background and race. A national task force on higher education observed in 1971 that "access alone does not lead to a successful education. It means only the exposure of a particular age group to whatever educational institutions there are and not the equality of the experience they are likely to find there." When one looked behind the tremendous growth in American higher education, one found a major phenomenon: "the surprisingly large and growing number of students who voluntarily drop out of college."[16] A national study of college dropouts by Alexander W. Astin, a professor at UCLA, outlined the principal predictors of persistence in higher education. They included grades in high school and scores on tests of academic ability; high aspirations at college entrance; financing college education chiefly via parents, scholarships or personal savings; not being employed during the school year; and being male.[17]

The problem of low college-going rates in rural areas was the focus of a number of national and regional studies. California long recognized the high correlation of local institutions and access rates. This understanding was one major reason for the proliferation of community colleges and the wide geographic distribution of state colleges and UC campuses. A study encompassing thirteen northeastern California counties revealed significant unmet demand for postsecondary education.[18] But there was also a relatively new concern about the pockets of poverty in urban areas and low access rates, again correlating with income and racial demographics.

The Carnegie Commission on Higher Education observed that "young people who live in suburban areas are more likely to attend college than those living in inner cities or in non-metropolitan areas, and that those living in the poverty portions of large metropolitan areas are especially unlikely to attend college."[19] In the early 1960s, Kerr and others professed the idea that America's great network of public universities, once devoted to agricultural development, might turn their attention to serving the needs of America's troubled cities. Here was a conceptual model inspired by the Great Society programs of the Johnson administration that might reshape the social contract of public universities. University researchers might help decipher the social causes of poverty. They could then educate urban teachers and create support services for schools in areas of poverty, train social welfare workers, and improve healthcare.

Bolstered by federal funding and an expanding network of public services in urban communities, universities did make some strides to focus their programs on urban problems. But it was only one more addition to the core research activities at universities. Research related to the sciences and engineering was a much more dominant concern of faculty. Indeed, the public universities in particular were rapidly changing in their academic culture and activities.

In his Godkin Lectures at Harvard in 1963 on "The Uses of the University," Clark Kerr noted that America's universities suffered a decline in their cohesive purpose and sense of community. Instead, the relatively new "multiversity" housed a multiplicity of separate communities of academic tribes with differing interests and increasingly focused on academic research productivity.[20] How to refocus faculty attention on the greater needs of society? It was a vexing problem for university leaders.

The academic achievements and reputation of the University of California continued to grow, largely because of its research productivity and the quality of its graduate programs. Campuses such as Berkeley and UCLA, and increasingly others in the UC system, attracted some of the best and most promising scholars in the nation, and the world, often fresh from doctorates received at other highly selective and many times from private universities. A natural drive of faculty, often with only a marginal understanding of the University of California history and its social contract, was to become more selective. These biases and the slow pace in enrolling minority groups increased the anger of lawmakers and others concerned with issues of diversity and socioeconomic mobility.

A Master Plan Review and an Attack

In 1973, a state legislative committee reviewing the state's master plan and chaired by Assemblyman John Vasconcellos offered a blistering attack on California's higher education system. Vasconcellos's committee cited the research of Astin and others on the barriers to higher education. "Our achievements in extending equal access have not met our promises," stated the committee's report. "Though we have made considerable progress in the 1960's and 1970's, equality of opportunity in postsecondary education is still a goal rather than a reality."[21]

The committee concluded that persons from low-income families were significantly underrepresented in California's public higher education system. There was a clear correlation between family income and the segment of California higher education a student attended. Armed with data collected in 1973 by California's coordinating council, Vasconcellos reported, "The average family income for a University of California student is $15,160 (nearly the family income for the average student attending a private institution); for a California State University and Colleges student, $12,330; and a California Community Colleges student, $11,420." The lack of access for minority groups to higher education in the state was a grave concern: "Blacks, Mexican-Americans and Native Americans represent 22.9% of the state's population," stated the report. "However, they comprise only 17.5% of the day enrollment in the California Community Colleges, 11.9% in the California State University and Colleges and 10.6% in the University of California."[22]

A strident liberal, Vasconcellos was an important leader among the activist Democrats that now dominated both the assembly and state senate. A frequent and almost universal complaint from students, Vasconcellos's committee stated, indicated that information and counseling on postsecondary education were not only seriously deficient but nearly nonexistent in poor urban schools. Attrition rates in higher education were much higher than previously understood, particularly at the community colleges. Transfer rates to the University of California were significantly down since 1960. The university had failed to meet the master plan objectives of enrolling at least 60% of its students at the upper division level. And the University of California's admission policies seemed overly biased toward traditional academic criteria and thereby served largely the privileged. "We are concerned with the racial imbalance in public institutions of higher education, especially with the increase as we move from community colleges through the California State University and Colleges to the University of California," concluded the report.

Vasconcellos, the primary author along with the committee's chief consultant, Patrick Callan, questioned the very purpose of California's tripartite system. "Many persons believe the three-tier system with its rigid admissions quotas is inherently racist because socioeconomic and cultural conditions in the early experience of minority persons leave them unable to measure up to the admissions standards of the four-year segments."[23] Vasconcellos and Callan intended the report to be an assault on the University of California and to a lesser degree the California State University. The combative tone was an unmistakable sign of the frustration among many lawmakers with the university, its selective admissions policies, *and* its high level of constitutional autonomy. Mission differentiation within California's tripartite higher education system, complained the report, was "dictated by institutional aspirations rather than by individual needs or any well articulated educational philosophy." Citing research that "indicates that the most selective colleges have the least effect on students," institutions like the University of California, stated the report, "make only a slight difference in the student's college achievements (academic and extracurricular), academic ability, likelihood of completing college, level of education achieved and choice of career." There was "almost no empirical basis for the contention that segregating students by ability, as measured by high school achievement, is educationally more effective than other approaches."[24]

Among the alternatives proposed by the report was an "open system" where "every public institution in all three segments" could be opened to "any high school graduate or 18-year-old seeking admissions."[25] Under this proposal, the University of California would, essentially, no longer set admissions criteria. California's tripartite system, vetted internationally as a model, would then joyfully collapse under the weight of egalitarianism, in Vasconcellos's view. As discussed in an earlier chapter, a similar populist proposal emerged at the City University of New York in the wake of ethnic battles over public higher education and ultimately resulted in confusion and a long-term decline in the overall quality of a once-robust CUNY. However, Vasconcellos's proposal was more a threat than a well-formulated plan. The constitutional autonomy of the university protected it from radical reform, and it appeared that few lawmakers wanted to dismantle the University of California or the tripartite system. Most recommendations of Vasconcellos's committee offered broad policy goals or program ideas that largely never came to fruition. The lambasting was strategic, intended to raise public interest in Vasconcellos and Callan's idea of reducing state funds and enrollment growth at the university in favor of the state's community colleges. "There is little evidence that the four-year institutions are more responsive to the learning needs of these students than are the community colleges," concluded their report. The issues of scholarship and research productivity and their influence on student learning, society at large, and the economy were of no concern to the majority of Vasconcellos's committee.

Vasconcellos's legislative review, however, did result in one particularly important policy directive: "Each segment of California public higher education," noted his report, should "strive to approximate by 1980 the general ethnic, sexual and economic composition of the recent California high school graduates." A bill was subsequently passed in 1974 with this exact language.[26] Legislation also urged consideration of expanded use of alternative admissions policies and required that each of the public segments report annually to lawmakers on progress toward the 1980 goal. For the University of California to ignore the target would be politically unpalatable. Some Democratic lawmakers noted a willingness to reduce the university's state budget if progress was not made. The intent was to place political pressure on the University of California and to a lesser extent on CSU to expand minority enrollment. And it worked.

The University of California needed to report its progress and plans by early 1975. With a little less than a year to create such a plan, university leaders launched in November 1974 a significant effort to assess the effectiveness of existing outreach efforts and admissions policies. But in doing so, the academic senate remained aloof, seemingly comforted that the problems of minority enrollment were largely the bailiwick of the university's president, Charles Hitch, and the campus chancellors and administrators.

Seeking Diversity

In early 1974, President Hitch directed Robert L. Johnson, Kidner's replacement as vice president for educational relations, to convene a group to "identify any barriers to the access or success of women, members of minority groups, and economically or otherwise disadvantaged students, and to recommend to the President means of eliminating those barriers."[27] In July 1975, Johnson offered their report. "Students from ethnic minority and low-income backgrounds," the group concluded, "are severely underrepresented in University programs at all levels, and that the enrollment of women in graduate programs is disproportionately low" (see Table 5.1).

Johnson's group offered another important finding. Data generated by the 1967 eligibility study indicated that there was a substantial pool of existing eligible students who, for one reason or another, did not plan to attend the university. A 1971 study by the university, focused on sixteen public high schools in Los Angeles, supported this observation and pointed to the need to work with urban schools. Based on information provided by high school counselors, it showed that approximately 10% of minorities were eligible for UC at their senior year in these schools, yet only 1.6% enrolled. Another 1.2% entered the university as special action admits. Special action remained a vital component for expanding diversity and possibly

TABLE 5.1
Estimate of California public high school seniors and UC freshmen by race/ethnicity:
1973–1974

	# Public HS	%	# UC Freshmen	%
African American	22,000	7.9	950	4.5
Asian American	8,800	3.1	2,200	10.5
Chicano/Latino/Spanish Surname	35,800	13.0	920	4.4
Native American	1,200	.4	120	.6
Euro-American and Others	213,700	75.9	16,800	80.0

SOURCE: Report of the Student Affirmative Action Task Groups, University of California, July 1975.

should be expanded, noted the task group. But more compelling was the idea of making a significant effort to tap into this already eligible pool of high school graduates.

President Hitch, his administration, and the campus chancellors saw that perhaps the key to expanding minority enrollment was to end "procedural barriers—real or imagined—to university attendance." The trick was to acquaint young high school students from underrepresented groups with university admissions requirements, encourage their application to the university, and expand the scope and reach of programs intended to improve their written and quantitative skills. Once at the university, there was a need for "minimal levels of support services" that could allow them to "achieve success at a rate similar to that of the student body as a whole."[28] This was a thought not much different from the motivations for EOP launched by Kerr in 1964. The difference was a greater resolve and commitment of resources. Johnson's report urged a "vigorous new outreach policy" and the bolstering of support services for enrolled minority students. The University also sought more data on the ethnicity and background of students. In their application, students were henceforth asked to voluntarily state their ethnicity, economic background, parental education, and physical and potential linguistic disabilities.[29]

In the area of admissions and selection at campuses such as Berkeley, Johnson's group was cautious. The university *might* consider "eliminating the use of those [standardized] tests which reveal ethnic biases" or seek methods for "normalizing test score data within ethnic subgroups" and "developing tests or test items which reveal academic potential of minority group applicants."[30] "Potential students with specialized talents in the arts or music, and students from non-traditional backgrounds," explained their report, "are frequently screened out of the University because of the exclusive reliance on a limited number of traditional academic subjects."[31]

A study of students at the Riverside campus of the university by Keith Sexton in the office of the president, for example, showed that overall grade point average in high school, excluding physical education and similar nonacademic courses, was as good a predictor of university GPA as completion of the university-required A-F courses.[32] Data cited by Vice President Johnson's group showed that the validity of testing was greatest for upper income Euro-Americans and correlated with a student's gender, ethnicity, socioeconomic status, and quality of his or her high school. High school GPA was a better predictor, particularly for low-income minority groups. Armed with this knowledge, how could the university, and BOARS, become more creative and flexible in opening the door to these students?

In the legislative mandated 1975 report to the California state legislature, President Hitch argued that the University of California was making progress in enrolling minorities. Since 1965, the university had spent a total of $40 million for financial and academic assistance to disadvantaged students. The number of EOP students grew from 100 on six campuses in 1965–1966 to 7,980 on eight campuses in 1975. Students in these programs showed a healthy rate of persistence, "with 85% of the Fall 1971 admittees returning in Fall, 1972." However, the president also noted that minority enrollment overall was growing slowly and that the "academic achievement of minority students [was] not equal to non-minorities."[33] A new effort by the university would, it was hoped, significantly expand the enrollment of underrepresented groups.

Following the report to the legislature, the University of California launched a number of new programs and increased funding for outreach programs. A general shift in priorities also occurred. EOP had the broad intent of serving "disadvantaged" students—students of all races and ethnic origins whose background (e.g., family income, parental education level, etc.) appeared to hinder their prospects for enrolling and persisting at the university. The post-1975 efforts, in the form of Student Affirmative Action (SAA) programs, focused largely on serving minority students. Race and ethnicity were slowly trumping economic disadvantage. A similar effort to expand SAA was undertaken in the California State University and the California Community Colleges. By 1981, $47 million a year were being spent on 137 specific EOP-SAA programs in California public higher education, with approximately 90% coming from state coffers.[34] (See Table 5.2 for a listing of major university-wide EOP programs and funding sources.)

TABLE 5.2

Major University of California EOP and student affirmative-action programs and funding sources: 1965–1979

	Program	Objectives	Funding Source
1964	Educational Opportunity Program	Increase enrollment and retention of low-income and ethnic minority students	Regents' Funds
1970	Mathematics, Engineering, Science Achievement (MESA)	Increase number of minority HS students prepared for math-based degrees	State and Private
1976	Student Affirmative Action Support Services	Increase number of ethnic and low-income students who complete their degree	State and UC Fees
	UC Early Outreach / Partnership Program	Increase ethnic minority enrollment by targeting students in 8th through 11th grades at 191 junior high schools and 140 high schools	State and UC Fees
1978	University Immediate Outreach	Increase number of students from underrepresented groups applying to the university	State and UC Fees
1979	Academic Enrichment Program	Involve faculty in the outreach programs and enrichment efforts for minority students	State Funds

A Growing Divide on Priorities

The University of California board of regents and the university presidents, chancellors, and administrative staff embraced the goal of diversifying undergraduate enrollment. A vast network of programs proliferated, largely decentralized and operated by campus student-affairs units, their numbers accentuated in part by the desire for minority-specific programs and support services. Ethnic groups tended to want their own support programs—a sign of both status and the frequently fractious relationships among minority groups seeking resources and political clout.

Despite this reinvigorated effort, by 1978 it was clear that the university faced a nearly impossible task in meeting the goal set by the 1974 statute. For many in the university, including its new president, David Saxon, there was a need to both continue EOP-SAA programs and rethink admissions. Saxon was a long-time faculty member in the physics department at UCLA and one of the original thirty-one faculty members who famously refused to sign a loyalty oath in 1950 demanded by conservative regents. He had served under Hitch for one year as the university's vice president.

He knew well the challenges of expanding minority enrollments and the considerable political pressure coming from Sacramento lawmakers.

Yet another statewide eligibility study offered a conundrum for Saxon and his colleagues. In 1976, the third eligibility study was completed, this time by the newly formed California Postsecondary Education Commission (CPEC), which replaced the earlier Coordinating Council. This study showed that the university was once again out of compliance with the master plan. The University of California was drawing from the top 14.9% of high school graduates, nearly the same figure as the 14.6% stated in the 1967 study. Using the data gathered by CPEC, a subsample study by the University of California showed that the pool might be approximately 17%. The university also failed to achieve the 40:60 ratio of lower division to upper division students set by the master plan to encourage community college transfers. In contrast, the CSU was in compliance with all aspects of the master plan's admissions goals and had been since the first eligibility study in 1961.[35]

Anticipating the publication of the 1976 eligibility study, President Saxon established a Task Force on Undergraduate Admissions, chaired by Academic Vice President Donald C. Swain and composed of Vice Chancellor Eugene Cota-Robles, two students, and two faculty members, including BOARS Chair Allen Parducci. The task force's mission was to consider the range of options the university might take to meet the master plan goal of reducing the eligibility pool while continuing the pursuit of affirmative action. The final report of the task force fully illuminated the differing values of administrators and faculty leaders.

Nearly a year later, the task force report was complete. In his transmittal letter to Saxon in March of 1977, Swain noted, "We aspired to unanimity but, in the end, there were fundamental differences of opinion within the group which could not be reconciled." Parducci was the sole dissenter. The majority advocated three policy options. First, they recommended marginal raises in admissions standards, including the addition of a fourth year of English for all freshman applicants. This would help in the academic preparation of all students, including minority students. Second, the task force argued for eliminating the use of standardized test scores in regular admissions. Although "applicants should be required to present scores on English and math achievement tests," these "scores should be used for diagnostic purposes, counseling, and course placement; they should not be used in making admissions decisions."[36] Swain's majority opinion was a clear attempt to thwart a growing interest in the senate and, within BOARS and by Parducci, to more fully integrate standardized testing into the regular admission process.

Swain offered a third recommendation: The university needed to consider alternative admissions practices. One option was to introduce the use of class rank, perhaps targeting the top 10% of each high school. Another idea was to create an "incentive model" as an alternative path for eligibility, wherein students who took more than a minimal number of academic courses would receive extra credit in the admissions process, in combination with A-F grades. This was thought to have "several attractive features, especially for minority students," including an added incentive for minority students to earn additional credit while upgrading their academic skills for success at the university.

Another alternative was to reintroduce "subjective judgment" of individual applications into the regular admissions process. "Special achievement or accomplishment, perhaps in the arts or science or even some nonacademic area," stated the majority report, "could pinpoint students with strong motivation and ability." Special circumstance might be more fully considered, along with outstanding letters of recommendation. All of these factors were commonplace in private colleges and universities and at one time at the University of California. The task force considered a formal proposal whereby 90% of regular admissions were through the contemporary admission policies and the remaining 10% were under these subjective criteria. Such flexibility might also afford opportunity "to conduct various admissions experiments to help identify valid, alternative predictors of academic success" while also offering a device for expanding diversity. Further, this new process would be in addition to special action—a selection process at the time conducted by each campus administration.[37] Parker Lee, a student body president at Davis and member of the task force, stated support for the so-called 90-10 model.

But most of the recommendations and options posed by the task force were strongly opposed by Professor Parducci. As the sole representative of BOARS, Parducci rejected any notions of ending or further limiting the use of standardized tests in regular admissions. In contrast, the majority of the task force concluded that the "University's admissions criteria should embody standards a student can attain through hard individual effort" and that, to some extent, "years of effort can be perceived as irrelevant in the face of seemingly arbitrary test requirements . . ."[38]

For Parducci, the antitesting tenor of the majority report simply reflected the biases of the university's growing EOP-SAA community. They ignored the paramount problem: the decline in academic standards in the high schools. "The students and administrators compose the overwhelming majority of the President's Task Force," stated Parducci in his minority report, myopically focusing their attention on affirmative action and not on the pressing issue of meeting the eligibility pool requirement mandated by the master plan. Parducci insisted that the recommendations of Swain and the rest of the task force would lead to "an aggravated violation of the Master Plan."

Parducci cited a number of indicators of an "alarming decline" in the preparation of students enrolling at UC. Their average test scores on the verbal portion of the SAT dropped some fifty points in six years, more than twice the drop reported for the rest of the nation. He also reported that, over that period, the university increased its total freshman enrollment by 30%, but the absolute number of freshmen with high SAT scores dropped by 40%. A similar decline was found in the less academically oriented high schools. Fewer than 10% of students at these schools were UC eligible, schools where "a B average is often no guarantee of the ability to read a freshman text or even to do elementary arithmetic."[39]

Parducci's arguments reflected the growing doubt among a sizable portion of the university's faculty regarding the merits of affirmative action. Giving preferences to minorities seemed intuitively against the very idea of a meritocracy. Further, how much did programs like EOP really help in making students truly competitive for entering the university? Layers of university programs administered outside the purview of academics seemed wasteful and perhaps ineffective. Arthur Jensen, a member of the psychology department at Berkeley, insisted that tests like the SAT were not biased against minorities. Furthermore, Jensen thought EOP and similar programs were bound to fail in large part because intelligence and academic aptitude were determined at an early age and through heredity. Richard Herrnstein at Harvard expressed a similar position. There was no surrogate for intelligence, which was hereditary.

Parducci did not share the controversial viewpoints of Jensen and Herrnstein. There was, however, a sense among faculty leaders like Parducci that the culture of affirmative action eroded the purity of the meritocratic ideal. While Parducci met with the task force, he and members of BOARS concurrently formulated a plan for raising the admissions requirements by establishing a new "eligibility index." The index combined an applicant's SAT scores and his or her high school grade point average in required courses on a sliding scale. Within the index, and for the time being, GPA would be weighted more than six times as heavy as the SAT. Grades remained the primary factor in determining eligibility under this model. The index, however, not only created a new threshold regarding a student's eligibility for acceptance to the university. Over time, it could be adjusted to account for grade inflation. For three years, BOARS and the senate's University Committee on Educational Policy had considered such a revision to admissions policy. A similar index already existed at the California State University system, adopted some ten years earlier.

While delegating the process of admissions decisions to administrative staff and largely removing itself from special action admissions, BOARS and the senate nevertheless retained the policy locus related to academic requirements. President Saxon and Vice President Swain attempted to engage the senate in a broader discussion on the potential impact of the eligibility index on minority admissions, but their overture garnered limited success. The different worldviews of the task force and BOARS were irreconcilable. Parducci and Academic Council Chair William B. Fretter earlier reminded the office of the president and others of the authority of the senate in admissions. Parducci explained to the task force that the "Regents have not delegated the establishment of admissions standards to administrators and students but rather to BOARS and the Academic Senate."[40] Before the regents, Fretter reiterated that the "Regents have delegated responsibility to the Academic Senate for policy on admissions, and the Senate has in turn delegated it to the Board of Admissions and Relations with Schools."[41] But these claims seem disingenuous: The senate by the mid-1970s was simply no longer interested in holistic management of admissions.

In July 1977, Fretter offered BOARS's recommendation for the new eligibility index to the university's governing board, only four months after Swain's task force report was published and submitted to the board. Fretter noted two general motivations for the new index: "first, the concern on the part of the faculty as to the quality and preparation of incoming freshmen." The second motivation was the urgent need to meet the 12.5% target mandated by the master plan. BOARS analyzed a number of options for raising admissions standards to meet these goals, he explained. One option "was to simply raise the grade point average from 3.1 to 3.2 to reduce the pool of eligible students to the Master Plan guideline of 12.5%. . . . Although we do not have good data on the subject," Fretter continued, "we expect that minority enrollments would be disproportionately diminished by that change. It would have some effect on raising the quality of incoming students, but would probably encourage further grade inflation in the high schools." Instead, BOARS proposed the eligibility index for regental action.[42]

The Arrival of the Bakke *Case*

Casting a huge shadow over all university deliberations on admissions, including the eligibility index, was the pending legal case of Allan Bakke. Undergraduate and graduate admissions operated in very different spheres. A general benchmark of grades offered a relatively transparent UC-wide guide for students and their families to gauge if they could enter not only the UC system but, usually, the campus of their choice. Graduate-level admissions criteria, however, were always the prerogative of individual departments and schools and their faculty. Professional schools like law and medicine most fully embrace the ideals of affirmative action, linked to their growing sense that a diversified workforce in these fields was vital for serving an increasingly diverse population. By the early 1970s, most medical school programs developed mechanisms for increasing minority admissions, including subjective criteria and point systems that gave extra weight to the race and ethnicity of the applicant. In some cases, a number of slots were simply set aside for minority or women candidates—essentially a quota system.

In the early 1970s, Allan Bakke twice applied to the medical school at UC Davis and was denied admission. It was not uncommon then, as now, for students and often their parents to write letters of protest to California governors, regents, university presidents, and lawmakers if they did not get into a campus such as Berkeley. Melvin Rush's 1975 letter to Governor Edmund (Jerry) Brown, quoted at the beginning of this chapter, was one example. Such protests are inevitable in a process of allocating a scarce and highly sought public resource. But Bakke took it a step further. In 1976, he sued the university's board of regents for discrimination, noting that his academic record, including test scores, made him more qualified than minority students admitted under an admission system that set aside for minority students sixteen places out of a total of one hundred.

A similar case against the law school at the University of Washington in 1973 reached the Washington State Supreme Court. In *DeFunis v. Odegaard*, a lower court found the law school's use of separate admissions procedures for students of color unconstitutional. The law school used a weighting system giving minority groups significant preferences in the admissions process. But the Washington State Supreme Court overturned the decision, ruling that it was in the state's interest to promote a racially balanced student body and specifically to address a perceived shortage of African Americans and Hispanics entering the legal profession.[43]

By 1978, the *Bakke* case was before the U.S. Supreme Court. Late that year, the highest court in the land ruled in Bakke's favor, stating that UC Davis's "quota" system was unconstitutional. But the court also stated that race could be considered, along with other socioeconomic factors, in the admissions process. Under a slim five to four majority ruling authored by Justice Powell, a precarious balance was struck that would frame the legal basis of affirmative action for some two plus decades. Although a series of lower court rulings in the late 1990s challenged the Supreme Court's 1978 decision, in the summer of 2003, the U.S. Supreme Court again essentially confirmed *Bakke*, a subject to which we will return in later chapters.[44]

On the one hand, the *Bakke* case highlighted the beginning of a long and divisive political battle over the merits and legal bases of affirmative action programs in both education and business. On the other, it formed a new understanding that race-based preferences, if crafted in a form that avoided quotas, were legal and publicly defensible. In the midst of this decisive court battle, the University of California's leadership, the majority of regents, and at least some faculty resolved to move forward with affirmative action. The university's presentation before the Supreme Court argued for the legality of the Davis medical school's admissions process, including the autonomy of the university in the process of selecting students, and the importance of racial and ethnic diversity in university enrollments. Yet BOARS and, in effect, the leadership of the senate were on a course that promised to erode any such efforts.

The SAT and the Eligibility Index

In early 1977, Parducci and BOARS proposed that the senate's legislative assembly adopt the new eligibility index and a proposal for a required fourth year of high school English, and prior to final approval by the regents. With the *Bakke* decision pending and continued pressure from lawmakers in Sacramento to increase minority enrollment, the proposal caused considerable debate. A small contingent of faculty, including Santa Barbara division Chair Robert Michaelsen, argued against the BOARS proposal. He was concerned about the "possible disproportionate adverse effects on some groups of applicants" and reiterated doubts about the "effectiveness of SAT results either as devices for encouraging increased preparation or as predictors of achievement in college." Michaelsen also stated a gnawing problem with the SAT: "It seems to me that some sort of competency test could relate more directly to school preparation than the SAT's do and might also do more to encourage students to prepare themselves more specifically and fully in those language skills needed for achievement in college—as well as in other walks of life."[45]

In the written proposal forwarded to the assembly, Parducci attempted to address these concerns.

> Critics of the proposed formula have expressed concern that any increased use of the SAT would have a negative impact on minorities. Proponents of the formula cite evidence that the formula is a better predictor of college grades than high school GPA alone. Proponents also argue that a standardized test would partially mitigate differential high school grading practices and partially compensate for grade inflation. . . . There is no agreement about the direction of these slight changes—whether in practice they will lead to slightly increased [or] slightly decreased numbers of minority students. There is agreement, however, that a cautious, carefully monitored approach is essential. The Academic Senate [should] recommend that data on all applicants under this formula be collected and carefully analyzed before further admission changes are proposed.[46]

The assembly proceeded to approve the proposal, but it was unclear what action the regents would take and how president Saxon would react. State legislators held hearings in Sacramento before the regents meeting, timed to influence the regents' decision. Assemblyman John Vasconcellos and Assemblywoman Teresa Hughes argued strongly against the new eligibility index. Hughes coauthored a concurrent resolution that called for an increase in the master plan guidelines from the top 12.5% to the top 15% of high school graduates and an end to the requirement for test scores in the application process. "Tightening admission requirements will affect those minority students the most who already are underrepresented at the California State University and Colleges and the University of California," stated the resolution, and would be "contrary" to the legislature's 1974 resolution "establishing a 1980 goal of overcoming underrepresentation of minority students."[47]

Although the concurrent resolution never passed and would not have been legally binding on the university, it provided an important context for the regents' July 1977 meeting, where they were to vote on the new eligibility index. At the regents' meeting, President Saxon stated his general endorsement for the BOARS proposal. It appeared more as a show of support for the authority of the senate than a strong belief in the merits of the eligibility index. Several regents noted deep concerns over the potential impact of the new index. Wilson Riles, the state superintendent of public instruction, stated his strong reservations and presented a resolution passed earlier by the state board of education requesting a delay in any decision. One regent asked why the university should be "tinkering" with admissions policy when the *Bakke* case was not yet resolved.[48] The regents delayed their vote on Parducci's proposal until their October meeting and, as a result, caused at least a one-year delay in its implementation.

Fretter reintroduced the BOARS proposal to the regents. In a memo to the regents, President Saxon again noted his endorsement. "Almost from the moment it became generally known that changes in the admissions requirements were under consideration," wrote Saxon in a memo to the regents meeting in October, "but especially in the last two months, this subject has provoked strong and vigorous debate, both within the University and without . . . Let me state unequivocally my firm commitment to equality of access for all qualified people of the State and my determination that the University will in no way diminish its active pursuit of this goal." "I am convinced," Saxon concluded, "that no ultimate conflict exists between equal access and educational excellence, and no message to that effect was ever intended, despite perceptions to the contrary on the part of some."[49]

At their October meeting, by a narrow vote of fifteen to twelve, the board approved the new eligibility index. The regents recommended that it become university policy in 1979.[50] At budget hearings in Sacramento, Assemblyman Vasconcellos created the impression that the university's state budget might be affected. "What have I learned from this experience?" asked Fretter at a later meeting of the academic council. "That the issue of admissions is deeply involved with the political forces in the State. . . . The Senate is not prepared to deal with such matters, and with seven new Regents on the Board, we can no longer count on them for protection."[51]

The Eligibility Index and Special Action

Reconciled with the change promoted by BOARS, President Saxon and members of his administration, like Hitch in 1968, considered the only major administrative mechanism that might compensate for the anticipated decline in minority enrollment under the new sliding scale of SAT scores and grades. He proposed increasing the special action limit from 4% to 6% to partially mitigate the impact and to demonstrate the university's commitment to broadening access to ethnic minority students.

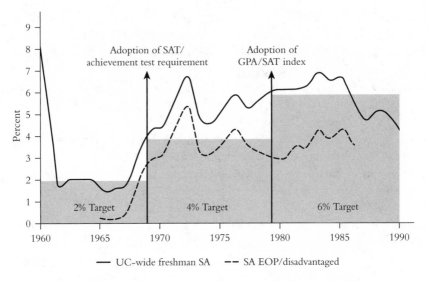

Figure 5.1.   University of California special action freshman admissions:
1960–1990

SOURCE: California Postsecondary Education Commission; University of California
Office of the President, Enrollment Reports.

Similar to 1968, the university president did not seek the approval of the
academic senate for raising the special action target; instead, he went directly
to the board of regents just months after their approval of the eligibility
index. Recognizing the need for a countervailing force to the effort to con-
strict access to the university, the board approved Saxon's request with the
new target, like the eligibility index, to go into effect in 1979. As explained
by James Albertson, the acting academic vice chancellor under Saxon, the
increase in special action would be for an experimental five-year term "to
encourage greater diversity in the student body."[52] Figure 5.1 provides data
on special action admissions between 1960 and 1990 and its significant and
varied role as a tool of affirmative action.

   With the regents' approval of the senate's proposal, the specter of any
substantial liberalization of regular admissions by the university's academic senate appeared not only limited but also closed for the immediate future. Outreach and special action remained the primary tools of the
university for increasing minority enrollments, and senate leaders made no
overtures to become more active policymakers in either area. Saxon knew,
however, that senate involvement was needed for any long-term hope of a
broader university commitment to diversity. "One of the important tasks

now facing the University," opined Saxon in 1981 before the regents, "is to determine what systematic experiments should be undertaken in Special Action admissions to test various alternative methods of selecting students for admission. The goal is to develop alternate means of assessing a student's chances of academic success, including factors other than grade point averages and test scores. Obviously, the academic senate must be deeply involved in designing these experiments." Saxon then requested the establishment of affirmative-action plans for each campus and the formation of a joint senate and administrative committee to report on campus progress to the university's academic council and the president's office.[53]

For university officials, there was room for optimism. A relatively new infrastructure of support services extended down to the schools, university guidance and recruitment efforts had grown, and the expansion of special action presented a revived effort to offer alternative routes into the university. But many problems remained, most of which extended outside the realm of the university. A significant decline in the national economy and momentous demographic shifts posed increasing challenges to funding and operating California's public schools. As one regent noted, "All the affirmative action programs in the world won't do any good if the University of California can't do anything to upgrade the primary and secondary education."[54]

At an annual meeting of administrators and staff involved in outreach programs, Karl Pister, then chair of the Berkeley division of the academic senate, noted his concern that faculty, and the academic senate specifically, were not fully cognizant of the need for affirmative action. "We are the heirs of an immense social problem—we are struggling for a solution, often looking for an easy solution to a complex problem," explained Pister. And although the senate possessed authority over admissions policy in collaboration with administrators, Pister complained that the faculty was not fully engaged in confronting the issue. "Individual faculty have been concerned with and active in student affirmative action," but the academic senate, he noted, "with minor exceptions, is just now awakening to the problem."[55]

The eligibility index, along with course requirements in areas such as English and math, formed the cornerstone of the university's contemporary admissions policy. But accompanying the establishment of the new index was yet another wave of calls that the university devise new administrative methods to increase the number of underrepresented students. These concerns resonated more with the administrative leadership than with the faculty and the academic senate, but this was about to change.

Chapter 6

For Every Action a Reaction: Race, Bakke, and the Social Contract Revisited

Each year, well over 20,000 students apply for admission into the freshman class at Berkeley. The sheer number poses formidable obstacles to the construction of a careful and deliberate decision-making process, and they have vastly increased pressure on the university to explain—and to justify—its selection practices. Never before has the zero-sum character of the admissions process been so visible, and never before has it so threatened the relationship between the University and the community it serves.

—Report of the Committee on Admissions and Enrollment, Berkeley Division of the Academic Senate, University of California, May 19, 1989

In 1957, Supreme Court Justice Felix Frankfurter saw value in a significant level of autonomy for universities, citing "four essential freedoms of a university." These included, "who may teach, what may be taught, how it should be taught, and who may be admitted to study."[1] Until the 1970s, the courts generally upheld Frankfurter's view, with a number of major exceptions, including a growing body of cases related to overt discrimination and denial of access to public universities, largely in the South. In 1950, for example, the U.S. Supreme Court forced the University of Texas Law School to admit African Americans for the first time. In doing so, the court ruled that the university's refusal to admit Herman Marion Sweatt would have been legal under the Fourteenth Amendment if the state could provide another and presumably segregated opportunity for him to pursue a law degree. Texas could not provide this option and therefore needed to admit Sweatt to its public law school.

The *Sweatt* case and a similar suit against the University of Oklahoma were strategic cases chosen by the leaders of the NAACP. They hoped to build a series of court decisions that would eventually force a decision by the U.S. Supreme Court on the inherent inequity of formal segregation. Two years later, in *Brown v. Board of Education of Topeka*, the court ruled unequivocally and famously against the concept of "separate but equal." And in 1956, in a federal case involving the state of Florida, the unconstitutionality of "separate but equal" was extended to higher education.[2]

120

In all of these cases, the courts ruled on whether a student was denied access to publicly funded higher education due to overt racial discrimination and demanded restitution and an end to policies barring entrance to any racial or ethnic group. Court rulings were narrow and focused on the question of access, not on the way universities made their decisions.

However, a new political and legal environment emerged in the 1970s, culminating in the 1978 *Bakke* case. *Bakke* barred quotas and also legitimized race and ethnicity, and gender, as factors in admissions. For the first time, the court passed judgment on the admissions process itself *and* suggested an appropriate approach. *Bakke* caused university leaders and administrators to ponder how they might construct admissions practices within a new legal environment and the growing glare of public scrutiny. *Bakke* "is the standard against which educational institutions must measure the legality of their admissions programs and procedures," wrote Alexander Astin, Bruce Fuller, and Kenneth Green in 1978, shortly after the decision.[3] But what exactly was that standard? For public universities already engaged in affirmative action in one form or another, the answer was not immediately clear. Was *Bakke* a defeat or a victory for affirmative action? Did it constrain or give license to university efforts to diversify their student bodies?

For both good and bad, America has shown a penchant for relying on the judicial system as a forum for resolving conflict more than any other nation. In exerting a central role in shaping admissions policy, America's courts increasingly immersed their decisions in the peculiarities of personal rights to the detriment of the broad issues of institutional purpose (see Table 6.1, listing major court cases).

After Bakke*: Ethnicity and Regular Admissions*

Shortly after the *Bakke* decision, the counsel of the Anti-Defamation League, Arnold Forster, welcomed the halt in quotas, perhaps influenced by their use in previous decades to exclude Jews. As "a practical matter," he noted, it appeared "difficult to allow race to be used as one factor in admissions without that factor eventually becoming the determining factor."[4] David Riesman, the famed Harvard sociologist, saw the decision as ambiguous and predicted future battles. What "we are now facing," noted Riesman, "is full employment for lawyers, as the rising sense of entitlement among groups and individuals takes hold with more bitterness at all levels."[5]

Forster's and Riesman's assessments would prove reasonably accurate, fueled by the earnest efforts of institutions to increase enrollment of minority

TABLE 6.1
Major court cases related to access and equity in higher education: 1954–1996

Brown v. Board of Education (1954)	The U.S. Supreme Court maintained that the precedent of "separate but equal" set in Plessy v. Ferguson (1896) was no longer constitutional. As a result of the Brown verdict, it was assumed that educational institutions would no longer resist the enrollment of African Americans.
Hawkins v. Board of Control (1956)	The unconstitutionality of "separate but equal" was extended beyond elementary and secondary schools to enforce higher education desegregation.
DeFunis v. Odegaard (1973)	The Washington State Supreme Court ruled affirmative-action admissions in professional schools justified by the need to promote a racially balanced student body and specifically to address a perceived shortage of African Americans and Hispanics entering the legal profession.
UC Regents v. Bakke (1978)	The U.S. Supreme Court ruled that admissions quotas were unconstitutional but that race and ethnicity, and gender, could be one factor among many in admissions decisions in public universities.
Podberesky v. Kirwan (1994)	The use of race-specific scholarships at the University of Maryland at College Park was questioned. A federal court ruled it was not permissible to maintain separate financial merit awards according to race.
Adarand v. Pena (1995)	The Adarand case applied the legal concept of judicial or "strict scrutiny" to argue that affirmative action should be applied only in documented cases of prior institutional discrimination and then only when carefully tailored to groups directly affected.
Hopwood v. Texas (1996)	Four Euro-American students filed suit in federal court against the University of Texas at Austin School of Law after being denied admission, charging the university used separate admissions criteria for African American and Hispanic applicants. The Fifth Circuit Court ruled in favor of the students. In 1996, University of Texas officials appealed the decision of the Fifth Circuit Court. The U.S. Supreme Court upheld the lower court's ruling, thereby continuing the ban on race and student affirmative action at public campuses in Texas.

groups. The effect of the Bakke case was a sense of liberation and license for the vast majority of public institutions intent on broadening their use of race in the process of admissions. Blatant quotas were to be avoided, but there were other mechanisms for broadening access to minority groups. In his majority opinion, Justice Powell not only validated the use of race and ethnicity in decision making, but he pointed to Harvard University's admissions program as an "acceptable" model. Harvard, he thought, treated "each applicant as an individual in the admissions process."

Like other private elite institutions, Harvard employed a point system that weighted scores to give favor to certain student characteristics, including grades, various talents, and race. The applicant "who lost out on the last available seat to another candidate receiving a 'plus' on the basis of ethnic background," noted Powell, "will not have been foreclosed from all consideration from that seat simply because he was not the right color or had the wrong surname. It would mean only that his combined qualifications, which may have included similar nonobjective factors, did not outweigh those of the other applicants."[6] Powell's opinion seemed to voice explicit rejection of quotas but not the idea of de facto quotas.

A consensus emerged within the higher education community and among affirmative-action supporters. *Bakke* appeared to end a period of legal uncertainty. Universities "have [a] constitutional blessing to stay the course," stated Andrew Fitt at a symposium organized by the College Board. "Those who may have hesitated, out of legal concerns, need do so no longer," he concluded. At the same symposium, the president of the American Council on Education, Jack Peltason, made a similar statement. The decision "left the options open. The overwhelming number of affirmative-action programs now in place will meet the standards outlined by the Court."[7] Clark Kerr, as head of the Carnegie Council on Policy Studies in Higher Education, said that the *Bakke* decision "supported a continuation of affirmative-action programs in higher education and diversity in college and university student bodies. This is good for higher education and the nation and allows efforts to increase social justice." UC President David Saxon announced that *Bakke* was a "great victory" and that "restriction on the use of race is going to make it more difficult, but not very much more difficult."[8]

UCLA Professor Alexander W. Astin pointed to challenges facing selective universities: how to define disadvantaged status and how to link any such definition to racial and ethnic background. In an edited volume on admissions after *Bakke*, Astin noted, "Although the term disadvantaged is frequently synonymous with membership in particular ethnic or racial minority groups, public resistance to special admissions appears to be much stronger when race rather than disadvantagement is used in the admissions process."[9] A new wave of research focused on how to build models that included a wide assessment of disadvantaged status, yet in the end, the models were heavily weighted toward race and ethnicity.

The *Bakke* case launched a wave of point systems that combined both academic and nonacademic factors to help determine admissions; the point systems both helped guide post-*Bakke* decisions and created a relatively transparent process of admissions defensible in the courts and in state capitals. Conceptually, the idea was to eliminate dual-track admissions in which minority groups were admitted under separate criteria. Instead, a holistic admissions process would include race and ethnicity as one factor weighed against other criteria. Besides Harvard, a number of public institutions already used academic indexes, including Michigan State University, Temple University, McMaster University in Canada, and Florida State University.[10] For the University of California and many other public universities, these institutions offered constr-ucts on which to build.

Race and the Parity Model

The University of California, specifically its most selective campuses, sought new admissions criteria that integrated race and conceptions of disadvantaged status into the regular admissions process. Until 1979, policy directives from the university's office of the president, the board of regents, or the university's academic senate made no explicit statement that race or ethnicity could be used as a factor in regular undergraduate admissions.[11] Only special action admissions could explicitly use race along with special talents. In the realm of admissions decisions, special action had thus far been the university's official affirmative-action tool.

Several months after the *Bakke* decision, however, President Saxon stated in a letter to the chancellors and academic council that race and ethnicity could now be used more broadly in the admissions process. "Grades and test scores alone," stated Saxon, "are not necessarily accurate predictors of potential to complete a program successfully. . . . Because of barriers and obstacles often associated with race, sex, and physical handicap," continued Saxon, "status as a member of such an underrepresented group may be regarded as indicative of the need for special scrutiny to determine whether the record accurately reflects the applicant's academic potential." Therefore, concluded Saxon:

In programs where the number of qualified applicants exceeds the number of available places, the selection of qualified applicants for admission should be designed to achieve a student body with a diversity of talents and characteristics appropriate to the needs of the field and the educational enrichment of the program. Sex and ethnic minority status may be taken into account where appropriate in establishing such diversity. Even in programs where there are large numbers of applicants, further efforts to attract a more broadly diversified applicant pool may be necessary in order to achieve the appropriate degree of diversity in the student body.[12]

Recall that in 1974 state legislators established a statutory goal mandating that enrollment more directly reflect the demographic mix of the state's

high school graduates. Lawmakers, particularly powerful Democratic legislators, wanted results fast. They demanded a student body that represented
proportionately the ethnic mix of the graduating class of high school seniors
by 1980. The university asked that the goal be pushed out into later years,
while reconfirming its general commitment to eventually meet the standard. Lawmakers obliged but again demanded significant progress. Saxon
and other university leaders then pondered what additional administrative
steps could be taken beyond the new university-wide policy opening regular admissions to include race and ethnicity. How might they make the
campuses accountable?

Different UC campuses possessed different geographic draws and hence
different abilities to recruit and admit students from the state's racial and
ethnic communities. In part, this was due to cultural and economic differences among ethnic groups. Asian American and Latino-Chicano high
school graduates and transfer students tended to apply to nearby UC campuses. Euro-American applicants had a greater tendency to apply to campuses located throughout the state.

Although a statewide institution in its mission, the university developed new campuses with the idea that each would disproportionately
serve a regional area. This conceptual framework proved crucial for justifying the development of each new campus and influenced the choice of
their locations—generally, in areas of substantial unmet local enrollment
demand. By 1979, however, the idea of each campus in a primary service area, where one might, as in Berkeley's case, have a higher concentration of African Americans and Asian Americans than Chicanos-Latinos
posed political problems. It meant that racial and ethnic groups might be
grouped by their academic ability. For example, university officials worried
that lower performing, on average, Latinos-Chicanos would tend to enroll at the Riverside campus, whereas higher performing, on average, Asian
Americans would congregate at Berkeley.

The prospect of segregating ethnic groups in correlation with the prestige
of the campus was not a politically viable position in the face of lawmaker
criticism and the university's inability to meet the mandates of the 1974 statute. This conclusion led to a new policy directive. President Saxon in 1979
established a parity model: Each campus was directed to "reflect" the racial
and ethnic composition of the state's high school graduates. Saxon's new
policy set an accountability framework to push campuses to recruit and enroll underrepresented groups. This put the onus on campus chancellors and
their staff to canvass the entire state to recruit underrepresented minorities,
regardless of a campus's location or its local constituency.[13]

Tiered Admissions at Berkeley and UCLA

Since its evolution as a multicampus institution with the inclusion of UCLA in 1919, the University of California's social contract had set requirements that determined a student's eligibility. Eligible students possessed a *right* to enter the university but not necessarily their first-choice campus. The establishment of new campuses in Santa Barbara, Davis, and Riverside by the late 1950s expanded the university's enrollment capacity considerably. Each campus, including Berkeley and UCLA, could grow and did. California's population continued to escalate at a spectacular rate. It surpassed New York as the most populated state in the union in 1963; two decades later, California was twice the size of its nearest state rival. Between 1960 and 1980, Berkeley grew from 24,000 to nearly 30,000 students. UCLA grew even more, enrolling nearly 10,000 additional students over that period. In total, the University of California grew from 55,887 students in 1960 to a total of 135,821 in two decades. Most UC-eligible students could attend the campus of their choice. But this option was quickly changing.

By 1980, Berkeley and UCLA reached their designated physical capacity for students at about 30,000—a limit influenced by local community concerns over population growth and by the University of California's own policies. Hence, Berkeley and UCLA were no longer able to grow at a time when applications from academically eligible students continued to climb. For these campuses, admissions became a zero sum game: Any effort to raise the admissions rate of one ethnic group would have to come at the expense of another. Beginning in earnest in the late 1970s and for the first time, significant numbers of qualified students were turned away from these two campuses. In 1975, for example, Berkeley received 5,035 applications to fill 3,064 freshman slots. Most students who applied were UC eligible; most were admitted, and most enrolled. In 1980, the campus received 9,115 freshman applications while its general target for freshmen stabilized at around 3,330 students. Applications continued to climb (see Table 6.2). In 1990, 19,946 students applied to Berkeley, a figure in part inflated by the University of California's move to a new application system discussed later in this chapter.[14]

For private institutions, such an increase in demand over supply was a phenomenon to flaunt—an indicator of the rising quality of entering students and the prestige of a campus. For public institutions, the net result was a policy conundrum. The fact that access to Berkeley, for ex-

TABLE 6.2
UC Berkeley freshmen applicants, admits, and enrolled: 1975–1995

	1975	1980	1985	1990	1995
Applicants	5,035	9,115	11,913	19,946	22,811
Admits	3,896	4,885	6,329	7,574	8,832
Enrolled	3,064	3,373	3,772	3,128	3,405
Ratio Admits to Applicants	77%	54%	53%	38%	39%

SOURCE: California Postsecondary Education Commission; University of California Office of the President, Enrollment Reports.

ample, became more difficult and more prized fueled the desire of many Californians to apply. Applications shot up. That meant more and more students would be rejected. The increased ranks of rejected students placed pressure on Berkeley, as a public university, to justify its admissions practices. Who was getting in and who was not?

At Berkeley and UCLA, adherence to a strict definition of academic aptitude, as determined by high school GPA and SAT scores in the selection process, would have resulted in an overwhelmingly Euro-American and Asian American student population. Such a path was not politically palatable for university leaders. But it was more than simply a political problem; the university had committed to making the university reflective of the state's burgeoning population. To increase the number of "underrepresented" students, primarily Chicanos-Latinos and African Americans, Berkeley and UCLA employed new methods to alter the composition of their undergraduate populations. Quotas were to be avoided, but there were other systematic ways to provide access to underrepresented groups.

Beginning in 1981, Berkeley's approach was particularly aggressive, relating to the strong desire of the campus's new chancellor, Ira Michael Heyman, to increase minority enrollment. "He just took the bull by the horns and went for it, and really turned [Berkeley] into a wonderfully diverse place," reflected William Baker, vice president of the university at the time. "He was clearly the leader in the university" regarding affirmative action. Baker also noted the tremendous political pressure. Sacramento required yearly reports on the university's progress. While legislators wanted increases in underrepresented students at Berkeley, a number of regents also demanded quick results. Regents Stanley Sheinbaum, Sheldon Andelson, Vilma Martinez, Yvonne Brathwaite Burke, and Yori Wada, stated Baker, "pressed us, even badgered us, urged us to reach out with affirmative action programs."[15]

Heyman first came to Berkeley in the late 1950s as a young law professor. He was a graduate of Dartmouth College with a law degree from Yale University. After serving in the U.S. Marines, he worked as a clerk under Earl Warren shortly after the former California governor was appointed Chief Justice of the U.S. Supreme Court. The experience of working with Warren was an important influence on his subsequent career at Berkeley. He joined the faculty at Boalt Hall in 1959. An active member of the academic senate during the tumultuous 1960s, he became the campus's vice chancellor in 1974. In 1980, he was named Berkeley's sixth chancellor—the first being Clark Kerr when the position of chancellor was established at both Berkeley and UCLA; previously, the president of the university was the head of each campus.

Although Berkeley was only one campus in the growing University of California system, Heyman saw Berkeley's responsibilities as distinct; the original campus in the system needed to be the most progressive in broadening access to minority groups. President David Saxon's 1979 directive set general parameters for admissions policies and asked that each campus venture forward as it saw fit. The idea that each campus might have different admissions practices was entirely new. The clarion call was to increase minority participation and pursue the parity model. It was the responsibility of the chancellors to get it done. "Responsibility for implementation of these special [affirmative-action] efforts is delegated directly to the Chancellors of the nine campuses of the University," noted one office of the president directive. The intent was to "eliminate underrepresentation."[16]

At the outset of his appointment as chancellor, Heyman publicly stated that increasing the number of underrepresented minorities was one of his major objectives. He noted this goal repeatedly. Berkeley's Long-Range Academic Plan gave him ammunition. Completed during the first year of his chancellorship, this plan was unlike previous plans. Past efforts focused largely on how to build academic programs and mused on possible curricular reforms. This new academic plan focused on affirmative action and the need to systematically diversify and improve the academic capabilities of incoming students. Berkeley "cannot, of course, control the deficiencies of the larger society which affect the motivation and preparation of students," explained the plan. "But, without lowering standards of academic admissions or academic performance, it can address those of its institutional practices that are obstacles to access and success at Berkeley if it has the will to do so."[17] The key was to reorganize the campus's affirmative-action effort.

Heyman established a new unit, the division of undergraduate affairs. He appointed Watson Macmillan ("Mac") Laetsch, a professor of biology and former director of Berkeley's Lawrence Hall of Science, as the new vice chancellor for undergraduate affairs and asked him to immediately inventory and better coordinate the affirmative-action efforts of the campus. More generally, Heyman directed admissions officers to stimulate an influx of minority students. In turn, Laetsch established a task force on minority recruitment and launched a significant new era in Berkeley admissions.[18] The relevance of the academic senate seemed, sadly, minimal if nonexistent to the new chancellor and Laetsch. In contrast to the administration, most faculty continued to demonstrate interest in one thing: getting smarter students with higher test scores. In Heyman's view, the senate and its leaders were marginal partners at best and potential opponents at worst.

In 1981, Laetsch and admissions officers created policies built around President Saxon's directives. Berkeley established three major categories, or "tiers," of admissions to help refashion the demographic mix of the undergraduate class.[19] The general idea was to create a number of avenues for incorporating racial preferences in the admissions process. The result was a greatly nuanced process that relied on subjective factors and the socioeconomic background of students. Tier 1 focused strictly on academic criteria. Approximately 50% of all freshman applicants would be accepted on this basis—a figure in line with the university-wide policy outlined by Frank Kidner in 1971. Building on the model of the eligibility index and formulas used at other universities, Berkeley created its own academic index, which produced a score based solely on GPA, the SAT, and the results of three achievement tests. The index gave approximately equal weight to GPA and test scores.

Tier 2 focused on a broader review of a student's application. Some 50% to 60% of regular admissions to Berkeley were reviewed based on their academic index score and a variety of "supplemental" criteria with their own scoring system. These supplemental criteria included California residence, high school coursework (e.g., did a student take advanced placement courses and were they available in her or his school?), and special talents in areas such as music and drama. Tier 2 also included the EOP status of the student (see Table 6.3). Although low-income Euro-Americans could be EOP students, the vast majority of these students were underrepresented minorities. In 1980, only about 15% of EOP students throughout the UC system were Euro-American. Some 28% were African American, 31% were Chicano-Latino, 20% were Asian American, and just over 3.2% were Native American. EOP status amounted to just over 15% of the total Tier 2 score a student could receive. But added to this was another element to increase the number

TABLE 6.3
Criteria and weighting for Tier 2 supplemental regular admission to UC Berkeley: 1980—1988

Criteria	Points	Relative Weight
California Residence	200	15.4%
Education Opportunity Program (eligible minority groups)	200	15.4%
4 Years of Math or 3 Years of Lab Science	100	7.7%
4 Years of One Foreign Language or 2 Languages	100	7.7%
Subject A Exemption (testing out of remedial English)	100	7.7%
Lack of High School Junior Year Honors Courses	100	7.7%
Essay, Honors, Public Service, and/or Special Circumstance	500	38.4%
Total	1,300	100.0%

SOURCE: "Freshman Admissions at Berkeley: A Policy for the 1990s and Beyond," May 19, 1980.

of underrepresented minorities: subjective criteria that included an essay and "special circumstance." Combined, they comprised 38% of the overall score.

Students admitted under the even more subjective Tier 3 needed only to be UC eligible and have one or more characteristics, including, and perhaps primarily, membership in an underrepresented group. The number of students admitted under this category varied over the years depending on the size of the Tier 1 and 2 pools.[20] Examples of Tier 3 groups included athletes, people with disabilities, students from rural areas, affirmative-action students (specifically, blacks, Hispanics, Native Americans, and for a period, low-income Asian Americans), and students with special talents in such fields as music, drama, and debating. Three of these groups—athletes, people with disabilities, and affirmative-action students—were guaranteed admission if they met UC eligibility requirements.

Berkeley's new admissions policy tilted a significant portion of the admissions process toward supplemental criteria, and those criteria were weighted heavily toward race and ethnicity. The growing excess of UC-eligible students offered a rich pool of academically prepared students. As the campus became more aggressive in diversifying its ethnic mix of students, it expanded the use of the Tier 3 category and to a lesser extent Tier 2. In 1986, for example, the campus reduced the percentage of freshmen admitted via Tier 1 from 50% to 40%. And between 1986 and 1988, the proportion of fall freshmen admits in Tier 3 grew from 28.1% to 38.9% (see Table 6.4). Students admitted under Tiers 2 and 3 and under special action were more likely to enroll at Berkeley than students admitted solely according to their academic index score. These students tended to come from more affluent families and applied to and were often accepted at other highly selective institutions, including Stanford.

TABLE 6.4

UC Berkeley freshmen admissions tiers: Admits and likelihood to enroll, 1988

	Admits	% of Total	Enrollment Yield
Tier 1—Academic Index Score (AIS) Only	3,015	39.0%	40.0%
Tier 2—AIS Plus Supplemental Points	1,260	16.3%	49.1%
Tier 3—Complemental Groups	3,007	38.9%	47.5%
Special Action	449	5.8%	62.6%
Total	7,731	100.0%	45.0%

SOURCE: "Freshman Admissions at Berkeley: A Policy for the 1990s and Beyond," May 19, 1980.

UCLA's Chancellor Charles Young and his staff sought a similar plan to expand campus diversity. In 1981, the Los Angeles campus launched a two-tier admissions system. UCLA proceeded to accept all underrepresented minority students (designated as student affirmative-action students, or SAAs) who were UC eligible. It was automatic. Berkeley's more elaborate admissions system appeared to do nearly the same. At the same time, UCLA upped the ante for academic standards for largely Euro-Americans and Asian American students by raising the required grade point average and giving increased weight to the SAT and achievement test scores. In 1984, UCLA decreased its admissions of low-income students, many of whom were of Euro-American and Asian backgrounds, to bolster the admission of minorities who came largely from middle-income families. Increasingly, the focus was on ethnicity at the expense of economic hardship.[21]

In 1990, the Los Angeles campus expanded considerably its two-tier admissions process. Approximately 50% to 60% of all freshman applicants within the College of Letters and Science were admitted on their "academic rank" as determined by an index of GPA and test scores. The campus selected the remaining applicants by reviewing their academic ranking and supplemental criteria in three general areas: (1) diversity (i.e., ethnic identity), (2) hardship (disabilities, educational disadvantage, and low income), and (3) special talents, interests, and experiences.[22] UCLA placed an increasingly high premium on race and ethnicity. For example, in 1994, a total of 21,000 UC-eligible students applied to the freshman class at UCLA. Yet only 9,860 of the entire pool of eligible students could be accepted—a 46% acceptance rate, with the anticipation that only about half would then actually enroll at UCLA. Admissions decisions were based on a scoring system that gave additional weight to UC-eligible students of African American and Chicano-Latino heritage without regard to economic plight. Although

6,800 (69%) of the admitted pool were based strictly on academic criteria, these students were almost entirely Euro-American and Asian American. Only 1.1% and 4.7% of the African American and Chicano-Latino students were admitted on academic criteria alone. The vast majority, some 2,140 students, gained admission over other UC-eligible students primarily because of their ethnicity.[23]

Aiding Berkeley and UCLA in their quest to increase minority enrollment was the establishment in 1985 of a new "multiple filing" application system implemented by the entire University of California system. Previously, students filled out a single application noting their first-, second-, and third-choice campuses. Under the new system, students applied to each campus separately. Criticism by families with students rejected at their first-choice campus brought political pressure from a group of lawmakers to alter the admissions system. An increasing number of highly qualified students were being rejected at their first-choice campus, usually Berkeley or UCLA. Often, their second-choice campus, for example, Santa Barbara or San Diego, was not available either. By the mid-1980s, both of these campuses either accepted a small number of redirected students or, for several years, rejected a number of UC-eligible students. Hence, many students with excellent academic qualifications were offered admissions only at their third- or fourth-choice campus. The result: Students and their families felt that UC did not offer them a viable choice, forcing them instead to look at other top-ranking and often private institutions with substantial tuition costs.[24]

The new application system provided greater choice for the most academically qualified; it was also intended to help campuses increase diversity. The most highly qualified high school graduates now could gain admission to both Berkeley *and* UCLA. At the same time, the number of minority student applications went discernibly up and provided the campuses with a chance to compete for these highly sought students. However, multiple filing accentuated some problems. For the student, multiple applications afforded greater choice. But the number of campuses to which a student applied varied significantly by ethnic group. In 1990, the average Asian American student applied to four campuses; in contrast, the average Chicano-Latino student applied to only 1.2 campuses. A correlation emerged between socioeconomic status and the number of campus applications a student filed. Reflecting the quality of schooling and counseling, cultural differences, and other factors, students from lower income families tended to apply to the fewest number of campuses and often at a campus nearest their home.

Multiple filing brought a dramatic increase in the number of applications, creating a tremendous workload for each campus. This in turn forced significant changes in admissions procedures that placed greater reliance on weighted formulas for admissions decisions. Within the University of California system, the number of applications jumped from 48,000 in 1980 to more than 168,000 in 1990, a 250% increase. Berkeley and UCLA each received just over 20,000 applications for the entering freshman class of 1986, with an average subsequent increase of approximately 1,000 applications per year. As a point of comparison, the number of applicants to Stanford and Harvard was in the vicinity of 16,000 and 14,000, respectively.

And finally, multiple filing substantially increased the number of UC-eligible students who received rejection letters from the University of California. In 1988, Berkeley and UCLA rejected approximately 20,000 UC-eligible students applying for the freshman year, or approximately two of every three applicants. "Record numbers of freshman applications have flooded the University of California this year," explained Larry Gordon in an article in the *Los Angeles Times*, "and more students than ever will be rejected from their first-choice campus, including thousands with perfect high school grades who aimed for UC Berkeley and UCLA."[25] These students were promised a place in the system or possible enrollment at a later date in the academic year. The average student redirected to a campus did not get an offer until late in the admissions process, often too late for entry in the fall quarter or semester and after many had already made plans to enter another college or to delay their college education.[26] In 1986, approximately 4,000 UC-eligible students fell into the redirection pool. Only a modest percentage ever enrolled in the university.[27]

Overrepresentation and the Case of Asian Americans

In formulating their new admissions policies, Berkeley and UCLA thought they devised publicly defendable approaches to expanding minority enrollment. But had they made race one factor among many—the legal dictum offered in the *Bakke* case? Or had race and ethnicity become first among equals?

One thing is for sure. During the 1980s UCLA's and Berkeley's evolving admissions policies successfully created a more ethnically diverse student population. In accomplishing this feat, both campuses bucked a national trend. From 1960 to 1977, minority enrollment at America's colleges and universities shot up from 6.4% of all enrollment to 13.8%. Of that total, African Americans represented most of the new minority enrollment. But in the early 1980s, increases in the number of African Americans, Hispanics, and Native Americans as a percentage of all enrollment leveled out and then dropped slightly, particularly at selective institutions. At Harvard, for example, minority enrollment dropped by 7%. At Cornell, the drop was approximately 10%.

Berkeley and UCLA, and the entire nine-campus UC system, experienced an increase in minority enrollment during the 1980s. Between 1980 and 1990, for example, the Berkeley campus increased the number of minority students from approximately 40% to 60% of all freshman admits. African Americans constituted 5.2% of all freshman enrollment in 1980; by 1990, that number was closer to 11%. Chicano–Latino freshman admits grew from 6% to nearly 20%. Native Americans grew only slightly, from 0.3% to 1.8%, in part reflecting their low numbers as a percentage of the general population.

One reason for the jump in minority enrollment was altered admissions policies championed by Chancellor Heyman. Another reason was the spectacular growth in California's minority population, bolstered by immigration and higher than average birthrates among some minority groups. California's pool of high school students was diversifying at a rate found in no other state. The only minority group not to grow in enrollment at Berkeley was Asian Americans. In 1980, Asian Americans already constituted 23% of the Berkeley freshman class, a percentage significantly higher than their overall population in the state. But by 1990, and despite population growth, their numbers declined to 20%. Asian Americans were among the first beneficiaries of affirmative action at the University of California. In the early 1980s, they arguably became the victims.

Did the Berkeley campus create new admissions policies to reduce Asian American enrollment in favor of Euro-American students, as Asian American interest groups claimed? Policies that would have a disproportionate effect on Asian Americans may have been considered, but there was no systematic effort to exclude Asian Americans in favor of Euro-American applicants. Did the campus create policies to reduce both Asian Americans and Euro-Americans in favor of underrepresented groups? The answer is yes. As stated later in a review of Berkeley's admissions policies by the academic senate, "A fair and equitable admissions policy is not, we wish to emphasize, a *neutral* one."[28]

Beginning in the early 1980s, and as previously discussed, the Berkeley campus administration made a series of adjustments in admissions policy. These adjustments included the invention of the Tier 1, 2, and 3 admissions categories. At first, this system helped Asian Americans. Berkeley admissions officers identified Asian Americans as an affirmative-action group. As such, they benefited from a Tier 2 supplemental admissions process that gave extra points for EOP status. Asian Americans also could enter Berkeley under Tier 3 criteria as a racial minority, and they qualified for minority-oriented outreach and support programs.

However, in 1984, university administrators, struggling with the parity model, removed Asian Americans from the list of underrepresented groups. Most outreach programs were now reserved for primarily Chicanos-Latinos and African Americans. Many EOP programs had become race specific, in part reflecting ideas that homogeneous programs gave a comfortable home for racial and ethnic groups in an otherwise alien cultural environment. Beginning in 1984, the campus administration had assigned targets for increasing the number of new black, Chicano, Latino, Filipino, and Native American students. The campus essentially sought to double their numbers over the five-year period 1984 to 1989. There were no similar targets for Asian Americans or Euro-Americans, but with Berkeley's enrollment capacity relatively stable, it was implied that their numbers would need to come down.[29]

The academic success of Asian Americans in California's high schools and their high SAT scores, particularly in math, were the primary reasons for their enrollments far in excess of their proportion to California's population. The majority was admissible under Tier 1. In the midst of Berkeley's effort to build the numbers of African American and Chicano-Latino students, an Asian American advocacy group noted the significant drop in Asian American students. They constituted 26.9% of Berkeley's freshman class in 1983, but a year later, the figure was only 24.1%.[30] But the year 1984 marked an even more pronounced drop. In 1983, Berkeley's admissions officers admitted 47.4% UC-eligible students of Asian American background; the next year they admitted only 34.4%. Reflecting the changing priorities of Berkeley's admissions processes, Euro-American admission rates dropped as well, from 61.1% to 48.1%.[31]

UC Berkeley Professor L. Ling-chi Wang observed the drop in student numbers with trepidation. Wang orchestrated a meeting of influential leaders in the Bay Area's Asian American community to discuss admissions at Berkeley. This led to the formation of the Asian-American Task Force on University Admissions (AATF) in late 1984, cochaired by Bay Area Judges Lillian Sing and Ken Kawaichi. The AATF requested information from the Berkeley admissions office and formulated a number of accusations intended to gain the attention of the campus and the media.[32] They charged Berkeley officials with constructing new admissions policies intended to reduce the number of Asian Americans. Specifically, the report claimed that the exclusion of Asians from EOP status was unjustified, essentially making EOP an entirely *race-based* program without regard to economic class or hardship. Further, they argued that Berkeley's Tier 2 supplemental criteria were decidedly skewed against Asian Americans, most of whom came from immigrant families. By requiring "four years of college preparatory English, four years of one foreign language or two years each of two foreign languages, exemption from Subject A [a remedial writing course requirement], and demonstration of leadership, character, motivation, and accomplishment," the AATF stated, Berkeley was being "unfair to most recent immigrants." The proof was in the numbers. Asian American undergraduate enrollment declined by 25% in a two-year period.

The AATF also thought that too much emphasis was given to SAT verbal scores. Asian Americans, in particular, immigrant groups, garnered only modest, often poor, scores in this portion of the test. Berkeley needed to change its admissions policies, it was stated, to "maintain the public trust." The AATF recommended the creation of a university-based task force with Asian representatives to "formulate, monitor and evaluate admissions policies."[33]

The national press generated first by the *Bakke* case and then by the charges of racial bias at Berkeley by the AATF brought a relatively new consciousness to many Californians. Affirmative action and race and ethnicity had arguably been used to create greater inclusion to a valuable public resource, a university education, and a prestigious campus. Now it appeared to many as an administrative means for exclusion. Throughout the 1980s, with record numbers of applications coming to the university, public criticism grew and, with it, growing demand by interest groups, not just the Asian American community, to reshape admissions policies. University officials were generally reluctant to begin a public dialogue about the details of the admissions process.

In reaction to public criticism, Berkeley officials added a form of delayed admissions to Berkeley in 1985. A student who narrowly missed admission as a freshman would be offered a provisional status that allowed the student to complete courses with transferable credit through the campus's extension program. Students could take this route the first semester and then enter with full status the following semester if they obtained adequate grades. It was a model long used by private institutions. This safety valve gave a second chance to many students and helped keep Berkeley's enrollments steady, essentially replacing students who, for one reason or another, dropped out.[34] Other than the delayed-admissions route, Chancellor Heyman and Berkeley officials kept to their plans and mounted a defense strategy.

In describing the initial salvos on the post-*Bakke* policies of University of California admissions, it is important to remember the context of what became an increasingly acrimonious debate. Within the higher education marketplace, the battle over affirmative action focused on a relatively small number of increasingly selective institutions. In 1985, Berkeley and UCLA represented the largest and most prestigious UC campuses. Combined, they enrolled 55,000 students. But in total, they represented only 3% of all enrollment in California's public higher education system. All UC-eligible students had access to other University of California campuses, all with growing prestige. Four campuses—San Diego, Santa Barbara, Davis, and Irvine—would eventually be elected to the American Association of Universities (AAU), a select group of approximately one hundred of the top universities in the United States. Access denied at Berkeley or UCLA did not mean access denied to the University of California. The university set eligibility criteria and then guaranteed access to a campus but not necessarily to the student's first choice. Yet this aspect of the social contract seemed irrelevant to many racial groups in California, in particular to the rising number of academically talented Asian Americans, many from immigrant backgrounds, many influenced by a cultural drive for socioeconomic mobility and status, and many located in the greater Bay Area. The prestige and the regional accessibility of Berkeley, in particular, created a huge demand for access to a campus that was increasingly rejecting more UC-eligible students than it could accept.

Research on the income and social status of college graduates indicates that, although there is a correlation between graduation from a prestigious institution and economic success, especially at the undergraduate level, it is generally exaggerated, particularly for students from higher and middle-income families.[35] This is not to deny that graduating from a prestigious institution does not confer advantages in postgraduate employment and entrance to graduate programs. Particularly in the realm of employment, much of the perceived advantage is not garnered by the quality of the academic program at a given prestigious or, in the lexicon of the modern era, a "brand-name" institution. Perhaps most influential is the high correlation with the enrollment of students from largely upper socioeconomic families with substantial "cultural capital" (e.g., highly educated parents with high expectations for their children). There are also regional considerations. In eastern and mid-Atlantic states, the vast majority of highly selective institutions are private. The percentage of students from high socioeconomic backgrounds in these institutions is substantially higher than in the few highly selective public universities. In western states, where public higher education institutions enroll the vast majority of students, the prestige correlation is even less meaningful.[36]

One can argue that the tremendous demand for access to Berkeley and UCLA by ethnic groups was unjustified because of the university's promise of access to one of its campuses and because the personal benefits of graduating from either campus are generally exaggerated. Further, and as discussed in previous chapters, the founders and shapers of the university's social contract never intended Berkeley or any campus of the University of California to be largely or exclusively accessible to a distinct group of applicants who, for example, scored well in a particular test. Such a narrow focus of merit would essentially alter the original purpose of the university as a dynamic agent for shaping society.

Such subtle truths and observations obviously did not alter the political discourse. Broad commitments to equitable social goals fell victim to the difficulties of individuals faced with the reality of a rejection letter from their chosen brand-name institution. This is where the rubber hit the road. "Rejection at UCLA sometimes produces anger, tears and threats of lawsuits," explained Rea Lee Siporin, director of UCLA's admissions, in 1988, "even if a student gets into a less-popular UC campus. This creates a lot of pressure, and enormous amounts of unhappy feelings and ill will." "It is very hard to tell someone who has a 4.00 [GPA], a valedictorian and class president that anyone else could possibly be more qualified," noted Edward Apodaca, the UC-wide director of admissions and outreach services, that same year.[37] "We now get letters all the time from alumni and angry parents who complain that because there are so many Asians their son or daughter wasn't accepted," stated Joyce Justus, then director of university relations at the office of the president.[38] Eligible students attempting to enter engineering programs at Davis and Santa Barbara also found that they were rejected, adding to the perception that the university's promise of access was dissipating.

Meanwhile, the AATF insisted that Berkeley needed to increase substantially Asian American enrollment, conveniently ignoring who might be rejected in favor of Asian Americans. Berkeley clearly designed its admissions process to include more underrepresented groups. Yet a number of the AATF members charged that the real motivation of Berkeley officials was to increase Euro-American enrollment. Supplemental criteria, stated task force member Henry Der, gave too much "latitude" in admissions decisions, were invoked "to the detriment of Asian American applicants," and likely were "manipulated to keep our numbers down." Ken Kawaichi, AATF cochair, stated that Berkeley officials, and presumably its chancellor, wanted to keep Berkeley "predominantly white."[39] A fear of Asian American dominance, they speculated, motivated Berkeley administrators. Similar charges of discrimination against Asian Americans were leveled at Harvard, Princeton, Brown, Stanford, and UCLA. In 1988, the U.S. Department of Justice opened investigations into admissions practices at Harvard and UCLA. Similar reviews of admissions at Berkeley and other universities were threatened by the Office of Civil Rights within the U.S. Department of Education.

University officials, including Bud Travers, the director of admissions, and Laetsch, the vice chancellor for undergraduate affairs, attempted to defend the admissions process. They stated that Berkeley took no overt actions to reduce overrepresented groups. Berkeley's Chancellor Heyman and University of California President David Gardner made similar statements. A meeting in March 1988 included members of the AATF, Gardner, Heyman, Laetsch, UC Regent Yori Wada, and Julius Krevans, the chancellor at the UC medical campus at San Francisco. The intention of university officials was to quell the rising rhetoric and to encourage dialogue with the AATF. Instead, task force members viewed the university as intractable, and they launched a successful campaign to have the board of regents and a committee of the state legislature separately schedule hearings on Berkeley's admissions practices. Their goal was to expand the number of politically powerful participants in the debate.

Simultaneously, San Francisco-based Assemblyman Art Agnos and state senate Pro Tempore Leader David Roberti from Burbank sanctioned an investigation by the state auditor general to review Berkeley's admissions policies. The auditor's report looked at admissions from 1981 through 1987. His conclusion: The admissions rate for Asian Americans was lower than that for Euro-Americans. But the difference was minimal, usually no greater than 5% in a given year. In total, the audit somehow concluded that perhaps eighty-three additional Asian Americans should have been admitted over a six-year period. The report essentially rejected the charges of the AATF. The auditor general still had harsh criticism for Berkeley. There was a lack of concrete criteria for the selection of Tier 2 applicants, he stated, and the university needed to better explain to the public its admissions process.[40]

With the auditor general's report in hand, in early 1988 the board of regents met on the UC Riverside campus to discuss Berkeley admissions practices. The campus's Vice Chancellor Roderick Park and Admissions

Director Travers staunchly defended the campus. Berkeley made no overt effort to reduce Asian American admissions, explained Park, but shaped admissions to broaden diversity under the guidelines issued by the office of the president. Berkeley had nothing to apologize for.

Neither Park nor Travers was prepared to respond to the divergent but pointed questioning that followed by Regents Yori Wada, Dean A. Watkins, and Frank W. Clark Jr. Wada was a strong supporter of affirmative action. Watkins and Clark were both conservatives who stated strong concerns about the university's use of affirmative action. All three regents criticized Berkeley's approach to admissions, in particular, the supplemental criteria under Tier 2. How did Berkeley justify its use of "special circumstances" to account for 500 of a total 1,300 points in its academic index used for admissions decisions? Park had not immersed himself in the details of Berkeley admissions practices. Travers offered only a vague response, stating that it depended on the student's application. Berkeley's use of supplemental admissions criteria appeared difficult to describe. Park and Travers seemed overly defensive.

Chancellor Heyman did not personally present Berkeley's case to the regents. Tired from a lengthy business trip, he had directed an ambitious and willing Vice Chancellor Park to take on the difficult task.[41] Thus far, they had relied on the notion of university and campus autonomy in making admissions decisions. It did not seem to them that every aspect of Berkeley's admissions process should be exposed to the light of day. They, and President Gardner, hoped that the regents' meeting might offer support for the Berkeley campus and be the beginning of the end of the confrontation with the AATF. Instead, it further fueled the fire.

Asian American representatives met with Gardner and demanded that Berkeley stop using subjective criteria, claiming they were unfair. The best students should be admitted, they demanded, and test scores and grades were the legitimate criteria. Predictably, Latino leaders argued a different viewpoint. They demanded proportional representation and asked that the university simply make it happen. Latino activists told Gardner, "We are 26% of the state's population. We should be 26% of the entering freshman class."[42] Gardner repeatedly exclaimed that the university never would turn away a UC-eligible student. But this assurance failed to deflect the intense interest in access to Berkeley and UCLA.

Per the request of the AATF, state Assemblyman Tom Hayden, chair of the state Assembly Education Committee, orchestrated a hearing to discuss admissions at Berkeley. As a student at the University of Michigan, Hayden helped to found the radical group Students for a Democratic Society (SDS). In 1962, he drafted the famous Port Huron Statement expressing the idealism of the New Left. And in the early 1960s, he participated in civil rights work in the South and in the black ghettoes of Newark. He had since made a political career in California seeking to attach himself to high-profile controversies that in some way matched his convictions and growing political ambitions, including a possible run for governor.

Hayden was a strong critic of the university, most notably for its lack of progress in enrolling minorities. There was every indication that he would use the venue of the hearing to lambaste Berkeley. Hayden's committee required personal testimony from Chancellor Heyman. Patrick Hayashi, an assistant in the chancellor's office recently appointed specifically to aid the chancellor with admissions issues, helped in the preparation of Heyman's statement. Hayashi had long experience at Berkeley as a student and as an administrator. In the early 1980s, he worked with outreach programs focused on poor and minority students and served on a task force that devised ways to bring more underrepresented students to Berkeley.

In January 1988, Heyman appeared before Hayden's committee and announced the establishment of a special committee to investigate Asian American concerns. The committee would be chaired by the head of the Berkeley library, Janice Koyama, and would include Professor Yuan T. Lee, a Nobel laureate in chemistry. Heyman also planned to create an admissions coordinating board to review Berkeley's admissions policies. But the chancellor did not end there. He offered an apology: "I wish we were more sensitive to the underlying concerns. While they did not manifest themselves as neatly as I now see them, Berkeley could have acted more openly and less defensively. I apologize for that."[43] Heyman added his hope "that we can work cooperatively to restore and enhance the confidence of the Asian Americans."[44]

Heyman's presentation set a tone of compromise. Assemblyman Robert Campbell, a member of the committee, later noted that the chancellor "just took the total thunder" from Hayden.[45] Expecting the chancellor to blindly defend campus admissions policies, Hayden had planned a surprise. His staff had unearthed a memo from Berkeley's director of admissions, Robert Bailey, to Vice Chancellor Laetsch in 1984, outlining a proposal to impose a minimum verbal SAT score of 400. The assumed purpose was to exclude a cohort of Asian Americans, whose verbal scores tended to be low, particularly among immigrant groups. Yet the proposal was simply one among many options considered by admissions officers in the quest for diversity but rejected.

Hayden circulated the memo just prior to the hearing. It sparked additional charges of conspiracy. Henry Der, an activist in the Asian American community and member of the California Postsecondary Education Commission, called it "a smoking gun," and the AATF demanded the resignation of Travers and Laetsch prior to the hearing in Sacramento. But at the hearing, Heyman's review of Berkeley's admissions process *and* his carefully crafted apology largely defused Hayden's planned attack. Even the AATF noted optimism for an improved dialogue after Heyman's qualified apology and plan.

Following the hearing, Heyman and other Berkeley officials began to more openly discuss the difficulties they faced in creating an equitable admissions process. "If we were to admit students completely on meritocracy alone, then the freshman class would almost be made up entirely of Asian American and white students," stated Park in a subsequent issue of the *California Monthly*, Berkeley's alumni magazine[46] Berkeley officials were "against quotas," stated Bud Travers in the same article, "and we have never used them against Asian-Americans." But Travers did admit that Berkeley had devised a method to apportion enrollment to targeted groups. "We are playing what is called the least-sum game," noted Travers. "If any ethnic group gains in admissions, then another ethnic group loses. We are supposed to service the top 12.5 percent of high school students *and* have affirmative action programs. Take these two things and add the fact that Asian Americans are at Berkeley in numbers four times higher than they graduate from high school, and you have a model that is unworkable."[47] Admission's Director Bailey insisted that if the campus never departed from the confines of admitting students strictly on the basis of GPA and SAT scores, "Could a Bechtel get into Cal now, could a Kaiser? These were good B students back in the '40s and '50s who would never be able to get in under these criteria."[48]

A Regental Statement on Affirmative Action

Neither Berkeley's division of the academic senate nor the senate's UC-wide admissions board, BOARS, had much to do with the profound shift toward racial preferences in admissions. For example, BOARS never passed judgment on UC President David Saxon's 1979 directive to chancellors and their administrative staff espousing the centrality of diversity. Saxon's memo stated, "ethnic minority status may be taken into account where appropriate in establishing such diversity."[49] The regents never acted on Saxon's authorization either, and prior to their meeting on Berkeley admissions, they did not engage in much discussion on the practices of the campuses. Within the context of increased scrutiny of university admissions, President Gardner and Berkeley's chancellor now sought a different approach. They wanted engagement and formal policy decisions from the regents and possibly the senate.

Five months after Assemblyman Hayden's hearing, President Gardner proposed that the regents issue a new statement on undergraduate admissions. The office of the president would then devise detailed guidelines giving each chancellor the ability "to establish selection procedures." "During discussion of undergraduate admissions at the regents meeting in February 1988," explained Gardner to the board, "it became evident that there was a need for a policy which would clarify the University's practice with respect to undergraduate admissions." The policy he now proposed "was developed in order to codify for the people of California and for the admissions practitioners on the University's campuses what, to date, have been unwritten historical commitments and practices."[50]

Gardner's proposal reflected the language of a bill pending in the state legislature, the Higher Education Equity Assessment Act, which reinforced the diversity goals of the university. The act was the third legislative amendment to existing statutes extending the stated deadline for meeting some form of parity; the first targeted for compliance in 1980, the second in the late 1990s, and this time a target of 2000. But there was a difference in the legislature's statement and that proposed by Gardner and university officials. The difference was in carefully selected wording.

The original 1974 legislation, most university statements, and the new act by lawmakers stated that all of California public higher education should "approximate" the diversity of the state's public high school graduates. Sometimes, the university used the word "reflect." This new proposal purposely substituted "approximate" with the word "encompass." The former implied proportionality—the parity model—and hence a potentially measurable goal by which to judge the university's performance. The latter was general. The difference may appear relatively minor. But for university officials repeatedly stung by the difficulties of actually reaching racial parity goals in undergraduate enrollments, this more general language appeared a potential tool for mitigating future battles. The regents' proposal also included the following statement:

> Undergraduate admissions policy of the University of California is guided by the University's commitment to serve the people of California and the needs of the state, within the framework of the California

Master Plan for Higher Education. Mindful of its mission as a public institution, the University of California has an historic commitment to provide places within the University for all eligible applicants who are residents of California.[51]

The regents approved the new policy statement at their May 1988 meeting. In consultation with BOARS, the university-wide administration proceeded to revise the administrative guidelines for admissions, replacing those issued in 1971 and 1979.[52] Three major elements were then incorporated into a directive to the chancellors from President Gardner and issued in July. The directive reiterated the requirement that *each* campus was to enroll a student body that "encompassed the broad diversity of cultural, racial, geographic, and socio-economic backgrounds characteristic of California." The office of the president stated that *up to* 60% of all freshmen, outside special action admissions, could be selected on "supplemental criteria" if they were UC eligible—a revision of university policy set at 50% in 1971. Campuses were given a statement on what these criteria should be. Three general categories were offered. The first category was special talents, defined as "interests or experiences beyond the academic criteria that demonstrate unusual promise for leadership, achievement, and service in a particular field such as civic life and the arts."[53] The second was special circumstances "adversely affecting the applicants' life experiences, including disabilities, personal difficulties, low family income, refugee status, or veteran status." And the third category was ethnic identity, gender, and location of residence. "These factors," stated Gardner's memo, "shall be considered in order to provide for cultural, racial, geographic, and socio-economic diversity in the student population."[54]

President Gardner's initiative created a more formal policy framework for campuses that retained affirmative action as a distinct part of the university's admissions procedures. The initiative also required drawing both the regents and the senate into a role in setting policy and ultimately solidifying the university's ability to defend the admissions process. In effect, Berkeley had found itself isolated and without the formal support of the regents or the senate. Faculty, generally, and the senate, specifically, had developed a distinct aversion to the debates swirling around affirmative action. The controversy related to Asian American admissions caused a long-dormant senate to awaken (if briefly) and, with the support of the admissions office, to defend, revisit, and modify Berkeley's admissions model.

New Policies at Berkeley

Chancellor Heyman's plans for an administrative review of Berkeley's admissions practices created the sense that a new deliberative process had begun. To some degree, the protests of the AATF seemed to have largely run their course. Democratic lawmakers in Sacramento, still a majority in both houses of the legislature, remained steadfastly supportive of affirmative action and were always willing to criticize the university for not making fast enough progress. Although Asian American activists wielded a base of political power, their overall influence was pale compared to that of a growing caucus of Latino lawmakers, a force that would continue to build and become more demanding. Berkeley's admissions policies clearly favored Chicanos-Latinos.

Heyman's promise for an administrative review and consultation with the AATF was soon upstaged by the actions of Berkeley's committee on admissions and enrollment, a standing committee of the Berkeley division of the academic senate. Chaired by ardent affirmative-action advocate Jerome Karabel, a professor of sociology at Berkeley, the committee issued a report intended to articulate more clearly the purpose and mechanics of campus admissions. Karabel wanted to reinvigorate the role of faculty in the affirmative-action debate, and he did so initially without any specific support from Heyman or other senate leaders. He simply used his position as chair to help force the issue. And he was well equipped to do so, having authored a number of important studies on issues related to educational opportunity and structural impediments for socioeconomic mobility, including a book with Steve Brint that claimed community colleges essentially tracked minorities and lower income students away from the university.[55] Once Karabel's committee proclaimed its intent to reinvigorate its role in the admissions debate, Heyman gratefully deferred.

As an entity of the academic senate, Karabel's committee had no obligation to engage in a dialogue with the AATF. Although the committee included Berkeley's director of admissions, Robert Bailey, it derived its authority from the senate's historical role as the once-primary voice in setting the conditions of admissions—authority delegated to the senate by the regents. Karabel and his colleagues created a document Berkeley sorely needed: a single guide for aggressively justifying its undergraduate admissions process.

The Karabel Report defended the past actions of the Berkeley campus and offered a modification to existing admissions practices. Karabel and his committee clearly rejected any substantial reform. As the "most prestigious

campus" within the UC system, they stated with no humility, and as "one
of the world's leading universities," Berkeley needed to lead the way by
rigorously pursuing affirmative action.

The report praised the efforts of Chancellor Heyman for attempting to
build a more diverse student body. The results, they thought, were impressive.[56] Berkeley needed to continue to assess the social consequences
of current and any proposed policies.[57] There should "absolutely" be no
"quotas or ceilings," and in a tone obviously struck for public consump-
tion, the report called such policies "immoral and illegal." "Berkeley will
not tolerate discrimination in the application of any of the criteria governing its admissions process." Yet any selective admissions process needed to
discriminate in some form, and the report noted as much. Berkeley could
not shrink from exercising human judgment in admissions.

The core recommendation of the Karabel Report attempted to modify Berkeley's existing tiered admissions policies. Reacting to criticism
that Berkeley had gone "too far" in its effort to expand minority enrollment, the report recommended increasing admissions by academic criteria
alone—so-called Tier 1—from 40% to 50%. That was simple enough and
within the parameters of regental policy. The second major recommendation was to create a new Tier 2 that combined and expanded what were
previously Tier 2 and Tier 3 admissions criteria and special admissions. The
new Tier 2 structure created an even more complex and subjective process
of evaluation for admitting the remaining 50% of Berkeley applicants, essentially students not admitted under Tier 1. The new Tier 2 included
four categories that required evaluation of supplementary information:
(1) outstanding accomplishment in a variety of endeavors—for example,
art, athletics, debating, drama, music; (2) socioeconomic background and
disadvantaged status; (3) reentry students; and (4) second review of students
narrowly rejected. In each category, evaluators were to consider a student's
academic index score (again, grades and test scores).

How would the Karabel Report translate into admissions decisions? In
total, Tier 2 included a set of ten "target" areas for admissions. Each target
area had a weighted score reflecting campus priorities. Race and ethnicity
secured the most significant weight. Approximately 50% of Tier 2 students
would be "affirmative action." Another 17% would be students who fit the
socioeconomically disadvantaged category. Eleven percent would be students of "special promise" (the barely rejected Tier 1 group eligible for a
secondary review), and 8% would be "athletes." Students from rural high
schools, along with Filipino students and "special talent" students (in music,
art, etc.) were given targets of approximately 5%, 3%, and 2%, respectively.

Students with a standard GPA in high school and reentry and students with disabilities were assigned a target of 1%. The targets meant, "no group would any longer enjoy 'total protection' (i.e., guaranteed admission on the basis of meeting UC's eligibility requirements)." Here was a response to Berkeley's previous practice, never publicly announced or decipherable in stated policy, of accepting any and all underrepresented minorities who were UC eligible—a practice that continued at other UC campuses in stealth mode and with political repercussions by the mid-1990s.[58]

The Karabel Report declared the need for transparency in Berkeley's freshman admissions policies and for placing the "details of its selection process in the public domain." But the net result was anything but clarity. The mechanics of the admissions process become even more complex. Still, for a period, Berkeley's revised admissions process, and the regents' 1988 proclamation, seemed to placate the discontent of lawmakers. Within the halls of Sacramento and in newspaper editorials emerged a general appreciation of the difficulties of setting the condition for admission at the university. As David Gardner famously quipped during a meeting of the board of regents, "For those of you who believe you have the solution to this problem, you do not comprehend the problem. And for those of us who do comprehend the problem, there is no solution. We are just doing the best we can."[59]

Other difficulties surfaced to replace the once-ubiquitous articles and editorials regarding admissions practices at Berkeley and UCLA, including the onset of a severe economic recession. President David Gardner also articulated an idea that gained salience, if only briefly, in the halls of Sacramento: Issues of access to Berkeley paled in relationship to the need for the university to grow and enroll more students as California's population grew. In the late 1980s, Gardner boldly outlined the need to establish three new university campuses. However, California's economic downturn and a period of yearly state budget cuts for public higher education slowly made discussion of funding new campuses moot. The University of California and the California State University raised student fees, cut staff and faculty salaries, and in the case of UC, launched a large-scale early retirement program. It was a period of retrenchment, not long-term planning.

But the seeds of a new and even more dramatic clash over affirmative action had been sown. Affirmative action was synonymous with race. Few talked of economic affirmative action for lower income students or even geographic affirmative action. Both had been cornerstones of admissions policy before 1960, a time when racial considerations were largely ignored. Now racial affirmative action was dominant. It was a politically vulnerable paradigm.

Part III

Modern Battles over Equity, Affirmative Action, and Testing

Chapter 7

California's Affirmative-Action Fight

The picture that emerged was that of an Institution which had *de facto* racial quotas, which refuses to acknowledge the true extent to which race is used in its admissions activities, and which is determined to maintain the status quo. I came to the conclusion that we are breaking the law.

—University of California Regent Ward Connerly, July 1995

In the early morning of Thursday, July 20, 1995, a moist and gray sky hung over the city of San Francisco. It was a typical summer day in the Bay Area; warm air from California's Central Valley met a cold ocean, creating a damp, cloudy, and stubborn marine layer. In the aftermath of too many unmanageable student protests, the board of regents had ceased holding most of its regular monthly meetings on the main campuses of the University of California. Instead, the board had elected several years earlier to use the confines of an auditorium hidden within a concrete and brick building at Laurel Heights, a satellite campus of the university's medical campus in San Francisco. Laurel Heights offered significant advantages for crowd control. UCSF also enrolls only graduate students who generally lack interest in the time-consuming and usually ineffective pursuit of protesting university policies. Better yet, the Laurel Heights facility is a research center located on a hill a mile or more away from the main UCSF campus. It was no accident that the regents and the president of the university chose Laurel Heights over a campus like Berkeley.

Nevertheless, on this occasion, a large group of some 1,000 students and supporters of affirmative action gathered outside the entrance to the auditorium, stretching into the parking lot and down an adjacent street. The cool air met the high emotions of the protestors. Signs reading "Access to Higher Education R.I.P." and "No Retreat: Speak Up for Affirmative Action" poked above the demonstrators. Among the crowd were members of a newly formed coalition with the semithreatening title "In Defense of Affirmative Action by Any Means Necessary." Members of Jesse Jackson's Rainbow Coalition were there, including Jackson himself. Some 500 police officers, including a SWAT team, bunched in various locations along the street and at entrances to the monolithic building. Television trucks lined the roadsides, and scores of reporters prepared to chronicle a national news event. A gavel thumped the meeting to order at eight in the morning, beginning what would become a marathon twelve-hour meeting.

Only two resolutions were on the regents' agenda. If passed, they would effectively end affirmative action at the University of California—specifically, the use of racial preferences in university admissions, contracting, and hiring. Augmented by the large crowd outside, nearly 300 people filled the auditorium to capacity. It was a colorful mix of protesters, worried university administrators, and nearly every major California politician. In the glare of the national press, the regents chose to be a bellwether on an issue that divides Americans to this day.

Regent Connerly, an African American businessman appointed less than two years earlier to the university's governing board by Republican Governor Pete Wilson, offered the two resolutions. One proposed that the university no longer use race as a factor in admissions; the other would end the use of race in the hiring of new faculty or in issuing university contracts for services. Ending racial preferences at UC was Connerly's and the governor's cause célèbre—a first step toward a statewide campaign to end affirmative action in California government and eventually in other states, including Washington, Florida, and later Michigan. Connerly was not only seeking the venue of the university's governing board to debate affirmative-action policies, but he was also using it as a springboard to mount a state constitutional amendment. With Wilson's support, Connerly led the campaign for a so-called California Civil Rights Initiative (CCRI), what would become Proposition 209. If passed by voters, Proposition 209 would ban the proactive use of race as a factor in decision making and in the allocation of resources in all public agencies. The campaign had problems. It failed to garner support from the state or the national Republican Party, and it needed a substantial infusion of financial support to gather the threshold of signatures required by law to place it on a ballot.

In virtually any other state, the debate over admissions at a public university would have bled beyond the confines of the governing board. The board would have deferred to lawmakers and an even more complicated public discourse. The University of California's unusual status as a "public trust" under the state constitution, however, meant that authority over admissions was the responsibility of the university and not subject to statutory law.[1] Both Connerly and the governor had an opportunity to have their debate within the confines of an increasingly conservative lay board that included both of them as voting members.

This chapter discusses the effectiveness of affirmative-action policies in admissions and the events leading to the regents' ultimate decision at that meeting in July 1995. Two themes are offered. The first focuses on the debate within the university community and the vulnerability of existing affirmative-action programs and policies, including a lack of unanimity among the faculty regarding the use of racial preferences. The second relates to the political tactics employed by Connerly and the salience of his arguments, which generally were addressed to a larger public and not to the academic community. Connerly cleverly attacked not only the idea of affirmative action but also the coherence of the university's existing admissions programs and the credibility of the university's administrative leaders.

The Impact of Affirmative Action

At least initially, affirmative-action policies within America's vast collection of public and private colleges and universities had a profound effect on the socioeconomic mobility of minority groups and women. Among a growing cadre of selective colleges and universities that represented some 10% of all higher education institutions, affirmative action "bore fruit," as William Bowen and Derek Bok chronicle in their 1998 book, *The Shape of the River*. African American enrollments in Ivy League colleges, for example, rose from 2.3% to 6.3% between 1967 and 1976. "Meanwhile, the proportion of black medical students had climbed to 6.3% by 1975, and black law students had increased their share to 4.5%," note Bowen and Bok.[2] Yet in the late 1980s, even as many colleges and universities, public and private, expanded programs and staff to recruit and retain underrepresented minority students, enrollment of these groups reached a plateau. Did the programs still work?

The influence of affirmative-action policies at the University of California is difficult to assess for three major reasons. First, some increase in minority and underrepresented enrollment at the University of California and all public higher education segments in the state were inevitable with or without affirmative action. Between 1964, when Berkeley established its first Equal Opportunity Program as a high school outreach effort, and

1995, when the regents deliberated the fate of affirmative action, California underwent a dramatic increase in its population *and* in the demographic mix of racial and ethnic groups. Immigration and the high birthrates of minority groups, particularly Latino-Chicano and some Asian populations, created a growing pool of minority applicants. A second difficulty is the incomplete nature of data gathering. University-wide data on enrollment by ethnicity were not collected until 1968 and then inconsistently until the 1970s. A third factor revolves around the difficulties of gathering information on racial identity. California is the nation's most ethnically diverse state. The simplistic categorization of ethnicity into six groups, reflecting federal legislation from the late 1960s, is arguably antiquated for analyzing the later demographic mix of the state and the enrollment in higher education institutions. For example, mixed race students, a growing proportion of California's population, had to choose what race or ethnic group they belonged to.

These variables noted one important gauge of the success of affirmative-action programs is the number of minority students who are eligible for the University of California upon graduating from high school. One might assume or hope that, over time and as affirmative-action programs have grown and matured, eligibility rates would increase for underrepresented minorities, which is a major goal of affirmative-action outreach programs. Under the parity model, the results are mixed at best. The first state-sanctioned eligibility study that included ethnicity focused on students who graduated from high school in 1983. The next study looked at students from the 1990 cohort. As shown in Figure 7.1, the rate of eligibility climbed from 3.6% to 5.1% for African Americans over that period. However, Chicano-Latino students dropped slightly in their eligibility rating from 4.9% to 3.9%. The next study of eligibility rates was conducted in 1996 and was even more worrisome. Both African American and Chicano-Latino populations decreased as a percentage of the eligibility pool.

Why the decline in black and Chicano-Latino eligibility rates? There are at least three major and interrelated influences: (1) the decline in the quality of California's public schools in part related to declining public investment on a per-student basis, (2) shifts in the state's economy and an increase in poverty rates, and (3) a correlated increase in immigrant groups, many without the cultural capital that spurs college-going patterns.

The first factor, the decline in California's schools—the so-called pipeline to higher education—has been startling and sad. One contributor is the precipitous decline in funding for public schools. In 1960, California ranked among the top five states in expenditure per student, and it pursued

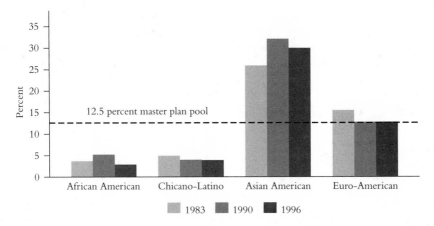

Figure 7.1. University of California freshman eligibility rates: 1983, 1990, and 1996

SOURCE: California Postsecondary Education Commission; University of California Office of the President.

a massive school construction program. The state aggressively anticipated and expected large-scale increases in enrollment growth at both the K–12 and postsecondary levels. By 1990, the state was among the bottom five states in spending per pupil. School construction had come to a virtual halt even as the state faced another massive wave of population growth. California slid from having one of the lowest state student-to-teacher ratios to having one of the highest. High school graduation rates declined, particularly among Chicano-Latino and African American students, often concentrated in poor and poorly funded urban school districts.

In the early 1990s and in the midst of a severe economic recession that hit California particularly hard, many critics of public schools argued that class size did not necessarily correlate with student performance. Indeed, a number of studies by economists with conservative leanings stated that funding is more than adequate; the problem is how money is spent and how students are taught. Many subsequent studies indicate the quality of the teaching staff is perhaps the most important single influence on student performance — as gauged by ubiquitous standardized tests. But there is also evidence that class size does matter. The practice of private secondary schools and elite colleges attests to some correlation and at least a sense of value in small rather than large classes. California's relatively low teacher pay in relation to living costs *and* large class sizes and deteriorating schools in much of California made teaching less attractive and, in part, led to an

TABLE 7.1
Percentage of undergraduate minority enrollment, University of California:
1968, 1975, 1980, and 1995

	1968	1975	1980	1995
Native American	0.3%	0.5%	0.5%	1.0%
Black	2.2%	4.1%	3.6%	4.0%
Chicano-Latino	1.8%	5.1%	5.5%	13.7%
Asian American	5.7%	9.5%	14.2%	34.9%
Total Minority	10.0%	19.2%	23.8%	53.6%
Total "Underrepresented" Minority*	4.3%	9.7%	9.6%	18.7%

* As designated in the early 1980s, Asian Americans were excluded from the underrepresented category.
SOURCE: California Postsecondary Education Commission; University of California Office of the President.

increasing shortage of credentialed teachers. Particularly in the growing number of poor urban schools, the percentage of the teaching staff with credentials declined, and the ratio of college counselors to students shot up in some communities to 1:800. The number of advanced placement courses, once relatively even across California high schools, varied greatly among school districts, with low-income communities, often heavily populated by minority students, offering the fewest.

Although the eligibility rates of Chicanos and Latinos declined between 1983 and 1990, it is important to note that their absolute enrollments at the university did not. A much larger force was at play: large-scale increases in the total number of minority students. In 1983, approximately 76,000 minority students graduated from California's high schools; by 1990, 108,000 graduated. Over that period, minorities grew from 42% of all California secondary school graduates to over 50%. Hence, while eligibility rates for Chicanos-Latinos fluctuated moderately, their actual enrollment, both in numbers and as a percentage of the entire undergraduate student body, continued to climb. Chicano-Latino students grew from 1.8% to 13.7% of the university's enrollment between 1968 and 1995, the year the board of regents considered ending the use of racial and ethnic factors in admissions. Most significantly, Asian American students grew from 5.7% to 34.9%. African Americans as a percentage of the university's total undergraduate enrollment grew from 2.2% in 1968 to only 4.0% in 1995. This anemic growth reflected the minor growth of the African American population in California and only minor increases in their UC eligibility rates.

Outreach programs and changes in the admissions approaches of the various campuses bolstered an inevitable flow of minority students to the University of California. Minority enrollments increased from 10% of the uni-

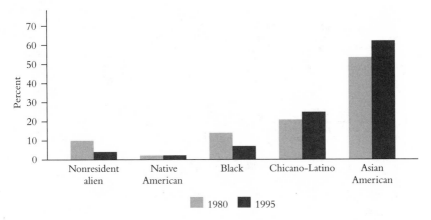

Figure 7.2. University of California total minority enrollment by racial group: 1980 and 1995

SOURCE: California Postsecondary Education Commission; University of California Office of the President.

versity undergraduate population in 1968 to 19.2% by 1975, the initial years of the university's affirmative-action efforts. But the largest increase was to come. Between 1980 and 1995, the university's undergraduate enrollment grew from 97,100 to 124,300 students. Over that fifteen-year period, minority enrollment grew from 23.7% to 54% of the total University of California student population, becoming the majority in 1993. This remarkable growth in minority enrollment was not equally distributed among ethnic groups, as indicated by the eligibility ratings shown in Figure 7.2. Although all minority groups grew in the total number of students enrolled, from 23,000 in 1980 to just over 70,000 in 1995 (an increase of over 200%), the majority of this growth was in Asian American students. In 1980, Asian Americans represented 54% of the university's undergraduate minority enrollment; by 1995, they represented 63%—a truly remarkable increase related to a variety of cultural and socioeconomic factors that remains a subject of debate.

Under the parity model, in 1995 Chicanos-Latinos remained the most underrepresented group: Although representing approximately 30% of the state's public high school graduates, they composed only 14% of the university's undergraduate population. Surprisingly and with no political discourse, Euro-Americans became the second largest "underrepresented" group, larger in number than African Americans (see Figure 7.3). However, there are caveats to consider. A rising number of UC undergraduate

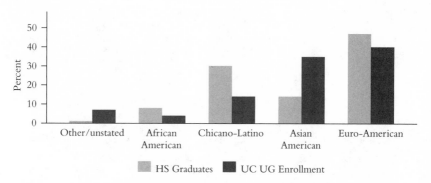

Figure 7.3.   California high school graduates and University of California
enrollment by racial/ethnic group: 1995

SOURCE: California Postsecondary Education Commission; University of California
Office of the President.

applicants declined to state their racial or ethnic background. There are
good anecdotal indicators that a large portion of those who failed to identify their race were Euro-Americans and Asian Americans, although there
was no systematic effort to find out. The affirmative-action debate undoubtedly raised the consciousness of white and Asian students that their
racial identity might inhibit their admission to a campus such as UCLA.
But there is another possible factor to consider: the growing population of multiethnic applicants. The University of California's application
asked that a student identify one racial category, presenting a quandary for
multiethnic students.

The problem with accurately identifying the racial composition of the
applicant pool illustrates some of the complications of assessing the success
of affirmative-action programs. Often purposefully vague policy goals also
demonstrate an ever-present political aspect to policymaking. What does
it mean to "encompass" California's population? Is the university's goal to
reach parity between the undergraduate population and the ethnic composition of the entire state's population or the high school graduating class?
This has proved a common point of confusion within the university and
in the discourse with lawmakers and the public. Should diversity be articulated into a university-wide policy goal and not a campus goal? What is
the appropriate definition of the "underrepresented" and "disadvantaged"
student? Answers to these types of questions were never fully vetted or an-
swered; some, one might argue, where purposefully avoided.

The affirmative-action policies of the University of California did bear fruit, but problems actually identifying the goals of the parity model and exogenous variables related to socioeconomic factors make any definitive assessment impossible.

The Vulnerability of Affirmative Action

Regent Ward Connerly was not particularly interested in the university's parity model. He focused exclusively on the morality of using race in admissions decisions and on any data that showed that affirmative action was essentially a misguided policy. In their book, Bok and Bowen presented results from a select group of institutions, mostly private, that showed affirmative action in a favorable light. But what were the realities of admissions policies and outcomes at the University of California? Bok and Bowen stated that 89% of affirmative-action students went on to complete their degrees—a relatively high persistence rate—but this was not the case at a campus like Berkeley. In the early 1990s, only 58% graduated, and some 42% of all African American students at Berkeley dropped out. At the same time, 84% of Euro-Americans eventually graduated.[3] As he considered how to generate a debate within the University of California's board of regents, Connerly sought to exploit this reality.

What was new about the deliberations over admissions in the 1990s? In the past, numerous groups had attempted to influence University of California admissions policies. At one time or another, legislators, governors, school administrators, student activists, and distinct communities sought changes. Individual grievances had also been filed over the years, culminating in the famous *Bakke* case. The difference was the willingness of a single regent to mount a concerted attack on the university's affirmative-action programs. The cumulative process of incorporating racial preferences into university admissions practices and faculty hiring did not create a coherent policy.[4] The regents sitting on the board in 1994 had little sense of ownership of the university's baffling array of affirmative-action policies and programs. Many if not most faculty had no sense of ownership either.

Affirmative-action proponents in the university often noted the need to get faculty involved in developing and implementing programs. A 1978 affirmative action plan lamented the fact that "the Faculty of the university [have] not been systematically involved in the Student Affirmative Action effort." While each campus division of the faculty's academic senate had a committee on affirmative action, the committee was one among an average of twenty or more senate committees. They had advisory powers but no direct authority over administratively run programs and marginal influence. For administrators and staff in the midst of what appeared an urgent need to increase minority enrollment, with the exception of a small core of proponents, most faculty seemed only remotely aware, sometimes completely ignorant, and some perhaps disdainful.[5]

In the wake of Connerly's attacks and proposed resolutions, the senate leadership at Berkeley and throughout the nine-campus system attempted to voice general support for affirmative action and for the efforts of the university president. Yet within the ranks of the faculty, most were hard pressed to defend specific programs and admissions practices operated in large part by administrative staff. Exposing the complexity of faculty, and the ability or inability of the senate to represent their constituents on a controversial issue, was the point of a survey conducted by the Roper Center for Public Opinion Research in January 1995. Opponents of affirmative action, including Martin Trow, a professor of public policy and a renowned scholar of higher education, collaborated with the National Association of Scholars (NAS) to sponsor the survey, well aware that it would likely show a diversity of faculty opinion. It was Trow's idea to do a survey. Through the senate, a subgroup of activist proaffirmative-action faculty, he predicted, would create the semblance of a united faculty front against Connerly's ban.

Trow had once served as the chair of Berkeley's division of the academic senate and had subsequently served as chair of the academic council, the executive body of the UC-wide senate. He therefore had held a nonvoting position on the board of regents as the faculty representative. Trow was no radical conservative but rather a sophisticated observer of higher education. In the case of affirmative action, he was an adamant opponent. The survey would help erode the ability of the senate's leadership to voice their support for the administration's affirmative-action policies.

The NAS emerged in the 1980s as an alternative association of faculty and academic researchers defined largely by their opposition to "political correctness." The association established a journal as a venue for discussing the perceived problems of an overly liberal academy. In the early 1990s, the NAS established a California chapter, providing a locus for Thomas E. Wood, an independent scholar turned affirmative-action activist, and Glynn Custred, a faculty member at the Hayward campus of California State University. Wood was motivated by his sense that affirmative action was a cause for his inability to secure a tenured faculty position, and Custred by his concern that affirmative-action faculty hires negatively affected the culture and scholarship in his own department of anthropology at Hayward. Wood and Custred mused over the idea of a state constitutional ban on racial preferences in the early 1990s, eventually launching the California Civil Rights Initiative. Connerly would later join their efforts and become the chairman and leading light of the campaign.

The Roper survey was sent to a sample group of 1,000 senate members less than six months before the regents would consider Connerly's resolution. They were asked whether they favored racial and gender preferences in admissions and hiring or whether they favored promoting "equal opportunities in these areas without regard to an individual's race, sex, or ethnicity." Some 31% said they did favor preferences, and 48% said they did not. A press release by the California chapter of the NAS announced that the Roper survey "found that a wide plurality of faculty at the University of California favors a policy of providing equal opportunity without resorting to racial and gender preferences."[6]

As predicted, the leadership of the academic senate, including the academic council and each of the campus divisions of the senate, did pass resolutions noting their general support for affirmative action. They claimed to be the voice of the faculty. Invited to speak on the Roper survey by Connerly before the regents, Trow made his point: "Let me begin by saying that on the issue of affirmative action, no one can speak for the faculty of this University, not myself, and not even, or perhaps especially not, those who claim to do so with the greatest passion."[7] Trow argued that the regents should simply ignore the admonishments of the senate.

Another weakness lurked in defending the university's admissions practices. The university arguably did not conform to *Bakke*, a charge leveled by Connerly repeatedly. "It is indisputable that we are applying far different standards to 'underrepresented' applicants being considered under the 'Supplemental Criteria' than we are applying to those who are not underrepresented (White and Asians, largely) applicants," wrote Connerly to a fellow regent in 1993. In the early part of his effort to sway the regents, he pointed directly at Berkeley's admissions program. "Look at the Karabel Matrix and you can see what I mean." Berkeley gave preference to "nonresidents who are wealthy and are underrepresented," and it purposely handicapped "Asian and White students who come from middle-class families." Similar policies at three other campuses made race a primary factor in admissions were a "clear violation of *Bakke*, because Asian and White students have a much higher standard to meet than African Americans, Hispanics, and American Indians."[8]

Connerly took the unusual role of a regent who not only asked tough questions of the university's president and administration but also became an aggressive personal investigator of affirmative-action programs. In forming his strategy, Connerly sensed a latent desire by the board to become more engaged in a major policy issue confronting the university. He argued that the board had been perhaps overmanaged by past university presidents. The previous president, David Pierpont Gardner, proved an extremely effective manager of the university and of the board. His approach was to focus the regents on broad policy issues and, where possible, steer the board away from policy implementation questions, including admissions policies.

Appointed as a regent in 1993, Connerly was disdainful of the regents' deference to the president. He implored the board to act more independently of the president and his staff, to essentially view the university's administration as merely one among many "constituencies." Past deference on issues "allows the public to believe that the Regents fell asleep at the wheel during the Gardner era," stated Connerly in a December 1993 memo to the board.[9]

The new president of the University of California, Jack Peltason, was appointed in 1992 and was a different breed than Gardner. Peltason served previously as a faculty member and founding vice chancellor at the university's campus at Irvine. He then served as the president of the University of Illinois before taking the presidency at the American Council on Education in Washington, D.C., from 1977 to 1984. He returned to the University of California with his appointment as chancellor of the Irvine campus. Peltason was a highly regarded political scientist and coauthor of a widely used college textbook. When Gardner announced his resignation in the wake of his wife's illness and death from cancer, a controversy erupted regarding his retirement package. Peltason was asked to quickly step in as interim president, and he reluctantly did so relatively late in his career and with the understanding it would be short lived. Adding to the difficulties of that era, California had fallen into a serious economic decline. The university faced state budget cuts of approximately 25% from 1992 to 1995. The budgetary problems and the emerging affirmative-action debate generated by Connerly reduced the attractiveness of the university presidency. The search for a permanent president proved difficult, with one candidate, Gordon Gee, pulling out at the last moment. Peltason's one-year commitment as interim president turned into a more than a three-year tenure.

Perhaps no president could have restrained Connerly's agenda, but Peltason's circumstance and temperament made containing Connerly particularly difficult. Peltason's ability to persuade was undoubtedly compromised by his interim status. Whereas David Gardner might have offered a stiff defense of the prerogatives of the president's office or recruited support from a majority of regents to isolate a rogue regent, Peltason sought compromise and dialogue. Peltason and the campus chancellors were not prepared for the gauntlet that followed.

Questions, Credibility, and a Proposal

In a memo to a fellow regent written in June 1995, Connerly pointed to a specific event as the seed to his campaign. He claimed it grew after he received a 1994 letter of complaint about a student who failed to get into medical school, a story that was similar to that of Allan Bakke. It sparked, he said, a moral crusade. But clearly, Connerly's viewpoint was formed well before this inspiring moment. Governor Wilson had specifically appointed regents who conformed to or supported his political viewpoint, arguably more so than previous governors. Most of Wilson's appointees had previously contributed to his various election campaigns. At one time a moderate on the issue of affirmative action as a senator in Washington, Wilson became a widely known opponent during his governorship, carefully crafting his position for a run at the Republican primary for the U.S. presidency. Connerly, a black businessman long associated with the Republican Party, had an engaging personality and a strong sense of loyalty. Could there have been a better man to lead a campaign on a divisive issue in American politics focused on race?

Even if Connerly were not doing the governor's bidding and their mutual interests were simply synergistic, much of the academic community and liberal supporters of affirmative action assumed a conspiracy. This in itself proved a source of resentment and some confusion within the university community. How should the university react to Connerly? Was he a regent concerned about affirmative action or a political operative?

In August 1994, Regents Clair W. Burgener and Ward Connerly reviewed the complaints of Jerry and Ellen Cook after receiving a letter from them regarding their son—the letter that Connerly claimed sparked it all. Jerry Cook was a professor at the University of California's campus at San Diego. Burgener was a former Republican congressman from southern California. The Cooks complained of unfair use of race-based admissions policies in the university's medical schools. Despite achieving significantly higher test scores than many admitted minority applicants, their son was denied admission to the university's medical school at San Diego. The

Cooks offered statistical information to back their protest. In his memo to Burgener, Connerly recalled how the Cooks plea proved a catalyst:

> As you know, I consented to meet with them, as did many other members of the Board . . . After our meeting, I very carefully weighed the material which they left with me and called the Office of the President to get information which would either validate or invalidate their findings, because on the face of their presentation it appeared to me that the University was guilty of violating the *Bakke* decision . . . you and I requested that the matter be reviewed and that a report be presented to the Regents . . ."[10]

In November 1994, President Peltason gave the regents the report on UC medical school admissions. At a meeting of the board, the president and other university administrators, including Cornelius Hopper, a vice president in charge of overseeing the university's various medical programs, stated that underrepresented students simply received a "bump" up in the admission process. A number of regents questioned the use of affirmative action in the university's medical schools, including Dean Watkins and Leo J. Kolligian. Watkins was an appointee of Governor Ronald Reagan and was an electrical engineer and professor at Stanford. Kolligian was a Boalt Hall graduate, a lawyer from Fresno, an appointee of Governor George Deukmajian in 1985, and part of a significant, generally conservative, group from California's Armenian community. Watkins and Kolligian asked if the university was practicing reverse discrimination.

Connerly stated there was a disjuncture between the complaint of the Cooks and what the office of the president and campus administrators were telling the board. "You didn't address the questions raised by the Cook Report," noted Connerly. "What we've just heard doesn't sound right and doesn't sound fair," he concluded. University administrators seemed "a little tetched," Connerly later wrote in his personal account, *Creating Equality*. The meeting ended with no clear resolution, just questions. University administrators, Connerly thought, seemed "smug" and appeared confident that they had extinguished "the Cook's little brush fire." Connerly, however, thought the board had "crossed a Rubicon even if we didn't know it at the time. This November 1994 meeting of the regents had let the genie of race preferences out of the bottle previously kept hidden away in the UC chamber of horrors."[11]

If university administrators thought they had contained the complaints of the Cooks and the concerns of Connerly, they were very wrong. As a regent, Connerly could place virtually any item on the agenda of future meetings of the board. Less than two months later, in early January 1995, Connerly informed President Peltason and fellow regents that he would request a general study of the university's affirmative-action programs. There was more: He requested that the board vote on the issue in June. Connerly planned for a period of debate on affirmative-action programs before submitting his own proposal for ending the use of racial and ethnic criteria.

Almost simultaneously, Connerly emerged as the head of the CCRI campaign. Governor Wilson had recently won reelection against Kathleen Brown, daughter of famed "pragmatic liberal" former California Governor Pat Brown (1959–1967) and a sister of past Governor Jerry Brown (1975–1982). Connerly, Kolligian, and others on the board of regents were active in contributing to and working for Wilson's reelection. Newspapers now talked of Wilson's presidential desires and his likely run in the Republican primary. For Wilson, the issue of affirmative action and reverse discrimination offered a route to national headlines. His stance on this issue and on an anti-immigrant initiative was credited, in part, for his reelection in California.

The political climate was ripe for a calculated political attack on affirmative action. There were a number of court cases winding their way through the legal system. Anti-affirmative action strategists sought select cases to test and hoped eventually to overturn *Bakke*. In early 1995, in *Adarand Constructors, Inc. v. Peña*, the Supreme Court provided an apparent building block for further legal efforts to limit or end group preferences. The court elaborated on the idea of "strict scrutiny," essentially requiring proof of historical patterns of discrimination by an employer or, by inference, a university before they could legally develop affirmative-action programs or make race-based decisions. Further, the court ruled that these programs needed to be narrowly tailored to those groups that could prove discrimination.[12] *Adarand* seemed to indicate a pattern of future rulings largely hostile to affirmative action. It also energized the CCRI campaign in California and Connerly's desire to tackle California first before moving to initiatives in other states.

The same month as the *Adarand* decision, Governor Wilson issued an executive order to "End Preferential Treatment and to Promote Individual Opportunity Based on Merit," essentially laying a precedent for ending affirmative action in personnel cases in public agencies. Its legal application, however, was not clear. It was not applicable to the University of California. The university's status as a public trust in the state constitution protected it from most executive orders. Wilson and his staff knew as much. His edict was a salvo against affirmative action following his successful campaign to pass Proposition 187, an initiative to end the extension of social services to illegal immigrants in California.

For Connerly and perhaps the governor, a period of six months of deliberations by the board beginning in January 1995 and leading to a regental action in June or so seemed a reasonable and defendable path. The debate would give momentum to Connerly's and Wilson's drive to place an initiative before California voters to end racial and ethnic preferences in public institutions. It also was timely for Wilson's presidential campaign.

At their January 19, 1995, meeting, the regents agreed to Connerly's request for a formal review and decision on the use of racial preferences in admissions and other university activities, placing the burden on the president to outline possible policy options. Yet the office of the president did not fully comprehend the building desire of the regents for a serious review. University officials focused simply on describing and defending the myriad affirmative-action-related programs—a strategic approach reinforced and encouraged by the council of chancellors, who met with the president regularly. At the outset of the debate, a sense prevailed among university-wide and campus administrators that any indication of fault with the affirmative-action policies would weaken their ability to defend diversity efforts. Anything but a strong defense might also draw significant criticism from students, faculty, legislators, and interest groups who strongly favored affirmative action.

Responding to Regent Connerly's request for a review, President Peltason stated to the regents that his office was "preparing an inventory and report on affirmative action programs, not because I intend to make recommendations for change—in my judgment, no changes are needed—but because we want to be prepared to answer any questions about them that may arise as a result of recently proposed legislation and constitutional amendments." He continued: "Over the past 30 years, we have established a series of programs designed to ensure that the University of California includes individuals from all backgrounds, both as an educational objective and as a matter of equity. We have done this partly in response to federal executive orders, congressional action, and legislative action by the State of California, and partly at the urging of the Board of Regents."[13] Peltason also told the regents that he would "accelerate" the completion of the report so that it would be available before the June 1995 meeting of the board—the meeting at which Regent Connerly noted his intention to submit his proposal. The president concluded that the university's policies derived from a "broad national consensus" and indicated that it would be premature for the regents to act: "If that consensus changes, so will federal and state policy and law. The University, as it is obligated to do, will respond at the appropriate time." [14]

At subsequent meetings of the board, heated and often acrimonious debate revealed significant division between a number of regents and university administrators concerning the proper scope and merits of race-based decision making. Other regents besides Connerly asked if the university's affirmative-action programs had gone too far, possibly violating the *Bakke* decision, and did not reflect the board's views. Although many long-term members of the board had supported President Gardner's 1988 resolution affirming the use of race and ethnicity in admissions (the last formal action of the board on the issue), it seemed to them a distant memory or an action that simply gave license to widespread abuse. [15]

The decentralized nature of affirmative-action efforts presented significant difficulties for the president and university-wide administrators. In the initial period of questioning by Connerly, university officials had difficulty accurately describing the breadth of programs that incorporated race-based and gender-based preferences or those created exclusively for a single ethnic group. Indeed, the true extent of racial preferences within the university was not fully understood by the academic and administrative leadership, a point Connerly effectively exposed. At one point, President Peltason and Provost Walter Massey stated in the deliberations with the regents that no campus admitted students solely on the basis of their race. It was simply one factor among many in choosing among UC-eligible students, they insisted, reiterating the mantra of the *Bakke* decision. The university's general counsel made the same unequivocal claim. These statements would prove a significant mistake. On further investigation, Peltason learned that at least two campuses automatically admitted all UC-eligible underrepresented students, including the Irvine campus, where Peltason had been chancellor. Further, both Berkeley and UCLA employed a tiered admissions process that heavily favored underrepresented groups.

As information surfaced on the differences in programs and approaches among the campuses, the credibility of the administration fell in the eyes of the regents. Did the president and his staff truly understand the vast array of affirmative-action programs within each campus? Did they purposely misrepresent the character of these programs? Connerly seized the opportunity and exposed a university culture that, arguably, was obsessed with the issue of race. Credibility and trust are key ingredients for an effective relationship between a university governing board and its president.

Connerly constantly reminded the board that they had not been told the true extent of racial preferences in admissions and other university decisions; they could not trust the president and his staff or the admonishments of the campus chancellors.[16] The board, argued Connerly, needed to strike out on its own and derive its own conclusions. Not until late in the debate would President Peltason concede that

> some of our programs need to be modified, either because we have concluded that a current policy or practice is inappropriate, or because we are convinced that the policy or practice is no longer necessary for us to meet our objectives. . . . most have to do with our undergraduate admission process. This should come as no surprise, since that process must balance a complex set of principles, policies and procedures.[17]

At the May 1995 meeting of the board of regents, Provost Massey and the assistant vice president of student academic services, Dennis J. Galligani, provided a package of materials on the university's affirmative-action programs and a number of presentations, including a review of admissions at UCLA and Berkeley's Boalt Hall School of Law and a report on "Policies and Procedures Governing Undergraduate Admissions." The regents also received a report on "The Use of Socio-Economic Status in Place of Ethnicity in Undergraduate Admissions." Prompted by the request of several regents for an analysis of the potential impact of ending the use of race-based criteria in undergraduate admissions, the report provided a simulation of what the freshman class at UC might look like, and specifically, the impact on minority enrollments, if economic factors replaced ethnicity in the admissions process. The simulation was based on data from the Berkeley and San Diego campuses.[18]

Opponents of affirmative action often pointed to the possible use of economic criteria as a morally acceptable substitute for race and ethnicity. The university's study attempted to refute this claim, focusing on the highly selective Berkeley campus and the San Diego campus, which was moderately selective at that time. Using economic criteria alone, the study projected a decline in Chicano-Latino and African American enrollment and a simultaneous increase in Asian American and Euro-American enrollment. One reason was the substantial number of white, low-income students from rural areas of the Central Valley and northern California. Another reason: A substantial number of underrepresented minorities applying to UC were not lower income students; most were from middle and upper income families.

For Connerly's opponents, the university's study offered proof of the disaster to come if race and ethnicity were removed as factors in admissions.

Underrepresented student enrollment would decline. There were a number of variables simply not assessed in the office of the president study. For example, it assumed that the college-going rate of Chicanos-Latinos would never change. Yet with the rise of a Chicano-Latino middle class and with possible improvements in the quality of secondary schools and hopeful increases in high school graduation rates, a slight increase in these rates could create a larger flow of UC-eligible students.

For critics of affirmative-action programs, the study appeared alarmist in intent and developed by university officials to draw media attention and increase pressure on the regents to avoid a decision. It also added to a perception that affirmative action was simply a special interest benefit. Preferences were being given to a racial group regardless of their family income or other indicators of privilege and social capital. Why should the university give preferences to upper income blacks? The study exposed the corrupting influence of racial preferences, essentially giving preferences and privileges to students from upper income groups over, for example, lower income Asian Americans who often had superior academic records.

California State Senator Tom Campbell, a Republican and former economist at Stanford (and a future dean of Berkeley's Hass School of Business), pointed to the university's analysis as proof of racial bias, using the example of a student from a "lower-income Asian family" who "worked extremely hard." Yet the student is insidiously denied access to Berkeley so as to provide a space for a "child of a professional couple of upper-middle income, no more academically qualified but possessing a different skin color."[19] "Affirmative action loses its credibility when benefits are distributed to those who have suffered no disadvantage, to the detriment of those who have caused no harm," noted Connerly in a memo to his fellow regents. Connerly explained that when he "brought this topic up for consideration in January, I concluded that the only way I could have any hope of ever affecting any change would be to increase its public visibility. . . . Right or wrong, I felt that I had no way of getting the University to take me seriously other than focusing the public spotlight on the problem."[20]

The net effect of the university's study was a precipitous decline in the working relationship between many members of the board and the office of the president. The report seemed to confirm Connerly's charge of intransigence. The administration's rigid support for existing programs reinforced the very ideological division that President Peltason warned against. Connerly never directly attacked President Peltason or other university officials. Instead, he consistently pointed to an internal bureaucratic culture blindly invested in affirmative action and driven by no direct federal or state law. "I have no doubt that President Peltason is operating in good faith," he wrote to the regents in a memo to Regent Burgener; "however, I have grave doubts about the wisdom of leaving this in the hands of the campuses, considering their failure to be forthcoming about their practices until now, and their absolute insistence on trying to preserve the status quo by whatever means possible."[21]

Governor Wilson also repeatedly pointed to institutional intransigence as a reason for regental action. The true extent of race-based decision making and its consequences had not been revealed to the regents by the administration. The regents must not tolerate university policies and practices that "violate fundamental fairness, trampling individual rights to create and give preference to group rights. It has become clear," he argued, that "despite official claims to the contrary . . . race has played a central role in the admissions practices at many UC campuses."[22]

In a May 23 letter, Ward Connerly urged the board to gather all the information necessary before coming to a decision. In June, he argued that the time had come. Connerly informed Peltason and the board of his plan to present a formal proposal to end preferences based on "race, religion, sex, color, ethnicity and national origin" in employment by January 1, 1996, and the same for admissions by January 1, 1997. As opposed to the normal path of offering a resolution directly to the board, Connerly chose a July 5 news release to present the language of his resolution—a mere two weeks before the regents meeting in which he would ask for a vote.

In his news release, curiously addressed to the regents, he again took direct aim at the credibility of the university administration. The intransigent university administration, Connerly claimed, required the regents to take action: "At the beginning of this evaluation, there were those who said no one is admitted to the University of California who is not eligible." But that "statement is not true. We were informed that no one was automatically admitted to the University of California solely on the basis of race or ethnic background. We have now confirmed the inaccuracy of that statement. We were told that race was never a major factor; it was only a 'bump.' Again, we have confirmed that on at least four of our campuses such a statement is blatantly false."[23] Connerly's gauntlet, formed by the self-proclaimed "Lone Ranger" among the regents, "pursuing what I felt I had to pursue as a matter of conscience and due diligence," caused further confusion within the university's office of the president.[24] How to react? On one side were a Republican governor and a regent; on the other a significant university community who adamantly supported affirmative action and a state legislature controlled by liberal Democrats still pushing the university to become more diverse.

Beginning in earnest in January 1995, Peltason's strategy successively moved through three phases. First was the impetus to circle the wagons, to defend any and all affirmative-action programs at the university. The second was to persuade the regents of the complexity of the problem and seek compromise, stating that a ban on racial preferences might risk the university's access to federal funds because affirmative action was a requirement of federal law and policies. Connerly would contest this and simply add to his draft resolution a clause stating that the board would take no action that would make the university ineligible for federal funds to mollify the potential concerns of his fellow regents. The third phase was to request that the board defer judgment on the issue of affirmative action in the face of a planned constitutional initiative (Proposition 209) and to allow the academic senate to review and recommend changes if the initiative passed.

In each phase, the president and his advisors thought they had a good chance to garner enough votes among the regents to defeat a proposal by Connerly. Why should the university be engaged in a politically divisive debate that could be settled by the California electorate? Why should the University of California become the first major American university to eliminate race and ethnicity in its admissions process? Peltason posed these questions to the regents at their January 19 meeting. "I believe that in our discussions of the University's programs and policies," Peltason warned, "we need to be careful not to embroil The Regents, and therefore the University, in a debate that is and should be taking place in the state and national arenas. Affirmative action is a volatile issue that generates strong feelings on every side." Still, he hoped "we can conduct our dialogue on this subject with the clarity, thoughtfulness, and precision it deserves." [25]

The Academic Senate's Response

The role of the senate in the deliberations on affirmative action offers another glimpse into the culture of the modern university. Connerly's initiative exposed the weakness of the faculty's ownership of admissions and its general aversion to a conflict that, at first, seemed to pit a president and his administrators against a rogue regent. In the fight over affirmative action, the senate was relegated to a minor role. The reasons were multiple: the effective efforts of affirmative-action opponents to demonstrate the frailty of any claim of faculty resolve through the Roper survey; the strategy of the president and administrators to be the front line of defense; and internal weaknesses within a senate largely forgetful of its once-dominant role in setting admissions policy. In light of the key role the faculty and the senate had played in shaping the university's social contract, this abrogation of authority and duties is a significant factor in the story of the regents' deliberation and final vote on affirmative action.

Until July, less than a month prior to the regents' vote, the president and the university-wide and campus administrations steadily defended affirmative-action programs independently of the academic senate. In their cause, the office of the president viewed the senate largely as a potential source of general support but not as a forum for reviewing university activities or for helping to develop a strategic response to the regents. The senate and faculty in general were not well informed on the issue, and their deliberations were often slow and unpredictable.

Although academic senate leaders independently could have taken action and offered options in light of their historic charge in the area of admissions, they did not. The regents began their dialogue with the office of the president on the form and merits of affirmative-action programs as early as August 1994. Committees of the university-wide academic senate did not broach the issue until a meeting of the academic council on January 18 of the following year. At that meeting, the council discussed how to respond to Regent Connerly's charges. "It is also expected that he will force a Regents' vote on the issue in June," stated Daniel Simmons, the chair of the council.[26] With seeming bravado, the council initially agreed that the senate should offer its formal view to the regents through the president. The relevant university-wide committees—BOARS, the coordinating committee on graduate affairs, and the committee on academic personnel—were asked to provide advice to Simmons on how to respond. In subsequent months, however, none of these committees reacted in any serious way, despite being informed of Connerly's intention to present a resolution to the board.[27] The only senate committee to respond to Simmons's plea was the previously dormant university-wide committee on affirmative action, a committee that rarely met.

In January, the senate's affirmative-action committee met for the first and only time during the 1994–1995 academic year. Simmons attended and asked that the committee take the lead role in forging the senate's response, possibly including a review of affirmative-action programs. Walter Yuen, the committee's chair and a professor of engineering at UC Santa Barbara, later summarized the committee's recommendations in a memo to Simmons, which in turn provided the strategic course the senate would follow. Yuen understood the difficulties of providing advice on affirmative action—what was in reality a vast network of programs within the university. "The committee is in agreement with you," he stated to Simmons, "that the Senate needs to play a role to support the University's past and present Affirmative Action efforts in response to Regent Connerly's attack and our committee is more than willing to play a leadership role in such an effort. But we do not feel that a 'hurry up' three-months effort to review *all* of the existing Affirmative Action programs will be the right strategy for the Senate." Yuen noted that the president's office "has probably accumulated most of the relevant data and their staffs should be able to generate a report for Peltason which is supportive of Affirmative Action. Since all the standing Senate Committees and our committee will start essentially from 'ground zero,' we do not believe that our efforts will add much to what the President's office can do."[28]

However, Yuen's committee did advocate issuing a strong and positive general statement by the academic council "to the Regents and the public" supporting the university's present and past affirmative-action efforts. Yuen stated the general need for the senate to later engage in reviewing affirmative-action efforts "independently of the President's office, whose staffs are directly responsible in running many of the AA programs (in effect, they are evaluating themselves!). I am in agreement [with] many skeptics of AA that many of the current programs are not effective and should be modified. In the spirit of shared governance, I believe that the Senate made a crucial mistake in letting staffs in the administration 'run away' with many of these programs with essentially no Senate input."[29]

The members of the university-wide committee on affirmative action then developed a general resolution for approval by each of the nine campus divisions of the senate. There was a need to "strengthen" the universities' affirmative-action programs—a hint that the university might need to carefully review its affirmative- action practices à la President Clinton's "mend it, don't end it" mantra. Presented at the February 15 meeting of the academic council held at UC San Diego, the resolution read,

> The affirmative action programs undertaken by the University of California have made the University a better institution by making it a more diverse institution in terms of the gender, racial, and ethnic makeup of its faculty, students, and staff. This work is not yet finished. The University should continue to act affirmatively to increase the participation of individuals from underrepresented groups, evaluating and modifying its programs in order to strengthen them.[30]

Simmons asked that the division chairs return to their campuses and gain endorsements from their divisions. By late May, each of the divisions, either through its executive committees or its representative legislatures, had endorsed a version of this resolution. Only ten days before the regents' historic meeting, and before the resolution by the divisions was formally presented to the board, President Peltason argued for the first time that further senate involvement was a necessity. He cited this need as a major reason for delaying the regents' vote, writing to the board "that any action now to dismantle our diversity programs would be premature and against the best interest of the University of California. . . . We should instead begin immediately the process of working with our faculty to decide how the University can best respond if the California Constitution is amended in the November 1996 election."[31]

The net effect of the senate's resolution was a general show of support for affirmative action. Arguably, this response also provided a sense of absolution. The senate provided no analysis of the extent of race-based decision making at the university, nor did it engage actively in devising an alternative strategy for consideration by the regents.

A Regental Decision

The weeks before the regents' meeting on July 20 were full of press statements, alternative proposals, and political posturing. The day before the meeting, and with an eye toward California, President Bill Clinton reiterated his theme of mending but not abandoning affirmative action. At a ceremony at the National Archives, he admitted that "affirmative action has not always been perfect and affirmative action should not go on forever. . . . it should be retired when its job is done." But he noted that clearly "the evidence suggests, indeed screams, that that day has not come."[32] The same day, Governor Wilson appeared on *Face the Nation* and other national shows to outline the extent to which race was used in University of California admissions and explained his determination to bring such practices to an end. They were "unfair" and "wrong." He planned to urge his "colleagues" on the board of regents to move "our nation forward toward a vision of equality, opportunity and fairness."[33]

Jesse Jackson promised to attend the regents' meeting to "guide" them and, if necessary, disrupt the proceedings as an act of civil disobedience. Jackson repeatedly charged that Wilson's interest in affirmative action was based solely on his personal drive to run for president. Jackson was not alone in this perception. The regents' meeting would provide Wilson with his biggest national spotlight yet, spiced by a confrontation with Jackson. "Governor Pete Wilson is using the dismantling of affirmative action as a cornerstone of his Republican Presidential bid," stated *The New York Times.* "Jesse Jackson is coming to town on Wednesday to lead protests," noted the article. Clinton "will deliver an important address on the subject on Wednesday. The twenty-six members of the Regents themselves appear to be sharply divided."[34]

Wilson decided not to chair the regents' meeting, although as the board's president, he had a formal right to this privilege. Clair Burgener—the incumbent chair of the board, a former Republican legislator, and an ally of Wilson and Connerly—would chair. Within a crowded theater on the Laurel Heights campus sat all but one member of the board, including eighteen appointees of the current and past governors, one student, and seven ex officio members. These included university President Jack Peltason; the speaker of the state assembly, Willie Brown; two representatives of the university's alumni association; Lieutenant Governor Gray Davis; and the state superintendent of public instruction. A Democrat, Davis was not only a strong supporter of affirmative action, but he also had his own political ambitions. While Wilson had the presidency in view, Davis had his sights on the governorship. The only regent not at the meeting was the speaker of the assembly, Doris Allen. Allen was a short-lived speaker, appointed in a compromise between Republicans and Democrats within an assembly almost evenly split between the two parties. Reflecting her weak political position, she abstained from attending the historic meeting.

Also participating at the board's meeting were nonvoting representatives of the faculty: the chair of the academic council, Daniel Simmons, and the vice chair of the council and chair elect, Arnold Leiman. The student and faculty representatives were added to the board in 1974, following the tumultuous student demonstrations of 1960s and early 1970s. Their presence, it was thought, might improve the board's connection to the students and the academic community. One hope was to mitigate future conflicts. Voting rights were extended to both the student and faculty regent in 1974; however, the academic senate chose not to have a voting representative lest he or she be compelled to formally join in decisions of the board that did not, and could not, accurately reflect the diversity of senate opinions.

The nine campus chancellors, as usual, also attended the meeting of the board, sitting along the front row but with no official capacity to speak unless recognized by the chair of the regents. The chancellors, and especially, Chang Lin-Tien at Berkeley and Charles (Chuck) Young at UCLA, had repeatedly voiced their full support for affirmative-action programs. Tien, in particular, had openly challenged Connerly on his facts and conclusions in meetings of the regents. The other chancellors included Richard Atkinson at UC San Diego (a future president of the university) and Karl Pister at UC Santa Cruz.

Representing the campuses with the most aggressive efforts at affirmative action, Tien and Young had suffered the brunt of difficult questions posed by Regent Connerly and other critics over the past year. In the months leading to the July meeting of the board, Connerly received encouragement from Regents Glenn Campbell, Frank Clark, Tirso del Junco, Leo Kolligian, David Lee, as well as Clair Burgener. Each held ties to the Republican Party. Campbell and Clark were affiliated with the Hoover Institution located at Stanford University, the first of a growing contemporary network of conservative think tanks. Campbell, del Junco, Kolligian, and Lee insisted that the regents weigh in on the affirmative-action debate, and they accused President Peltason of playing politics by requesting that the regents await an "election that may or may not occur."[35] Connerly's proposed proposition had not yet garnered sufficient signatures to place it on the California ballot.

Regent Meredith Khachigian indicated on the morning of the vote that her mind was not entirely made up. Yet she openly questioned the use of racial preferences at the university. Would she follow the admonishments of Governor Wilson? Her husband, Ken Khachigian, was a former speechwriter for Ronald Reagan and remained an important political advisor to the state Republican Party and Republican candidates, including Wilson. A simple count of regents by their party affiliation indicated an edge for Connerly and Wilson. At least six regents had contributed to the governor's most recent gubernatorial campaign: Connerly, Howard Leach, Stephen Nakashima, John Davies (who also served as the governor's advisor for the appointment of judges), Clark, and William Bagley. Leach had given $82,000; Connerly contributed $73,000.[36] Although appointed as nonpartisan and independent actors on a board of high prestige, regents usually aligned with the governor who appointed them on an issue he strongly cared about. Over the many decades of the university's existence, it was not an unusual practice for a governor to appoint an old friend or political ally to the board, but increasingly, a litmus test seemed to be a financial contribution to a governor's election war chest.

Still, President Peltason and others in the office of the president thought they could secure the necessary votes to block Connerly's motion. Regent Roy Brophy appeared to be an influential swing vote. Brophy noted his general support for affirmative action but, like Khachigian, worried over the university's use of race in admissions. A Sacramento real estate developer, Brophy was a rare breed—a Republican appointed by a Democratic governor, Jerry Brown. He had served previously on both the California community college's board of governors and the California State University's board and had long been a supporter of Wilson. Brophy and fellow Regents Bagley (a moderate conservative) and Ralph Carmona (the incoming alumni representative) appeared sympathetic to Peltason's call to leave the matter to voters if and when the CCRI got on the ballot. They worked together to find an alternative action the regents could pursue in the weeks before the June meeting.

Just days before the historic July meeting, Peltason offered a substitute motion to Connerly's resolution. It again asked the regents not to embroil the university in a decision they need not take. Instead, he asked that the board instruct him "to develop, in consultation with the Academic Senate, appropriate changes in undergraduate, graduate, and professional school policies governing admissions." The proposed action item also stated that these policies would take effect on or before January 1997, subject, of course, to "possible changes in state or federal law"—that is, a state initiative or a possible federal court ruling on affirmative action.

In a last show of unity, the chancellors, the president, and his vice presidents also issued a joint statement. They returned to a question discussed throughout this book's historical review of a public university's social contract: how to balance the needs of individual opportunity with the university's larger social purpose. In their statement, they reflected on the thoughts of earlier university leaders, in particular Daniel Coit Gilman. "The explicit democratic mission of the public university challenges us to serve 'the people' who represent a diverse and dynamic constituency," announced Peltason and his compatriots. It was the university's duty to create outreach programs *and* admissions policies that "ensure a diverse pool of students" who "reflect California society in the broadest possible sense, not just for the sake of diversity, but because the democratic value of a public education lies in the strength of its access to all qualified students."[37]

Adding to the mix of voices and to the confusion five days before the historic regents' meeting, the University of California's systemwide student government (the UC Student Association) offered its own substitute proposal. As a voting member of the board, student Regent Ed Gomez submitted a proposal that reflected the anger and frustration of student activists with the course chosen by Connerly and possibly the board. He reiterated the "imperative to have the population of the University of California truly represent the people" and the need for forceful action to have the "students, faculty, staff, and administration" reach parity with the state's population. "Nondiscrimination is a passive process toward equality, one whose timeline is intolerably slow, indefinable and unenforceable." The proposal demanded that the university "continue to implement its current Affirmative Action policies without direct intervention by the Regents."[38]

Leading up to the regents' meeting, student activists led dozens of demonstrations on the campuses of the university and formed a variety of new associations to battle Connerly, including the Coalition to Defend Affirmative Action by Any Means Necessary. These demonstrations often resulted in sit-ins, attracting a host of nonuniversity organizations and people, from Jesse Jackson to busloads of high school students from largely minority areas brought in to bolster the number of demonstrators. The effort of protesters, and Jackson's admonishments in particular, was not particularly productive. In the view of university officials, Jackson's presence was divisive and, indeed, a potentially fatal blow to their effort to persuade politically moderate regents to reject Connerly's proposal.

Regent Clair Burgener gaveled the meeting to order. All 300 seats in the room were occupied. The regents' secretary, Leigh Trivette, received innumerable requests to speak. The initial portion of the meeting was devoted to public comment. But Governor Wilson asked to speak first. With the full attention of the audience and the media, Wilson offered a rebuttal to Peltason's earlier pleas. Wilson stated that in this "matter of fundamental fairness and justice," only the regents could act. "We cannot ignore or duck that responsibility nor temporize in making the required decision." Wilson reiterated his earlier charge: "Race has played a central role in the admissions practices at many UC campuses. Indeed, some students who don't meet minimum academic requirements have been admitted solely on the basis of race."[39]

Then came a cavalcade of statements from some forty speakers, each lasting ten minutes or more, often spiced by repeated shouts of support or derogatory comments by student activists—acrimony that brought repeated gaveled demands by the chair for order and pleas for courtesy. In the midst of the public statements, Regent Roy Brophy asked Wilson to meet with him in a private room just outside the auditorium. Wilson obliged. While noting his general support for Connerly's proposals, Brophy urged the governor to seek a rather subtle compromise: The regents could vote on approving the ban on affirmative action, but give the university president and his staff a year to study its potential impact before it became formal policy. By then, Proposition 209 would be decided, presuming it got enough signatures to appear on the ballot. If it failed, the board might revisit its decision. Wilson said no to the idea. There was no room for compromise, and he wanted an up or down vote that day.[40]

Jesse Jackson was the last to speak during the public comment period. Wilson and Brophy had returned to their seats to hear Jackson. "Let us stand together and join hands and have prayer," Jackson announced. The reverend's invitation presented an awkward moment, with regents slowly standing and glancing at other board members to gauge the appropriate collective response. Only Wilson remained seated as Jackson launched his prayer, calling on the heavens for guidance. He then launched into a forty-minute plea for affirmative action.[41] When Jackson finished, the board began its own deliberations. Disruptions intensified. One by one, motions to table, substitute motions, compromise language, and the alternative proposals offered by President Peltason and the student regent were discarded. Nine hours into the marathon meeting, a bomb threat forced the evacuation of the meeting hall. After a nearly two-hour delay, university police gave clearance for the regents to meet in a room down the hall prepared for just such an event. Deliberations could legally continue in a secluded room, stated UC General Counsel Jim Holst, if security for the board could not be guaranteed. Live radio and a TV link still preserved the right of the public to witness the board's deliberations. Though some regents protested, Wilson insisted that the board get on with its business.[42]

Two hours later, in the room down the hall, the board voted to close off debate. A steady stream of proposed amendments to Connerly's proposal came to an end. Only one amendment was passed: a statement drafted by Regents Bagley, Connerly, and Governor Wilson reasserting the university's commitment to attaining a diverse student body. The amendment read: "Because individual members of all of California's diverse races have the intelligence and capacity to succeed at the University of California," the actions of the board were intended to achieve a student body that "reflects this state's diversity." It was hardly a compromise. It included the statement that such diversity should be achieved through the "preparation and empowerment of all students in this state to succeed rather than through a system of artificial preferences."[43] Connerly reportedly agreed to the change on the chance that the new language might influence the final vote in his favor.[44]

In the last hour of a thirteen-hour meeting, and without the threatening glare of student protestors, the board voted on the two motions offered by Connerly, with the sole amendment noted. The first, SP-1 (nomenclature for a special regental action number one) removed race, ethnicity, and gender related to university admissions, "ensuring equal treatment." It also set new parameters on the percentage of students admitted solely on academic criteria—test scores and grades. "Effective January 1, 1997," stated the resolution, "not less than fifty (50) percent and not more than seventy-five (75) percent of any entering class on any campus shall be admitted solely on the basis of academic achievement."[45] Connerly's resolution also called on the president to "confer with the Academic Senate of the University of California to develop supplemental criteria for consideration by the Board of Regents."[46] In this request, the regents appeared not only to confirm the historic role of the senate in admissions policy but also the ultimate authority of the board to set policy in a major area of the university's operation. The second motion, SP-2 removed race, ethnicity, and gender in the realm of employment and contracting.

By a vote of fifteen to ten, the regents proceeded to abolish affirmative action in hiring and contracting. And by a vote fourteen to ten, with one abstention and with only the amendment devised by Connerly, Wilson, and Bagley, SP-1 passed. Regent Bagley voted for the end of racial preferences in hiring and contracting but abstained on SP-1. The votes reflected the party affiliations of the regents, with those voting for approval almost exclusively appointees of Wilson and the previous Republican governor, George Deukmejian; those opposed were mostly appointees of Jerry Brown.

Connerly and Wilson orchestrated a major victory. The University of California became the only public university to have its board formally ban the use of race and ethnicity and gender in admissions decisions. The next day, the *Sacramento Bee* reported that Reverend Jackson led an "impromptu march through the streets of San Francisco." An estimated 350 people joined Jackson: "The crowd was spirited—there were six peaceful arrests—but relatively small."[47]

The Initial Meaning of California's Debate

Critics of affirmative action focused on the seeming injustice of providing preferences for specific racial groups. Their most poignant protests, however, centered on the perceived violation of individual rights. In this view, affirmative action is not a question of public benefits but of private benefits denied. Individual merit, rather than group identity, should be paramount in admissions decisions. Merit, furthermore, is not a broad and subjective notion but should be determined according largely to two quantifiable factors: grades and test scores.

This narrow approach to the role of public universities and the increased dependence on test scores for determining merit potentially formed a profound paradigm shift in the historical purpose of public universities. What would it mean (to provide one extreme example) to accept only students with high test scores to America's most selective public universities? It would mean precluding factors related to a student's socioeconomic background, proclivities, and academic engagement not reflected in a standardized test. It would mean less diversity in thought and achievement and in the economic and ethnic backgrounds of students. It would mean a profound narrowing of institutional mission and, in short, the death of the original ideal of public universities as agents of social change.

As chronicled in earlier chapters, the purpose of public universities, their governance, and the breadth of their academic programs are all the result of public resolve and investment over time. Universities were created for a reason and in the spirit of broad access and broad social benefits. These institutions have accumulated responsibilities that have been purposely and publicly declared. Historically, they have attempted, and often struggled, to promote the ideals of meritocracy and inclusiveness by establishing admissions requirements that are sufficiently broad to allow access to the disadvantaged or to those who show talents outside traditional academic norms. Few conservatives openly argue against these traditions and values; rather, their desire is to tip the scales even more toward measurable academic standards.

The advocates of affirmative action, on the other hand, often manipulated the concept of the social contract as solely a matter of race and racial representation. In the course of their arguments, affirmative-action supporters also dangerously and unnecessarily narrowed the concept of the social contract of public universities. Although external pressures, including lawmakers and racial interest groups, influenced this course, universities developed internal cultures that inordinately elevated race in admissions and other decision making. To a marked degree, institutions such as the University of California lost their bearings in their ardent effort to become more inclusive of underrepresented racial and ethnic groups; their advocacy inadvertently diminished the viability of affirmative action within the political culture of present-day America.

Together, both critics and advocates of affirmative action created a polarized debate with little middle ground for pragmatic compromise. Both sides placed emphasis on the mechanics of the admissions process and their outcomes—for example, on the plight of individuals denied access, on the perceived fairness of the admissions process, and on the number of underrepresented students enrolled. In the resulting politicized environment, many higher education institutions were distracted (to be kind) or simply negligent (to be harsh) in probing and articulating their historical purpose in society. Is the purpose of public universities simply to provide an education to those who have the best test scores, even if those scores are only marginally predictive of academic success at the university and are also correlated closely with socioeconomic privilege? In this model, the tendency is to view the entrance gate to a public good as a reward.

In the short run, the losers in California's fight over affirmative action were the university itself and the growing population of minority students in the state. The administration lost much of its credibility with the board, a crucial element for an effective working relationship. As discussed in the next chapter, the effect on minority applications and enrollment at the university, particularly at campuses such as Berkeley and UCLA, was a sharp downward trend.

For the winners, not all was achieved. Wilson's presidential hopes briefly brightened. The governor gained name recognition in national polls conducted over the summer of 1995. There also was a small surge in campaign contributions, mostly from Californians. But Wilson dropped out of the race in September. The eventual Republican candidate for president, Bob Dole, also weighed in on affirmative action, calling it "a corruption of the principles of individual liberty and equal opportunity upon which our country is founded."[48] Bill Clinton won reelection with relative ease.

For Connerly and the CCRI campaign, however, the decision by the board brought much-needed media attention. It helped boost financial contributions and momentum at a critical time. Enough signatures were gathered to place Proposition 209 on the November 1996 ballot. California voters passed the proposition by a 54% plurality. Was the regents' decision a decisive factor in the eventual success of the proposition? Lydia Chavez, in her book on the anti-affirmative-action campaign in California, credits the regents' action as an important component in the march to victory. Most significantly, the decision proved the salience of the issue for the Republican Party in both state and national politics. Ultimately, she notes, "Wilson and the state Republican Party could take the credit for putting CCRI on the ballot. It was they who pumped nearly $500,000 into the campaign and paid the signature gatherers to stay on the street."[49]

Within the university, students groups organized a new round of demonstrations. Proponents of affirmative action continued to predict a decline in underrepresented students at Berkeley and UCLA. More or less left out of the media was consternation among University of California faculty not so much on the merits of affirmative action but on the appropriate locus of admissions policymaking. The concept of shared governance, and the appropriate role of the senate in setting admissions policy, appeared to be victim of an aggressive regent.[50] The Berkeley division of the academic senate considered a proposal to censure the board of regents—an action with no formal authority other than to state the displeasure of faculty with the board. A meeting of the division approved moving forward with a vote of all Berkeley faculty. But the vote never came. It was deftly tabled by Berkeley's senate leadership at the behest of Arnold Leiman, Simmons's successor as chair of the university-wide academic senate. Such a condemnation would not have been constructive; the animosity between a number of key members of the regents and the senate was already deep enough, thought Leiman.

Reflecting the sentiments of one side of the affirmative-action debate, an angry and politically powerful state senator, John Vasconcellos, wrote to the regents the day after their decision, "How dare you rush to judgment—according to no public interest timetable—to join the desperate effort of a presidential candidate to jumpstart his nonstart campaign. How pathetic!" But there was more: "You have committed the most destructive act in modern California history," he intoned, and after a night of "outrage and agony," he now stated that as chair of the state senate's committee on the budget, "the regents action yesterday makes it virtually impossible for me to vote for any 1995/96 budget that provides the University of California['s] Board of Regents any money whatsoever."[51] It was an empty threat.

The Clinton White House initially stated that it might rescind some $4 billion the University of California received in federal grants—highly unlikely but a mild show of protest. The American Association of University Professors convened a commission to study the action of the regents and then issued a report. Chaired by Robert Atwell, the former president of the American Council on Education, the commission's report argued that the regents had broken the rules of shared governance, even though their knowledge of the deliberations was marginal. Lawsuits were filed against the regents and against Wilson for breaking the state's sunshine laws that prohibit private lobbying among fellow lay board members with no result.

Politics had proven a decisive force in refashioning the university's admissions policies. The subsequent backlash against the regents' decision proved an insufficient force to undo their decision on racial affirmative action. The university community needed to comply with dispatch. The board and then the people of California had ended racial preferences. There was no available end run—exactly as opponents of Proposition 209 had predicted. Or was there? Despite earlier claims to the contrary, might revived forms of economic and geographic affirmative action offer a route for progress on racial and ethnic diversity?

Chapter 8

The First Aftermath:
Outreach and Comprehensive Review

Government may treat people differently because of their race only for the
most compelling reasons.
—*Adarand Constructors, Inc. v. Peña*, 515 U.S., at 227

"Further efforts to defend affirmative action will be immensely difficult,"
wrote political scientist and ardent liberal Andrew Hacker a little less than
a year after the University of California's 1995 decision to end racial preferences. Among American voters, he concluded, "its defenders are still having difficulty making a convincing case for it."[1] Five months after Hacker's
statement, Ward Connerly's campaign to pass Proposition 209 succeeded.
California's state constitution was amended to ban the use of race and ethnicity in all public agencies. Voters in the state of Washington followed
with a similar initiative. In Florida, Governor Jeb Bush issued an executive
order in 1999 banning the use of race and ethnicity in public university and
college admissions.

Opponents of affirmative action seemed to ride a reactionary wave of
discontent with the concept of racial preferences among the public and a
group of powerful lawmakers. The conservative *New York Post* gave Connerly much of the credit. The regents' ban and Proposition 209, exclaimed
one editorial, "is a revolutionary development. And it seems likely to be
the inspiration for a nationwide rejection of the high-minded but grossly
unfair and un-American reverse-discrimination regime."[2] Even a portion
of the liberal left noted that Connerly's methods might be suspect, but he
raised important questions. Jesse Douglass Allan-Taylor, a black journalist,
wrote that "progressive people of color ought not to let disagreement with
Ward Connerly's political and social goals blind us to confronting the very

legitimate and timely questions he raises on race and ethnicity." Connerly proved "an anomaly for a black person of his generation." Yet Allan–Taylor thought he fit in well with "some elements of the hip-hop generation, that part which brags that it has 'moved beyond' the confines of race."[3]

State initiatives such as Proposition 209 offered only one front in the battle over affirmative action. The courts offered another. The right lawsuit, Connerly and others thought, might result in a nationwide ban. In the post-*Bakke* era, a growing number of court cases added to a sense of a limited future for racial preferences in all public agencies, with possible implications for the private sector. Opponents anxiously looked to the Supreme Court to revisit the issue and reverse *Bakke*. "I pray to God the Supreme Court rules on it one way or another, win, lose or draw," stated Connerly to the press and his followers. "This is something the court needs to act on."[4]

Cases such as *Adarand* focused on hiring and contracting practices, with implications for higher education.[5] However, the most salient issue for the courts and among the public was the use of affirmative action at selective public universities. In the mid-1990s, a suit in Texas appeared to be the likely test case. In 1996, a federal court considered a charge of reverse discrimination directed at the University of Texas School of Law in Austin. There were similarities with the *Bakke* case: With the help of a conservative legal defense fund, four white students filed a suit against the university after being rejected at the law school. Based largely on their standardized test scores, they charged that the university operated a dual admissions process, one for whites and another for African American and Hispanic applicants. In *Hopwood v. Texas*, the Fifth Circuit Court ruled in favor of the plaintiffs, effectively placing a ban on affirmative action in the court's jurisdiction of Texas, Mississippi, and Louisiana. The Fifth Circuit's decision was appealed and then upheld by a federal district court. Two of the three judges who formed the majority opinion in *Hopwood* argued that prior decisions by the Supreme Court related to hiring and contracting essentially made affirmative action in admissions unconstitutional. Their decision was again appealed, this time for consideration by the U.S. Supreme Court. But the highest court in the land refused to hear the case. The lower court's ruling therefore stood.

By the late 1990s, a number of other cases made their way through the courts, most threatening to restrict further the use of affirmative action in public university admissions.[6] It seemed inevitable that the Supreme Court would hear one or more of these cases. "Is affirmative action doomed?" asked Ronald Dworkin, a professor of law at New York University. "Does it violate the Fourteenth Amendment's guarantee of 'equal protection of the laws' for universities to give preferences to blacks and other minorities in the fierce competition for student places, as the best of our universities have done for years?" Dworkin was not sure, but the likely votes among the sitting Supreme Court justices would probably overrule *Bakke.*[7]

Both opponents and supporters of affirmative action prepared for a hearing before the court, launching new studies and searching for evidence to support their respective positions. Among observers of the court, many saw possibly one or two swing votes, including Justice Sandra Day O'Connor. Appointed by President Ronald Reagan, O'Connor was the first woman on the court and had not proven the stalwart conservative that many in the Republican Party had anticipated.

The anticipated test case started as not one but two lawsuits filed in 1997 against the University of Michigan. Both cases went through a series of lower court rulings before being appealed to the U.S. Supreme Court. This time, the court agreed to hear the case in the summer of 2003. Proposition 209 and the *Hopwood* and Michigan cases provided an important context for states such as California. How to bolster access to underrepresented and disadvantaged groups without the tool of affirmative action, particularly in states with quickly growing minority and immigrant populations? That is, is there a surrogate for race and ethnicity?

Three responses emerged in states that fell under either legislation or court rulings that restricted or eliminated affirmative action. The first was an attempt to expand university outreach programs to local schools; the second was a revival of school-based criteria, so-called "percentage plans" that guarantee admission to top students of each public high school in a state; and the third was shifting admissions policies to incorporate more fully the context of a student's academic achievements. What emerged out of these possible responses was no single reform to mitigate the effects of the end of affirmative action. There was no silver bullet.

After SP-1 and Proposition 209

As discussed in previous chapters, the University of California's social contract grew out of a desire by state governments to expand opportunity and to shape society—to make it more equitable, productive, and prosperous. In the course of pursuing these goals, a number of "principles" emerged between 1868 and the 1970s, all oriented toward expanding opportunity and clarifying the university's role within a progressive system of public higher education. Women were to be admitted on the same basis as men; admission of students was to be selective, while also free of sectarian and political influences; the university was to assure a place to all students admitted under standards set by the faculty; the university's student body was to reflect the larger society it served. These and other principles guided a relatively transparent commitment to the people of California. The board of regents' 1995 decision was a restrictive edict, a policy that in some ways ran contrary to or made it more difficult to pursue its other principles.

A subtext of many conservative attacks on affirmative action was that representation by a particular racial group might be an erroneous goal. Let the market decide based on quantifiable gauges of merit, defined exclusively by test scores and grades. Yet there has been no major effort to overturn the general concept of representation as a core part of the social contract. Broad access remained a salient goal, codified in legislation and in the institutional missions of universities. The question is how to achieve this goal.

During the University of California regents' affirmative-action debate, university officials and analysts predicted dire results. Admissions of underrepresented groups would decline. Not only would the admissions process no longer favor these groups; the university's board, it was charged, sent a chilling message that minority students were not welcomed. There might be a decline in underrepresented minority applications. The majority of regents, including Ward Connerly, insisted on almost immediate implementation of the ban. However, the university's new president, Richard Atkinson (appointed shortly after the board's decision) hoped for a delay.

Atkinson served as the chancellor at the university's San Diego campus for fifteen years and helped build an institution rapidly growing in its academic prestige and national ranking. Prior to his tenure at San Diego, he served as the director of the National Science Foundation during the Carter administration. Upon his appointment as the university's seventeenth president in October 1995, Atkinson was confronted with the difficulties of rapidly implementing the regents' edict on affirmative action. The regents' resolution, SP-1, stated that the new admissions policies would go into effect for undergraduate and graduate students admitted for fall 1996, with the actual process of making admissions decisions completed largely by April and May of that year. Fearful of a precipitous decline in underrepresented minorities and in the midst of devising new outreach programs and admissions policies, Atkinson proposed a one-year delay on the deadline by conferring with key regents, both liberal and conservative and including Connerly. With an agreement seemingly close at hand, Atkinson still

needed to privately seek Governor Pete Wilson's approval. There were indications that Wilson would agree.

But prior to that consultation, Atkinson's proposal was prematurely
leaked to the press. Wilson reacted angrily to the president's plan. For-
merly sympathetic regents, including Connerly, then condemned delay as
deliberate obstruction. Yet Atkinson stuck to his insistence on a postpone-
ment. Within the media, there was conjecture on his possible firing by the
board. In the end, a compromise was reached. The dropping of racial preferences in graduate admissions would begin in fall 1996 for selecting the
following year students; but for undergraduate admissions, the new policy
would not begin until 1997 for selection of the 1998 class.

In the spring of 1998, Atkinson sent a personal letter to 13,000 promising high school seniors encouraging them to consider UC and to apply to
more than one of its campuses. The chancellors, faculty, students, and various UC regents were making widespread contacts with potential students
to urge them to attend the university.[8] Yet such efforts seemed to have a
marginal effect. As predicted, at Berkeley, UCLA, and San Diego,. application rates among many minority groups declined. Of the 10,509 undergraduate applicants who were offered a slot in 1998 at Berkeley, only 2.4%
were African American, down from 5.6% a year earlier. Chicano students,
about 11% of the applicants accepted in 1997, made up just 6% a year
later. Taken together, African Americans, Native Americans, and Latinos
of all backgrounds, who constituted about 34% of the state's population,
accounted for just 10% of admissions at Berkeley.[9]

Even more precipitous declines in underrepresented minority groups
occurred at San Diego, UCLA, and to a lesser extent Santa Barbara. However, a substantial portion of these real declines in minority representation was offset by gains at Santa Cruz, Irvine, and Riverside. In general,
these were less selective institutions with plans for large-scale enrollment
expansion but also with high-quality, nationally ranked academic programs
(see Figure 8.1).

The University of California's social contract has long included the concept of providing access to one or more campuses of the university for
all eligible students but not necessarily to a student's first-choice campus.
Hence, although the end of racial preferences had a significant impact
on five campuses, the overall impact was a relatively moderate three-year
decline in underrepresented students of 3%. Still, this was a decline that
California and the university as a whole could ill afford and that might
compound with each entering class. California's minority population was

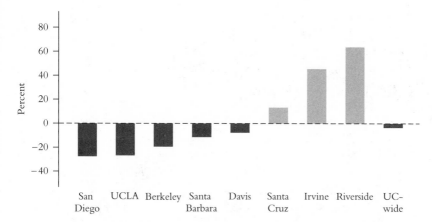

Figure 8.1. Post-Proposition 209 changes in underrepresented minority enrollment in the UC system by campus: 1997–1999

SOURCE: University of California Office of the President, Enrollment Reports.

and is growing and should, as noted previously, spur a corresponding increase in university enrollment.

For proponents of affirmative action, the declines at Berkeley and UCLA appeared catastrophic. Media accounts focused almost entirely on these two campuses. At Berkeley, minority admissions plummeted. For critics of affirmative action, the significant decline in underrepresented admissions and enrollment at the most selective campus confirmed the charges of Connerly and others that previous admission practices were overly dependent on race in admissions decisions. For university officials and lawmakers, conservatives and liberals alike, the questions were how to revitalize outreach programs to local schools and refashion admissions to mitigate predicted and real decline in underrepresented groups.

The Problem with the Schools

Although much of the public attention is on the entrance gate to UC campuses such as Berkeley and UCLA, the defeat of affirmative-action policies at the ballot box spawned a renewed focus on how to improve the quality of California's schools. One component of the regents' 1995 policy statement ending the use of race in admissions was to bolster university outreach. SP-1 called for the creation of a task force to develop proposals "for new directions and increased funding" for outreach. The purpose was "to increase the eligibility rate of underrepresented groups." The hope was that the university and other higher education institutions could improve the pipeline for disadvantaged students.

Like most land-grant institutions, the University of California had a long history of interaction and programs intended to support and improve the academic quality of local schools. As recounted in earlier chapters, university faculty at one time accredited local public high schools. However, such formal interaction between UC faculty and California's school officials dissipated over time. What emerged beginning in the 1960s was a series of targeted outreach programs largely for underrepresented students. The scale of the effort was relatively modest, reflecting national norms. Most outreach strategies focused on enhancing college awareness, building self-esteem, providing role models, and improving academic skills; most were largely funded by federal programs established in the 1960s.[10]

In California, federal funds supported early intervention programs, Upward Bound, and similar programs targeted at minorities and low-income sectors of the population. State funds supported a variety of program to improve the skills of these students: statewide programs such as Mathematics, Engineering, Science Achievement (MESA), Early Academic Outreach, the Puente Project, and a variety of campus-based initiatives. A 1994 study cataloged some 800 different outreach programs across the University of California system.[11]

The renewed attention on outreach in the late 1990s primarily focused on improving the quality of the teaching staff in local schools, on college counseling, and perhaps most important, on a new university-based initiative: school partnerships intended to improve the preparation of students for college. It also included a new effort to expand the interest of disadvantaged students in going to the university or other postsecondary institutions. Buttressing this effort was the return of a healthy California economy. State lawmakers wanted the University of California and the California State University (CSU) to make a difference and now had a flow of tax dollars to fund new programs. Indeed, while supporting a number of initiatives to bolster the funding and programs of local school districts, lawmakers allocated an inordinate amount of hope and money to the higher education segments and to the University of California in particular. Might they be the main catalysts to intervene and somehow reshape and fix a troubled school system?[12]

The problems facing California's public schools were enormous, unprecedented, and long term. The University of California's historical role as the state's most selective public higher education institution depended in no small measure on the overall quality and vibrancy of the state's schools. Yet the entire public education system, including the community colleges and the California State University, was showing significant signs of eroding quality, the victim of long-declining public investment, significant enrollment growth, and a major and complex demographic transition.[13] California's once-famed public school system now ranked at the bottom of the pile in most measurements of organizational and institutional health and productivity. Between 1960 and the late 1990s, the state's high school graduation rates had slumped from among the nation's highest to among the lowest. California ranked forty-seventh in the number of sixteen to nineteen year olds who gained a high school diploma. Only Florida, Georgia, and Nevada ranked lower. Arizona and Texas were only slightly better—both states with high concentrations of immigrants and rising poverty rates.[14] Per-student spending in California, through most of the twentieth century among the top five in the nation, sank to well below the national average. Huge enrollment increases in California's schools, combined with efforts to reduce class size in grades one through three and a period of stagnant teacher salaries, resulted in a dramatic shortage of qualified teachers. By 1998, more than 21% of the teachers had no teaching credentials, with even higher rates in poor urban schools.

For the first time since the late 1800s, California's college-going rate for high school graduates actually started to drop beginning in the early 1990s. Once the national leader in this important category, by 1997 the state ranked well below the national average. The root of the problem is complicated. There was not only the erosion of school funding over some thirty years, a pattern that was briefly reversed during the economic boom of the late 1990s. Other problems included a complicated and growing educational bureaucracy, relatively new levels of poverty within California's rapidly growing population, and the difficulties of educating a tremendous influx of immigrants and students from families with low educational backgrounds. By the 1990s, California was by far the largest state in population with some 33 million people, nearly twice the size of New York. It was also the most diverse, with the largest number of English as a second language students, usually the children of the poorest families.

In California's high schools and in most community colleges, once-robust academic counseling services had all but disappeared among the many low-income districts. "Urban high schools have a ratio of about 1,040-to-one students to counselors," explained Robert Taranishi in a study of college-going patterns among poor communities in the Los Angeles area. Taranishi observed that in many schools with a high concentration of low-income students, counselors often told students they should not apply to the University of California. Particularly after Proposition 209, they told students the admissions bar was too high.[15]

The disproportionate growth of advanced placement (AP) courses offers another important indicator of the disparities in California's huge network of public and private high schools, a system with some 1.8 million students in 1999.[16] Whereas virtually all public high schools in the state at one time offered a small number of AP courses, the number of courses offered ballooned, disproportionately growing within wealthier school districts. Originally, college and universities designated AP as a method for "superior" students to gain college credit by first taking a college-level course in a local college and then passing the AP exam in that subject. The Educational Testing Service developed AP exams in the mid-1950s. In the 1960s, high schools began to offer their own AP courses. Not until the 1980s, however, did AP become a significant factor in the admissions process of selective institutions such as the University of California.[17] In 1981, UC wanted to encourage seniors in high school to take more rigorous courses during their senior year in preparation for entering the university. Following the lead of private institutions, the academic senate changed the university's admissions policies, weighting grades in AP courses significantly higher than regular college-preparatory courses. Suddenly, the traditional four-point scale for grades became a five-point scale. An "A" in a regular course generated a 4.0 grade, but the same grade in an AP course generated 5.0 points. The change, which was adopted by most selective colleges and universities, created increased interest by high schools in providing AP courses to make their students more competitive. And it increased the interest of students in taking such courses.

Between 1985 and 2001, the number of AP exams taken by students in California grew from 42,950 to nearly 260,000.[18] There were two unintended consequences. First, the popularity of AP courses among students seeking entrance to increasingly selective institutions created a significant influence on grade inflation. For example, by 2001, the average GPA for students admitted to Berkeley was a one-time unfathomable 4.31. A second problem was a growing disparity in the range of AP courses offered among California's 900 public schools. Not surprisingly, in low-income communities, there were fewer AP or honors courses. In 1998, some schools offered no AP courses; some 10% did not even offer the full range of courses required to be UC and CSU eligible.[19]

The lack of AP courses in low-income communities and the general disparity between rich and poor school districts resulted in a class-action suit by the American Civil Liberties Union, *Daniel v. California*. In 1999, the ACLU sued the state of California for essentially creating a separate and decidedly not equal public school system based largely on the significant disparity of AP course offerings.[20] The ACLU joined with the Mexican American Legal Defense and Educational Fund (MALDEF) to sue the Berkeley campus as well. They and three other civil rights groups charged the campus with discrimination against minority applicants by relying on advanced placement courses *and* SAT scores in the admissions process. A Philadelphia court ruling added momentum to their charge. In that case, the National Collegiate Athletic Association was successfully sued; test-score eligibility requirements for freshman athletes were found racially discriminatory. The prospect of similar rulings caused ETS to float the notion of giving extra credit to poor and minority test takers, an idea so fraught with methodological and political difficulties that it was quickly dropped.[21]

Outreach in Overdrive

With seemingly few options available for mitigating the effects of the ban on racial preferences, University of California officials ventured to reformulate their outreach programs. With Democrats in control and influenced by the priorities of a powerful Latino caucus, lawmakers poured money into outreach as separate budget items above the university's normal operating budget. Indeed, university officials were given funds for outreach programs that they had not even asked for, an unusual twist in the higher education budget process. In fueling the outreach machine, lawmakers wanted a healthy return; they wanted to see numerical increases in the number of minority students applying to the university.

Within the university's academic community and among its leaders, worrisome questions lingered. Could UC possibly meet the growing expectations of lawmakers? Was UC capable of effecting change at the local school level? School reform had been the subject of ubiquitous study, and the conclusion of such research is uniform in one dimension: Schools are complex organizations not easily influenced or redirected. How was the university going to influence a school system with so many maladies?

Two years after the regents' 1995 decision, a four-point outreach effort emerged. As in admissions, each needed to be race neutral. The first component of UC's revived effort included establishing new partnerships with low-performing schools, so-called "school-centered" outreach. A second was expanding existing college-preparatory programs in areas such as math and science, so-called student-centered programs focused on academic development. This included tutoring and extracurricular opportunities and placing AP courses offered by UC online. A third component was enlarging efforts at "informational outreach," including new publications and online sources of information on how to qualify for college. This entailed concerted efforts to bolster college counseling for students in disadvantaged communities. And the fourth prong of UC's outreach effort was supporting research on the causes of disparate levels of eligibility and college participation as a means to evaluate outreach programs.[22]

More initiatives were later added, in large part due to the lobbying of lawmakers and Governor Gray Davis—Pete Wilson's successor. Following a model found in other states, UC was asked to establish new teacher and school-management training programs, including new "principals' institutes" targeted to preparing school leaders in poor urban communities. In 1999, Davis also successfully pushed to fund a new initiative to train 70,000 teachers.

A number of key lawmakers championed large increases in the state's Cal Grant program. The program was first established in 1955 to provide financial aid to make college affordable for poor and middle class students with moderately high grades in high school. Modeled on the GI Bill, Cal Grants subsidize the costs of a public or private college or university in the state.[23] In the late 1980s and early 1990s, lawmakers failed to sufficiently fund the program or to adjust the grants for inflation, a particular problem for students entering private colleges and universities where tuition fees had increased dramatically. More students applied than could be funded under a formula managed by the California Student Aid Commission. The legislature passed a bill in 1999 that promised some $1.2 billion for the grant program over five years, but the promise was made with little effort to analyze the actual need for such a large boost in the program.[24] The expanded Cal Grant program appeared progressive, but could the state maintain such an expansive financial commitment?

Revitalizing outreach became a mantra among public university leaders and a number of major foundations. If affirmative action was to wither, what other options were there? "There is still so much we can do to improve access to our universities," stated Larry Vanderhoef, the chancellor of the University of California's campus at Davis. Vanderhoef served on the twenty-seven-member Kellogg Commission on the Future of State and Land-Grant Universities, which offered a report on outreach in the early part of 1998, in the midst of UC's effort to construct its outreach efforts.[25]

California was one of a number of states where lawmakers looked to their public research universities to do something about K-12. North Carolina's university system put up $5 million to bolster teacher education programs and entice professionals in the private sector into becoming teachers. The University of Washington developed a number of new initiatives in the late 1990s, many garnering federal funding.[26] Yet the political dynamics of California were arguably unique.

In Texas and Florida, legislative mandates altered the admission process wholesale — in Texas in the wake of *Hopwood* and in Florida under a proposal offered by Governor Jeb Bush. The University of California's board of regents, led by activist board member Ward Connerly, had on its own accord ended racial preferences independently of lawmakers and in advance of Proposition 209. This created an environment of frustration among lawmakers, threats of budgetary consequences, and anger over the seemingly premature ending of affirmative action in admissions. To a degree not experienced by other major state universities, the University of California bore a political burden to develop a statewide approach to outreach and to produce results. Another difference was the scale of public funds committed by California lawmakers to expand financial aid and outreach efforts. Governor Gray Davis and democratic lawmakers disagreed on many issues, including Davis's opposition to the size of the Cal Grant funding commitment, but they agreed to spend money on a scale that, as we will see later, proved not sustainable.

In return for the largess offered by the state, the university needed to establish a variety of accountability measures. UC President Richard Atkinson established the proverbial task force to help in this endeavor.[27] Based on their report, Atkinson announced a number of ambitious benchmarks. Each was negotiated with legislative leaders in Sacramento, and all were to be reached by the summer of 2003, five years after the initial funding by lawmakers. Two of the benchmarks related to increasing eligibility rates among underrepresented students, which meant in large part Chicano-Latino and African American students. University officials stated an objective of a 100% increase in UC-eligible students from partner high schools and other academic development programs throughout the state. Within this cohort, the university would achieve a 50% increase in the number of students eligible for admissions to UC's most competitive campuses, such as Berkeley. They also promised a 200% increase in the number of contacts each campus had with elementary and middle schools and community college students.

No other state university established a similar set of benchmarks for its outreach programs. The deal was struck. Sacramento opened its checkbook to help put the University of California's outreach programs into

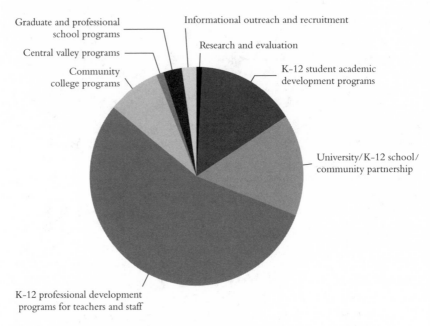

Figure 8.2. Funding allocations for University of California outreach by program area: 2000–2001

SOURCE: University of California Board of Regents Budget, 2000–2001.

overdrive. The university's budget designated for outreach ballooned from approximately $60 million in 1997 to $328 million in 2001. This increase included about $183 million from the state and another $144 million in matching and other funds from federal agencies and foundations. While there were state funds going directly to the California State University for similar programs, the UC office of the president became the central granting agency for the state's outreach cause, distributing funds to both university programs and similar efforts at CSU and in the community colleges.

Many outreach programs existed in one form or another in the pre-209 era. Some were race specific and needed to be modified. The most significant new program area was the notion of school partnerships. Of the $328 million budgeted for outreach in 2001, 55% was allocated to a host of new professional development programs for teachers, some of which passed through UC to CSU (see Figure 8.2). Another 30% was evenly divided between university-school partnerships and a host of academic development programs such as MESA, the math and science program for disadvantaged high school and community college students. Funding was also provided for outreach programs in the Central Valley. UC hoped to gain significant increases in Latino enrollment through a new campus in Merced planned for opening in 2005. Some 15% of the funds allocated in 2001 were targeted for low-performing schools with large numbers of students whose parents never went to college. Some 10% of the roughly $175 million allocated for K-12 professional programs was discretionary for campus chancellors.

In the midst of formulating this new outreach plan, Atkinson asked Karl Pister to lead the university's new outreach effort. Pister had been a member of the task force that formulated the program, and he carried the right credentials to move it forward within a highly politically charged environment. A former dean of engineering at Berkeley, Pister had recently stepped down as the chancellor at the university's Santa Cruz campus. He hailed from California's Central Valley, having grown up in an area historically underserved by the university in terms of enrollment and where a growing Latino population might eventually be tapped to increase their numbers at the university.

Atkinson, Pister, and many others, including chancellors and those working in the trenches of university admissions and outreach, saw grave problems if UC did not keep better pace with the state's demographic shifts. The state's land-grant university was not adequately serving California's growing lower income and minority population. There were also practical political consequences: "The other side of the issue is what are the political stakes if we don't do this," asserted Pister. "This is what you always face. The legislature and the governor will kill us [budgetarily] if we don't accept this responsibility."[28] Democratic lawmakers threatened budget cuts and public lambasting if the university failed to place significant effort into outreach and admissions reforms beneficial to minority groups.

Not all saw the urgency. Pister heard the worries within much of the university community. UC was accepting special appropriations and promising what it could not deliver, argued critics. For Pister, improving K-12 education was the new frontier, the land-grant idea revisited. UC could use its research capabilities to delve into K-12 curricular activities and teacher and administrator training. But neither he, nor Atkinson, nor Larry Vanderhof, the chancellor at Davis, perhaps truly knew how enormous the undertaking would be. The cause required lofty goals and rhetoric for a fighting chance. They offered concrete indicators of institutional commitments. But that was the easy part. There were the problems of actually producing research and programs that could influence local schools. Another difficulty was the inherent predilections of the academic community itself.

How to excite and engage faculty in outreach and policy-relevant research related to education?

The focus of lawmakers and state funding on UC perturbed many within the California State University system, not least its president, Charles Reed. The bulk of teacher training and professional development, although historically an important component for UC, was CSU's bailiwick. The fact that lawmakers and Governor Gray Davis concentrated on UC as the conduit for improving the schools and, arguably, neglected CSU's teacher training programs was an affront to many in the system. As noted previously, 55% of UC's new outreach budget from the state was to go to CSU as subgrants for expanding its teacher professional development programs, a total of some $180 million. This flow of funds was not the idea of University of California officials but of Davis who apparently viewed UC as offering some sort of quality-control mechanism. UC dutifully funneled funds to CSU for existing and new outreach programs. Still, this policy generated significant tension between the two four-year segments in the state's public higher education system.

UC and CSU did agree on one thing: California higher education could influence teacher education, support professional development, and increase student interest in and knowledge about how to apply to college. With this agenda in mind and in the context of large-scale shortages of qualified teachers in the state, UC and CSU rushed to build their own outreach programs. By 2000, UC counted 286 "partnership" schools, including seventy-six high schools, most of which were chosen because they ranked in the bottom two quintiles of California schools based on performance measures such as standardized tests. The criteria for picking these schools were cloaked in nonrace-based factors, but the correlation with minority student populations was high. CSU had about 124 partnership high schools of its own. Such a designation qualified a school for special programs intended to improve the skills and professional development of teachers and included various counseling and college preparation programs. Until 2001, however, UC and CSU did not even know which schools they shared under their separate partnership programs.

What was the reaction of teachers and administrators in the public schools to these outreach efforts? School officials and teachers were already in the throes of yet another spate of reforms characterized by new accountability mandates and demands for statewide tests for students and teachers alike. They remained hardened by numerous intervention schemes from outside agencies and regulators. University of California officials and faculty involved in admissions and outreach were warned early on not to orchestrate outreach simply to "cherry-pick" the best and brightest students for recruitment purposes. Outreach should benefit a wide spectrum of students and not be just a recruiting tool for UC. Yet most of the accountability measures and expectations of state lawmakers remained fixed on the goal of increasing the applicant pool to UC and ultimately on the admission of underrepresented groups—particularly at the most selective campuses, UCLA and Berkeley.

As measured by the ambitious goals announced by Atkinson, progress was modest. The university was to double the number of UC-eligible graduates at partner high schools from 1998–1999 to 2003–2004 or increase the UC eligibility rate in these schools by 4%, whichever was greater. But by 2001, approaching this goal appeared a near impossibility; by 2003, budget cuts to outreach programs put success out of reach. There was progress in the overall goals of the outreach effort, focused on "bridging the achievement gap." By 2001, freshman applications to UC were up for African American and Chicano-Latino students, increasing by 15% and 22%, respectively, since 1999—the nadir of the post-209 decline. Transfer student applications also showed increases for these groups: African American and Chicano-Latino student applications were up 20% and 16%, respectively. As a review of the university's outreach efforts since 1997 noted, nearly 40% of Latino and African American students enrolling as freshmen at the university in 2001 participated in one of the university's major outreach programs.[29]

One needs to put these gains in perspective. Increases between 1999 and into the early part of the new century were fueled in part by growth in the number of Chicano-Latino high school graduates. Yet gains also clearly related to outreach programs. Collectively, they generated a sense that the university was determined to recruit and enroll students from disadvantaged backgrounds, even if they did not participate in an outreach program. The review of outreach programs completed in 2001 noted that this message was perhaps the most important net effect of outreach programs.[30] This finding reinforced the argument among proaffirmative-action groups, and some regents, that the university's governing board should rescind SP-1 symbolically, even though doing so would not change California law.

Percentage Plans Revived

Outreach was one response to the end of affirmative action in California and other states. Percentage plans adopted in California, Texas, and Florida were another. By the latter part of the twentieth century, most state universities depended on undergraduate admissions policies that attempted to evaluate and rank student applications with reference to a state's entire pool of high school graduates. Percentage plans attempted to evaluate student academic performance within the context of their local school—a recognition that the quality of schools and the environment they offer for student learning vary. Why not guarantee a fixed percentage of each school's top graduates a place in the state university? It was a concept particularly attractive to law-makers and proaffirmative-action activists.

School-specific percentage plans are, in fact, an old idea, although few contemporary policymakers apparently knew this. Following the 1996 *Hopwood* decision, Texas was the first state to revisit the idea. Proaffirmative-action interests such as the NAACP and the Mexican American Legal Defense Fund (MALDEF) charged that the University of Texas system proved faint supporters of affirmative action. In the midst of defending the university in the *Hopwood* case, the UT board of regents did vote to appeal the Fifth Circuit's *Hopwood* ruling all the way to the Supreme Court. Reflective of a board divided on the merits of race-based admissions, the university's subsequent defense revolved largely around the concept that the inability to use racial considerations in admission put UT at a competitive disadvantage with other universities and colleges nationally. A number of regents stated that their support of an appeal to the Supreme Court was for one purpose: gaining a ruling for or against affirmative action, thus creating a "level playing field" for all public universities.

Governor George Bush seemed to welcome the end of affirmative action. Texas State Attorney General Dan Morales declined to represent UT, saying that he opposed racial considerations and did not think UT could win.[31] When the U.S. Supreme Court upheld the Fifth Circuit's ruling by refusing to hear the case, Morales banned affirmative action not only in admissions but also with regard to financial aid and scholarships at Texas public institutions of higher learning. Within this political environment, Texas adopted a Ten Percent Plan in 1997 for implementation the following year. The initiative came not through the university community but from state legislators in the capital in Austin.

Although lawmakers disagreed on the merits of affirmative action, liberal and conservatives alike sought to mitigate the inevitable decline in minority enrollment, particularly at the flagship campus in Austin. Under the plan developed in the state senate, supported by Governor Bush, and shaped by political action groups such as MALDEF, Texas high school students who graduated in the top 10% of their class were guaranteed a slot at the state public university of their choosing, including the highly selective

University of Texas at Austin and Texas A&M University. Only grades went into figuring a student's class rank; college entrance exam scores were not considered. Legislation provided guidelines to selective public universities for admitting students who did rank in the top 10% of their class. Each institution could consider seventeen other factors in their admissions, including socioeconomic background.[32] Compared to other states, Texas has historically low college-going rates among the traditional college-age cohort. Sponsors of the plan hoped the new law would boost minority higher education enrollments to new highs despite the *Hopwood* ruling.

A similar plan was under consideration at the University of California, in part influenced by the events in Texas. However, the process of policymaking and the scope of the proposed plans proved very different. In Texas, the Ten Percent Plan replaced existing statewide admissions policies, making eligibility totally dependent on student performance at the local level. A subsequent University of Texas report suggested that, after a slow start, the law was boosting minority enrollment—this after UT-Austin, for example, declined in minority enrollment immediately after *Hopwood*.

There were some real political problems with the Texas plan, however. The new admissions regime essentially capped the number of students deemed eligible at a given high school. In affluent areas, there were a significant number of highly talented students who suddenly were excluded from the state's most selective public universities. By 2004, Rick Perry, the new Republican governor, argued for radically reforming the Texas plan. The loudest complaints came from parents of students with high SAT scores who fell short of the top 10% in competitive high schools. It was charged that these students were leaving the state to attend other selective colleges and universities and paying higher tuition rates. "I clearly think it is a problem in the state of Texas when you've got highly qualified young men and women leaving the state of Texas," argued Governor Perry, "because they can't get into the University of Texas." UT President Larry Faulkner essentially agreed: "We're admitting far too high a fraction of the freshman class on the basis of one criterion. And that's not healthy for Texas or this university."[33]

In California, percentage plans were embraced as an additional measure, not as a replacement for statewide criteria. In the case of the University of California, any percentage plan would be the result of the university's own internal decision making. The legal autonomy of the university did not stop lawmakers from trying to inspire reforms. With Texas committed to its 10% plan and lobbied by advocates such as MALDEF, in 1998 California State Senator Teresa Hughes (an African American Democrat from

Los Angeles) offered a bill proposing a 12.5% plan for each high school and reflecting the master plan statewide target. This new method of determining eligibility, argued Hughes, might create a new flow of students from lower performing high schools, often with high percentages of Latino and African American students. Many urban and rural schools sent only one or two students to the University of California; some sent none. If passed, Hughes's bill would not be binding on the university, but it would require the university to offer a measured response.

While Hughes and other legislators held hearings in the fall of 1997 and issued press releases regarding their desire for a percentage plan, the university's academic senate was already in the process of considering its own plan. In 1996, Richard Flacks and Rodolfo Alvarez offered a formal proposal to the academic senate's board of admissions, BOARS. Both were professors of sociology, Flacks at the university's Santa Barbara campus and Alvarez at UCLA. Both had a history of activism dating back to the 1960s. Flacks had been a young professor and a compatriot of Tom Hayden at the University of Michigan. Flacks and Alvarez suggested a revival of the 10% plan or possibly a 6% plan, in part informed by a history of admissions at the University of California.[34] Their argument revolved around two observations.

First, they noted, like Senator Hughes, that a sizable number of high schools sent very few of their graduates to the university. Second, the university's reliance on SAT test scores in determining UC eligibility and for the selection of students at campuses such as Berkeley and UCLA favored students from certain races (Euro-Americans in particular) and upper income families. In their view, the SAT was race biased and UC should simply drop it as a requirement.[35] They also saw a school-based admission policy as a motivator for many schools to improve their curriculum. "Community pressure might mount to have all of the 844 public high schools in California offer the full complement of courses that are required for UC and CSU admissions," argued Alvarez and Flacks in an editorial.[36] In promoting school-specific criteria for admissions, Flacks and Alvarez argued that simply promoting outreach programs could not sufficiently mitigate socioeconomic barriers to UC admissions. A 1997 "eligibility study" by the California Postsecondary Education Commission (CPEC) estimated that the University of California was admitting only 11.1% of the state's top students (just below the statewide target of 12.5%). According to the study, another 9.4% were not eligible because they did not take the battery of standardized tests, in particular the SAT II, required to become UC eligible. For CSU, students needed to take only the SAT I; there was no requirement to take any standardized tests at the community college level. Many students in various parts of the state simply did not aspire to enter the University of California.[37]

The Flacks-Alvarez proposal coalesced with similar ideas floating among other faculty, university analysts, and administrators in the office of the president. The university needed to develop arguments in Sacramento as to why it should or should not develop a percentage plan. President Atkinson proved adept at embracing various reforms and then pushing for them within the senate and ultimately to the regents. He was supportive of some sort of percentage plan. Guided by its chair, Keith Widaman, BOARS began extensive deliberation on a wide range of options for modifying university admissions in the post-Proposition 209 era, supported by a cooperative administrative staff at the office of the president. An analysis conducted by Saul Geiser in the office of student services predicted a significant overall decline in student academic ability if the university abandoned statewide criteria in favor of accepting all students among the top 12.5% of each high school, as proposed by Hughes. There would be a positive increase in underrepresented minorities, but many might find it hard to succeed at the university. A simulation estimated that UC graduation rates would decrease by 6% to 8%.[38]

Adding to the worry of BOARS's members, past statistical trends indicated that students at the margin of UC eligibility who were admitted were those most likely to enroll. Students at the higher end of the freshman eligibility pool tended to apply to other selective institutions and to have more options. In the eyes of Widaman and his committee, the 12.5% plan would create a surge of students whose academic abilities were marginal. Any proposed change, such as a percentage plan, would need to be brought to the university-wide academic senate's executive committee and ultimately to the senate's legislative body, the academic assembly. How would they react to the simulations and effects on the quality of the student body? How would the regents react, including a skeptical Ward Connerly?

Widaman proved a fortuitous choice as chair. A professor of psychology at UC Riverside, his field was psychometrics. He brought an astute understanding of the possible implications of various policy options, including the possible political reactions. In his May 1998 report to the academic assembly, Widaman stated that Senator Hughes's 12.5% plan might result in increases in minority students to UC. It might also increase the enrollment of students from both rural and urban schools with historically low participation rates. However, the negative aspects of the proposal overwhelmed the positive; it was a "well intentioned but poorly thought out alternative."

Why? "A high percentage of students who are not now UC eligible, and hence do not meet minimum academic requirements, would now become eligible. In turn, it appeared a strong likelihood that the number of students matriculating and graduating would also decline." The proposal might also result in new inequities, he stated. High schools that do a good job teaching and preparing students for college and for applying to the university, for example, would have an artificial and arbitrary limit placed on the number of students who could attend a UC campus. This would become the rule irrespective of the talents and achievements of their cohort of graduating seniors.[39] Indeed, this was a problem that eventually created a political backlash to Texas's percentage plan years later.

BOARS was more receptive to the idea of accepting students from the top 4% or 6% of each high school's graduating class, which was a less problematic proposal. Simulations indicated that students would be much more academically prepared than at 10% or 12.5%. The plan would offer a new mechanism for increasing the enrollment of high school graduates from rural and urban schools with historically low participation rates. As Flacks and Alvarez had argued, determining eligibility by high school rank might change the internal culture of schools with high numbers of disadvantaged students, encouraging greater UC involvement in the quality of the curriculum in A-F courses. Simulations also showed, however, that adjusting the definition of UC eligibility in this manner would result in only marginal changes, if any, in the admission of underrepresented groups. This was because the admissions standards would be raised for students who were not ranked in the top 4% to 6%. BOARS would need to adjust the criteria (GPA primarily) for UC eligibility for the remaining students, for example, so that UC remained in compliance with the master plan guidelines of selecting from the top 12.5% statewide. Raising the statewide admissions standards, it was postulated, would have "a disproportionate impact on students of African-American and Latino/Chicano background who did not rank among the top 6 percent of their high school class—students who tended to have lower GPA's in A-F courses and lower test scores."[40]

With pressure on the University of California to initiate some type of reforms in admissions policies, Widaman announced on May 5, 1998, that BOARS would recommend to President Atkinson and the UC board of regents a 4% plan. It would create a new admissions path—eligibility to the UC system determined by "superior academic performance" in the local context of the individual high school. The proposal was dubbed "Eligibility in the Local Context" (ELC). Anticipating criticism by Hughes and others that the ELC proposal had not gone far enough, Widaman testified at a legislative hearing chaired by Senator Hughes that, "Based on the success of the program and of student success at UC in the future, we may wish to [later] alter the percentage of students at each high school who achieve eligibility in this fashion."[41]

School-specific admission plans drew the public criticism of anti-affirmative-action activists. Once again, Regent Connerly was the most visible skeptic. Connerly constantly questioned the intentions of university officials at meetings of the board and in numerous editorials and interviews with the press. He generated his own proposals to ensure adherence to Proposition 209. Connerly wanted the regents to eliminate any questions related to race in a student's application, an item commonly asked by universities on a voluntary basis. Admissions officers, Connerly argued, might use the information in making their admissions decisions in violation of Proposition 209. "I suspect there are a few people who want to use this information in impermissible ways," stated Connerly in the *Los Angeles Times*. BOARS and university officials opposed eliminating any data that helped analyze the effects of admissions changes or the composition of the university's student body. "Let us not bury our heads in the sand and preclude the university administration and the public from knowing which students are seeking an education at the university," wrote thirteen state lawmakers when they learned of the proposal. "It benefits no one to hide from the truth."[42]

University officials offered a compromise, and Regents Connerly and Meredith Khachigian successfully endorsed it for consideration by the board of regents: Although more than 60,000 high school seniors checked a box indicating their race in 1998, the information would be electronically erased from the applications before they reached admissions staff. Four years later, Connerly would dream up yet another proposition banning the collection of racial data by all California government agencies. This became Proposition 54 on an October 2003 statewide ballot and was entitled by Connerly the "racial privacy initiative." It failed to pass.[43]

And what of the ELC plan? Its fate was not clear. As chair of the regents' educational policy committee, the group that would make a recommendation to the full board, Connerly would have a strong voice. With BOARS now making a recommendation, Atkinson embraced the 4% plan and presented it as a formal part of his proposed admissions reforms. On May 15, 1998, ten days after Widaman's announcement of the ELC plan at the hearing chaired by Senator Hughes, BOARS formally presented the 4% plan to the board. Early on, President Atkinson had noted his general support for some form of a percentage plan. "Before we close escrow on this, I think you've got to give us more assurance that quality is not going to be affected," said Connerly. Widaman stated that some two-thirds of the students who made it to the top 4% of their high school class were already eligible under UC's regular admissions criteria, so offering admission to the remaining third would not significantly lower standards. But it would add perhaps between 300 and 700 black and Hispanic students to the pool qualified for admission—a drop in the bucket within a pool of some 40,000 high school students projected to be UC eligible in 2000. ELC would also act as a magnet, drawing students to the idea of meeting UC's regular admissions criteria.[44] The regents proceeded to approve the ELC program in 1998.

Holistic to Comprehensive Review

With the 4% plan established, one more reform was emerging—the notion of "comprehensive review." Shortly after the 1995 decision by the regents to eliminate affirmative action in admissions, the Berkeley campus announced that it wanted to more fully integrate factors such as economic disadvantage, extracurricular and civic engagement, and school-specific criteria in considering applications. Under regental policy, no more than 50% of freshman admissions could include such "holistic" factors. The rest of the pool would be admitted on "academic merit" alone, defined as grades and test scores. The Berkeley campus proposed that the regents remove the 50% restriction. Admitting a class with an array of desirable characteristics is a model most highly selective private universities and colleges have pursued for years. But it requires investing in sufficient staff to allow for more than a perfunctory review of a student's application. If Stanford and Harvard could do it, then why not Berkeley?

Following Berkeley's lead, a university-wide task force jointly chaired by Berkeley Professor Arnold Leiman and Dennis Galligani, associate vice president for student services, generated guidelines for selecting among UC-eligible students in the postaffirmative-action environment. They recommended a general expansion of university selection criteria. Previously, campuses such as Berkeley and UCLA had relied on weighted formulas and carefully reviewed only a fraction of the large inflow of applicants, with the most attention and resources given to studying applications from students at the margin of being accepted or rejected. The task-force report placed emphasis on developing admissions policies and practices that reviewed all applicants using "holistic" criteria "sufficiently broad and varied so that applications from differing backgrounds have the opportunity to evidence qualities in a variety of ways . . ." And they sought new policies that would balance individual merit and the university's larger social contract. "In other words, concern for individual accomplishments and circumstances, as defined by academic or non-academic criteria, may be subordinated to concern for institutional goals," stated their report.[45]

Within the board of regents, the idea was well received among many, yet a majority of the board thought the policy should be restricted to the 50% target.[46] Regent Connerly and others professed a deep worry. The institutional *Zeitgeist*, he argued, remained fixated on issues of race at the cost of academic merit. Lifting the cap would lead to greater administrative discretion in admissions and stealth-like schemes to simply get more underrepresented minorities at the most selective campuses. Any such change would also require amending SP-1, a prospect that Connerly and other regents wanted to avoid. The majority of regents generally agreed. In 1995, the board approved the task force's proposal for holistic review for up to 50% of all freshman applicants, but they would not expand it further.

However, President Atkinson, and in turn the academic senate, looked to revive the proposal beginning in 1999. The composition of the board's membership was changing marginally but with important implications. Democrat Gray Davis succeeded Republican Governor Pete Wilson, and Democrats increased their numbers in the state assembly. Davis appointed a number of new regents. Atkinson considered requesting that the regents revisit the expansion of holistic admissions. Berkeley Chancellor Robert Berdahl believed that the shift would not lower academic standards and insisted that the proposal was not intended as a back door to affirmative action. "We are not about to take race into consideration," he said. "We don't, and we won't."[47]

Helping President Atkinson formulate a formal proposal for the regents was Patrick Hayashi, an associate president who worked closely with the president. As described in a previous chapter, Hayashi had proven an important advisor and confidant to Berkeley Chancellor Ira Michael Heyman during acrimonious debate with the Asian American community over campus admissions in the 1980s. He served on the task force on undergraduate admissions established by Peltason and was soon recruited by Atkinson to help navigate the treacherous post-209 waters. Now he assisted the president in formulating a number of major changes in admissions, including expanding holistic review and later possibly dropping the SAT as a requirement.

By early 2001, Atkinson proposed lifting the 50% limit, repackaging the proposal under a new nomenclature: "comprehensive review," a term suggested by Hayashi. Atkinson felt that *comprehensive review* conjured a better sense of the proposed admissions process. Simultaneously, Atkinson added a second and controversial initiative: The university should reconsider the use of standardized testing in the admissions process and possibly eliminate the SAT I as a requirement. At the same time, a third initiative emerged, proposed by a number of regents with significant political pressure from Sacramento lawmakers: The board was asked to vote on a proposal, forwarded by Regent Judith Hopkins, to rescind its 1995 ban on racial preferences, SP-1. Atkinson and other university administrators did not publicly promote this initiative lest they anger the more conservative members of the board. But it was clear they would welcome the symbolic move of rescinding the regents' policy. SP-1 continued to irk Democratic lawmakers who controlled the assembly, the senate, and the governorship, even if Proposition 209 usurped it.

Although comprehensive review and a reconsideration of the SAT in admissions would have the greatest influence on admissions, the proposal to rescind SP-1 drew the most attention. In the midst of the bargaining for a surge of funds for outreach, incensed Latino lawmakers on key budget committees threatened to cut the university's state funding unless the regents formally ended their ban on racial preferences and altered admissions criteria to those thought more open to nonacademic factors. The regents' 1995 edict, SP-1, however, was largely moot as a policy issue with the passage of Proposition 209 but potent as a signal of the university's commitment to minorities. Some revision to it was also necessary to change the 50% rule.

The May 2001 meeting of the regents proved a huge success for Atkinson. The board voted in principle to expand comprehensive review to all admissions decisions. They also voted to rescind the 1995 policy banning race and ethnicity. All twenty-two regents, including Ward Connerly, voted in favor of rescinding SP-1.[48] Connerly worked with Regent Hopkinson, Lieutenant Governor Cruz Bustamante, and Assembly Speaker Robert Hertzberg to fashion the final language. The university would "seek out and enroll, on each of its campuses, a student body that demonstrates high academic achievement or exceptional personal talent, and that encompasses the broad diversity of backgrounds characteristic of California," stated the regents' new resolution.

After the vote, Connerly explained, "The Latino caucus especially made it very clear [that] if the resolution did not contain what they wanted, our budget would be affected."[49] With the university coping with declines in minority enrollment, particularly at UCLA and Berkeley, Connerly conceded that the affirmative-action ban "may have created the perception that students are not welcomed, and it is time to change that."[50] Connerly also saw another reason for his vote: "We have to move on. We're spending enough energy on this thing that we could light the city of Los Angeles for weeks."[51]

In the headlines of the *Sacramento Bee* the next day, the regents' action was largely seen as a concession to lawmakers and not a principled stand by the board. "Under pressure by lawmakers who threatened budget cuts," wrote *Bee* staff writer Terri Hardy, "University of California regents Wednesday voted to rescind the system's ban on racial preferences and, in a surprise move, called for an end to admissions based on academic criteria alone." Student Regent Odessa Johnson clearly welcomed the pressure from lawmakers. "This is a great day for the students of California and the prospective students—for all the people of California. I wore black today because I hoped I was coming to a funeral."[52] "The welcome mat is back. Hallelujah!" stated Speaker Robert Hertzberg. An Associated Press article stated one motivation. "The board also sought a graceful exit from being in the thick of the national debate on affirmative action," noted reporter Michelle Locke.[53]

In his successful "comprehensive review" proposal, President Atkinson was careful to defer to the academic senate for the ultimate judgment on its viability and worth. The board of regents endorsed the idea of specifically allowing campuses to decide what percentage of their applicants might be reviewed under the policy. But it was up to the academic senate to determine how this would be done, subject to final approval by the board.[54] Activist lawmakers worried about this process. Might the board later reject the senate's proposal? Bustamante and Hertzberg insisted on and were given the university president's promise in writing that comprehensive review, in one form or another, would become operational by fall 2002.

In the immediate aftermath of the board's May meeting in San Francisco, Bustamante spoke with the aid of a bullhorn to a large crowd of protesters gathered outside. He announced the end of the regents' previous 50% rule, saying that if Atkinson and the university did not follow through, "we could drag them into court and win." Connerly and other regents complained of political interference, citing the regents' constitutional autonomy. "It is inappropriate for anyone to threaten" the university in this manner, he explained. The irony was clear. One assemblyman who pushed for comprehensive review and rescinding SP-1 retorted that if one side (namely, Connerly) could play politics with the university, certainly the other side could as well: "If you open the doors of politics, expect politicians to get involved."[55]

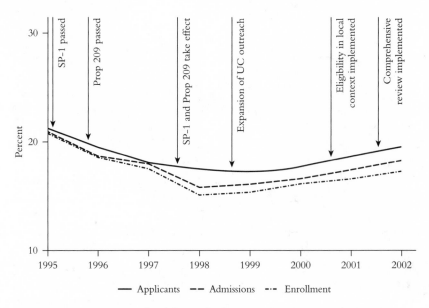

— Applicants   — — Admissions   –·– Enrollment

Figure 8.3.   University of California freshman underrepresented minority applications, admissions, and enrollment and post-Proposition 209 policies: 1995–2002

SOURCE: University of California Office of the President, Enrollment Reports.

The Impact of the New Admissions Regime

A look at admissions and enrollment trends at the University of California over the last decade or so helps assess the effectiveness of post SP-1 shifts in admissions policies. As discussed previously, in the immediate aftermath of the regents' affirmative-action decision, applications by underrepresented minorities dropped from 21.1% of all freshman applicants in 1995 to a low of 17.5% by 1998 (see Figure 8.3). Admissions and actual enrollment of these students also declined precipitously. Total underrepresented freshman enrollment fell from 20.8% to 15.1%.[56]

Yet SP-1 and Proposition 209 did not go into effect until the fall 1998 admissions cycle. As critics of the regents' action predicted, the perception by minority populations of a reduced commitment to recruit and enroll African Americans and Latinos appears to have been a major factor for explaining the downturn in applications and in turn enrollment.

The expansion of outreach efforts, followed by the adoption of Eligibility in the Local Context, and then comprehensive review each appear to have contributed to a partial recovery. By 2002, applications to the University of California by underrepresented groups increased to 19.7%, admissions to 18.4%, and actual enrollment to 17.4%. These percentages still lagged behind 1995 figures. Further, California's population continued to grow, and the percentage of minority students graduating from the state's public high schools swelled. In 1995, some 78,350 African Americans, Latinos, and Native Americans graduated from California's public high schools; in 2002, that number grew to nearly 145,600.

Hence, the disparity between the ethnic and racial composition of the state's high school graduates and university enrollment grew despite the efforts of university officials. Comprehensive review appears as well to have been a marginal influence in promoting the admissions and enrollment of first-generation college students and students from low-income families and low-performing schools (see Table 8.1). And reflecting previous simulations of the impact of various alternative admissions processes, the percentage of students from underrepresented minority groups admitted to UC between 2001 and 2003 grew only slightly. Berkeley and UCLA had marginal increases; San Diego had the largest, yet still a meager jump: from 11.1% to 14.5%.[57]

There are other factors to consider. For one, differences between the quality of high schools in rich and poor neighborhoods have grown, as noted previously. Competition is another important factor. The University of California's ability to enroll admitted underrepresented students in the top third of the applicant pool slipped. In 1999, 55.7% of admitted underrepresented students who placed in the top third of UC applicants accepted the university's admission offer. In 2002, this figure was only 50.1%. Berkeley and UCLA, in particular, appeared to be losing a significant number of these high-achieving minority students. Why? Among African Americans, one reason appears to be the perceived lack of a critical mass of similar minority high achievers. But perhaps most important is the highly competitive market for these students. One analysis showed that in 1999, some 16% of high-achieving underrepresented admits to UC chose to attend private selective institutions; by 2002, this figure had increased to nearly 24%.[58]

Selective private colleges and universities, most with sizable endowments, are now placing significant resources into recruiting this relatively limited pool of minority students, offering not only race-based scholarships but also the advantages of smaller classes and personal attention that a Berkeley and UCLA can no longer match. Again reflecting the vast differences in autonomy and market advantage between private institutions and public, Stanford and Harvard could still offer scholarships tailored to, for example, talented African Americans; Berkeley and UCLA

Table 8.1

California underrepresented high school graduates and University of California enrollment by admission status: 1994–2002

	1994	1995	1996	1997	1998	1999	2000	2001	2002
Underrepresented CA HS Grads	38.3%	38.7%	39.1%	39.4%	40.2%	40.7%	40.9%	41.8%	42.8%
Underrepresented UC Minorities	20.7%	20.8%	18.4%	17.5%	15.1%	15.4%	16.2%	16.7%	17.4%
First-Generation College	32.2%	31.4%	30.6%	29.8%	28.9%	30.7%	30.5%	31.0%	31.5%
Low Family Income	23.8%	22.6%	21.0%	20.5%	18.7%	18.9%	19.6%	18.9%	18.9%
From Low-Performing Schools	na	na	na	na	16.6%	17.3%	18.0%	17.0%	18.7%
California Rural Students	5.7%	6.1%	6.6%	7.2%	7.5%	7.9%	7.8%	8.0%	8.0%
California Urban Students	39.3%	39.3%	38.6%	38.0%	37.3%	37.8%	37.5%	37.7%	38.4%
California Suburban Students	47.7%	48.4%	49.3%	47.8%	47.9%	47.4%	48.4%	48.2%	48.1%
ELC Students	na	na	na	na	na	na	na	18.2%	20.9%
Outreach Participants	na	na	na	na	9.5%	10.3%	11.0%	13.4%	na

SOURCE: *Undergraduate Access to the University of California After the Elimination of Race-Conscious Policies*, University of California Office of the President, Student Academic Services, March 2003; California Department of Finance, High School Graduates By Ethnicity, 2004 Series.

could not. In California, Proposition 209 had no legal ramifications for Stanford.

In the midst of analyzing the marginal influence of the university's reformed admissions policies and practices, a question remained: What options were potentially left? University officials had placed significant political capital in the outreach programs, in launching the ELC program and comprehensive review, and in orchestrating the symbolic end of SP-1. In essence, the university had returned to a more dynamic admissions process that was reminiscent of the pre-1960s admission regime with its various alternative paths to the university's entrance gate. What remained was another familiar area of controversy: standardized tests.

Chapter 9

The Second Aftermath:
President Atkinson Versus the SAT

Contending that standardized college tests have distorted the way young people learn and worsened educational inequities, the president of the University of California is proposing an end to the use of the SAT's as a requirement for admissions to the state university he oversees, one of the largest and most prestigious.

— *The New York Times*, February 2001

In the fall of 2004, the burgeoning test-preparation industry began to warn students and their parents that planned revisions to the SAT I would raise the stakes for getting into a prestigious college or university. The new test's debut was set for March 2005. "As you may have noticed, this isn't your parents' SAT," noted an advertisement by one large test-prep company. One could only become "Harvard material" if one spent a sizable sum to be formally prepared. The new test is "longer, harder, and with a new Writing section that is much more demanding than the SAT versions of the previous years." It is downright "risky to rely on yourself only to cover all the pitfalls throughout the test." Test preparation offered by professionals will decidedly "help you overcome your weaknesses (be they time management, organization experience or specific skills)."

After years of defending the SAT against data that showed the test is, at best, a marginal tool for predicting the collegiate success of students at selective institutions, the Educational Testing Service, its purveyor, decided to make the first significant modification in its content in decades. Some fifteen years earlier, in 1990, ETS did make some modifications to the SAT. They recalibrated the scoring system but made only minor modifications in the content of what was once billed as a scholastic aptitude test. (ETS no longer uses the full title but retains the SAT moniker.) And to compete with the ACT, which offers subject-specific tests, they created the SAT II.

Why change the highly successful SAT I, which dominates the admissions market? The reason was the activism of one major university, the University of California, and in particular, the complaints of its president, Richard C. Atkinson. Atkinson had an unusual fascination with standardized tests. As a graduate student at Indiana University and then as a faculty member at Stanford, Atkinson focused his research on psychometrics—the effort to quantify and assess the process of learning. As a young cognitive psychologist at Stanford, he published works entitled "Adaptive Instructional Systems," "Problems in Mathematical Learning Theory with Solutions," and "A Mnemonic Method for the Acquisition of a Second-Language Vocabulary." At one time, he was a visiting scholar at Educational Testing Service (ETS). He left Stanford to take the position of associate director of the National Science Foundation and later became its director. Then in 1980, he accepted the position of chancellor at the University of California's up-and-coming campus at San Diego, now a major hub for science and technology centers that serves as a catalyst for numerous computer and biotechnology businesses.

During his time as chancellor, Atkinson wondered privately about the appropriate use of the SAT, but he made no public statements even as it grew as a factor in admissions at Berkeley, UCLA, and eventually, San Diego. After becoming president of the University of California in 1995 and during dinner conversations with his friend Arnie Leiman, a fellow psychometrician, professor at Berkeley, and a former chair of the academic senate's executive committee, Atkinson professed to taking the SAT occasionally.

Atkinson attended the University of Chicago as an undergraduate at a time when the university did not require the test. Now, as president of the largest multicampus research university in the United States, he wanted to personally see how it was written, what it tested, and what biases it might contain. He also found the mental exercise of the test a form of entertainment. His academic background, curiosity, and position as the president of the largest and arguably most prestigious system of research universities put him in a unique position to question and reevaluate the uses of testing in admissions.

A First Look

With the shock of SP-1, University of California officials and faculty began to seriously rethink the use of the SAT and similar standardized tests, such as the ACT. Atkinson's latent interest would soon blossom. Keith Widaman, like Atkinson also a psychometrician, was chair of BOARS in 1998. Study after study showed that the SAT was, at worst, culturally and racially biased and, at best, reflective of gross differences in the schooling and opportunities for learning among the nation's demographically diverse population. African Americans and other minority groups, with the important caveat of Asian Americans, consistently scored lower than white students. A report by the Educational Testing Service reiterated long-known data. The percentage of African Americans scoring above 500 points on the SAT I in math, for example, was a mere 21%; for Mexican Americans, it was 35%; and for Euro-Americans and Asian Americans, it was 62% and 70%, respectively.[1]

Latino interest groups lobbied hard for the university to drop the test. In the post-Proposition 209 era, it was a symbol of exclusion. Eugene Garcia, the dean of Berkeley's School of Education, helped produce a number of reports that insisted the university end the SAT and the ACT as a factor in admissions. Representing the Latino Eligibility Task Force, Garcia made a presentation to BOARS arguing vehemently that test scores were part of the problem for expanding underrepresented minority enrollment. He alleged the tests were racist; UC should abandon their use in any form. The frustration with the regents' edict to end affirmative action, and then Proposition 209, infuriated a significant cadre of faculty, political activists, and lawmakers. For Garcia and others, it seemed self-evident that dropping standardized scores would offer a significant mitigation. "We have a devastating disjuncture and California Latinos are concluding: Enough is Enough," stated the task force report. "Things cannot remain the way they are. Ya basta." Without major reforms to admissions, they claimed that the "viability of the University of California" was in question.[2]

Garcia's proselytizing was not particularly well received by the members of BOARS and, in particular, by its chair. The pleas of proaffirmative-action groups were often tinged by oblique threats, empowered by the gathering political strength of the fast-growing Latino population and lawmakers. Garcia reported on a study conducted by the Latino Task Force that "Eliminating the SAT requirement would greatly expand Latino student eligibility . . ."[3] Widaman knew differently. Ending the use of the SAT in admissions at UC was no panacea for underrepresented minorities. The data Widaman analyzed showed that it would only marginally alter the eligibility rate of minority students. Garcia's claim was exaggerated, and the task force study was self-serving. UC's "eligibility index," the sliding scale of required GPA in required courses and required test scores to identify university eligibility, was and remained heavily weighted toward grades.

A student needed to achieve a GPA of 3.3 or higher to be eligible for the university. They needed to take the SAT and three subject-based tests, but the scores where inconsequential. Over 91% of the students applying to the university became eligible in this manner. Those with a GPA between 2.82 and 3.29 in required courses also needed to achieve a minimal combined verbal and math SAT score determined by the sliding scale. Students could also take the ACT instead of the SAT, and their score would be calibrated accordingly. But most college-bound students in California took the SAT. As discussed in previous chapters, ETS had successfully cornered the market in California and most western states by the late 1960s. At UC, the lower the GPA, the higher the required standardized test scores. Only 8% became eligible under this category. A small percentage, fewer than one-half of 1%, became eligible simply by achieving high standardized test scores.[4]

A university-generated study that included Widaman as a coauthor concluded that dropping the test would initially enlarge the pool of students, including underrepresented groups. But the university would make other adjustments to remain in the 12.5% pool outlined in California's master plan. The university would then need to raise the required GPA in required courses to nearly 3.7, eliminating most of the gains in underrepresented groups. Latinos and African Americans would not fare well under this new system unless accompanied by other reforms. The variables were many and complicated, and for Widaman, additional research was essential.[5]

Campuses such as Berkeley also depended on testing as a means to help rationalize their admissions process and deal with some 35,000 freshman applications. Perhaps even more important was the culture of the institution, and in particular, the faculty, which placed significant faith in tests as a marker of the quality of the student body. That faith was shared by a larger public, and by the 1980s, it emerged in a new form: commercial rankings of institutions, such as *U.S. News and World Report*, which leaned heavily on test scores as a proxy for the quality of a college or university.

A number of high-quality undergraduate colleges, such as Bates, Bard, Connecticut College, and Bowdoin made great fanfare of their choice to drop the SAT and the ACT as requirements for admissions. But no large and highly selective public or private university had followed suit. These institutions clung to test scores. There were other big political concerns around dropping the test at the University of California. A number of key regents who supported SP-1 and Proposition 209 would likely view ending the use of standardized testing as a ploy, part of a perceived stream of ploys to somehow reincorporate racial criteria.

With the wide disparity in the quality of California's schools, Widaman and other members of BOARS were reluctant to give up standardized testing. Such tests remained the one nationwide measure for student abilities, a way to normalize grading practices that varied significantly from school to school. As he stated before legislators and the board of regents, "Simply eliminating the SAT and other standardized tests altogether . . . would pose several major problems, and despite the claims of some would not improve student diversity at the University."[6] Not the least would be the political battle it would spawn within the board.

The 4% plan, or what was called Eligibility in the Local Context, was a compromise that appeared to have minimal influence on the quality of the UC eligibility pool and could be argued as within the bounds of the regents' policy barring race and ethnicity in the admissions process. Indeed, and in part to balance out possible effects of the ELC program and to keep to the 12.5% master plan target, BOARS recommended increased dependence on the testing. For students selected on statewide criteria, the board planned to require a minimum score in the SAT I and three SAT II subject-area tests (previously, students only needed to take the SAT I if they achieved a GPA of 3.3 or higher). They also planned to give more weight to the SAT II.[7]

Yet there were three festering reasons the University of California would soon take a hard look at dropping the SAT I. First, standardized tests, and in particular, the SAT I, long promoted by the ETS as an aptitude test, provided virtually no additional information on a student's future academic success at the University of California. In the post-Proposition 209 world, UC studies showed that grades provided the best single indicator of academic achievement, as judged by the academic performance of students during their freshman year. And a combination of grades and subject-area tests provided the best indicator—if marginally.[8] Similar studies conducted by BOARS in the early 1960s, as discussed in previous chapters, had come to the same conclusion. Curiously, university officials were ignorant of these earlier research efforts and the extensive debates on the negative and positive policy implications of using test scores in the admissions process. Such "validity" studies, then and now, focus on the freshman year, when the curriculum is generally more uniform for students.

A second reason for dropping the test related to an old question: Was the SAT I truly a measure of the innate mental abilities of a student? President Atkinson thought that such abilities are probably not measurable. "Few scientists who have considered these matters seriously would argue that aptitude tests like the SAT I," stated Atkinson at a conference on standardized testing, "provide a true measure of intellectual abilities. Nonetheless, the SAT I is widely regarded as a test of basic mental ability that can give us a picture of a student's academic promise." Atkinson thought the test, and in particular, the verbal component of the SAT I, a more culturally biased version of the IQ test, dominated by questionable word analogies.[9]

A third reason for dropping the SAT I was more philosophical. Why should a public university require the SAT or any other test that did not actually test the knowledge of a student in subjects required by the university? Atkinson was not against tests. However, "We should use standardized tests that have a demonstrable relationship to the specific subjects taught in high schools. This would benefit students because much time is currently wasted in and outside the classroom prepping students for the SAT I; the time would be better spent on learning American history and geometry."[10] By requiring the SAT I for admissions, the University of California sent a powerful message to schools and students to prepare for a test. Yet it offered limited value for the institution or for the student—except as a tool for arbitrarily culling student admissions. Atkinson recalled one inspiration for his subsequent battle with ETS. He visited an upscale private school in Florida where twelve-year-olds were studying analogies in preparation for the SAT I. By requiring the SAT, the university was adversely influencing the curriculum of California's schools. There were also obvious inequities generated by requiring such a test.

The College Board and ETS long have insisted that one could not "teach to the test." Because it gauged aptitude, ETS claimed there should be no invidious influence on the high school curriculum and what students studied. Yet as standardized tests became an increasingly significant tool in admissions, a private industry arose to prepare candidates hoping to apply successfully to selective institutions. Kaplan, the Princeton Review, and Sylvan Learning Systems are three large enterprises offering test preparation services; all are major corporations traded on the New York Stock exchange. Students from upper income families are the primary clients, those who can afford an array of services, including private tutoring, classes, and online programs. Costs can range from $400 to $5,000, and even higher. Kaplan and the Princeton Review claimed they could raise a student's SAT I score by one hundred points or more out of a possible total of 1,600. In 2000, some 150,000 students enrolled in such programs, generating more than $100 million in revenues.

In the immediate post-Proposition 209 period, BOARS considered dropping the SAT I as a requirement for admissions while retaining subject-based tests. But nothing came of it. Instead, energy was spent on discussing new outreach programs, developing percentage plans, and designing the university's new comprehensive review process. By early 2001, however, Atkinson chose a national venue to discuss the merit of the SAT.

Starting a Controversy

In February 2001, Atkinson gave the keynote address at the eighty-third annual meeting of the American Council on Education (ACE). The ACE meeting was held in the nation's capital, and Atkinson made his argument: The higher education community needed to "rethink" the use of the SAT. He announced that the University of California might drop the SAT I altogether. *The Washington Post* and *The New York Times* obtained an advance copy of his prepared talk and, the day before his appearance at ACE, offered excerpts and the initial reactions of a wide variety of higher education leaders.

Before a large crowd of higher education leaders and administrators at ACE, Atkinson pondered "the appropriateness of the SAT in college admissions." "Many students spend a great deal of time preparing for the SAT," he noted. "But students are not the only ones affected. Teachers, knowing that they will be judged by the scores their students achieve, are under pressure to teach to the test. College admissions officers are under pressure to increase the SAT scores of each entering class. They know that their president, faculty, and alumni pay attention to how scores affect their standing in college rankings . . . and some parents go to great lengths to help their children score high."[11] The SAT and AP courses were all part of the "educational arms race," Atkinson complained, characterized by students and their families seeking every advantage to gain entrance to selective colleges and universities. But how did the SAT I in particular fit the needs of the University of California? What were the disproportionate effects on disadvantaged groups?

Prior to his speech, Atkinson requested that UC's academic senate, and BOARS in particular, consider eliminating the SAT, while keeping the SAT II and ACT tests (both subject-based exams), or possibly develop or adopt a new test built on the curriculum offered in California's high schools. This last option was not unrealistic. The vast majority of California high school graduates who go on to college do so in their home state. Only about 8% travel to another state to attend college. Most states retain their native cohort of high school graduates who then attend college. Nationally, only about 15% of students leave their home state to attend college.

Developing a new test, however, also posed significant difficulties. The process would be long and undoubtedly fraught with political fighting over content and design. Atkinson was not particularly concerned about the bumpy road to such a solution. There was a matter of principle. At a minimum, he stated, the university, and the senate, should "require only standardized tests that assess the mastery of specific subject areas, rather than undefined notions of 'aptitude' or 'intelligence.'" In a later article in *The Presidency*, a publication of the ACE, Atkinson charged that an "overemphasis on test scores hurts all involved, especially students."[12]

The Educational Testing Service was quick to respond. Kurt M. Landgraf, president of ETS, insisted that the "SAT I is too valuable a tool for any college or university to discard." Reiterating earlier ETS themes in defense of the test, the real issue, Landgraf stated, "is not test use"; it is "test misuse." Universities, high schools, and students and their parents had falsely created the "hype and hysteria swirling around SAT scores, which is fueled by almost everyone except the sponsor and administrator of the test." Relying only on subject tests such as the SAT II, concluded Landgraf, "would not work. As valid and important as they are, the curriculum-based tests simply do not measure the same set of critical reasoning skills assessed by the SAT I."[13] Gaston Caperton, president of the College Board, argued that nothing could replace the SAT: "It is a national standard that cuts across state lines, and it really measures high achievement."[14] He called Atkinson's threat to drop the test "a mistake." The problem was not the test. Differential tests scores reflected "unfairness in our educational system. It is urgent that we focus our energy on raising standards for everyone, rather than on eliminating tools that help reveal unequal educational opportunities."[15]

The prospect of the University of California dropping the SAT I, and possibly the SAT II if it generated its own test, would be a significant blow to ETS and the College Board. With the largest population in the United States, California represents the single largest testing market. Some 11.4% of all those taking the SAT I in the United States were in the state. Californians constituted 34.4% of all SAT II takers, and combined with AP exams administered by ETS, they generated approximately $20 million in revenue for the College Board.[16]

If UC were to drop the test, others in the state might also do so. The California State University system, with similar course requirements for admissions purposefully coordinated with UC's requirements, would likely follow suit. Although many Californians would still take the SAT I—particularly more affluent students considering private institutions or other colleges and universities outside the state—the number of those taking the test would undoubtedly fall significantly. Revenues might marginally increase if UC required more subject-area tests offered by the SAT II. They required three subject tests, and there was discussion of expanding that to five if the SAT I was abandoned. But that would not make up for the market loss of the SAT I. And if the largest land-grant university in the country actually abandoned the SAT I, it would surely start a movement in other states.

Shortly after Atkinson's speech, Ward Connerly argued against dropping the SAT I at the University of California. "While Atkinson downplays the immediate effects of this policy change on racial 'minorities' in 'majority-minority' California," wrote the regent in an opinion piece, "the bottom line effect for 'underrepresented' groups is too often the driving force for such calls for change." Atkinson and other university officials, he noted, "won't admit it publicly, but a considerable number of race-preference advocates hold the following disgraceful position: Black and Latino students are incapable of mastering aptitude tests and, therefore, such tests should be abandoned." Connerly accurately noted that dropping the test, despite common perceptions, could actually reduce the competitive position of some underrepresented groups. Their GPA tended to be lower, on average. But the stealth plan of university officials, he and other critics insisted, was to expand the importance of subject-area tests. That would likely benefit multilingual students like Latinos. Most if not all would take Spanish as one of their subject-area tests and, of course, score extremely high.[17]

Connerly decried a "constant whittling away of academic merit." Administrators were pushing an array of strategies to achieve this, including a "misery index that emphasizes obstacles over achievement."[18] The only purpose of dropping the SAT and the move to comprehensive review admissions were part of a larger invidious plot. Other critics agreed. "Texas and California show what occurs when educators and politicians committed to 'diversity' lose in court or at the polls," argued Jack Citrin, a professor of political science at Berkeley. Two years earlier, Citrin had quit Berkeley's admissions committee in frustration. The majority of the committee and Berkeley's administrative staff still seemed obsessed with finding ways to increase minority admissions by hook or crook. The reasons were twofold: One was the constant pressure of racial interest groups and their supporters in the legislature. The other was the persistent administrative culture that placed greater value on race than on academic standards. In Citrin's view, Atkinson, other university administrators, and complicit faculty serving in the senate wanted to lower standards, "first by expanding the pool of high school students eligible for the more selective public universities, and then by reducing the use of objective measures of ability such as standardized tests." In California, continued Citrin, "the Latino caucus bluntly told the University that more of 'our people' at Berkeley and UCLA is the price of budgetary support."[19]

The College Board Responds

Observers of American higher education wondered about Atkinson's motives. Was Atkinson's proposal to "rethink" the use of the SAT an attempted end run around Proposition 209? Was it an attempt to prompt real reform in university admissions? Was it a philosophical statement against aptitude tests? Or was it simply political grandstanding—a vehicle to gain political currency with a powerful Latino caucus in California and gain national headlines but with no real prospect of instituting change at the University of California? There is no doubt that Atkinson's proposal to drop the SAT I did relate to political circumstances, but it also derived from university analysis and a conviction that there are major problems with the design and use of standardized tests. The two motivations were not mutually exclusive.

Pat Hayashi, Atkinson's special assistant, a veteran of UC's admissions wars, and a member of the College Board, approached ETS and the College Board prior to Atkinson's speech in Washington. Armed with data that indicated the SAT I offered no additional predictive value at the University of California, he asked if ETS might assist UC in developing a new test. The initial reaction of the College Board and ETS was negative. But the resolve of Atkinson and the University of California to take a hard look at the existing standardized testing program seemed real enough to eventually force the board to rethink its initial resistance.

The anxiety bred by the SAT and similar tests, and Atkinson's plea, made good press. Controversy regarding the test continued to generate national headlines. A feature story in *Time* magazine was one result, this at a time when Bush's poor academic record at Yale was generating its own cycle of news. "Usually one side says the SAT should die because it's racist; the other says it should flourish because it maintains standards," wrote reporter John Cloud. Yet those that criticized the "aptitude" test seemed to make little headway; indeed, Cloud thought them largely pointless, "since the number of SAT takers has increased virtually every year since Pearl Harbor."[20]

Educators had long known the "rap sheet on the SAT," noted Peter Sacks in an article in the *Nation*. "Since its inception, the SAT has become among the most scrutinized and controversial of standardized tests.

And yet, the exam—and the mental testing culture that has sustained it
in the United States—has been remarkably impervious to the attacks on
it over the years." But finally, Sacks postulated, "the SAT suffered a body
blow when the president of the University of California system proposed
dumping the exam." It might not lead to a wholesale defection from the
SAT; yet Atkinson's announcement was far-reaching and "legitimized open
discussion of a heretofore taboo subject for large and selective universities:
whether they (and society) would be better off without the test."[21]

In making his pitch to regents, lawmakers, and the press, Atkinson told
anecdotal stories that highlighted the negative influence of the SAT. He
knew of attorneys, businesspeople, engineers, and academics who at one
time scored "less-than-brilliant" SAT scores yet went on to brilliant careers,
including a member of the National Academy of Sciences. Their low scores
had proven an obstacle at one time, limiting their choice of what college
they could attend. Many felt a personal stigma. A potential employer asked
for a candidate's disappointing test scores more than a decade after he had
proven himself as a professional in his field. "Clearly, the SAT strikes a deep
chord in the national psyche," observed Atkinson.[22]

Although making national headlines and drawing wide praise and criticism, Atkinson's proposal still needed a hearing first among the faculty of
the University of California's academic senate and then the regents. The
chair of the academic council, Michael Cowan, a professor of American
studies at UC Santa Cruz, predicted that faculty would likely embrace
the president's goals but would need to look at the alternatives carefully.
"There is no question that first and foremost in the faculty's mind will be
to do nothing that reduces quality."[23]

In the first months of 2001, BOARS and university analysts began to
look harder at the predictive powers of the SAT and other tests and to
explore Atkinson's proposal. By the summer, Atkinson was presenting additional evidence of the limitations of the SAT. Before a special hearing
of the California Postsecondary Education Commission in Sacramento in
June 2001, he displayed the predictive power of grades, test scores, and
various combinations of the two. Warren Fox, the director of the California Postsecondary Education Commission, orchestrated a two-day meeting
at the state capital that featured both Atkinson and College Board President
Gaston Caperton, but Fox had difficulty getting them both scheduled in
Sacramento on the same day.

The University of California was arguably a perfect laboratory for analyzing the usefulness of standardized tests. It was the largest multicampus
research system in the country, with university-wide admissions standards.

TABLE 9.1
Explained variance in UC first-year GPA:
Fall 1996–Fall 1999

Predictive Variables	Percentage Explained Variance
High School GPA	14.5
SAT I	12.8
SAT II	15.3
SAT I and II	15.6
High School GPA + SAT I	19.7
High School GPA + SAT II	21.1
High School GPA + SAT I + SAT II	21.1

SOURCE: California Postsecondary Education Commission, *Examining Standardized Testing in the Context of University Admissions: A Panel Discussion* (Sacramento: California Postsecondary Education Commission, August 2001).

Since the late 1970s, the university required both the SAT I and II or the ACT, with most students taking the two ETS products. In assessing the college success of some 82,000 first-time freshmen entering a UC campus between 1996 and 1999, Atkinson explained that alone or in combination with high school grades in required courses, the SAT I "adds nothing to the admissions process." Grades and the SAT II offered virtually the same predictive value, about 21% of the explained variance (see Table 9.1). Why require both? Why require the SAT II over the SAT I, or vice versa?

Atkinson's answer: The SAT II and all subject-based tests, including the ACT, were better and, therefore, the SAT I was expendable. In principle, he reiterated, the University of California should only require tests that test a student's knowledge in subjects required by the university. By doing so, he argued, "We will be encouraging students to spend time on coursework rather than focusing on things like verbal analogies that are on the SAT I." And to the charge that his advocacy for achievement tests was simply to devise ways around Proposition 209, UC analysis showed that the change would have little influence on increasing underrepresented minorities.[24] In Atkinson's view, and that of his advisors such as Pat Hayashi, the philosophical, indeed moral, argument of the link between required subject matter and admissions criteria was their key argument. It was the principle of the thing.

Literally hundreds of studies conducted or sponsored by the College Board showed the SAT was an important predictor of success in college. A report sponsored by the board with results published in 2000 claimed that all of the past "validity studies consistently find that high school grades and SAT scores together are substantial and significant predictors of achievement in college."[25] Yet the predictive value of the SAT I, or grades for that matter, was least meaningful in the most selective institutions and more powerful in less selective institutions. Most important for Atkinson and university officials was the question of whether the SAT I was a better predictor when combined with grades than the SAT II. There were many studies on the SAT I, but as a groundbreaking analysis by Saul Geiser and Roger Studley explained, there were few that examined the predictive power of achievement tests, such as the SAT II and the ACT battery of tests.

Atkinson's presentation in Sacramento relied on Geiser and Studley's analysis. SAT I scores "add very little, if any, incremental power in predicting UC freshman grades *after* SAT II scores and High School GPA are taken into account," they explained. When socioeconomic factors were included in the analysis, "the predictive weights for both the SAT II and High School GPA are undiminished (and in fact increase slightly)." SAT I scores, however, were more sensitive to socioeconomic factors, with upper income groups consistently scoring higher.[26] The findings further empowered Atkinson and helped to hone his message. In reality, there was only a marginal difference in the sensitivity of the two tests.[27] At first, Atkinson had fixated on the claim that the SAT II was a better predictor. But follow-up analysis showed that there really was no substantial difference.[28] The most powerful theme was the appropriateness of using subject-based tests.

Gaston Caperton appeared the next day at the hearing, never crossing paths with Atkinson. Caperton was a former two-term governor of West Virginia, leaving office in 1996. The following year, he taught as a fellow at the John F. Kennedy Institute of Politics at Harvard. He then moved to Columbia University, where he founded, managed, and taught at the Institute on Education and Government. He was hired by the College Board in 1999 in part to help defend the SAT and to expand its markets. In this venture, he revamped the organization of the College Board, replacing an older cadre of staff with a more entrepreneurial group of employees. Charges that the SAT perpetuated and promoted inequities in admissions prompted Caperton to develop a campaign to alter this perception. The board established showcase college-preparatory programs in low-income schools to help in this cause.

Atkinson's attack on the SAT was, obviously, not welcomed. Since Atkinson's speech before the ACE, the College Board and ETS were sure to appear as often as possible at any and all public forums on the testing in California, particularly if Atkinson or other UC officials planned to participate. As an experienced politician, Caperton recognized that the board needed to respond to every criticism. What were Atkinson's motives and end game? This was not clear to Caperton. And in fact, Atkinson's criticism of the SAT and what it might eventually lead to was not entirely clear to Atkinson himself or his immediate group of advisors. He was feeling his way, often surprised by how much attention he received. The diffuse authority in the University of California, with a tradition of shared governance with faculty, their academic senate, and at times contentious governor board, also made any proposal to drop the SAT I precarious. But the fluid nature of Atkinson's criticism and his general lack of authority over admission were not perhaps entirely clear to Caperton.

At the two-day hearing in Sacramento, Atkinson talked of the need to develop a new test. The next day, Caperton reiterated that the SAT I was not culturally or racially biased. "Dropping the SAT I may be politically smart, but it won't change anything." Repeating his mantra, the real challenge, noted Caperton, was equity in the schools. Caperton pointed out that the UC president "didn't say how much it could cost to build a new test . . . He didn't say how a new test would be a better predictor and better tool for the admission process."[29] When it was over, the press rushed to interview Caperton. But Caperton instead pulled Warren Fox aside and quickly departed for the sanctuary of a local bar. He asked Fox what Atkinson intentions were.[30]

At a conference sponsored by the University of California's academic senate on the SAT and held at the UC Santa Barbara campus in November 2001, Atkinson and Caperton again appeared. Each reiterated their seemingly irreconcilable themes. "University of California President Richard Atkinson is gradually becoming one of those rare figures in higher education," wrote *Sacramento Bee* columnist Peter Schrag, "a university president who, maybe by accident, maybe by design, has grown into a national force for educational innovation and social policy."[31] Caperton and the College Board said publicly that they had no plans to change the most successful standardized test ever invented. Behind closed doors, however, the College Board and ETS were discussing with University of California officials on how the SAT I might be modified or if they might be contracted to create a new test. It was all a preliminary discussion. UC officials explained that they wanted to keep talking with ETS and keep their options open. At the same time, BOARS announced plans to bring a proposal for dropping the SAT I in spring 2005 to the president and eventually to the regents.

The largest future market for the SAT I was in Europe and possibly Asia. The SAT I was marketed as a test that measures general aptitude that cuts across cultures. With continued controversy regarding England's admissions system—"A-Level" exams reeking of the nation's old class system—Caperton would soon be selling the SAT to those who would listen in London. How might the College Board retain its market for the SAT in California? Creating a California-based achievement exam would erode the board's ability to sell the SAT nationally and internationally.

Caperton and his colleagues at ETS began a discussion on a possible modification to the SAT I, bent on satisfying or eroding Atkinson's complaints. ETS had earlier debated possible revisions to its hallmark test. In 1990, a blue-ribbon commission established by the board produced the report "Beyond Prediction." Four years later, three recommendations were incorporated into the SAT I: elimination of antonyms in the verbal section of the test, addition of an open-ended response for a few select questions, and allowing students to use a calculator in completing the math portion. But one suggestion was rejected: the addition of a writing test. This would require the development of a quantifiable process for grading the written portion and add significant costs that would be passed on to those taking the test—already about $75.

By April 2002, a little over a year after Atkinson's ACE speech, the College Board announced it was changing the SAT. The test would now include a new written section. Modifications were made to the verbal section to eliminate analogies and to assess "reading for understanding," and the test now had a greater emphasis on "mathematical problem solving." This included the introduction of math questions that were modeled on "real-life situations." The best preparation for the new SAT, stated the board, was rigorous courses, implying that test-preparation courses were not a route for improved scores. The hope was that these changes would satisfy the University of California and counteract the increasingly negative press. The new test was so innovative, stated the board, schools and teachers should teach to the test. Another *Time* magazine cover story emphasized this point: "Caperton's ambitious agenda for the big test [has] launched another great social experiment . . . the idea is that the test's rigorous new curricular demands will lift all boats—that all schools will improve because they want their students to do well on the test."[32]

The College Board stated that the changes would go into effect in March 2005. In public announcements and in subsequent print materials on the SAT I, the board emphasized that the new and improved SAT was simply part of the board's normal process of having the test evolve "along with educational and social practices and innovations."[33] "The current SAT I is the most rigorously and well-researched test in the world," stated Caperton in a College Board press release, "and the new SAT I will only improve the test's current strengths by placing the highest possible emphasis on the most important college success skills—reading and mathematics, and, now, writing."[34]

The College Board portrayed the new SAT as its own innovation. Some begged to differ, including the conservative *National Review*. "As our most important standardized admissions test, the SAT is the critical barrier to the complete triumph of a racial and ethnic spoils system in the academy," wrote the editors. California voters tried to reject the "spoils system when they banned affirmative action in 1996, but Richard Atkinson, the president of the University of California system, has sought a way around the ban through elimination of the SAT as a requirement for applicants. With the nation's largest university system about to withdraw its business, the College Board, creator of the SAT, has caved in. The test is now set to be transformed in ways designed to boost minority performance."[35]

Larry Summers, president of Harvard, and prior to an uproar over his comments on the ability of women to conquer the sciences, offered his congratulations to Caperton and his board. "The College Board has taken a strong step recently in making changes to the SAT itself," he stated at a speech in Chicago to help celebrate the board's fiftieth anniversary. "The new test is designed to be less coachable and to capture more accurately what students learn in school. It also promises to demonstrate more clearly the kinds of skills students need to succeed, such as writing."[36] And Harvard's dean of admissions spoke similarly. "The new SAT will be a better yardstick of what people here have accomplished . . . The symbolic importance of stressing writing on the SAT is critical. I think it will lead to real reform."

Many higher education leaders had a different take. Selective public universities needed to both reduce their dependence on the SAT and become more sophisticated in assessing an individual's application, stated Juan E. Mestas, chancellor of the University of Michigan's Flint campus. "These are complex decisions that should take into account qualities that do not lend themselves to quantification, such as determination, good judgment, the ability to overcome obstacles, creativity, and common sense." The SAT told university admissions officers nothing about these qualities, argued Mestas. Yet the new SAT I was sold as measuring practical and creative abilities. "Soon we may learn that Michelangelo was 20 points more creative than Shakespeare. God help us."[37]

Some three years later, the revised SAT was administered for the first time in early 2005 and included a twenty-five-minute essay and forty-nine multiple-choice questions that require students to improve sentences and identify errors. Scorers were instructed to read all essays "holistically" and to disregard minor factual errors in favor of the overall coherence and structure of the student's effort. Fair Test and other critiques of the SAT hoped that the national attention Atkinson brought to the topic and worries over the new test would provide a tipping point for making the test optional or even an eventual wholesale rejection. A small number of small liberal arts institutions, including the College of the Holy Cross in Massachusetts and St. Lawrence University in New York, did drop their tests requirements, joining Bates, Bard, Connecticut College, and Bowdoin. In 2006, some 700 universities and colleges did not require all applicants to submit SAT or ACT scores. But at the vast majority of these institutions, those admitted without submitting scores are generally a small percentage of the total admits—often fewer than 10%. MIT said it did not trust the scoring for the written essay, and for the 2006 freshman admissions class, it eliminated that portion of the test in evaluating the brilliance or lack thereof of student applicants.

The National Council of Teachers of English stated that the writing test is unlikely to improve the teaching of writing in schools. Yet the transition to the new test went relatively smoothly for ETS. Only a few leading higher education institutions balked at the new test. In 2004, approximately 1.4 million college-bound seniors took the SAT I, and some 1,424 four-year colleges require all applicants to submit standardized test scores. More students are projected to be taking the SAT each year. The market will grow because of both population growth and the increasing value of higher education in the job market. Young adults are taking the test at younger ages than in the past under the rubric that practice makes perfect or at least brings a higher chance of improvement. Prospective college students can take the test as many times as they can manage, with colleges and universities using only the highest scores achieved. Some students, invariably from upper income families, are taking it even before they enter high school. In recent years, the number of eighth graders taking the SAT I increased by nearly 20%. "The pressure itself is just absolutely amazing," remarked the College Board's executive director, Brian O'Reilly. "Parents want to give their kids an inside edge."[38]

In revising and repackaging the test, the College Board and ETS forged a brilliant if not familiar move. They appeared to respond to criticism, modified the existing test at the margin, and most importantly, added a writing section. They preserved the market for the SAT I. And although the changes have driven up the cost of administering the test, those costs are passed on to students and their families in the form of a higher fee.

Meanwhile, the University of California and its faculty need to consider the merits not of the old SAT I but the new test. The University of California could have developed a test just for California. But this route posed significant problems; devising its content and satisfying divergent political interests, including neoconservatives and minority advocate groups alike, would prove difficult and would take a number of years. Simply using a new statewide high school graduation exam would not avoid such a debate; the test is a general high school accountability tool, not a device for assessing potential collegiate success. The path of least resistance for BOARS and the university leadership was to await the new SAT and then evaluate its predictive validity. It would mean waiting more than two years after students started to take the test in spring 2005. Students would need to enroll and complete their freshman year. The university would then analyze their grades and, based on the results, potentially propose to the regents to drop the test and offer alternatives—for example, greater dependence on subject-area tests, a university-generated test, or one developed with other entities in the state.

BOARS vowed to continue its quest of evaluating the university's options. But by late 2003, Atkinson had stepped down as president. In 2006, Michael T. Brown, chair of the university's admissions committee, along with other faculty members on the committee, stated their interested in a serious review of the new SAT. At a minimum, there needed to be an analysis of the influence of the writing component on entering student competencies. But it is unclear at this time if the university's leadership, and specifically the office of the president and the faculty senate, will sustain the interest in dropping the SAT I. Atkinson's successor, Robert Dynes, a physicist and former chancellor at the university's San Diego campus, immediately found that he had other problems to confront, including retaining university management of three national laboratories in a competition with a University of Texas–based consortium and, by 2006, a major controversy over salaries and other forms of compensation for the university's top brass.

In a world where public resources are generally declining for public universities relative to costs and there are continued calls by legislators and governors to do more with less, a prolonged fight over standardized testing is arguably a distraction. And no other major public or private university has stepped up to the plate to ask why it should be so dependent on the test. That's exactly how ETS likes it.

An important moment passed, leaving the testing regime in place and, indeed, continuing to grow in its influence on schools and on admissions practices. In light of the University of California's extensive studies and debates on the predictive value of standardized tests in the 1960s and the analysis offered in more contemporary times, one can argue that there is no compelling reason for the university to require the SAT or the ACT. It is clearly more a tool to exclude than to include students—a requirement that essentially further erodes the social contract of a public university. If test results proved of significant value in predicting academic success and other gauges of collegiate engagement, then the rationale for requiring the test would be sound.

An alternative approach for advancing that social contract, in part informed by the historical account in previous chapters, could have and might still include: (1) simply dropping the test (therefore relying more on high school grades, civic and academic achievements, and socioeconomic background); (2) actually adhering to the special action targets of 6% or revising the special action criteria and raising the target back to its historic, pre-1960 target of 10% (in 2006, Berkeley still only admitted around 3% of its class under special action); and (3) a more aggressive reviving of the University of California's original concept of regional service areas in which each campus might provide disproportionate access to low-income students. There is also the recurring proposal that the University of California might revise the 12.5% admissions pool upward, in part in recognition of the expanding needs in the U.S. and California economies for a better educated workforce. Each option, however, poses difficulties and requires extensive analysis. And any reforms must be broadly conceived not only around race and ethnicity but greater economic, geographic and regional inclusion, student motivation and engagement, and perhaps most important, the future socioeconomic needs of California and the nation.

In the post-SP-1 debate, affirmative-action opponents saw admissions reform efforts as largely about race, charging conspiracy and subversion in most if not all proposals forwarded by University of California's academic leaders. Eligibility in the Local Context (ELC), comprehensive review, and the possibility of dropping the SAT were each viewed by critics as a concerted effort to lower academic standards with one goal: boosting underrepresented minority enrollments. Connerly and other opponents of affirmative action, although not adverse to increased eligibility rates and enrollment of underrepresented minority groups, remained particularly suspicious of the seeming black box of comprehensive review. How could the regents, for example, really be sure that race did not remain a factor in admissions decisions at the most competitive campuses? As we have seen, the politicization of admissions is not a terribly new phenomenon. Indeed, it is a natural outcome of an increasing demand for a scarce public good. And universities, such as California's land-grant university, have in the past made strategic mistakes highlighted by an overdependence on race as a factor in admissions, a dynamic discussed at length in previous chapters. As a result, affirmative action became less politically viable, harder to defend, and more open to attack.

But the polarizing nature of the debate over affirmative action is not the singular fault of good policy aims implemented badly. And such debates are not fueled simply by philosophical differences over addressing complex social problems. There are also the behaviors and interests of individuals and groups who hold or seek significant levels of political power, whether it be a cabal of lawmakers or a regent. Public universities, and in particular, highly selective institutions, not only must distribute an increasingly scarce resource; they must also deal with a wide group of real and perceived stakeholders.

How can these universities create coherent and socially responsible admissions policies within this political environment? This is only part of the challenge facing public universities with important implications for their social responsibilities, historically rooted in their charge to broaden access within a state. As discussed in the final part of this book, there are also the invidious influences of declining public investment and potentially significant shifts in higher education markets and the priorities of public universities.

Part IV

Whither the Social Contract? The Postmodern World and the Primacy of Higher Education

Chapter 10

Perils and Opportunities:
Autonomy, Merit, and Privatization

We have long recognized that, given the important purpose of public education and the expansive freedoms of speech and thought associated with the university environment, universities occupy a special niche in our constitutional tradition.

—Justice Sandra Day O'Connor, *Grutter v. Bolinger,*
U.S. Supreme Court, June 2003

Is the historical social contract of public universities, including the primary devotion to meeting the particular needs of a state, still relevant, or is there a need for serious revision? Do shifting notions within and outside the academy regarding the national and global role of research universities, and the increasing wealth of a core of private research universities, mean that they must operate differently to compete for students, for income, for prestige, and to retain or perhaps boost their relevance in a postmodern society?

In the following, I venture to discuss the contemporary vitality of the social contract and focus on four interrelated issues. The first is the appropriate *level of autonomy* that public universities should have for setting admissions policies. The second revolves around how *merit is defined and used* in the process of selecting among qualified students. The third issue is what can be called the *crisis of the publics*—the significant decline in public funding for higher education relative to costs. In turn, this last phenomenon, long in the making, generates a fourth issue: the relatively new interest by selective public universities in the process of *privatization*. In pursuing privatization, will these institutions increasingly act like private institutions in their admissions practices, in their perceived clientele, in their fund-raising, and in their assessment of what academic programs are financially viable?

The Courts and Autonomy Revived?

An old adage says that politics is about who gets what, where, and when. This trinity requires an addition: who gets to decide. With such a wide variety of stakeholders and with demand growing, it is not surprising that admissions policy, practices, and their defense have become increasingly political. In the midst of Proposition 209, a spate of court cases indicated an eventual decision by a relatively conservative Supreme Court banning the use of racial and ethnic criteria in university admissions. Among anti-affirmative-action forces, having the courts create a nationwide ban was a seemingly achievable goal. But this did not happen. In *Grutter v. Bolinger*, the Supreme Court issued a landmark affirmative-action decision in the summer of 2003. Proaffirmative-action interests claimed a major victory. The actual meaning of the court case, however, is complicated, and its clarity is exaggerated. The decision is, arguably, more important in the autonomy it granted institutions in setting their admission policies than in its rather vague defense of affirmative action.

When the University of Michigan's Law School denied admission to a white Michigan resident with a 3.8 GPA and a high score in the LSAT, she filed suit. Barbara Grutter and her lawyers alleged that the law school had knowingly discriminated against her on the basis of race and in violation of the Fourteenth Amendment Title VI of the Civil Rights Act of 1964. Like Allan Bakke more than twenty years earlier, Grutter based her case on the fact that she had achieved higher grades and test scores than other applicants who gained admission, particularly African American and Hispanic students. The law school, it was charged, used race as a "predominant" factor, "giving certain minority students a significantly greater chance of admission than students with similar credentials from disfavored racial groups; and that respondents had no compelling interest to justify that use of race."[1] The court considered a similar case at the same time, which charged racial discrimination in the University of Michigan's undergraduate admissions process.

The two cases were argued before the court beginning in April 2003. On June 23, the court issued its ruling. While condemning the use of weighted formulas in the undergraduate admissions processes at the University of Michigan, the court upheld the admissions practices at Michigan's law school. The law school used a holistic admissions process that included race and ethnicity as criteria. What are the differences between the undergraduate and graduate admissions process? One was formulaic and gave clear advantages to underrepresented minorities on a mass scale; the other was more subjective and focused on a more detailed and time-consuming review of an individual's merit. A slim majority essentially reaffirmed the *Bakke* decision: Race and ethnicity and gender could be used as factors among many. The court's majority stated, "The Law School's narrowly tailored use of race in admissions decisions to further a compelling interest in obtaining the educational benefits that flow from a diverse student body is not prohibited by the Equal Protection Clause, Title VI."[2]

Writing the majority opinion, Justice Sandra Day O'Connor reiterated two justifications similar to those offered twenty-six years earlier by Justice Powell in the *Bakke* case. First, O'Connor recognized the "principle of student body diversity as a compelling state interest" and that universities "can justify using race in university admissions" largely for their role in creating a more equitable society. "Effective participation by members of all racial and ethnic groups in the civic life of our Nation," wrote O'Connor, "is essential if the dream of one Nation, indivisible, is to be realized." Second, O'Conner focused on the "constitutional dimension" of institutional autonomy and, specifically, the proper authority of universities in the realm of admissions. In her written opinion, she cited Powell: "The freedom of a university to make its own judgments as to education includes the selection of its student body."[3] O'Connor also cited Justice Felix Frankfurter's 1957 opinion identifying the selection of students as one of four freedoms essential for the academic enterprise, the others being "who may teach, what may be taught, how it should be taught."[4]

Past judicial judgments identified the need to balance the protection of individual rights with the rightful authority of organizations and individuals with "special knowledge" and experiences, in this case, the academic community that set the standards for admissions. O'Connor wrote that the courts should avoid "complex educational judgments in an area that lies primarily within the expertise of the university." "The Law School's educational judgment that such diversity is essential to its educational mission is one to which we defer," she continued. "Our holding today is in keeping with our tradition of giving a degree of deference to a university's academic decisions, within constitutionally prescribed limits."[5]

The *Grutter* case returns us to the focus of this book: What is the purpose of America's public universities, and how might we understand their unique position to influence and shape society? What locus of decision making is most appropriate in setting the general mission of public institutions and in setting admissions policies and making decisions? Should it be the state, the courts, public opinion and referenda, interest groups, or the institutions themselves?

It is important to note what the court did and did not find compelling. Data and arguments regarding the overall success of students (e.g., graduation rates, professional success after graduation) admitted under affirmative-action programs were largely ignored. The court's majority opinion also made only passing reference to the supposedly critical nature of diversity for the educational process. The court essentially made no effort to determine the strength of that argument and instead "deferred" to the law school's judgment on educational benefits.[6] Understanding that public universities and colleges will always be subject to considerable external and internal political pressures, the court's landmark decision gives renewed salience to the importance of considerable institutional autonomy in setting admissions policies. Greater legal authority, however, must be accompanied by a larger public sense that the admissions processes are reasonably transparent and fair—that collectively, decisions on admissions relate to a larger, comprehensible institutional mission. Only then can public universities, and in particular, highly selective institutions, gain sufficient levels of trust from the public, lawmakers, and members of their governing boards that they are rationally balancing the needs of the individual with their larger social purpose.

Yet also looming is the prospect of a return to the issue of affirmative action by the U.S. Supreme Court. The Michigan case is not considered a definitive judgment. With the continued packing of the court with ideological conservatives (at least that is the goal of the Bush administration), another test case may make its way to the highest court in the land thereby revisiting this contested area of American domestic policy.[7] Nevertheless, public universities need to exert their views on the meaning of their social contract, renew their historical role as agents of pragmatic social engineering, and link their contemporary and future salience with their authority to set the conditions of admission.

Choosing a Student Body and Rethinking Merit

Thus far, much of the debate about admissions revolves around the rights of individuals or groups to have access to selective universities, whether they are students with high SAT scores or students of a particular racial background. But another important question relates to the engagement of students once they arrive at the university. How well do they meet the expectations of the institution as motivated and high-performing students, as contributors to the academic community, as potential leaders and contributors to society?

In its amicus brief to the Supreme Court, the University of Michigan ventured into this territory. But the arguments they used were myopic. Lawyers and the university's administration essentially clung to the primacy of race and ethnicity and the need for a "critical mass" of underrepresented minorities. That critical mass, it was argued, was beneficial, even crucial, to the academic experience of all students at the Ann Arbor campus. Their personal experiences and views, it was believed, would enrich the experience of their fellow Euro-American students within the classroom. There just had to be enough of these students. However, few studies effectively show that exposure to a more or less diverse group of peers fosters the development of new viewpoints or in some significant dimension furthers the educational experience and achievement of individual students. The general notion has merit, yet it is hard to prove.

Within the classroom, there is arguably only a marginal influence exerted by ethnic and racial diversity, with perhaps a greater influence in the social sciences and humanities than in the sciences and engineering. Indeed, the traditional ideal of scholarship and higher learning, if not always the practice, is to strive toward the removal of personal background bias in the cause of analytical study. This is the very core of the scholarly enterprise, although it should be noted that postmodernists view all academic inquiry as hopelessly built on individual biases.

There is some evidence, however, that outside the classroom a diverse student body—racial, economic, and otherwise—has a beneficial impact on the social behavior of students, on the process of enculturation, and perhaps on tolerance. A number of studies have shown a "positive" correlation regarding "developmental benefits" based on surveys of students. This notion is not new. In his famous 1852 tome on the importance of community within the English college, Cardinal Newman insisted that students from different backgrounds learning and living together were important in both the classroom and the boarding house. Students, he remarked, "are sure to learn from one another, even if there be no one to teach them; the conversation of all is a series of lectures to each, and they gain for themselves new ideas and views, fresh matter of thought, and distinct principles for judging and acting, day by day."[8] Yet how can we gauge the benefits of learning and living among a diverse student body? What is the relative role of race and ethnic differences versus other socioeconomic factors, such as economic background?

While recognizing that socializing among those with different racial or ethnic backgrounds likely has a positive influence on a campus, Anthony Lising Antonio notes "relationships on diverse college campuses are not

well understood." Indeed, the complexity of the issue has caused a generally liberal caste of scholars to recognize the criticism of conservatives. Although students at "diverse" campuses note inevitable interaction with students of other races and ethnic backgrounds, they state that their campuses
still have racial conflict and isolation. They report racial balkanization often
encouraged and supported by organizational structures on campuses, and
they still experience prejudices—perhaps magnified by America's fixation
on race over issues such as class.[9] In fact, almost all work in the field defines
diversity in racial and ethnic terms. Yet race and ethnicity are, frankly, not
diverse enough notions of diversity. What other elements of diversity contribute to a "critical mass" of underrepresented students required for creating learning and living environments that measurably influence student
outcomes?[10]

In a society undergoing yet another demographic transformation with
countless racial and ethnic groups and many multiethnic families, simply cat-
egorizing groups is increasingly problematic. For example, in California—
one of the most demographically diverse states, although other large states
are not far behind—Latinos have the highest birthrates, but the second
highest birthrate is among multiethnic families.[11] California's higher education system is already majority-minority; Texas, Florida, New Mexico, and
a number of other states will soon follow.[12]

As noted, the legal briefs in support of the University of Michigan
placed tremendous emphasis on the idea of the educational benefits of diversity and critical mass without ever defining what they might be. This
defense of affirmative action, specifically in justifying racial preferences
in admissions, proved a slippery slope. If one could imagine a definition
of that critical mass, would it become a floor or a ceiling for justifying a
percentage target for the admission of underrepresented students? Because
this notion posed legal problems for proaffirmative-action forces, University of Michigan administrators and lawyers drifted into the mist in arguing for the educational benefits of diversity. They testified that "critical
mass" meant "meaningful numbers" or "meaningful representation" and
that "there is no number, percentage, or range of numbers or percentages
that constitute critical mass."[13]

A more fruitful path in shaping admissions policies—and more generally, in creating a student body suitable to the mission and ideals of the
public university—may be found by investigating more fully how admissions standards and practices affect actual student academic performance.
That is, what admissions criteria result in a student body that is diverse in
talent and fully engaged in meeting the academic and civic expectations of

the university? Within the academy, however, the difficulty of disentangling the specific effects of the college experience from personal influences has long been recognized. The variables are many and familiar: a person's early experience, family relationships and friends, social origins and advantages. "The effects of higher education," once wrote Martin Trow, "may be very subtle and difficult to measure: effects on mind, character, sensibility, competence, horizons, and ambitions—effects, that is to say, on the whole range of moral, emotional, and intellectual skills and qualities that a person takes with him into his adult life."[14]

Yet it is possible to decipher some of the influences on what can be termed academic *and* civic engagement of students—to measure how their prior achievements and social backgrounds influence their learning and experience once they began their undergraduate careers. Surveys to measure student engagement and experience have been conducted for many years. They generally show a wide variation among students and academic institutions. What might they show if such data were linked with more robust information on the socioeconomic background of students?

A recent survey and study of undergraduates at the University of California attempted to explore this link. It generated some intriguing findings. First, it found that the socioeconomic and ethnic background of students was much more diverse than previously thought. Some 55% from a representative sample stated that they had at least one parent who was an immigrant; on the two most selective campuses within the system, Berkeley and UCLA, the figure was approximately 65%. About 25% learned another language before learning English, and another 25% grew up speaking English in addition to another language. Although students reported a median parental income of $72,000, about 25% of the student body was drawn from families whose incomes were below $35,000. About 25% of the students were the first generation of their families to enter college, and about 30% identified their families as "working class" or "low income."[15]

Most important for this discussion, students from relatively disadvantaged backgrounds were likely to rank higher on indicators of academic engagement (e.g., time studying, class attendance, interaction with faculty, completion of assignments) than students from more affluent backgrounds. They also had similar and sometimes better time-to-degree rates. All of this was true despite the fact that the less privileged cohort was more likely to be working more hours to finance their education. They also typically had more family-related responsibilities than their more affluent counterparts.

The study also found that time invested in studying and preparing for class was inversely related to students' scores on the SAT I verbal test—a provocative finding. Students from different social class backgrounds also prioritized their goals in college somewhat differently. Students from more disadvantaged backgrounds emphasized career-oriented goals and learning for its own sake, whereas those from more affluent backgrounds tended to emphasize "fun" and "social" goals.[16]

These findings corroborate existing assumptions about student attitudes and behaviors. They also help emphasize the importance of a more nuanced understanding of merit. What are public universities attempting to achieve in their admission practices? In part, the goal should be to distribute access (when choosing among students) to those who are not only talented but who will be the most engaged, who will have the most to gain or contribute to the academic milieu. In choosing among many, one threshold is who will have a reasonable chance of success at the university, a principle incorporated by the University of California almost from its founding, although it came later for many other state universities. But one might also assume that universities, public and private, must also take some chances and provide exceptions to the general rules of admissions. The goal is to seek admissions policies that can take into account the great variety of human talents and abilities, the desire for learning, and the potential contribution of a student to the larger academic community, which include the ideals of representation (but not as an edict) and ultimately balance individual merit with the larger needs of society.

Within the political realm that is unique to selective public universities, one dictum stands out: No matter how well constructed admissions policies and practices are, there will be some element of arbitrary decision making, particularly at universities with high demand for access and relatively few openings. Students who apply to highly selective institutions are already a largely self-selected group; they meet or exceed general academic requirements. For example, in 2004 at Berkeley, some 38,000 students applied at the freshman level for only 4,800 enrollment spots; more than 20,000 of these students had high school GPAs in required courses of 4.0 or higher (bolstered by additional credit for advanced placement courses). Statistically, students who are of this caliber, and irrespective of standardized test scores, generally do well within a demanding university curriculum.

Admissions policy is not just about selecting students based on their academic performance in high school or their projected academic ability; it is also about rejecting students and explaining why. As we have seen, rejecting so many able students has real political consequences, even if the students have other equally viable routes to a quality public or private institution. Public universities must defend their policies and actions, but under this dynamic, they will always be vulnerable to criticism. The key is not simply to detail the mechanisms of admissions policies but to cogently argue both the larger social purpose of these institutions *and* the need for significant levels of autonomy in making their choices.

The Crisis of the Publics: Funding and Access

Throughout this book, we have explored the differences between private and public institutions in their governance and expected levels of accountability, in the character and breadth of their academic mission, in their relationship to a larger system of schools, in their sources of funding and management of internal resources, and finally, in their defined market for undergraduate students and admissions policies. The great state universities, both highly and moderately selective, have always served a distinct constituency: the youth, adults, businesses, and communities within the state that chartered them and sustained them financially. This has been a core element in the social contract—a compact between the states and their public universities.

Another distinction between the public and private higher education sectors is the dominant role of public colleges and universities in providing access. Private institutions, including for-profits, are important partners in America's higher education system. The diversity of institutional types is a great strength. However, this should not blind observers and policymakers to the increasing (not diminishing) primacy of public institutions. In 2005, more than 75% of all enrollments in the United States were in the public sector; some 42% were in a four-year public university. The private or independent sector, including accredited institutions such as Stanford, Harvard, and a vast array of small colleges, is focused almost exclusively on the four-year schools and enrolls approximately 20% of all students in the United States.

For-profit institutions with accreditation, such as the University of Phoenix, are a growing and important sector, yet they remain relatively small in overall enrollments when compared to the public and independent sectors. In 2005, they accounted for less than 5% of all enrollments in degree-granting institutions. These institutions are also largely focused on niche markets of vocational and professional programs with relatively low operational costs and for which moderate to high fees can be charged. Thus far, these providers have not significantly altered the market for public institutions, in part because the overall demand for educational services is rapidly growing.

It is not an exaggeration to say that the health of America's economy and the character of social stratification will remain dependent on the vibrancy of its public schools *and* higher education institutions. Indeed, it is probable that the public sector will grow in its overall share of the higher education market. Public higher education, in all its forms, also is the most important route for socioeconomic mobility. Students from wealthy families congregate at the most prestigious private and public institutions, with significant variance depending on the state and region of the nation, reflecting the quality and composition of state systems of higher education. For middle and lower income students, public institutions remain the primary entry point. And although selective or "brand-name" private institutions have worked to expand access to low-income and other disadvantaged groups, offering increasingly generous financial aid packages to offset their considerably higher tuition rates when compared to the publics, there is evidence of an actual decline in enrollment by these lower-disadvantaged and middle-income students.[17] Public institutions remain the most viable path upward.

But what is the vibrancy of public higher education to meet future enrollment demand—to maintain and perhaps expand their social contract? Historically, the core constituent base for public universities has been the government and people of their respective localities. This public paradigm may change not because of a well-conceived refinement of the social contract but because of finances. Some institutions are beginning to act like or argue that they should operate more like private entities, seeking markets and funding where they can. In part, state universities are responding to decreases in state funding, long the bread-and-butter source for funding faculty salaries and other core instruction and research operations. One direct consequence of this shift is steep raises in tuition rates for in-state students. Traditionally, state governments have heavily subsidized public universities to keep tuition low for state residents. Some states, including California, established and maintained tuition-free policies—excluding the cost of housing and the increasing array of fees for student services. The objective has always been to lower economic barriers to access. With the erosion in these subsidies and rising operational costs, tuition for in-state residents has increased sharply over the past two decades. In 1981, tuition represented just 21.5% of total revenues for public higher education; by

2001, it had risen to nearly 30% and, in 2006, to 36.7%. But new revenue is not being generated at a sufficient rate to cover the rising costs. Across the nation, per-student spending in public universities is declining in real terms. On average, total funding (from all sources) per full-time equivalent student declined by 8.8% in public institutions between 2001 and 2005.[18]

Why has the operating cost of public universities gone up so drastically? One reason is that higher education, thus far conceived, is a labor-intense activity and dependent on highly skilled professionals that include faculty, research staff, and administrators. Higher education operating costs have roughly reflected rising costs in similar highly specialized economic sectors. Another cause is the disproportional and important growth of the sciences and engineering. State-of-the-art research and instruction in science and technology fields require an ever-expanding dependence on expensive instruments, technical support staff, properly equipped buildings, and team approaches to research. There are other more mundane reasons for increased costs, including rising housing costs and the expansion of public services, such as outreach programs, often subsidized by the operational budget of a public university. And in states such as California, Texas, and Florida, where the population is quickly growing, there are up-front costs for expanding higher education systems to accommodate increasing enrollments.[19]

Rising operating costs explain one reason tuition rates have gone up at public institutions. But the most important influence on tuition rates, arguably, has been the corresponding decline in state and local government subsidies. At public universities, jumps in tuition correlate with economic cycles and fiscal crises within state governments. In turn, this has generated desperate attempts by universities to both cut costs and quickly raise tuition to reduce (but never eliminate) the impact on university programs. This has resulted in "efficiencies," including substantial increases in student-to-faculty ratios at most public institutions. There is much room for efficiencies and seeking cost containment in academia, to be sure, but there is no clear revolution in the near future and much exaggeration regarding the efficacy of, for example, technological solutions.[20] In essence, states and their public universities have backed into tuition increases without a broader plan or idea about what the proper contribution might be from the state, from students and their families, and from other sources.[21]

How can public institutions compensate for the seemingly irreversible decline in public subsidies—an investment intended to support the social contract? They can continue to look for ways to become more efficient by reallocating resources. They can and will continue to look for new revenues, including raising their endowments and generating new income through commercial ventures and the sale of intellectual property. But by far the most significant and logical source of additional income will be tuition. And there is a conundrum in any significant expansion of tuition. In contrast to private institutions, public universities and colleges face barriers to setting tuition rates, including the potential deleterious effects on access and significant legal and political limits; for example, in most states, fee increases need the approval of lawmakers.

Private universities have long embraced a model of differential fees and have used tuition revenue to provide financial aid to needy students or to attract top students. Many selective private colleges and universities have incorporated "need-blind" admissions practices—initially making admissions decisions without regard to information on what a student can afford. Only after a student is admitted does the institution consider financial information to assess what a student and his or her family will be charged and what direct or loan-based aid might be offered. Even in moderately selective private institutions, few students actually pay the full tuition price posted, or the so-called "sticker price"; but few also pay no tuition!

Public universities and colleges are in the early stages of charging substantial fees and consciously generating fee income as a source for financial aid. Previously, they relied almost completely on state subsidization of a student's education and on federal and, to a lesser degree, state funding for financial aid. It seems inevitable, barring a political and budgetary renaissance, that public universities will consciously move to a similar private institution archetype, what one might call a *moderate-fee and high-financial-aid model*. The distinction between public and private fee policy will, and should, relate to greater public subsidization and the primacy of maintaining tuition levels that are affordable to all economic classes.

Tuition has increased significantly at both private and public institutions. An important gauge will be the relative costs of attending private and public colleges and universities. "The pattern here is clear," note Michael McPherson and Morton Schapiro in a study of tuition trends. "Tuition has been replacing government spending at both public and private institutions."[22] However, even after significant percentage increases in tuition rates among public institutions (from a relatively low base) over the past decade, tuition rates remain substantially below those of private institutions. Among selective public and private universities, the differential in price is now between $20,000 and $28,000 per year.

Much of the increase in tuition within the privates has been used to maintain low student-to-faculty ratios and to enhance the undergraduate experience. In the public sector, however, one sees direct evidence of a decline in competitive position relative to private institutions. As noted, in the public sector, student-to-faculty ratios are climbing significantly. In the 1960s, the University of California had a ratio of approximately 14:1, a bit higher than institutions such as Stanford and Harvard that have maintained and, in some cases reduced, this ratio. At the University of California, the ratio is now more than 22:1.

One can argue that within most major state universities, the quality of instructional programs is declining as more and more students are pushed into larger classes. Direct student contact with faculty has decreased, although instructional technologies and new modes of communicating over the Internet may mitigate the harmful effects of reduced student-to-faculty ratios. To help reduce costs, the number of part-time faculty has escalated. As federal and state financial aid programs have drifted from grants to loans, more students in the traditional age cohort of eighteen to twenty-four are attending part time, many are working part time, and these students tend to have higher attrition rates.

Within this scenario, selective public universities share a number of peculiar maladies. They are finding it increasingly difficult to compete for highly qualified graduate students. Even though their tuition rates generally remain substantially below elite private institutions (for the time being), publics are at a distinct disadvantage in recruiting. Private institutions use their revenue, subsidized by undergraduate student fees and endowments and to a lesser extent federal financial aid, to offer scholarships and other forms of direct aid that are increasingly more attractive to prospective graduate students. There are also growing disparities in faculty pay rates between the selective public and private universities, indicating a future concentration of talent in the privates.[23] Resources for start-up funds in the sciences are more plentiful in the privates as well.

Such disparities did not exist in the 1960s and into the 1970s. "The basic economics of private institutions—high tuition coupled with fundraising in the billions—seems to be working much better than the model of slowly rising tuition and fast-declining state aid found so often in the public sector," notes Steven Brint in a study on the how public universities might compete in the new environment.[24] "State support for public higher education on a per-student basis has dropped steadily," recently lamented David Ward, president of the American Council for Education, "and, at the federal level, there has been a dramatic shift in the emphasis from grants to loans for promoting college access. As a result, the United States has witnessed an unraveling of the successful higher education financing partnership among government, institutions, and families that has served our nation so well over the last century."[25]

The crisis in the funding of public higher education reflects larger problems that pit the promise of education as a great engine of opportunity against the realities of contemporary society. "Traditional American fiscal federalism is straining state resources," notes one study on public higher education, "and there is a reluctance to re-engineer state revenue systems to match changing twenty-first century economies. Coupled with hostility on the part of the federal government to helping states, these pressures have produced a decade of retrenchment and improvisation in state policies and support of higher education."[26]

Public investment rates are declining not just for higher education. America has increasing rates of poverty, inequalities in income, inequalities in schooling, and as Norton Grubb notes, "relatively laissez-faire and under-funded welfare states." The larger problems of society in an age of "small government" mean that "universities must cope with the differences among students caused by various inequalities without being able to counter those inequalities themselves, and without being able to rely on a strong welfare state to provide health care, housing stability, family support, income support for 'new students' in colleges and universities, and other support necessary for all individuals to take advantage of the opportunities provided."[27] Certainly, a rejuvenated welfare state is not the answer to all of society's problems; one could argue, however, that government policies over the last several decades have accentuated structural problems that in turn hinder access to higher education, public and private.

The intense attention on preferential admissions at institutions such as Berkeley and the University of Texas at Austin masks a much larger issue: the declining ability of states to be the primary funding source for public higher education. The population of the United States continues to grow. States like California, Florida, and Texas project large-scale increases, and the demographic mix within these states is rapidly changing. These states will soon become minority-majority states, where ethnic minority groups will collectively outnumber Euro-Americans.

The prospect of a continued decline in investment in public higher education by state and federal government is having deleterious effects on access. The issue of investment in public higher education may be the most important affirmative-action issue in the first decades of the twenty-first century—a demand and supply problem that will likely not be solved by private institutions that service a relatively small share of the undergraduate population and that do not bear the social responsibilities of public universities and colleges. Unfortunately, within this new reality, public universities, particularly the most prestigious and selective, see a successful future in which publics increasingly act like privates.

The Specter of Privatization

For more than a century, state governments and their flagship universities had a deal, notes Mark Yudof, president of the University of Texas. "In return for financial support from taxpayers, these universities would keep tuition low and provide broad access, train graduate students, promote arts and culture, help solve local problems and perform ground breaking research."[28] Now, many public university leaders are essentially saying that the deal is nearly dead and with little hope for resuscitation. They muse and sometimes argue that the social contract needs redefinition in light of the decline in state funding. Leaders in public higher education talk of moving from "state-supported" to "state-assisted" or even "state-located" status and a corresponding shift in institutional priorities. In part, the threat is intended to gain the attention of lawmakers and the public. It also reflects a realistic assessment of a funding paradigm that has been seemingly lost permanently.

State and local governments are unlikely to revive their former role as the primary funding agent of public higher education. States face increasing costs for services, including prisons, transportation, and probably most significantly, medical and pension expenditures. The federal government is unlikely in the near future to expand in any significant manner its student loan and grant-in-aid programs, such as Pell Grants for low-income students. Raising tuition at public universities and colleges in some combination with expanding institutional aid is the most likely scenario that will be vigorously pursued by institutions faced with declining government funding—barring a dramatic shift in federal policy.

The process of seeking new funding sources, and hence potential new constituencies, has gained the anointed title of *privatization*. For those worried about the fate of America's public universities, particularly its most selective institutions, a process of convergence in which the publics become more like the privates is not necessarily a completely bad thing. In essence, the resources a university gains from society influence its quality, effectiveness, and the scope of programs. Where those resources come from influences institutional behavior and, in effect, its general understanding of its role in society.[29] Less funding from government and more from students, or from industry, should mean a shift in priorities. What does it mean to be a public university today?[30] Some elements of privatization, including seeking a greater diversity of funding sources and raising tuitions, are manageable and inevitable. But public institutions must retain their unique role in America's impressive diversity of public and private institutions, based on their public purpose and the values of their *social contract.*

Raising fees and increasing institutional aid—the model long used by private higher education—are only two components in the privatization model for public universities. Other components include actively seeking extramural support for research (funded both privately and federally and to a lesser extent through state and local government initiatives), forming start-up companies and ventures related to university research discoveries and teaching and learning expertise, and seeking greater freedom from regulatory controls of government. And linked to the privatization movement are numerous influences on the way universities and colleges approach their internal organization, practices, and funding, including boosting professional school fees and, in some cases, allowing these schools to operate as relatively independent administrative units within a university.

Prior to the current shift in tuition policy and authority, most public institutions charged either nothing or a relatively modest flat fee for all students, whether they were undergraduates, graduate students, or professional degree candidates. Low tuition was viewed as the most effective means of lowering economic barriers to attending a university. A flat fee (or the lack of differential fees) also ensured against or reduced potential biases in a student's choice of subject and degree preference. Students' academic abilities and interests were expected to guide their choice of subject at a time when, at least in the United States, salary differentials among professions were relatively small. Since low tuition was made possible by tax-based subsidies, differential rates were established for noncitizens—that is, out-of-state students and foreign nationals.

The first major break in this across-the-board low-fee policy at public universities came with the introduction of specific and higher tuition levels in the 1980s and early 1990s for professional degrees, following the lead of many independent institutions. Three factors have influenced this shift. First and foremost, there is the increased private benefit afforded to the student with a professional qualification. It is assumed that graduates of a professional program will generate a sizable income over their careers and can therefore afford the higher initial cost (investment) in their university education. The second factor is the higher cost of maintaining the pro-

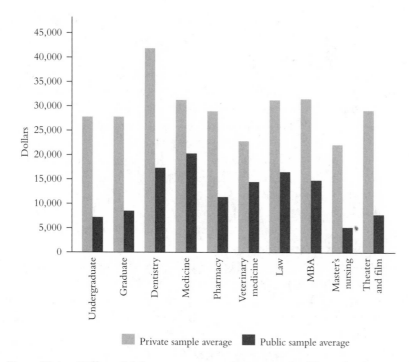

Figure 10.1. Differential fees among a sample group of public and private universities: 2003–2004

SOURCE: David Ward and John Aubrey Douglass, "The Perils and Promise of Variable Fees," *Perspectives: Policy and Practice in Higher Education* (UK) 9, no. 1 (2005): 29–35.

gram, including rising costs in some professions for recruiting and retaining faculty. The third factor is the financial opportunity for the institution in lucrative fields in which fees more than cover costs.

Figure 10.1 offers the fee levels of a sample group of twenty-six relatively selective public and private institutions. It includes fourteen public universities and eleven private institutions, with Cornell as a hybrid (with both state statutory programs at the undergraduate level and professional programs with private endowments).[31]

The privatization movement and the relatively new market thrust of public universities mean that the differential fees between public and private institutions will likely decrease in coming decades—at the undergraduate *and* graduate and professional levels. The push by institutions to raise revenue through tuition will be significant, and the price for students will

increase. If the average tuition fee of the public sample group were to increase to approximately 75% of the private sample group, the undergraduate sticker price (not counting financial aid offsets) would be $21,100,
which is an increase of more than $14,000. At the graduate level, the in-
crease would be similar, just over $13,000. And in a professional program
like pharmacy, the tuition rate at a public university would be $17,200,
an increase of over $5,800; in nursing, the fee level would be $16,800, an
increase of $11,800. The tuition fee for an MBA in most elite public uni-
versities is already close to that of privates. Baring a cultural and financial
revolution, the path to some form of market parity in tuition fees between
private and public universities seems inevitable.[32]

Although some observers of higher education worry about how higher
fees will influence access, two contemporary factors are driving the push
upward in fees and trump such concerns. The first is a desire and a sense of
legitimacy to calibrate tuition and fees based on what a comparable group
of institutions (within a state, within a nation, and increasingly, internationally) charge. This is a competitive model devoid of any larger sense of
the relationship of revenue generation to the specific financial needs of an
institution or to its influence on affordability and access. The second and
related factor is a relatively new thought: Public universities should eventually be able to charge what the market will bear, while mindful of the
need to generate funds sufficient for a robust financial aid program that also
draws on institutional, state, and national sources. Generally, the increased
acceptance of the market model among public institutions, including differential fees, has prompted government policies to limit the total amount
that can be charged, either as a ceiling or as a percentage change per year.
But particularly at the graduate level for professional programs, convergence with privates seems to be a strong desire of many public universities,
particularly among the faculty and academic leaders within those professional programs at elite institutions.[33]

This path has largely gained the tacit (sometimes formal) approval of
state lawmakers in a number of states. Without any foreseeable ability or
political interest in returning to state investment rates found in earlier decades, they recognize the need to generate more revenue. Hence, there are
the experiments of allowing the University of Michigan to move toward a
private model (free to charge variable rates for different academic degrees)
and a similar plan in Virginia for a number of public universities. Already,
state lawmakers have agreed to allow the law school at the University of
Virginia to operate as a distinct financial operation.[34]

If higher tuition rates and convergence with the privates are the future route of American public higher education, an important question is how this will affect the market—specifically, access and opportunities for students and their families from lower and middle class and disadvantaged backgrounds. There is evidence that robust financial aid programs can offset the potential negative effect of higher fees at the undergraduate level. For example, the University of California's experience with raising fees in the early 1990s did not result in a reduction in demand or in a discernible decline in access by lower income groups, in part because for each dollar raised through fees, $0.35 was placed into an expanded financial aid program. (The average among U.S. universities is about $0.25 for each dollar raised through fees and tuition.)

A key factor is the elasticity of pricing. Research on costs of and access to higher education indicates that there is a range in which fees can be charged with limited impact on access and the actual costs to students from lower income groups. If higher education is priced correctly for a family, the real and perceived socioeconomic gains of a higher education, particularly by high-quality providers, make such an investment appear reasonable to students and their families. Creating a logical fee and financial aid structure also requires a phased-policy approach that is consistent and avoids wild fluctuations in the rules. Changes in fees and student aid programs need to be done gradually, with significant academic advising. An increase of $1,000 in tuition in a single year, for example, may result in a reduction of 5% or more in enrollment by lower income students according to recent studies on U.S. public higher education.[35]

This said, there are few well-designed economic studies on the elasticity of tuition and its potential effect on low and middle-income students.[36] And beyond calculating an acceptable price and appropriate financial aid models, there are larger questions regarding the appropriate mix of public taxpayer financing, the appropriate contribution of students toward the cost of their education, and what other sources of income will be sufficient to maintain high-quality academic programs. Low fees can have a beneficial impact on lower income students; but they can also represent an inordinate subsidization of students from wealthy families, which is a cohort that is more likely to be admitted and enrolled in a selective public university.

Beyond the important questions raised by the inevitable rise in tuition at public universities, there is another side of the equation that, thus far, has not been adequately examined: how will the new income be used within institutions? For most of the history of universities, public and private, revenue sharing and cross-subsidization have been crucial for supporting the academic enterprise. Generating funds through state subsidies or tuition to fund the broad spectrum of academic programs, from the humanities to the hard sciences, will remain crucial to the economic viability of institutions, but the interests of professional schools and other potential "for-profit centers" will both generate new funds and will tear at the edges of this model. They are not as interested in revenue sharing and are aggressive at retaining any additional revenue streams.

How will privatization influence the social contract of public universities? An increasing number of critics of American higher education lament the growing efforts by universities and colleges to expand their income sources. In this view, striking deals with industry and business to promote university research useful to business and the economy offer the greatest threat to academic freedom and the purpose of universities. Whether public or private, bemoans David Kirp in a recent book on the market and higher education, "What is new, and troubling, is the raw power that money directly exerts over so many aspects of higher education." Although significant public attention is paid to heated debates over affirmative action and the SAT, he notes, America's leading public universities are more quietly "reinventing" themselves as more businesslike enterprises.[37]

On the heels of Sputnik, higher education leaders worried about the influence of a surge in federal research funding for higher education. Clark Kerr, then the president of the University of California, noted in 1963 what many feared: a growing dependence on the federal largess that might unduly influence academic research and instructional programs. There was irony in the observation that America's research universities, "which pride themselves on their autonomy . . . should have found their greatest stimulus in federal initiative."[38]

Perhaps the interaction of universities with the outside world, including business, is not so much a new transgression as it is an old activity redefined. As in the past, the worry is that the search for income, both for the institution and for individual university-based researchers, creates conflicts of interest and further commercializes the academic enterprise. Yet the actual income generated by such relationships with business, for example, is still relatively small compared to the total revenue generated by public and private universities. "Compared to this transfer of the cost of supporting universities from the taxpayers of our states to the students who attend them," notes Berkeley's Chancellor Robert Berdhal, "the 'commercialization' that the critics have warned against pales into insignificance."[39]

This raises the prospect that a much greater impact of privatization will not be the incursion of industry and business interests into the public university. Rather, the more important policy consideration is how these institutions might redefine their social contract, and specifically, how they might redefine their market for students in the search for general operating funds. Influenced both by declining public funding for undergraduate education and by surging enrollment demand, many public universities now select from a pool of eligible students and, at the same time, seek new pools of out-of-state and international students.

In certain regions of the country, there have always been streams of students crossing state borders to go to college. A number of state universities, such as the University of Wisconsin at Madison, have long enrolled a relatively high percentage of out-of-state students for a public institution precisely because the state's economy and state subsidies were not large enough to fund a large-scale research university. However, recently, there is a much more deliberate effort at public institutions to recruit out-of-state students because they bring in more revenue. Tuition rates for these students, again reflecting the historical role of public universities to serve their state constituency, are higher and usually pegged to the assessed cost of educating a student. The institutional desire to recruit these students, and international students as well, will likely grow if state subsidies continue to decline and if tuition fees for in-state students continue to be restricted by legislative mandates. Rising costs and the decline in state funds are forcing public institutions to become more market driven and less public in this regard.

Will public universities adopt the formal policies of private institutions and offer special admissions routes for alumni and the offspring of the wealthy and influential? Children of alumni at Harvard, for instance, are still about three times more likely to be admitted than "nonlegacy" students—students who had no legacy of parents or other close relatives who attended the institution.[40] What is the reason for this special and privileged standard for the children of alumni? America's private colleges and universities have long recognized that admissions is not only about academic potential but is also a means to build a sustainable and often wealthy community devoted to the institution and willing to donate toward its preservation, quality, and prestige.

Although there are no well-researched studies on legacy admits at public universities in the United States, it appears that there have been few formal policies or significant efforts to admit these students or others who might eventually provide financial gifts. The ethos of the public university has made legacy admissions an exception to the rule. For example, a 1996 audit of University of California admissions practices showed that only two campuses had developed an admissions process that was linked to either political ties or potential funding: UCLA and Berkeley. At both campuses, the number of actual admissions relating to these factors was marginal. In large part to create a system to deal with the inevitable special requests of lawmakers, regents, and the economically powerful, in the early 1990s, Berkeley established a review committee and made judgments on seventy-eight cases in 1996. A total of twelve came from the regents, ten from legislators, ten from UC faculty or administrative officials, thirty-four from donors, and twelve from miscellaneous sources. Two were accepted at the junior transfer level, and nine were accepted at the freshman level out of a total freshman class of some 4,500. All were UC eligible. Nevertheless, after the heated debate over affirmative action and increasing demand for access to Berkeley and UCLA, the board of regents ended any special review process, stating that "no gift, contribution, gratuity, or other consideration either made or contemplated to the University or any of its operations, functions, or programs shall play any part in any admissions decision."[41]

In part, public institutions largely avoided the moral dilemma of allocating a scarce public resource based on family ties (often to a socioeconomic elite with many other educational choices) because of ample state funding. There was no funding imperative, and any open or large-scale use of such admissions practices was against the very idea of the public university and a political liability if exposed. But as public universities become increasingly concerned with raising tuition, building endowments, and new facilities, the pressure will grow to influence the admissions process for financial purposes.[42]

Another variable to consider is a growing international demand for higher education, part of the process of globalization. Public universities and colleges are developing relatively new programs to recruit from or offer services to international markets. This trend includes not only increases in the number of foreign nationals enrolled in undergraduate and graduate programs but an increasing array of off-campus programs, typically either online courses or off-campus centers in other countries or programs that combine both. Although many programs are rationalized as a natural extension of the mission of universities—to serve a larger good within a global society—most are rooted in business plans intended to generate new revenue streams. For less notable institutions, the attraction is expanding recognition and creating prestige; for the brand-name institutions, the attraction is more about leveraging international recognition into profits.

University extension programs once targeted for state residents and businesses are expanding, sometimes beyond state borders. Academic departments seek similar markets and offer new degree programs largely in professional fields such as business, drawn by an operational profile of low overheard and high earnings. Privatization is thus not just about seeking revenues; it is the active commercialization of higher education products, principally degrees, knowledge, and access to the network of academic talent. Privatization also means competition—new commercial competitors who fish in the same waters for profits—typically provided by adults seeking continuing education in professional fields. The search for profits and influence includes U.S. public and private institutions operating abroad and, most significantly, Australian and UK universities. Critics argue that such ventures by public and private universities and colleges not only distract institutions from their core values and practices, but they are often conducted with less vigilance regarding quality and academic freedom.

Increasing fees, changing markets for students, commercialization, incentives to reduce the burden of academic programs that serve broad social needs and are costly, and differential fees are all influences altering the social contract of public universities. Put another way: Will the seeming necessity of "privatization" distract public universities from serving their core constituency? Are these institutions entities of the state that gave them their birth, or are they becoming (and do they indeed want to become) free-market and global enterprises?

One irony of the contemporary era is that while most public colleges and universities seek more diverse and robust funding portfolios and naturally desire greater autonomy, state lawmakers seek greater accountability in public higher education institutions and systems, largely through outcome measures. Their concern is efficiencies and costs for the state and for parents and families paying tuition. They are less concerned about quality—what their investment buys—or with the ability of public institutions to meet their broad social contract. In this view, rising student-to-faculty ratios are a sign of greater cost efficiencies. Further, there is significant skepticism regarding the ability of the higher education community to organize itself for public purposes. "Institutions are perceived by the public and elected officials as inwardly focused, self-serving cases," notes a recent study by the American Council on Education, "where goals such as workforce and economic development often are met with disdain."[43] Within the crosscurrents of privatization, autonomy, and accountability are the seeds of a potentially significant conflict.

One senses that the fate of public universities and the coherence of their social contract lie largely within the academic community. Such a vision will likely not come from external forces. Gaining the interest of lawmakers and the public in the vitality of America's public universities will require more than an articulation of the problems facing these institutions. Perhaps it could also be fueled by an understanding of the significant strides recently made by other nations to meet and exceed the higher education participation rates of the United States. America has long had a higher education system that was the envy of the world. But that once dominant role is waning.

Chapter 11

The Waning of America's Higher Education Advantage

We don't even know what skills may be needed in the years ahead. That is why we must train our young people in the fundamental fields of knowledge, and equip them to understand and cope with change. That is why we must give them the critical qualities of mind and durable qualities of character that will serve them in circumstances we cannot now even predict.

—John W. Gardner, *Excellence: Can We Be Equal and Excellent Too*, 1961

"The great advantage of the Americans," wrote Alexis de Tocqueville in the 1830s, "is that they have arrived at a state of democracy without having to endure a democratic revolution, and that they are born equal instead of becoming so."[1] The caveats to this romantic observation are absolutely huge. Yet the spirit of democracy and equality of an earlier age does help us decipher why America created a network of public higher education systems unique in the world. The astounding success of this venture had a tremendous impact on the nation only partially assessed in this book. Throughout most of the twentieth century, more Americans went on to a college or university education than did citizens of any other country. Particularly in the later part of the twentieth century, America's technological prowess was heavily rooted in the long-term investment, productivity, and quality of its public research universities.

American higher education produced much of the science vital for the nation's most productive and creative economic sectors, past and present. It has been the primary source of scientific and professional labor and has attracted a great pool of talent from throughout the world. Perhaps most important, America's venture into mass higher education, the first in the world, offered an essential route for socioeconomic mobility and, ultimately, created a more equitable and prosperous society. The United States has long enjoyed the advantages of being the first mover in the contemporary devotion to building higher education systems.

"In the technological society," wrote famed British sociologist A. H. Halsey in 1960, "the system of higher education no longer plays a passive role; it becomes a determinant of economic development and hence stratification and other aspects of social structure."[2] At that time, it was widely recognized that America had taken the lead among the world's nations in creating mass higher education, in making universities and colleges a necessary component for economic prosperity and social equality. The diversity of institutional types (public and private, two- and four-year, vocational and liberal arts), their ubiquity, and their general affordability existed in no other part of the world. As a result, and in concert with societal norms that have tended to ignore class distinctions and reward those with strong work ethics, America gained the most productive labor force and enjoyed an unparalleled level of socioeconomic mobility among its population.

Broad access, high levels of productivity, the ability of students to bank credits and matriculate between institutions, the diversity of institutional types, and the general understanding of the social contract of universities (their greater purpose in society) are among the great strengths of America's pioneering higher education system. At the root of the social contract of public universities is the concept of pushing *and* facilitating demand for higher education through a variety of institutional types, buttressed by the ability to matriculate from one institution to another.

In his 1971 survey of American higher education for the Carnegie Commission on Higher Education, British university administrator Sir Eric Ashby saw bumps in the road for America's leadership position, with demand growing and problems of financing for public higher education around the corner. It was an accurate prediction. Yet he also sensed a trajectory "toward a conclusion with the inevitability of the plot in Tolstoy's *War and Peace*. The conclusion is universal higher education, equality of opportunity, proliferation of graduate education and research, corporate involvement in helping to resolve the dilemmas of society."[3]

After a century of leading the world in participation rates in higher education, however, there are strong indications that America's advantage is waning. The academic research enterprise remains relatively vibrant, although there are important global shifts even here that are eroding the U.S. advantage. More important for the focus of this book, participation and degree attainment rates have been stagnant and have declined over the past decade among younger students—seemingly more than just a bump or short-term market correction. Ashby optimistically thought in 1971 that the next phase of American higher education was to finance and plan expansion "until privileged and underprivileged children of similar ability have similar opportunities to go to college."[4] But we find that these disparities are growing.

Meanwhile, other nations with developed economies, in essence America's direct competitors, are attempting as a matter of government policy to match or exceed U.S. participation rates among their younger populations. Many are taking proactive steps to more fully integrate higher education into national economic and social policy with a fervor that has dissipated in the United States. Within the context of their own political culture and national development, many of the members of the Organisation for Economic Co-operation and Development (OECD, a consortium of thirty nations with mostly developed economies), and in particular the members of the European Union, have looked across the ocean and sought inspiration and models. Many have set national and multinational goals for higher education reforms intended to increase participation rates, degree attainment, and targets for investment in basic and applied research. Although not without problems, their efforts are paying off. For the first time since the late 1800s, America no longer has the world's highest rate of young students going on to a postsecondary institution.[5]

Here is a major global trend that has garnered little attention in Washington or in the halls of state capitals and has yet to infiltrate the rhetoric of America's higher education community in any significant way, with the scientific community being the most vocal. It has implications both for socioeconomic mobility in the United States and for national economic competitiveness. What are the factors that explain this waning of America's leadership position in promoting higher education? What are America's competitors attempting to achieve? And what course might the United States pursue?

Participation Rates and Competitors

International comparisons are fraught with difficulties, in part because there have been differing national views on what constitutes higher education, with the United States the most liberal. Europeans, for example, have tended to think of a distinct class of universities as constituting higher education, whereas in the United States, anything after secondary school is deemed tertiary education. There is also a significant time lag in capturing data on enrollment and graduation trends. But a host of national higher education reforms throughout the world and efforts to improve international data collection by agencies such as the OECD are beginning to offer a better picture and a sense of trajectories.

Overall, the United States still retains a lead in the number of people with higher education experience and degrees. But at the younger age cohort, a different story emerges. On average, the postsecondary participation rate for those aged eighteen to twenty-four in the United States is approximately 34% according to a 2005 study, down from around 38% in 2000. There is substantial variation among the states. In 2002, Rhode Island had the highest rate at 48%, and Alaska had the lowest at 19%. California, Florida, and Texas—states with large and the fastest growing populations—had approximately 36%, 31%, and 27%, respectively, attend some form of postsecondary education. In the majority of states, these participation rates have flattened or marginally declined over the last decade. More students today are part time, and more are in two-year colleges; the wealthiest students are in the four-year institutions, and students from lower and even middle income families are now more likely to attend a two-year college, less likely to earn a bachelor's degree, and now take much longer to attain a degree than in the past.[6]

In contrast, within a comparative group of fellow OECD countries, many nations are approaching or have exceeded 50% of this younger age group's participation in postsecondary education, and most are enrolled in programs that lead to a bachelor's degree. One reason for the U.S. lag is that it ranked only nineteenth in secondary graduate rates, with some evidence that this is an optimistic estimate. When compared with other industrialized nations, in 2004, the United States ranked only fourteenth in the percentage of the population that enters postsecondary education and then completes a bachelor's degree or higher.[7] As noted, it appears that this is not a short-term trend. The United States still affords a much more dynamic higher education system than most nations. Students in the United States often transfer from one institution to another or delay entry into a postsecondary institution, coming in and out of higher education during the course of their lives. This system is much more forgiving than in the vast majority of other countries, where young adults are often tracked into a university or nonuniversity path very early in their student careers, although this is also beginning to change. But many Americans and the growing number of immigrant groups are not getting their degrees.

The United States is one of the few OECD nations in which the older generation has achieved higher tertiary education rates than the younger population.[8] A recent study looked at the tertiary degree attainment rates of the high school graduating classes of 1972 and 1992. On average, those who graduated from high school in 1972 were more likely to

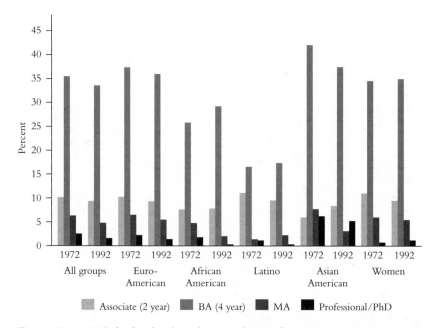

Figure 11.1.   U.S. high school graduating classes of 1972 and 1992 and accumulative higher education degree attainment nine years later (in percentage)

SOURCE: Cliff Adelman, *Principal Indicators of Student Academic Histories in Postsecondary Education: 1972–2000* (Washington, DC: Institute of Education Sciences, U.S. Department of Education, 2004).

gain a bachelor's degree over a twelve-year period. This fact held true for both Euro-Americans and Asian Americans (see Figure 11.1). There were, however, increases in degree attainment rates for Latinos and African Americans—evidence of a rising middle class and perhaps the benefits of affirmative action. Women also increased their degree attainment. A similar pattern is evident for those achieving a master's and professional degree or a doctorate: declines for Euro-Americans and Asian Americans and, generally, increases for African Americans and women but, interestingly, a decline for Latinos.[9]

In some states, such as California, access to higher education for the traditional age cohort has declined significantly over the past two decades. In 1970, some 55% of all public high school graduates in California moved directly to tertiary education, among the highest rate in the nation; in the year 2000, the rate was a mere 48%, with the vast majority going into community colleges, most as part-time students and most destined never to attain a two-year, let alone a bachelor's, degree.[10] Since 2000, the college-going rate of high school graduates has probably declined further, influenced in part by the large number of high school dropouts. This has occurred in an economic environment in which demand for a labor pool with a postsecondary training and education is expanding. A 2006 study estimates that by the year 2022, one in three new California jobs generated will require an associate's degree, bachelor's degree, or higher. Jobs requiring higher education are already growing faster than overall employment in the state.[11]

There is some good news. In the United States, there are healthy increases in the participation rate of older students over the past decade— important for lifelong learning in the postmodern economy and for facilitating socioeconomic mobility. The United States also has among the highest rate of the labor force participating in some form of continuing education and training in nondegree and usually short-term programs often funded by employers. But even in this regard, a number of OECD countries are attempting through national policies to expand participation of older students with the goal of meeting or better yet exceeding the rates found in the United States.[12]

Within the European Union, the push to increase participation rates in higher education transcends national borders. So important is the expansion of universities for EU nations that many countries are now integrating degree standards (influenced by the American model) under the 1999 Bologna Declaration. That year, European ministers of education convened in Bologna to voluntarily seek common higher education reforms, including creating comparable degrees, programs to ease student mobility between countries, and efforts at reviewing and improving the quality of academic programs. The objective of the declaration is to "ensure that higher education and research in Europe adapt to the changing needs of society and advances in scientific knowledge" and to "increase international competitiveness of a European system of higher education."[13] Since the initial adoption of the Bologna Declaration in 1999 by twenty European countries, additional countries have joined the process demonstrating the willingness for Europe's universities to work together to create a common higher education and research area. As of May 2005, the total number of signatory countries in the Bologna Process is forty-five.

Although the rhetoric of markets and deregulation pervades much of the talk in Europe about how to promote higher participation rates, it is largely governments that are forcing reforms and creating bureaucratic regulatory regimes focused on access, productivity, and quality. Government plays a heavier hand in Europe than in the United States, in part because of his-torical and cultural differences: The development of public higher educa-tion in America has been a largely organic process of building institutions and creating self-regulated systems over a long time, whereas in Europe and most of the world, higher education was until the 1960s (and arguably, later in many countries) an elite function forcibly transformed by governments. European Union members seek their own "social contract" built around their cultural and education institutions while looking to the American model for ideas.[14]

European integration is a complicated political process with many co-nundrums, obstacles, and no clear end result. But it is also a powerful force that, along with the rise of China and India as economic powerhouses, will significantly alter the world economy and the flow of skilled labor. It is clear that proactive national policies of EU members have produced a surge in participation rates, particularly over the last two decades. To some ex-tent, the higher education community in each country has been a reluctant or ambivalent partner in these government-initiated attempts to increase access. The results, however, are astounding. Higher education enrollment has grown by over 30% in England over the past two decades and in France by a staggering 72%.[15] One important question: There is increasing access, but access to what? The quality and efficiency of higher education systems in Europe are not uniform, with many students in France, Spain, and Italy, for example, never completing a degree. But reforms are being undertaken in places such as Italy and Germany to radically change degree structures in part to address high attrition rates. As a consequence, many OECD coun-tries are approaching or exceeding degree productivity rates found in the United States.

Another indicator of the differences between the U.S. and EU higher education markets is illustrated in Figure 11.2, which provides data on en-rollment increases by major continents. Even with significant population growth in North America (dominated by the United States), overall post-secondary enrollment grew by only 2.6% between 1990 and 1997—this at a time when immigration has contributed to an 11.4% overall increase in the number of students in elementary and secondary schools. In sharp con-trast, European higher education enrollment has increased 15.2% over this short seven-year period, while growing at only 3.1% at the elementary and secondary levels, On the one hand, this reflects relative slow population growth, and on the other, the significant emphasis on expanding access to tertiary education.

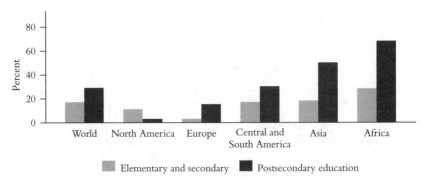

Figure 11.2.   Percentage change in student enrollment by area of world: 1990–1997

SOURCE: Education at a Glance (OECD 2001).

One sees even greater increases in Africa, Asia, and Central and South America. Such growth in these parts of the world reflects relatively recent large-scale increases in schooling in "developing" nations *and* the building of nascent higher education systems. Few regions of the world currently match the postsecondary participation rates in the United States, the European Union, and a collection of economies like Canada, South Korea, and Japan. But this may slowly change.

The OECD estimates the role of education in increasing labor productivity, measured as GDP per person employed. One important cause of rising economic productivity, it is argued by economists, is educational attainment of the working population—a correlation embraced by national governments. In 2004, the United States ranked sixth in the role of educational attainment in productivity growth, behind Portugal, the United Kingdom, Italy, France, and Finland. In previous decades, it had ranked number one. "By many measures, since 1980, the quality of the U.S. workforce has stagnated, or its growth has slowed down dramatically," note economists Pedro Caneiro and James J. Heckman.[16]

There are other indicators that America's leadership position is faltering. Relative to most other nations that are economic competitors, significantly smaller proportions of college-age students are entering scientific fields. In 2005, it is estimated that China had nearly three times and India over two times the number of college graduates in engineering, computer science, and information technologies as the United States.[17] The Chinese national government is engaged in a large-scale effort to expand higher education through both building native institutions and cleverly created limited partnerships with foreign providers—partnerships in which the national government retains significant institutional control. In the midst of its rise as a major economic player in the world, China also has stated an intention to eventually create twenty MITs—a mighty task to be sure.

At the same time, many high-technology-based conglomerates, including IBM and Nokia, have started new research and development centers in major Chinese cities and in other developing economies where higher education is growing, such as in India, and where academic programs are largely focused on science and technology. A 2006 study by the National Academies (a consortium that includes the National Academy of Sciences and the National Academy of Engineering in the United States) notes that in 2005 chemical companies closed down seventy facilities in the United States and planned to close forty more; at the same time, 120 chemical plants were being built around the world with price tags of $1 billion each or more, with some fifty in China and only one being built in the United States.[18] More lax environmental regulations play a part, but so does the availability of skilled labor and technical knowledge.

There is increasing evidence that the quality of these academic programs in other parts of the world, and the clusters of research expertise that entice international companies, is growing and becoming increasingly competitive with the U.S. institutions and research centers. This has led critics of shrinking state and federal funding for higher education in the United States to argue that the nation is at the edge of losing its long dominance in basic science.[19] For example, of the articles in the world's top physics journal published in 1983, some 61% were authored by scholars in American universities; in 2003, that proportion dropped to 29%.[20] As a percentage of GNP, federal funding for basic research in the United States in the physical sciences and engineering has been declining for the past thirty years to less than 0.05% in 2003. Asia's developing economies are placing increasing percentages of the GNP into science and technology. The payoff? Their share of global high-tech exports rose from 7% in 1980 to 25% in 2001. According to National Science Foundation figures, the U.S. percentage fell from 31% to 18%.[21] The United States is still competitive; it is just that others have become more competitive.

Some observers see benefits in what appears to be the edge of a sea change. The increased quality and concerted efforts of governments to build their higher education sectors mean a richer global supply of scientific and technological expertise, much of which will be drawn to the United States. Some even predict a "glut of technical sophisticated human capital." But few policymakers, thus far, would view growing and significant reliance on the international market for scientific and technical labor and innovation as sound long-term national economic policy and, in essence, turning their backs on producing native talent. Investing in native talent and attracting and seeking skilled labor in the global market are not mutually exclusive objectives.

As the global production of scientists and engineers grows, the rise of new high-technology industries and research clusters outside the traditional hegemony is altering the flow of talent. Some worry that the U.S. attractiveness, and that of Europe, for drawing global talent will decline in relative terms. As a recent OECD report notes, how can the United States retain "a strong knowledge economy without a stronger education system?"[22] As emphasized throughout this book, higher education is not just a tool for meeting immediate labor needs and for promoting economic innovation, although that is an important role; it also is a vital route for socioeconomic mobility, for creating a more inclusive society and promoting democracy itself.

Explaining the Stagnation

Beyond the rise of concerted competitors, what factors contribute to this erosion in America's once dominant position in higher education? There is no one cause but, rather, an array of interrelated causes. However, they can be boiled down to four main factors. One is the stagnation and, in many states, significant *declines in high school graduation rates*, which in turn erode the demand for higher education. A second cause is *declining political interest and government investment in public higher education* (where some 75% of all American students are enrolled). This factor helps generate a third cause: *increased fees without adequate increases in financial aid*. And a fourth cause is the possibility that all mature higher education systems, such as that in the United States, may reach *a point of equilibrium*—a leveling off of participation rates, reflecting in some measure a point of saturation. The following sections discuss each of these factors.

SECONDARY SCHOOL ATTRITION RATES

As noted, the United States has among the lowest secondary school graduation rates among the most developed OECD countries. Based on U.S. Department of Education reports, the OECD reports a 75% completion rate in 2004. A 2005 study by Paul E. Barton, however, estimates that the percentage is possibly as low as 66.1%, down from an estimated peak of

77% in 1969. Burton and others insist that previous and current estimates by the Department of Education, and in turn by state governments, of high school completion rates are too high.[23] Federal data for 1970 through 2001 show only a marginal decrease in the number of eighteen- to twenty-four-year-olds who have completed high school.[24] But because of disparities in data collection among the thousands of schools districts and the fifty states, there are good indicators that federal data artificially inflate the nation's claimed high school graduation rates.

In more optimistic times, it was thought that the United States might reach a high school completion rate of 90%, which was a goal set by President George H. W. Bush and the nation's governors in 1990. However, according to Barton's analysis, between 1990 and 2000, the completion rate declined in forty-three states, and in ten states, it declined precipitously—by more than 8%. Only seven states experienced increases.[25] There are few indications that this trend has bottomed out. Among the causes cited by a growing body of literature are not only significant socioeconomic shifts in the American population but the overall vitality and focus of America's high schools.

Many argue that the declining pool of potential college students relates to inadequate curricular demands among a large proportion of the nation's secondary schools, particularly, but not exclusively, in lower income communities. One assessment is that 40% of American high school graduates are not prepared for college work. A 2004 survey of all fifty states by Achieve Inc. reports that no state "requires every high school student to take a college and work-preparatory curriculum to earn a diploma. While some states offer students the option to pursue a truly rigorous course of study, a less rigorous set of course requirements remains the standard for almost every state."[26] Before a meeting of the nation's governors in early 2005, Microsoft Chairman Bill Gates claimed that the American high school system is "obsolete" compared with education abroad. America's system, he stated, was undermining the workforce of the future and "ruining the lives of millions of Americans every year."[27]

The high attrition rates of male students are yet another wrinkle in the story. Males are more likely than females to drop out of high school. They tend to get lower grades and take fewer college-preparatory courses. Females are now the majority in chemistry and advanced math courses. In 1960, males represented 64.1% of all college and university students; they now represent less than 43%. A similar trend can be seen among the other OECD countries.[28] There is some evidence that this phenomenon reflects pent-up demand and the opening of the job market to females. But increased enrollment by the female cohort is more exaggerated in the United States and correlates with rising levels of poverty, the complexities of growing immigrant populations, and other social factors not clearly understood.

High school attrition rates are tied to socioeconomic trends and public investment patterns. There have been significant demographic changes in the United States over the past four decades, along with a significant increase in the gap between the rich and the poor and, arguably, erosion in the financial position of the middle class. "Economic inequality in the United States is higher today than at any time in the past sixty years," notes a 1999 study by economists Claudia Goldin and Lawrence F. Katz. "One would have to return to the period just before our entry into World War II, still during the Great Depression, to find inequality measures comparable in magnitude to those at the current time."[29] In 1999, some 34 million people, or 12.4% of the population, lived below the federally determined poverty line, and that figure is creeping upward.

Shifts in demography and income have influenced the socioeconomic mix and in turn the college-going rates of various subgroups. Some immigrant groups have fewer real and perceived opportunities and expectations of entering postsecondary institutions; other immigrant groups lack the *cultural capital* but also exhibit a substantial drive to enter public higher education, most notably, recent Asian immigrant groups. Most significantly, blacks and Mexican immigrants and their children have extremely low high school graduation rates relative to the general population. In states such as Florida, Texas, and California, the low participation rates of the fastest growing minority group, Chicanos-Latinos, pose a major problem. And for reasons even more complex, African American high school and college participation rates correlate even more directly with economic status.

Low high school graduation rates result in low college access and degree rates, and that means general exclusion from the mainstream of American economic and social life—a pattern experienced by a significant portion of African Americans. Nationally, only 14.7% of Chicanos-Latinos have earned either an associate's or higher degree; for African Americans, the number is 20.0%, and for Asian Americans and Euro-Americans, the numbers are 50.5% and 33.6%, respectively.[30]

ECONOMIC SWINGS AND POLITICAL PRIORITIES

Economic downturns and shifts in political priorities are additional factors for explaining the general stagnation of participation rates among the younger age cohort. After years of building mass education systems, many states have shifted much of their energy toward other policy problems such as the escalating cost of Medicare and prisons and the debates over tax reform and immigration.

At the federal level, government has reduced over time the level of funding available for financial aid relative to the cost of tuition in both public and private institutions. Despite opinions to the contrary, tuition at public higher education institutions has grown at a rate roughly equivalent to the rate of inflation in most other high-skilled service sectors; yet the amount of aid provided by both federal and state governments, either as grants or as loans, has been well below the general rate of inflation. As a result, financial aid provided by institutions (at public universities, largely generated by the tuition paid by more affluent students) has grown substantially. As discussed in the previous chapter, the relatively new source for financial aid is, thus far, inadequate in reducing the economic barriers for lower and many middle class families. And increases in tuition at public colleges and universities have not been enough to offset large declines in state investment in higher education on a per-student basis.[31] Government is most interested in attempting to control or reduce services, not in increasing them or becoming more active in shaping future labor supplies.

While state governments have the greatest influence on the fate of their public higher education institutions, there is a role for the federal government when it comes to meeting national needs. Seemingly with that thought in mind, U.S. Secretary of Education Margaret Spellings established in 2006 a Commission on the Future of Higher Education charged with "developing a comprehensive national strategy for postsecondary education." Yet the final report did not seriously look at the competition abroad or garner ideas for significant new investments in higher education. Reflecting in some form the political agenda of the Bush administration, many of the recommendations simply mimic the No Child Left Behind initiative—essentially looking for a federal regime to "measure institutional performance" and seeking ways to squeeze "the most out of our national investment in higher education."[32] Those are not necessarily bad goals; they are just not enough.

The Spellings Commission did propose an increase in existing Pell Grants—federal grants to low-income Americans for college. Yet President George Walker Bush's proposed 2007 federal budget offered large cuts in federal student loans and indicated that the priorities of his administration lie elsewhere.

The November 2006 national elections gave the Democratic Party a majority in the House of Representatives and the Senate. Democratic leaders have promised to confront the president about reducing student federal loan rates and to amend or overturn his executive order severely limiting stem cell research using federal research funds. The ability of Washington lawmakers to focus on major higher education related initiatives may be difficult, with the executive and legislative branch likely locked in a stalemate. The conflagration in Iraq, astounding increases in the national debt and lack-luster exports, school systems perpetually struggling with finances and performance, uncontrollable medical costs, and the growing disparity between rich and poor, *and* higher education participation rates, all are major problems in search of solutions. Bold moves on the domestic front will perhaps need to await the next presidential administration. The result is that some of America's big domestic problems essential for long-term economic competitiveness and socioeconomic mobility languish or go unrecognized, at least in the near term.

FEES AND ACCESS

Public institutions have attempted to make up for a portion of the decline in government investment and the impact of rising costs by raising tuition. In 1980, fees and tuition made up approximately 15% of public university operating costs; they grew to about 28% by 2000. At the same time, student debt has increased. In the face of rising fees at both public and private institutions, the policies of government and colleges and universities have perhaps made things worse. The federal government moved precipitously toward loans over grants, raising the interest rates in a move largely calculated to reduce the federal debt. Many institutions, particularly the privates, have also devoted more of their own institutional financial aid to "merit" over "need-" based grants and loans.

As a result of the combination of these forces, two-thirds of the students graduating from college now have student loans, carrying an average debt of close to $20,000, an increase of 60% in just seven years. Graduate students carry average debt of $45,000. Almost every college-qualified, high-income high school graduate enrolls within two years, but more than 20% of qualified low-income students do not go at all.[33] Not surprisingly, the net cost of attending a college or university is taking a larger share of family income at a disproportionate rate. One estimate indicates that the net cost of attending a college or a university (fees minus financial aid) absorbs 38% of the total income of families and individuals in the lowest income quintile, and that figure is 45% in the second lowest quintile. The lower figure for lower income groups reflects in some form more readily available financial aid, yet both are arguably large percentages with deleterious influences on access. Families in the middle, fourth, and highest income quintiles devote 30%, 20%, and 14% of their family income to college costs.[34]

Criticism of increased tuition has focused on the impact on middle-income families, prompting various congressional hearings. But arguably, the biggest influence is on the growing number of low-income Americans. Rising fees, for example, appear to be accentuating the tendency for students from more affluent families to congregate at the higher priced and most prestigious colleges and universities, both public and independents.[35] "At a time when the financial payoffs of a college education have risen," notes Rupert Wilkinson in his study of the history of financial aid in the United States, "widening the economic gulf between college graduates and others, many qualified young people are not going to college because of lack of money and fear of debt."[36]

It has long been assumed that higher tuition fees in public and private institutions will negatively influence access among lower income groups. As fees at public institutions began to creep up in the 1980s, one study published in 1987 indicated that for every increase of $100 at a four-year institution, one might postulate an almost 1% decrease in participation among eighteen- to twenty-four-year-olds.[37] A 1995 study on price sensitivity indicated that a $1,000 increase at four-year institutions resulted in a decline in demand by lower income students of 1.4%.[38] Both studies indicated the obvious: Lower income students are the most sensitive to price changes. As a group, part-time students, many of whom are from lower or middle class backgrounds, are also heavily influence by price increases. In the United States, part-time students are now the majority and the fastest growing higher education cohort.

As discussed in the previous chapter, rapid and unpredictable increases in fees at public universities, as opposed to gradual and planned increases, may be the biggest culprit negatively influencing access. Private colleges and universities can establish a funding plan and keep to it; publics are subject to the political and economic vacillations. After severe state budget cuts to most public universities in the early 1990s, an improved economy caused lawmakers in a number of states to force fee reductions largely for political gain and not as part of a long-term plan for financing higher education. Virginia, California, and Massachusetts all followed this path. Previously, rapidly rising fees helped to suppress demand: after the fee reductions, demand then grew. But the effects appeared temporary—more an indicator of price sensitivity and confusion on the availability of financial aid. Marginal fee increases in subsequent years resulted in relatively stable demand for higher education. In short, students and their families could better plan for educational services and their cost.

There is a great need for expanded research on the relationship between tuition levels, affordability, and access in public colleges and universities. There are very few good studies focused on microeconomic questions related to pricing and student (consumer) choices in higher education within the modern context. For example, might an overall decline in resources for public institutions, and resulting reductions in academic staff and the number of courses offered, be a bigger threat to access than moderate increases in fees over time? Might access and equity be achieved best by raising the costs for the affluent to attend selective public universities and redirecting the resulting augmented resources to expand financial aid for the needy? It is a complex problem with many social and economic variables; nonetheless, there are economic models that could provide guidance. It is perhaps not an overstatement to say that we are entering a new era of moderate or high fees at public institutions without a strong sense of what may transpire.

MARKET SATURATION AND DEMAND

Two other explanations for the leveling off and marginal declines in higher education participation rates in the United States are worth exploring. One explanation is that perhaps there is a point at which a national higher education system serves all those capable of benefiting from a university or college education. As a national system approaches this thus-far inconceivable point, increases in participation rates inevitably slow down and eventually level off. This model assumes a certain limit in the intellectual powers of the general population—an argument, as we have seen in earlier chapters, reiterated in historical debates over the purpose and proper scope of higher education. The problem with this concept is, of course, that in building mass higher education systems, particularly in the United States, we have essentially redefined higher education to mean a vast array of academic and applied programs that serve the varied proclivities of a nation. Old arguments regarding the intellectual capability of the general population are rendered nearly meaningless. Further, America's commitment to course accumulation and the transfer function exudes the idea that people develop their talents and intellectual ability at different rates and in different ways. The model also assumes a match of supply (institutions and programs) with demand. Lack of supply, and the lack of readily available financing, means an artificial suppression of demand and participation rates.

Another explanation is more relevant: Perhaps the perceived value of a higher education for potential students has declined relative to other potential pursuits. In the 1970s, a provocative study by Richard Freeman, an economist at Harvard, discussed the cycles of the labor market, the demand for higher education, and the notion of the "over-educated" American.[39] Two factors colored Freeman's analysis and those of other higher education observers. First, demographic projections indicated that the number of young people entering elementary schools would decline throughout the 1970s and perhaps beyond, leading to an eventual decline in postsecondary enrollments. Second, the job market for college and university graduates appeared to wane. The boom era of the 1950s and 1960s, in which participation rates increased considerably, thought Freeman, created an oversupply of graduates. This surplus, combined with shifts in the economy, including declining demand for teachers and for technical and professional fields once funded by robust federal research and development budgets, meant a leveling off of jobs in which a college or graduate education was useful or required.

Data from the early 1970s indicated to Freeman that, "Real and relative earnings of graduates dropped, employment prospects and occupational attainment deteriorated, and large numbers were forced into occupations normally viewed as being below the college level."[40] Freeman observed a short-term decline in participation in higher education and predicted a longer term leveling of total enrollment in the United States. The economic value of higher education had declined, perhaps permanently, and with it demand. Freeman largely focused on the educational benefit provided to individuals by a tertiary education.[41]

Freeman offered two important observations. Not only could there be an oversupply of higher education graduates, but there could also be cycles of undersupply and oversupply—if the main objective was to correlate degree production rates with immediate employment and, ultimately, economic growth. Why push demand and the associated costs for individuals, government, and society if there was no evidence of employment demand? And why encourage individuals to postpone entering the job market if their investment of time and money—essentially, time lost in gaining an income—would not result in suitable employment and measurable economic benefits?

A main function of public universities, and other components in America's vast network of schools and colleges, was to push and meet demand, under the assumption that there is an economic *and* social need. Freeman argued that governments and higher education institutions needed to more adroitly monitor the market for graduates (both generally and in specific fields like engineering). They might even, and at times, consider consciously reduce participation in higher education.[42]

The projected downward trends in demand among younger students, and declines in government funding, caused most higher education leaders to lament "a new era of constraints." It all seemed to portend a stark future in which mergers and closings of campuses seemed inevitable. A 1974 survey of presidents of colleges and universities offered a pessimistic view of the future both in funding and student demand. The only hope, they thought, was to help create and serve "nontraditional" populations, specifically adult education largely linked to professional needs.[43]

However, the predicted long-term decline in higher education enrollment demand did not happen. The projected shortfall in the college-age cohort, based then on the assumption of relatively meager birthrates and a brief flattening in school enrollments, was offset by unpredicted increases in America's total population, largely fueled by immigration. In turn, many immigrant groups have proven the most insatiable consumers of education, clearly seeing college as a route to socioeconomic mobility.[44] Generally, Freeman and others, including most higher education leaders in the United States, significantly underestimated the growing demand for higher education among every kind of student: undergraduate, graduate, professional, and adult learners training for a purpose or simply for edification. The employment market for students with a bachelor's or professional degree also grew.[45]

The question, then, is whether the contemporary flattening of participation rates, and in some states, their actual decline, is the result of temporary or long-term market forces or of social and economic forces, including the declining quality of secondary schools, rising tuition rates, and lagging financial aid programs. In other words, have government policies and social woes in the United States artificially constrained participation rates?

Do Participation Rates Matter?

Particularly since World War II, a growing number of studies showed the relative importance of increasing participation rates in higher education. Developing *human capital* for both economic and social benefits was an idea as old as the nation itself, but it was not until the 1960s that economists began to offer significant analysis of its key role in economic development. Garry Becker and T. W. Schultz famously offered evidence that more than 30% of the increased per-capita income between the 1930s and the 1960s was attributable to increased schooling. They also claimed that investment in a college-educated workforce provided a greater rate of return than any other single economic investment, including machinery. They also predicted that the private rate of return for an individual of attending and graduating from college would grow substantially when compared to those who attained only a high school diploma.[46]

The following sections discuss public and private benefits, debates regarding supply and demand, and the role of higher education in building a culture of aspiration in modern economies. All demonstrate that participation rates do matter and will be a key factor in creating more equitable and economically competitive nations.

PRIVATE AND PUBLIC BENEFITS

The work of Becker and Schultz and others spawned a significant body of economic research on human capital formation and the role of education in the U.S. economy, with increasing interest in the link of investment in higher education with technological innovation. It is important to note, however, that there are other variables beyond education and training that provide complexity to the notion of human capital. There is *cultural capital*, defined as family traits and cultural backgrounds that influence individuals, including perceived ethnic and racial ties, language, neighborhoods, and community. An increasing number of studies indicate that what happens in early childhood, including socioeconomic and family influences, often determines chances later in life and is perhaps more influential than a student's school experiences. This is why programs such as Head Start in the United States and its equivalent, Sure Start in England, have gained broad political support. As one observer of higher education, Alan Ryan, notes, preschool "programs will do more for higher education than any directly related program; but it is a long run."[47]

There is the factor of *social capital*, essentially, behavioral knowledge on how to best use opportunities, to understand the workings and manners of society and its institutions, and perhaps most important, the ability to navigate through the treacherous waters of growing bureaucracies. There is also the notion of *cognitive capital*. There are different kinds of intelligence. Their distribution is not even, or localized in one particular social, racial, or economic group. Social capital and cognitive capital are also influenced by ambition or lack thereof. Ambition plays an important role, in part influenced by environmental factors (e.g., real opportunities) and by personal traits. The combination of social and cognitive abilities with ambition helps explain why a significant number of successful CEOs in the United States were not particularly stellar students or did not come from elite universities and colleges. Some have even argued that there is such a thing as *moral capital*, what conservative journalist David Brooks calls "the ability to be trustworthy . . . Brains and skills don't matter much if you don't show up on time."[48]

Obviously, there is great complexity to understanding how humans interact within society and how their personal development contributes to economic development. The promotion of higher education has increasingly turned on the promise of financial benefits—arguably, too much so. Yet there are strong indicators that educational opportunity has been, and remains, a key ingredient for economic growth and for shaping the cultural, social, cognitive, and perhaps even the moral capital of a society. A 1999 study by Claudia Goldin and Lawrence F. Katz estimated that during the last century, about a quarter of U.S. growth in income per worker was due to the rise in educational attainment.[49] Similarly, David Mitch found that investment in secondary and postsecondary education in Europe over the last century had a large impact on general economic growth, although not as large as in the United States.[50] "Education plays an important role in accounting for the time pattern of economic growth and the cross-country variation in income per capita," explains economist Elhanan Helpman.[51] And that assertion holds not just for those who attend college; there is evidence that in U.S. cities with large concentrations of college graduates, wages are higher for other workers. "This implies," notes Helpman, "that the social rate of return on higher education is higher than the private rates of return."[52]

Other recent studies continue to demonstrate the importance of college participation rates and how they produce both private and public benefits vital to nations, particularly those with postmodern economies. The private benefit afforded individuals who participate in higher education, and particularly those that graduate with a degree, continues to grow.[53] Salaries for all Americans have generally been stagnant since 2001, but the gap between the lifetime income of college graduates and that of high school graduates has increased and is the highest among OECD countries. The income gap is also, not surprisingly, rising dramatically between college graduates and the nation's growing pool of high school dropouts.[54] In 2004, the workforce population over age twenty-five with a bachelor's degree had an average personal income of $48,400; those with only a high school diploma earned, on average, only $23,000.[55]

Those who attend college have, in addition, much higher rates of employment and much greater opportunities for both social and economic mobility and status. They have longer life spans and vote at higher rates than other portions of the population. And their children are more likely

TABLE II.I
Private and public benefits to higher education participation

	Private Benefits	Public Benefits
Economic		
	• Greater Economic Mobility • Higher Lifetime Income • Higher Employment Rates • Higher Levels of Personal Saving	• Greater Economic Equity • Lower Unemployment Rates • Greater Productivity • More Flexible Workforce • Lower Welfare Rates
Social		

	• Greater Social Mobility
	• Improved Health / Lifespan
	• Improved Economic/Health
	  Chances for Offspring
	• Improved Consumers
		• Greater Social Equity
		• Greater Social Tolerance
		• Greater Civic Involvement
		• Increased Charitable Giving
		• Lower Crime Rates
		• Higher Education Persistence
		  Rates Among Next
		  Generation

to attend and graduate from college, essentially receiving from the previous generation the cultural capital that spawns a general desire for education and self-improvement.[56]

Society has a vested interest in encouraging a significant proportion of the population to go to college and gain a degree because college education creates a more flexible, talented, and productive workforce; encourages both social and economic equity; and reduces unemployment rates and welfare rolls. It places downward pressure on crime rates, increases social tolerance, and correlates with high voter participation and rates of charitable giving. These are all general benefits that are now widely recognized by national governments and higher education leaders and advocates. Table 11.1 provides a simple matrix that outlines these and other private and public benefits of high participation rates.[57]

BALANCING SUPPLY AND DEMAND

Understanding that these benefits are substantial for both the individual and society, we confront Freeman's question: Can there be too many overly educated individuals who, encouraged to enter higher education, subsequently find they cannot find the appropriate employment? Contemporary critics of those who profess the panacea of education have reiterated the question of whether there is a finite percentage of the population actually capable of participating or gaining any robust financial return from higher learning. Historically, this is an old debate. In the 1930s,

Robert Maynard Hutchins, then the president of the University of Chicago, provocatively opposed the idea of the community college, in part because he thought the number of those academically capable was rather small. Later, while promoting greater participation, President Harry Truman's commission on education stated in 1947 that "at least 49 percent of our population has the mental ability to complete 14 years of schooling," and another 32% could complete a bachelor's degree in a liberal arts or professional field.[58] At the time, 19% of all eighteen- to twenty-one-year-old Americans were participating in some form of postsecondary education, many on the GI Bill.

Some thirty years after Freeman's analysis, in a critique of British policies on boosting higher education participation rates, Alison Wolf, a professor at King's College in London, expressed a concern that the Labour government in England was pursuing an irrational quest. The Labour Party's 1997 manifesto stated a goal of having 50% of all younger students participating in higher education (in some form). Similar goals exist in many other EU countries (there is no stated goal in the United States at the federal or by state governments, yet). In France, there is a goal that some 80% of the secondary school population should enter the baccalaureate level; Germany has a more modest 40% target, and Sweden 50%.[59]

Such targets are in part framed by the structure of their postsecondary systems; none are based on a careful analysis of the supply and demand related to labor needs. In an age of increased global competition, national governments and political leaders, Wolf observes, have become unrealistically enamored with higher education. In the rush to promote education as a key component of national economic policy, they are focused on pushing access and graduation rates, are generally unconcerned about the quality of their educational enterprises, and she notes, are largely devoid of any true understanding of the limited market for university graduates. One result: There is a growing cohort of students who feel compelled to go to a university by social and family pressures, but have little real initial interest or motivation to gain a degree and perhaps little chance of employment related to their studies.

There is the real possibility of diminishing rates of returns among countries with mature education systems and advanced economies. Wolf's argument, like Freeman's, largely targets the match between the number of postsecondary graduates and labor-market needs. She and many others are skeptical about the link of higher education participation with productivity and economic growth.[60] The postmodern boosterism of politicians seems to avoid such a consideration and, in the view of critics, instead mindlessly embraces "Education, Education, Education"—the campaign words of Prime Minister Tony Blair, which, incidentally, were first uttered by Andrew Carnegie in the early twentieth century as the panacea for America's socioeconomic ills. Wolf states, "The main conclusion must be that, while (almost) nobody would deny that education creates 'human capital,' the relationship between this and what happens in the labour market, or the real economy, is far more complex than a simple input-output model."[61]

The fascination of governments, and economists, with developing human capital relates to tenets of *new growth* theory—essentially, that postmodern economies are driven by "knowledge accumulation," leading to technological innovation and adoption. Higher education produces much of the science and know-how required to create innovation and the future workers to apply it in the marketplace. In large part, Wolf's concern is with overly aggressive ministries in Europe that are increasing their regulatory powers and expectations for their national higher education systems without adequately funding the enterprise. Specifically, she advocates, "governments need to abandon their love affair with quantitative targets."[62] Wolf and other critics of government officials are, in part, also protesting the spreading of limited public resources around in the interest of expanding access, which in turn could mean declining investment in elite universities. It is a question of where to invest, and clearly, quality over quantity is the viewpoint of the existing elite universities.

There are two important and related questions to consider in our discussion. First, can a nation, or state, provide (and fund) too much higher education regardless of how it structures its investment? And second, should governments and higher education institutions attempt to more aggressively regulate access and graduation to more directly fit immediate and projected labor market needs? Certainly, there is a need for national systems, and in turn individual institutions, to correlate their degree production to, in some form, match existing and perceived labor needs in a country, particularly in professional fields—ignoring for the moment global labor markets.

But it is also clear that anticipating market needs is a precarious and complex endeavor. Who should decide: governments or institutions? Is an undersupply better then an oversupply? In a number of European countries with traditional ties to command economies (where the national government has had a heavy hand in regulating its economy) and where public higher education is dominant, national ministries of education (and not institutions themselves) have set quotas and targets for how many students should enter a particular field—sometimes by limiting admissions to specific universities and colleges or by restricting funds for student positions.

But might this lead to a suppression of demand in fields that are some-times difficult to predict? In disciplines such as the humanities, social sci-ences, and even in science and engineering, matching supply and demand is difficult to assess. Particularly at the undergraduate level, students gain knowledge and skills with wide and often serendipitous uses over their work-ing careers—a trend that may become more dynamic in the coming years.

National governments tend to see the advantages of an oversupply. China is experiencing a huge surge in demand for higher education facilitated by national government policies, and families often invest large sums of their personal savings and incomes. College going rates have shot up from around 12% in 2002 of the traditional college age cohort (18-24 years of age) to pos-sibly 19% in 2006 according to the World Bank. But there is also a large lag in the immediate job market for people with a college degree. This disjuncture is causing significant stress for university graduates, hardship for their fami-lies, and status anxiety. Still, the Chinese government continues to push for large-scale increases in access to a tertiary education.[63] In this case, it appears that the long-term economic gains are deemed more important than a pos-sibly short-term disjuncture in the supply of graduates and the labor market.

A CULTURE OF ASPIRATION

A top-down attempt to match supply and demand is one model. An-other might be called a "structured opportunity market." The majority of OECD countries have moved toward "open admissions" systems increas-ingly accompanied by fees and evolving attempts to create differentiation in their array of tertiary institutions. In turn, fees not only generate new funds; they help in some form to decipher the motivated student from the casual user, influencing the market and, it might be argued, creating greater efficiencies. Differentiation in institutional missions helps to match student skills and interests to academic programs, and focuses institutions on their role in a larger system of higher education—in theory. In some form, this is the model emerging in most nations.

Most governments in developed and increasingly in developing econ-omies support some sector of postsecondary institutions that are open to all graduates of secondary schools. In a growing number of nations, a second-ary diploma is not a requirement for an expanding array of postsecondary programs. There are, of course, constraints on the ability of students to enter specific universities or other institutions determined by admissions standards, financial aid, institutional financial resources, physical capacity, and other limits. But most nations are committed to broad access and ag-gressively pushing demand. Why?

The reasons transcend immediate or even long-term job-market needs or the recognition that most workers will change jobs numerous times in the course of their working lives, often with the need for retraining under the rubric of *lifelong learning*. The primary reason is, or should be, the desire to promote a *culture of aspiration*, which in turn influences socioeconomic mobility and creates a more talented and entrepreneurial population, global competitiveness, and the hope for a more prosperous and equitable society.[64]

This ethos is front and center for many EU member states in their conscious efforts to boost participation rates and refashion their national higher education systems, often battling the legacy of overt class distinctions and biases. "All those who have the potential to benefit from higher education should have the opportunity to do so," states an influential white paper issued by the Labour government in England in 2003. "This is a fundamental principle which lies at the heart of building a more socially just society, because education is the best and most reliable route out of poverty and disadvantage."[65]

In effect, the goal of most postmodern governments, with only the tacit and sometimes reluctant support of the higher education community, is even larger in scope: to make broad access to higher education, or at least the opportunity at virtually any age, a part of citizenship. Just as compulsory education has moved from the elementary school level to the first two years of secondary school in most OECD countries, perhaps it will eventually include some form of postsecondary education. Alone, the economic arguments for such a policy shift are, in the contemporary era, not convincing because not all jobs require such an expansion. But the extension of compulsory laws to secondary schools in the early twentieth century was not explicitly formulated for economic reasons alone; rather, it related to broad ideas of citizenship, to fostering equality and socioeconomic mobility, and to assorted other national priorities, including the integration of immigrant populations in America.

Cultural differences abound in the socioeconomic aspirations of the population in different nations. The United States offers one case example. In part because of the relatively low social consciousness of class differences, the historically robust nature of its economy, demographic trends (including succeeding surges of immigrants), and arguably, because of its particular mass higher education system, one sees incredibly high rates of socioeconomic aspirations among Americans. Indeed, their aspirations exceed the ability of the contemporary economy to actually fulfill their expectations. Data from the OECD indicate that the occupational

TABLE 11.2

Percentage of fifteen-year-olds' occupational expectations by age thirty
in selected OECD countries: 2000

	All Students			
	White-collar, high-skilled	White-collar, low-skilled	Blue-collar, high-skilled	Blue-collar, low-skilled
OECD Countries				
Australia	65.0	11.7	10.4	12.9
Canada	70.9	10.2	7.1	11.8
Denmark	58.5	17.5	19.6	4.3
Finland	60.4	15.8	12.2	11.5
France	48.9	14.7	9.9	26.5
Germany	48.8	20.9	17.2	13.2
Italy	69.1	15.2	5.8	9.9
Japan	45.8	12.9	4.0	37.4
Spain	66.6	12.2	8.2	13.1
Sweden	63.2	10.3	8.1	18.5
United Kingdom	57.1	16.3	7.6	19.0
United States	80.5	8.2	5.1	6.2
Country mean	62.2	13.9	10.1	13.8

SOURCE: Education at a Glance (OECD 2004).

expectations of fifteen-year-olds in the United States are that, by age thirty, 80% anticipate high-skilled jobs that require postsecondary education (see Table 11.2). Only 8% believe they will have white-collar low-skilled jobs; a meager 6% expect to be in low-skilled service and manual labor jobs. In contrast, 57% of those in the United Kingdom expect to have high-skilled and professional jobs; in Sweden, the figure is 63% and in Germany and France 49%.[66]

Analysis of labor needs in postmodern economies like that of the United States indicates that the job expectations of America's youth are probably unrealistic. According to one perhaps conservative projection, only 21% of the U.S. job market in 2010 will require a bachelor's degree or higher. Only 13% of jobs will require subbaccalaureate degrees and credentials. That leaves some 66% of the job market requiring a secondary diploma or less, or depending on employers for training.[67]

Yet we know that encouraging educational aspirations benefits the individual, society, and the economy in a variety of ways. Generally, estimates of the future educational needs of a national workforce outline minimum requirements. In an analysis of the difficulties of projecting the need for college graduates, Economist John Bishop notes that the Bureau of Labor Statistics and other projections have a track record of underestimating market demand. "The task of projecting the number of jobs 'requiring a college degree' into the future is essentially impossible," he notes. Employers set out minimum requirements for a particular job but almost always desire the most educated and competent worker they can possibly hire.[68] To be sure, there are dangers in creating a caste of overqualified (the term *overeducated* seems to relegate education to a strictly vocational purpose) workers in terms of an overinvestment in an individual's education and training and in the potential mismatch of personal ambitions with actual job possibilities. The archetypal example is the history or English Ph.D. who has invested eight to ten years of postbaccalaureate education, only to drive a taxi in the immediate aftermath of graduation.

We also know that the postmodern economies are constantly changing, and most workers will switch jobs numerous times during their careers; in the face of that fact, it's reasonable to assume that for most workers, the more education, the better. The old paradigm "once a factory worker, always a factory worker" or "once a plumber, always a plumber" no longer applies. Education, and postsecondary education in particular, offers an avenue for general edification, with its own merits for the individual *and* the possibility of additional socioeconomic mobility in the future. And from a purely economic viewpoint, it offers the best chances for improving worker productivity and for fostering the entrepreneurial ethos. And although there are limits in the job market for those with higher education degrees, there is also evidence that this cohort is more likely at least to be in the labor force. For example, in the United States, participation rates among twenty-five- to sixty-four-year-olds with upper secondary education are about 60%; among those with postsecondary education experience, the rate is 88%, and for those with university-level experience, the rate exceeds 90%.[69]

One might also argue that robust levels of postsecondary education, and the promise of access, are particularly important in postmodern economies that are or will experience a large influx of immigrants. The dynamic in relatively open societies and developed economies is that in-migration of foreign nationals correlates not only to job opportunities and improved standards of living. It also correlates with rising educational levels of native populations, a corresponding expansion of high-skilled service and high-technology sectors.

Although some immigrant groups are highly educated and fill job needs in high-skilled and professional areas, more often they provide a labor force for low-skilled jobs that grow as the national economies of these countries grow. This is a dynamic long prevalent in the United States but relatively new in the European Union and other OECD countries. Robust mass higher education systems help in the assimilation of these new populations and other disadvantaged groups. They help mitigate a sense of permanent lower or ethnic class or caste. As the process of globalization continues, marked by increasingly open markets and the flow of migration, education in all its forms will increase as a tool of creating a healthy, more equitable, and productive society.

In 1960, John W. Gardner, then president of the Carnegie Corporation insisted on the centrality of creating a culture of aspiration. "If the man in the street says, 'Those fellows at the top have to be good, but I'm just a slob and can act like one'—then our days of greatness are behind us. We must foster a conception of excellence that may be applied to every degree of ability and to every socially acceptable activity. A missile may blow up on its launching pad because the designer was incompetent or because the mechanic who adjusted the last valve was incompetent. The same is true of everything else in our society. We need excellent physicists and excellent mechanics, excellent cabinet members and excellent first-grade teachers. The tone of our society depends upon a pervasive, an almost universal, striving for good performance."[70]

Economists and sociologists are increasingly interested in the question of how one accounts for societies characterized by high levels of social aspiration, actual socioeconomic mobility, and economic growth and technological innovation. How can we account for economic growth, social progress, and the differences among nations? One widespread interpretation, and building on Becker and earlier work on human capital, is that political cultures that build and expand institutions over time, such as higher education but also democratic legal frameworks, are the key factors that account for historical differences in the economic performance of nations. Further, investment rates in these institutions (politically and economically) will influence future performance and the competitive position of nations and regions. That is, particular political cultures both create social and economic institutions and are fundamentally shaped by them over time. It is a long-term and cumulative investment.[71]

Globalization, supranational entities, and international frameworks, such as the European Union and the General Agreement on Trade and Services (GATS), are tugging at the once dominant role of nation-states in shaping political culture and institutions. Yet nations remain the most significant influence on the extent and vibrancy of educational institutions, particularly in more advanced economies that owe much of their present position to previous investment rates in education. The nation-state is not dead yet; indeed, its resilience or transformation into regional alliances may surprise globalists.[72]

A Matter of Priorities?

Whether one agrees with the highly interventionist efforts of national governments in the European Union to corral and direct their tertiary institutions, it is obvious that among the EU nations higher education is a major policy issue. EU countries are engaged in national and international debates regarding the future of higher education, setting goals for expanding access, considering and implementing alternative funding policies, and negotiating cooperative initiatives, such as the Bologna Agreement.

With the exception of political battles in America over admissions to a few selective public universities and concerns over cost containment, American higher education remains a second-tier political issue. The crisis of the publics—the underinvestment in public colleges and universities, which are the primary providers of postsecondary education—is not a mainstream political concern. For this and a variety of other reasons, the United States has become relatively complacent in maintaining its higher education advantage.

A full discussion of policy options for bolstering America's already mature mass higher education system lies beyond the scope of this book. Instead, I present only a few thoughts on a difficult problem. Although this and earlier chapters have outlined many maladies of the U.S. system, there are many strengths. Arguably, America's brand of higher education is not in need of the kind of top-down regulatory reforms recently and currently pursued in European and other nations. What is needed is the interest and attention of national and state governmental leaders and some consensus in the higher education community on how to improve the nation's school system, how to create a national agenda focused on increasing higher education participation and degree-attainment rates, and a sustainable financial model for public universities and colleges.

America's population continues to grow, reaching 300 million in 2006. A study by the Education Commission of the States estimates that some 2.2 million additional students will enter accredited public and private colleges and universities between 2000 and 2015 if national participation rates hold steady. Yet current rates of participation within the traditional age cohort (eighteen- to twenty-four-year-olds) and older students (twenty-five and older) are arguably too low. If the participation rates nationally

TABLE 11.3
Projection of U.S. postsecondary participation, steady state and benchmark: 2000–2015

	2000 # Students	2015 Projection	2000- 2015 Increase	2015 Benchmark	% Change	Total Potential Increase
Age 18–24 Students	9.2 million	10.4 million	1.2 million	14.6 million	+59%	5.4 million
Age 25+ Cohort	8.2 million	9.2 million	1.0 million	13.1 million	+60%	4.9 million
Total	17.4 million	19.6 million	2.2 million	27.7 million	+59%	10.3 million

Steady State = U.S. average participation rates for age 18–24 students (34.0%) and age 25+ (4.5%).
Benchmark = Top state U.S. participation rates for age 18–24 Students (47.7%) and age 25+ (6.5%).
SOURCE: *Closing the College Participation Gap*, Education Commission of the States, 2003.

were to reflect the best-performing states, the result would be 10.3 million additional students in accredited postsecondary institutions by 2015 (see Table 11.3). That large projected difference demonstrates how poorly many and heavily populated states are doing in their participation rates.[73]

Yet another projection by the U.S. Department of Education estimates that there could be some 15 million additional students who will *want* (if given the chance) to enter some form of higher education by 2020 — public, independent private institutions, and private for-profit. In both the Education Commission of the State's and the longer-term U.S. Department of Education projections, they estimate that the greatest increase in demand will be at the two-year, postsecondary level, yet with sizable increased demand at the four-year level. One might postulate that these are modest predictions. Most past projections have significantly underestimated demand, in part because the population has grown faster than anticipated, job-skill requirements have escalated, and perhaps most important, individual aspirations have grown.

Whether there are 15 million additional students seeking entrance into higher education or a higher figure, the most likely scenario is that public universities and colleges will take the bulk of them if they have the funding, political desire, and capability to meet that demand. The number and type of providers, including for-profits, will undoubtedly increase, further diversifying the nation's higher education system. But in no small part, educational attainment in the United States will depend on the vibrancy of its public higher education sector. In my view, it is also critical that, as the higher education sector grows over time, selective public universities need to retain in some major form their historical role in society as broadly accessible agents of social change; conversely, they must avoid near convergence with their private counterparts, which is the possible outcome of privatization.

A Concluding Thought

Since the founding of the American union, promoting education, including the university, formed a core component of our democratic experiment. "Knowledge is in every country the surest basis for happiness," stated George Washington in his message to Congress in 1790. In the expansive American view, education could perpetuate social and class distinctions or it could break them; colleges and universities could simply preserve knowledge, or they could be a great catalyst for new ideas and for expanding America's economic and democratic experiment. The *social contract* of America's public universities, in tandem with the nation's vibrant network of independent private higher education institutions, has remained true to these ideas. Now much of the world has embraced them too.

Most contemporary pundits agree that there are significant problems with access and financing public colleges and universities. In the United States, as noted, these are second- or third-tier national policy issues. In many EU countries, they are first-tier issues, with concerted efforts to, in the words of the Bologna Agreement, "increase international competitiveness of a European system of higher education." They have formed supranational forums for debating and forming policies to assess and reposition the European Union. Arguably, the U.S. federal government has a greater historical and contemporary role in supporting higher education than in supporting K-12. Although such a suggestion cuts against the current political ethos of free markets and less government and raises the danger of another stifling round of accountability bureaucracy, one might reconsider how a national strategy could strengthen American higher education.[74]

On their own, states generally lack a broader understanding or concern regarding the issue of national competitiveness and the larger problems of growing social and economic stratification. Individual states may seek increased participation rates and recognize the need for additional resources for public higher education; but most are financially incapable (because of competing needs, political gridlock, and legal restrictions on generating revenue) of launching a rate of investment similar to the post–World War II and 1960s eras. Indeed, the resources and political commitment in that period that significantly expanded access required a collaboration of state and federal government—neither could do it on their own. Certainly, those political eras and policy approaches could not and should not be directly replicated. However, the specter of privatization and market models will probably not generate the investment rates and political commitment needed to adequately bolster American education and to retain its leadership position.

Or perhaps the world economy and priorities of competitor nations have permanently eroded America's once distinct higher education advantage. Even if this is the case, a new sense of resolve by political and higher education leaders in the United States is paramount, both as a key route for economic development *and* socioeconomic vitality. What would it mean for the United States to continue its downward trajectory relative to other developed economies in secondary graduate rates, in access to higher education and degree production, and what would be the resulting ramifications for socioeconomic mobility? How will the growth of new science clusters and the shift in the production of science and engineering degrees to new areas of the world shape future economic activity? The answers to these questions will profoundly influence the future development of the nation's economy and, eventually, political influence. America should look across the oceans and to other continents for ideas, inspiration, and a pragmatic sense of the globalizing and increasingly competitive world.

Chapter 1

1. "Inauguration of the New President, D. C. Gilman, Late of Yale College," *San Francisco Morning Call*, November 8, 1872.

2. Ibid.

3. Daniel C. Gilman, President of the University of California, "The Building of the University, an Inaugural Address Delivered at Oakland," November 7, 1872 (University of California Archives, henceforth UCA).

4. David Starr Jordan, "University Tendencies in America," *The Popular Science Monthly*, 63 (June 1903): 143–44; see also Edward McNall Burns, *David Starr Jordan: Prophet of Freedom* (Stanford, CA: Stanford University Press, 1953): 154–58.

5. Charles R. Van Hise, Commencement Address, University of Wisconsin, 1910.

6. Historians of higher education have focused largely on general surveys, on institutional histories, or on specific issues such as gender and race. The role of these colleges and universities, public or private, in socioeconomic mobility and in the nation's economic development has yet to be competently explored. In terms of general histories, John Thelin has provided the most recent chronicle in *A History of American Higher Education* (Baltimore, MD: Johns Hopkins University Press, 2004). A number of recent books have focused on one era or a set of institutional types, such as the small private college in the 1800s. See J. Bruce Leslie, "*Gentleman and Community: The College in the 'Age of the University'*" (State College: Pennsylvania State University Press, 1992); Julie A. Reuben, *The Making of the Modern University: Intellectual Transformation and the Marginalization of Morality* (Chicago: University of Chicago Press, 1996). Beyond a series of state surveys completed largely before World War II, there are only three relatively recent studies on how and why states nurtured and developed higher education: John Aubrey Douglass, *The California Idea and American Higher Education* (Stanford, CA: University of Stanford Press, 2000); David G. Sansing, *Making Haste Slowly: The Troubled History of Higher Education in Mississippi* (Jackson: University Press of Mississippi, 1990); Richard M. Freeland, *Academy's Golden Age: Universities in Massachusetts, 1945–1970* (New York: Oxford University Press, 1992).

7. U.S. Department of Education, National Center for Educational Statistics, *Digest of Education Statistics, 2005*, Table 188; James L. Duderstadt and Farris W. Womack, *Beyond the Crossroads: The Future of the Public University in America* (Baltimore, MD: Johns Hopkins University Press, 2003).

8. G. Gaither (ed.), *The Multicampus System: Perspectives on Practice and Prospects* (Sterling, VA: Stylus Publishing, 1999): xix.

9. See Alexander W. Astin and Leticia Oseguera, "The Declining 'Equity' of American Higher Education," *The Review of Higher Education*, 27, no. 3 (Spring 2004): 321–41.

10. For a discussion on the nature of the colonial college and its private and public characteristics, see Jurgen Herbst, *From Crisis to Crisis: American College Government 1636–1819* (Cambridge, MA: Harvard University Press, 1982).

11. Benjamin Silliman Jr., "The Truly Practical Man, Necessarily an Education Man: Oration Delivered at the Commencement of the College of California, June 5, 1867," in *Pamphlets on the College of California*, Bancroft Library, Berkeley, p. 18 (UCA).

12. An Act to Create and Organize the University of California, California State Legislature, March 23, 1868, sect. 13.

13. Ibid.

14. Ibid., sect. 14.

15. Cited in Michael Bezilla, *Penn State: An Illustrated History* (University Park: Pennsylvania State University Press, 1985): 6.

16. *The Berkeleyan*, January, 1874, p. 10 (UCA).

17. *The Occident*, October 2, 1891, p. 4 (UCA).

18. Biennial Report of the Regents of the University of California, for the Years 1873–1875, (Sacramento, 1875): 114.

19. See Douglass, *The California Idea and American Higher Education*.

20. Cited in William Warren Ferrier, *Origin and Development of the University of California* (Berkeley, CA: Sather Gate Book Shop, 1930): 322.

21. Andrew J. Moulder, Secretary, *Regents of the University of California Report of the Regents of the University of California, Relative to the Operations and Progress of the Institution* (Sacramento, CA: T. A. Springer, State Printer, 1872).

22. Ibid.

23. As quoted in Ferrier, *Origin and Development of the University of California*, p. 333.

24. *Foltz v. Hoge* (1879) 54 C 28.

25. James Bryce, *The American Commonwealth*, vol. 2 (London: Macmillan, 1891): 600–601.

26. Ibid., p. 605.

27. Ibid.

28. Cited in Reuben Gold Thwaites, *History of the University of Wisconsin* (Madison: University of Wisconsin Press, 1900).

29. Ibid.

30. Ibid.

31. Charles H. Brown, "Penn State Centennial History," Penn State University Archives, 1953.

32. Act to Create and Organize the University of California, sect. 18.

33. Minutes, University of California Board of Regents, April 12, 1870, vol. 1, pp. 133–34; a total of eighty-eight students enrolled in the university's preparatory school during the 1870–1871 academic year, sixteen of whom had Hispanic surnames.

34. See Herman Adolph Spindt, "A History of the University of California and the Public High Schools of California, 1872–1945" (unpublished Ph.D. dissertation, University of California-Berkeley, 1946).

35. Report of the President for the Board of Regents: 1881–1882 (UCA).

36. Minutes, University of California Board of Regents, May 23, 1884 (UCA). The regents "allowed the Faculty to hold examinations in different parts of the state at their discretion."

37. "Historical Sketch of the Policies of the University of California with Respect to the Admission of Freshmen," Minutes, Special Committee on Admissions of the Academic Senate, University of California, November 17, 1928 (UCA).

38. Ibid., p. 5.

39. Verne A. Stadtman, *The University of California: 1868–1968* (New York: McGraw-Hill, 1970): 95.

Chapter 2

1. Cited in John Aubrey Douglass, *The California Idea and American Higher Education* (Stanford, CA: Stanford University Press, 2000): 119.

2. James McKeen Cattell, "A Statistical Study of American Men of Science," *Science*, 24 (1906): 739; Edwin E. Slosson, *The Great American Universities* (New York: Amos Press, 1910): 148–49.

3. Alexis F. Lange, "Our Adolescent School System," *University of California Chronicle*, no. 1 (1908): 2–14.

4. Alexis F. Lange, "The Junior College," circa. 1915 in the Lange Collection, University of California Archives (henceforth UCA).

5. Ibid.

6. Alexis F. Lange, "The Unification of Our School System," *Sierra Education News*, 5 (June 1909): 346.

7. "The Fresno Junior College," *The California Weekly*, July 15, 1910, p. 539; Merton E. Hill, "The Junior College Movement in California," *Junior College Journal*, 16, no. 6 (February 1946): 254.

8. Carnegie Foundation for the Advancement of Teaching, *Report of the California Commission for the Study of Educational Problems*, California State

Printing Office Sacramento, 1932 p. 62. William Wallace Campbell, "The Junior Colleges in Their Relationship to the University," *California Quarterly of Secondary Education*, (January 1927): 117; David O. Levine, *The American College and the Culture of Aspiration, 1915–1940* (Ithaca, NY: Cornell University Press, 1986): 174–75.

9. Douglass, *The California Idea and American Higher Education*, pp. 135–69.

10. John Aubrey Douglass, "A Tale of Two Universities of California: A Tour of Strategic Issues Past and Prospective," *Chronicle of the University of California*, no. 4 (Fall 2000).

11. Jesse B. Sears and Elwood Cubberley, *The Cost of Education in California*, (Washington DC: American Council on Education, 1924) p. 17; Verne A. Stadtman (ed.), *The Centennial Record of the University of California* (Berkeley: University of California Press, 1967): 3.

12. James Sutton, "Historical Sketch of the Policies of the University of California with Respect to the Admission of Freshmen," Minutes, Academic Senate Special Committee on Admissions of the University of California, November 17, 1928 (UCA).

13. See Douglass, *The California Idea and American Higher Education*.

14. "Announcement of the University of California: Academic Year 1923–24," *University of California Bulletin*, 5, no. 1 (UCA).

15. Harold S. Wechsler, *The Qualified Student* (New York: Wiley, 1977): 124–25.

16. Ibid. These powers were vested in the academic senate in the standing orders of the University of California regents both before and after the so-called "Berkeley Revolution" of 1920. Standing Order 105 read: "It shall be the duty of this board to examine and classify applicants for admission to undergraduate status, whether regular, at large, or special; and to report thereupon to the Academic Senate. The Board shall have power to grant supplementary examinations, where necessary, to ascertain the qualifications of applicants for admissions; and shall have power in exceptional cases to admit applicants with minor deficiencies."

17. Minutes, Academic Council of the University of California, April 17, 1920 (UCA).

18. Oliver M. Washborn, Chairman of the University of California Academic Senate Committee on Schools, to the Academic Senate Board of Admissions, September 18, 1939 (UCA).

19. Minutes, Board of Admissions and Entrance Examinations, University of California, May 10, 1920 (UCA).

20. Herman A. Spindt, Principal, Kern County Union High School and Junior College, to Mr. B. M. Woods, Chair, Board of Admissions, November 11, 1928 (UCA); Report of the Committee of the High School Principals Association, "Accreditation of High Schools," *California Quarterly of Secondary Education* (June 1928): 395–403.

21. Oliver M. Washburn to the Academic Senate Special Committee on Admissions of the University of California, April 12, 1928 (UCA).

22. Clarence Paschell, Office of the Examiner of Schools, to the Academic Senate Special Committee on Admissions of the University of California, June 9, 1928 (UCA).

23. Minutes, Academic Senate Special Committee on Admissions of the University of California, November 17, 1928 (UCA).

24. Liaison Committee of the State Board of Education and the Regents of the University of California, *A Master Plan for Higher Education in California, 1960–1975* (Sacramento: California State Department of Education, 1960): 70.

25. Wechsler, *The Qualified Student,* p. 240.

26. James Gray, *Open Wide the Door: The Story of the University of Minnesota* (New York: G. P. Putnam's Sons, 1958): 138–39.

27. Frank Aydelotte, "The American College of the Twentieth Century," in Robert Lincoln Kelley (ed.), *The Effective College* (New York: Association of American Colleges, 1928): 6; Seymour Martin Lipset and Reinhard Bendix, *Social Mobility in Industrial Society* (Berkeley: University of California Press, 1974).

28. Robert Gordon Sproul, Inaugural Address on Becoming President of the University of California, October 1930 (UCA).

29. Robert Gordon Sproul, speech before the Commonwealth Club of California, July 25, 1930.

30. Sproul, Inaugural Address, October 1930.

Chapter 3

1. Delegates to the 1849 Constitutional Convention, "Address to the People of California," quoted in *Constitution of 1849* (San Marino, CA: Huntington Library, 1949).

2. Ibid.

3. David O. Levine, "Discrimination in College Admissions," in Lester F. Goodchild and Harold Wechsler (ed.), *The History of Higher Education* (New York: Pearson, 2003): 523.

4. Marcia Graham Synnott, *The Half Open Door* (Westport, CT: Greenwood Press, 1979): 17; see also Jerome Karabel, *The Chosen: The Hidden History of Admission and Exclusion at Harvard, Yale, and Princeton* (Boston: Houghton Mifflin, 2005).

5. Ibid., p. 17.

6. Clyde Furst, "Tests of College Efficiency," *The School Review,* 20, no. 5 (May 1912): 320–34.

7. Cited in Synnott, *The Half Open Door,* p. 21.

8. Cited in Levine, "Discrimination in College Admissions," p. 513.

9. Ibid.

10. Cited in Wechsler, *The Qualified Student,* p. 230.

11. Seymour Martin Lipset and David Riesman, *Education and Politics at Harvard* (New York: McGraw-Hill, 1975): 143.

12. Synnott, *The Half Open Door*, p. 21.

13. Cited in Wechsler, *The Qualified Student*, p. 230.

14. Alexander Meiklejohn, "What Does the College Hope to Be in the Next Hundred Years?" *Amherst Graduates' Quarterly* (August 1921): 337–38.

15. Ibid., p. 219.

16. Record of the 1938 New York State Constitutional Convention, Albany, NY, 1939.

17. *Higher Education for American Democracy*, A Report of the President's Commission on Higher Education, vol. 1, Washington, DC, December 1947, p. 34.

18. Ibid., p. 35.

19. Synnott, *The Half Open Door*, p. xix.

20. Levine, "Discrimination in College Admissions," p. 523.

21. Wechsler, *The Qualified Student*, pp. 255–65.

22. Ibid.

23. A public school of optometry and a medical school in Brooklyn operated outside the CUNY network.

24. Wechsler, *The Qualified Student*, p. 260.

25. Author's interview, Albert Bowker, April 7, 2004.

26. Wechsler, *The Qualified Student*, p. 260.

27. Minutes of Proceedings, CUNY Board of Higher Education, July 9, 1969.

28. The City University of New York, University Senate, "Report on Special Admissions Policy," February 12, 1969, 1.6–7, cited in Wechsler, *The Qualified Student*, p. 287.

29. Minutes of Proceedings, CUNY Board of Higher Education, July 9, 1969.

30. *Ward v. Flood*, 48 Calif. 36 (1874); see also Charles M. Wollenberg, *All Deliberate Speed: Segregation and Exclusion in California Schools* (Berkeley: University of California Press, 1976).

31. Irving G. Hendrick, *The Education of Non-Whites in California, 1849–1970* (San Francisco: R&E Research Associates, 1977): 41.

32. Irving G. Hendrick, *California Education* (San Francisco: Boyd & Fraser, 1980): 20–21.

33. See Wollenberg, *All Deliberate Speed*, pp. 125–32.

34. John Caughey and LaRee Caughey, *To Kill a Child's Spirit* (Itasca, IL: F. E. Peacock, 1973): 9–10; Wollenberg, *All Deliberate Speed*, pp. 134 and 157.

35. Daniel C. Gilman, President of the University of California, The Building of the University, an inaugural address delivered at Oakland, November 7, 1872 (University of California Archives, henceforth UCA).

36. Benjamin Ide Wheeler, address delivered at Dartmouth College, June 27, 1905, in *The Abundant Life* (Berkeley: University of California Press, 1926).

37. Benjamin Ide Wheeler, message to the Japanese Students of the University of California, published in the *Berkeley Lyceum*, June 1909, in *The Abundant Life* (Berkeley: University of California Press, 1926).

38. University of California Board of Regents' Special Meeting, "Tuition on Aliens and Non-Residents," January 4, 1921 (UCA).

39. Verne A. Stadtman (ed.), *The Centennial Record of the University of California* (Berkeley: University of California Printing Department, 1967): 300.

40. University of California Report of the President, 1926 (UCA).

41. Lucy Warf Stebbins, Report of the Dean of Women, July 1, 1926, in University of California Report of the President, 1926 (UCA).

42. This estimate of Asian American enrollment at Berkeley is based on a visual scan of the yearbooks that also provide information on students' major and city of origin.

43. University of California Academic Senate, Academic Council Minutes, September 18, 1963 (UCA).

44. University of California, Academic Council Minutes, December 11, 1963 (UCA).

Chapter 4

1. Edward L. Thorndike, "The Measurement of Educational Products," *The School Review*, 20, no. 5 (May 1912): 289–99.

2. For a detailed analysis of the negotiation process, see John A. Douglass, *The California Idea and American Higher Education* (Stanford, CA: Stanford University Press, 2000).

3. Master Plan Survey Team, *California Master Plan for Higher Education, 1960–1975*, prepared for the Liaison Committee of the State Board of Education and the Regents of the University of California, Sacramento, 1960, p. 67.

4. See John A. Douglass, "How California Determined Admissions Pools: Lower and Upper Division Targets and the California Master Plan for Higher Education," CSHE Research and Occasion Papers Series, CSHE.2.01 (September 2001).

5. Ibid., p. 63.

6. Report of the Committee on Educational Policy, Representative Assembly Minutes, January 10, 1961, p. 9 (University of California Archives, henceforth UCA).

7. George D. Strayer, Monroe E. Deutsch, and Aubrey A. Douglass, *A Report of a Survey of the Needs of California Higher Education* (Sacramento, CA: State Printing Office, 1948).

8. Douglass, *The California Idea and American Higher Education*, pp. 201−6.

9. Nicholas Lehman, *The Big Test: The Secret History of the American Meritocracy* (New York: Farrar, Straus and Giroux, 1999): 104.

10. David Royce Hubin, "The Scholastic Aptitude Test: Its Development and Introduction, 1900−1948" (unpublished Ph.D. dissertation, University of Oregon, 1988): 120.

11. Richard Pearson, Oral History, conducted by Gary Saretzky, ETS Oral History Program, December 27, 1979.

12. *A Restudy of the Needs of California in Higher Education: Prepared for the Liaison Committee of the Regents of the University of California and the California State Board of Education* (Sacramento: California State Department of Education, 1955).

13. California Coordinating Council for Higher Education, "The Flow of Students in Higher Education," (Sacramento: CCCHE, May 20, 1968): 19−20.

14. *A Restudy of the Needs of California in Higher Education*, p. 108.

15. Richard W. Jennings, Alfred E. Longueil, et al., "Educational Problems Related to Size," report given at the Eleventh All-University Faculty Conference, April 27−29, 1956.

16. Minutes, Board of Admissions and Relations with Schools, University of California Academic Senate, July 1956 (UCA).

17. Minutes, Board of Admissions and Relations with Schools, University of California Academic Senate, May 10 and 11, 1957 (UCA).

18. Ibid.

19. BOARS Report, Representative Assembly, Meeting October 28, 1958, p. 39 (UCA).

20. BOARS Report, Representative Assembly, Meeting October 23, 1961, p. 10 (UCA).

21. BOARS Report, Representative Assembly, Meeting October 28, 1958, p. 39 (UCA).

22. BOARS Minutes, December 8 and 9, 1961, p. 2 (UCA).

23. BOARS Report, Representative Assembly, Meeting May 22, 1962, p. 22 (UCA); Academic Senate, Representative Assembly, Northern Section, January 8, 1962 (UCA).

24. Minutes, Board of Admissions and Relations with Schools, January 11, 1963 (UCA).

25. Minutes, Board of Admissions and Relations with Schools, "University Eligibility and Rank in Class," May 20−21, 1963 (UCA).

26. Minutes, Board of Admissions and Relations with Schools, "Progress Report on the Fall 1963 Achievement Test Study," February 25−26, 1965, pp. 9−11 (UCA).

27. Ibid.

28. Ibid., p. 11.

Chapter 5

1. John David Skrentny, *The Ironies of Affirmative Action: Politics, Culture, and Justice in America* (Chicago: University of Chicago Press, 1996): 107.
2. Ibid., p. 108.
3. Hugh Davis Graham, "Affirmative Action for Immigrants? The Unintended Consequences of Reform," in John David Skrentny (ed.), *Color Lines: Affirmative Action, Immigration, and Civil Rights Options for America* (Chicago: University of Chicago Press, 2001): 55.
4. Record of the Assembly of the Academic Senate, 6, no. 1, November 18, 1968 (University of California Archives, henceforth UCA).
5. Record of the Assembly of the Academic Senate, 1, no. 2., January 10, 1964 (UCA).
6. See University of California at Berkeley, Office of Admissions and Records, "History of the Admission Policy for Educational Opportunity," 1988 (UCA).
7. "Socio-Economic Characteristics of Student Groups Relevant to the Question of Equality and Access," University of California, October 1967 (UCA); see also Student Affirmative Action Task Groups, "A Report to the President of the University of California," July 1975, pp. 28–29 (UCA).
8. Meeting of the Assembly of the Academic Senate, Barrows Hall, Berkeley, May 22, 1967 (UCA).
9. H. W. Iverson, K. Lamb, and H. Reiber, "Broad Aspects of Admissions," to BOARS, University of California, March 16, 1966, in BOARS Minutes, March 18, 1966 (UCA).
10. Minutes, Academic Assembly, meeting on the Riverside campus, November 3, 1969 (UCA).
11. On March 4, 1967, BOARS approved the proposal that the university expand the special action category to an additional 2% of students to provide greater opportunities to "disadvantaged" students. On March 15, 1968, regents approved the change.
12. Coordinating Council for Higher Education, "The Flow of Students in California Higher Education," (Sacramento, CA: CCCHE, May 20, 1968): 37.
13. Elements of the 1971 "administrative policy" issued by Vice President Kidner reflected the action of the senate's university committee regarding "Basic Principles of Enrollment Policy," submitted to the University of California Academic Assembly at their November 17, 1970, meeting (UCA).
14. Frank L. Kidner, Vice President for Educational Relations, to Chancellors, University of California, May 1971 (UCA).
15. Ibid.
16. Frank Newman et al., *Report on Higher Education* (Washington, DC: U.S. Government Printing Office, 1971): 1.

17. Alexander W. Astin, "College Dropouts: A National Profile," *ACE Research Reports*, 7, no. 1 (February 1972).

18. Northeastern California Higher Education Study, "Council Report 72-77," Coordinating Council for Higher Education, Sacramento, December 1972.

19. Carnegie Commission on Higher Education, *New Students and New Places* (New York: McGraw-Hill, 1971): 97.

20. Clark Kerr, *The Uses of the University* (Cambridge, MA: Harvard University Press, 1964).

21. Joint Committee for Review of the Master Plan for Higher Education, Report of the Joint Committee on the Master Plan for Higher Education, California Legislature, September 1973.

22. Ibid.

23. Ibid.

24. Ibid.; The Joint Committee cited K. Patricia Cross's observation that "the best way to graduate a bright class is to admit a bright class." K. Patricia Cross, "The New Learners," *Change*, 5 (February 1973): 31.

25. California State Legislature, "Report of the Joint Committee on the Master Plan for Higher Education," Sacramento, 1973.

26. Passed as ACR 150 and ACR 151 in 1974 by the California State Legislature.

27. Student Affirmative Action Task Groups, "A Report to the President of the University of California," July 1975, p. 1 (UCA).

28. Ibid.

29. Ibid., p. 14.

30. Report of the Student Affirmative Action Task Groups, University of California, p. 13 (UCA).

31. Ibid.

32. Keith Sexton and J. Goldman, "Archival Experiments with College Admissions Policies," University of California Office of the President, 1975 (UCA).

33. "Report to the Legislature in Response to Item 349 of the 1974 Budget Conference Committee Supplemental Report: Student Affirmative Action at the University of California," January 1975 (UCA).

34. California Postsecondary Education Commission, "1982–83 Budget Report on Equal Educational Opportunity Programs," March 1982; Minutes, University of California Board of Regents, June 1980 (UCA).

35. Minutes, Assembly of the Academic Senate, University of California, June 2, 1977 (UCA).

36. "Final Report of the Task Force on Undergraduate Admissions," University of California, Office of the President, March 1977 (UCA).

37. Ibid., pp. 28–29.

38. Ibid.

39. Ibid., pp. 15–16.

40. Ibid.

41. William B. Fretter, presentation to the University of California Board of Regents, July 15, 1977 (UCA).

42. Ibid.

43. *DeFunis v. Odegaard* (1973) 507 P.2d 1169 (Wash. 1973), dismissed as moot, 416 U.S. 312 (1973), on remand, 529 P.2d 438 (Wash. 1974).

44. *Regents of the University of California v. Bakke*, 438 U.S. 265, 295 (1978).

45. Robert Michaelsen, Chair, Santa Barbara Division, to Wilson Riles, State Superintendent of Public Instruction, July 18, 1977 (California State Archives).

46. Minutes, Assembly of the University of California Academic Senate, June 2, 1977 (UCA).

47. Proposed Assembly Concurrent Resolution No. 28, March 14, 1977.

48. William B. Fretter to the University of California Academic Council, July 19, 1977 (UCA).

49. President David S. Saxon to the University of California Board of Regents, September 23, 1977 (UCA).

50. Minutes, University of California Board of Regents, October 1977 (UCA).

51. William B. Fretter, Chair, University of California Academic Council, to Academic Council Members, July 29, 1977 (UCA).

52. Ibid.

53. Minutes, University of California Board of Regents, June 1980 (UCA); Minutes, University of California Board of Regents, "Report on UC Admissions: Impact on the Current Undergraduate Admissions Policy," May 6, 1981 (UCA).

54. Minutes, University of California Board of Regents, June 1980 (UCA).

55. Karl S. Pister, "Student Affirmative Action—A Faculty Member's Perspective of Past Failures, Current Problems and Opportunities for Future Success," at the forth annual Fall Outreach Services Conference, UC Irvine, September 3, 1980 (UCA); William E. Broen Jr., BOARS Chair, to Donald C. Swain, Academic Vice President, University of California, February 10, 1981 (UCA).

Chapter 6

1. *Sweezy v. New Hampshire*, 354 U.S. 234, 236 (1957).

2. *Florida ex. rel. Hawkins v. Board of Control*, 350 U.S. 413 (1956).

3. Alexander W. Astin, Bruce Fuller, and Kenneth C. Green (ed.), *Admitting and Assisting Students After Bakke* (San Francisco: Jossey-Bass, 1978): vii.

4. Quoted in Terry Eastland and William J. Bennett, *Counting By Race: Equality from the Founding Fathers to Bakke and Weber* (New York: Basic Books, 1979): 178.

5. Ibid.

6. Cited in Astin, Fuller, and Green (ed.), *Admitting and Assisting Students After Bakke*, p. 2.

7. Cited in Eastland and Bennett, *Counting by Race*, p. 176.

8. Ibid.

9. Cited in Astin, Fuller, and Green (ed.), *Admitting and Assisting Students After Bakke*, p. 75.

10. See Bruce Fuller, Patricia P. McNamara, and Kenneth C. Green, "Alternative Admissions Programs," in Astin, Fuller, and Green (ed.), *Admitting and Assisting Students After Bakke*, pp. 1–27.

11. Frank L. Kidner, Vice President for Educational Relations, to the Chancellors, University of California, May 1971 (UC Archives, henceforth UCA).

12. President David S. Saxon to the Chancellors, "University of California Guidelines on Fair and Equal Opportunities to Participate in Undergraduate and Graduate Programs," June 12, 1979 (UCA).

13. "University Policy on Undergraduate Admissions," adopted by the University of California Board of Regents, May 25, 1988 (UCA).

14. Berkeley Division of the Academic Senate, University of California, "Freshman Admissions at Berkeley: A Policy for the 1990s and Beyond," May 19, 1980 (henceforth the Karabel Report), p. 2 (UCA).

15. In Stephen A. Arditti, William B. Baker, Ronald W. Brady, William R. Frazer, and Cornelius L. Hopper, *The University of California Office of the President and Its Constituencies, 1983–1995. volume 1: The Office of the President.* University of California, Berkeley, Regional Oral History Office, 1997–1998.

16. University of California Systemwide Administration, Office of Outreach Services, "University of California Student Affirmative Action Plan," May 1978, p. 17 (UCA).

17. Long-Range Academic Plan, University of California, Berkeley, 1980, p. 4 (UCA).

18. Patrick Saburo Hayashi, "The Politics of University Admissions: A Case Study of the Evolution of Admissions Policies and Practices During the 1980s at the University of California, Berkeley" (unpublished Ph.D. dissertation, 1993), pp. 55–58.

19. Karabel Report, pp. 22–25.

20. Ibid.

21. Academic Senate Committee on Undergraduate Admissions and Relations with Schools, "1990 Freshman Admissions to the College of Letters and Science," University of California, Los Angeles (UCA).

22. Philip Curtis, Chair, UCLA Academic Senate Committee on Undergraduate Admissions and Relations with Schools, Statement Before the Regents, Minutes, University of California Board of Regents, July 10, 1990 (UCA).

23. Christopher Shea, "Under UCLA's Elaborate System Race Makes a Big Difference," *Chronicle of Higher Education*, February 1995; see also *UCLA Today*, March 10, 1995.

24. Minutes, University of California Board of Regents, "Report on the Establishment of a New Admission Application System," June 20, 1985 (UCA).

25. Larry Gordon, "Many Top Students Are Losing UC Campus Bid," *Los Angeles Times*, February 12, 1988.

26. Helen Henry, BOARS Chair, to Fred Speiss Academic Council Chair, April 4, 1990 (UCA).

27. BOARS Report to Academic Council, University of California, on the California Articulation Number System (CAN) and the New Admissions System, June 18, 1986 (UCA).

28. Karabel Report, p. 29.

29. Dropping Asian Americans from the designation of underrepresented minorities was outlined in a five-year plan developed in 1983. See W. R. Ellis and F. J. Hernandez, *Five-Year Plan for Undergraduate Affirmative Action*, University of California, Berkeley, Office of Undergraduate Affairs, April 4, 1983 (UCA).

30. Michael Manzagol, "Sins of Admissions," *California Monthly*, April 1988.

31. Report of the Asian American Task Force on University Admissions, San Francisco, June 1985, p. 6.

32. Dana Y. Takagi, *The Retreat from Race: Asian-American Admissions and Racial Politics* (New Brunswick, NJ: Rutgers University Press, 1992): 33–35.

33. Report of the Asian American Task Force on University Admissions, p. 6.

34. Michael Ire Heyman, Oral History, Regional Oral History Office, The Bancroft Library, University of California, 2003; see also Karabel Report, p. 53.

35. Alan Krueger and Stacy Dale, "Estimating the Payoff to Attending a More Selective College: An Application of Selection on Observables and Unobservables," *Quarterly Journal of Economics*, 117, no. 4 (November 2002).

36. See Alexander W. Astin and Leticia Oseguera, "The Declining 'Equity' of American Higher Education," *The Review of Higher Education*, 27, no. 3 (Spring 2004): 321–41; Ernest Pascarella and P. T. Terenzini, *How College Affects Students* (San Francisco: Jossey-Bass, 1991).

37. Gordon, "Many Top Students Are Losing UC Campus Bid."

38. Ibid.

39. Cited in Takagi, *The Retreat from Race*, pp. 73–74.

40. California State Auditor General, *A Review of First Year Admissions at the University of California, Berkeley* (Sacramento: State of California, October 1987).

41. Author's interview with Patrick Hayashi, April 4, 2004.

42. David Pierpont Gardner, "A Life in Higher Education: Fifteenth President of the University of California, 1983–1992," an oral history conducted in 1995 and 1996 by Ann Lage, Regional Oral History Office, The Bancroft Library, University of California, 1997, p. 427.

43. Irene Chang, "Heyman Apologizes to Asians," *Daily Californian*, January 1, 1988.

44. Ibid.

45. Roy T. Brophy, Robert J. Campbell, George C. Deukmejian, Richard G. Heggie, Walter E. Hoadley, Meredith J. Khachigian, Howard H. Leach, Steven A. Merksamer, Dean A. Watkins, and Harold M. Williams, *The University of California Office of the President and Its Constituencies, 1983–1995, Vol. 3: Regents and State Government Officials*, University of California, Berkeley, Regional Oral History Office, 1997–1999. Available from the Online Archive of California at http://ark.cdlib.org/ark:/13030/kt30000428.

46. Michael Manzagol, "Sins of Admissions," *California Monthly*, April 1988.

47. Ibid.

48. Ibid.

49. President David S. Saxon to the Chancellors, "University of California Guidelines on Fair and Equal Opportunities to Participate in Undergraduate and Graduate Programs," June 12, 1979 (UCA).

50. Minutes, University of California Board of Regents, May 25, 1988 (UCA).

51. University of California Board of Regents, "University Policy on Undergraduate Admissions," May 25, 1988 (UCA).

52. Mark Wheelis, BOARS Chair, to Murray Schwartz, Academic Council Chair, on "Draft Guidelines for Implementation of University Policy on UG Admissions," June 14, 1988 (UCA).

53. President David Gardner to Chancellors and Academic Council, "Guidelines for Implementation of University Policy on Undergraduate Admissions," University of California, July 5, 1988 (UCA).

54. Ibid.

55. Steve Brint and Jerome Karabel, *The Diverted Dream: Community Colleges and the Promise of Educational Opportunity in America, 1900–1985* (New York: Oxford University Press, 1989).

56. Ibid., p. 25.

57. Ibid., p. 29.

58. Ibid., p. 41.

59. David Pierpont Gardner, "A Life in Higher Education: Fifteenth President of the University of California, 1983–1992," an oral history, Bancroft Library, p. 427.

Chapter 7

1. California Constitution of 1879, art. IX, sect. 9.

2. William Bowen and Derek Bok, *The Shape of the River: Long-Term Consequences of Considering Race in College and University Admissions* (Princeton, NJ: Princeton University Press, 1998): 7.

3. Office of the Assistant Vice President, Student Academic Services, Office of the President, University of California, "Reports on Enrollment, 1990–1995." (University of California Archives, henceforth UCA).

4. David A. Hollinger, "Group Preferences, Cultural Diversity, and Social Democracy: Notes Toward a Theory of Affirmative Action," *Representations*, no. 55 (Summer 1995): 31–40.

5. Office of Outreach Services, University of California Systemwide Administration, "University of California Student Affirmative Action Plan," May 1978, p. 22 (UCA).

6. California Association of Scholars, press release, January 15, 1996.

7. Martin Trow, presentation before the Board of Regents of the University of California, January 18, 1996 (UCA).

8. Ward Connerly to Chairman Howard Leach, Board of Regents of the University of California, December 21, 1993 (UCA).

9. Ibid.

10. Ward Connerly to Clair W. Burgener, Chair of the University of California Board of Regents, June 30, 1995 (UCA).

11. Ward Connerly, *Creating Equality: My Fight Against Race Preferences* (San Francisco: Encounter Books, 2000): 126–28.

12. *Adarand Constructors, Inc. v. Peña*, June 12, 1995.

13. Minutes, University of California Board of Regents, January 19, 1995 (UCA).

14. Ibid.

15. See John Aubrey Douglass, "Setting the Conditions of Admissions: The Role of University of California Faculty in Policymaking," University of California Academic Senate, February 1997 (UCA).

16. Minutes, University of California Board of Regents, statement of President Peltason to the Regents, July 20, 1995 (UCA).

17. Ibid.

18. Office of the Assistant Vice President, Student Academic Services, Office of the President, University of California, "The Use of Socio-Economic Status in Place of Ethnicity in Undergraduate Admissions: A Report on the Results of an Exploratory Computer Simulation," May 1995 (UCA).

19. State Senator Tom Campbell, press release, July 17, 1995.

20. Connerly to Burgener, June 30, 1995.

21. Ibid.

22. Minutes, University of California Board of Regents, July 20, 1995 (UCA).

23. Ward Connerly, news release, July 5, 1995.

24. Connerly, *Creating Equality*, p. 131.

25. Minutes, University of California Board of Regents, January 19, 1995 (UCA).

26. Minutes, University of California Academic Council Meeting, January 18, 1995 (UCA).

27. Minutes, University of California Academic Council Meeting, April 12, 1995 (UCA).

28. Walter W. Yuen, Chair, Universitywide Committee on Affirmative Action, to Daniel Simmons, Chair, University of California Academic Council, February 5, 1995 (UCA).

29. Ibid.

30. Minutes, University of California Academic Council Meeting, February 15, 1995 (UCA).

31. President Jack Peltason to the Regents, July 10, 1995 (UCA).

32. *Los Angeles Times*, July 20, 1995.

33. Ibid.

34. *The New York Times*, July 19, 1995.

35. Regents Campbell, del Junco, Kolligian, and Lee to President Peltason, July 13, 1995, cited in Pusser, "The Contest over Affirmative Action at the University of California: Theory and Politics of Contemporary Higher Education Policy" (unpublished Ph.D. dissertation, Stanford University, 1999): 250. Along with Chavez's book *The Color Bind*, Pusser's dissertation and later book, *Burning Down the House: Politics, Governance, and Affirmative Action at the University of California* (Albany: State University of New York Press, 2004), offer the most detailed discussion of the regents' debate.

36. This according to Jesse Jackson's statement before the regents at their June 20, 1995 meeting.

37. Statement of the President, Chancellors, and Vice Presidents of the University of California, July 10, 1995 (UCA).

38. Ed Gomez and the University of California Student Association to the University of California Board of Regents, July 17, 1995 (UCA).

39. Minutes, University of California Board of Regents, July 20, 1995 (UCA).

40. Chavez, *The Color Bind*, p. 64.

41. Minutes University of California Board of Regents, July 20, 1995 (UCA).

42. Ibid.; Chavez, *The Color Bind*, p. 66.

43. Minutes, University of California Board of Regents, July 20, 1995 (UCA).

44. Chavez, *The Color Bind*, p. 65.

45. President David Gardner to the University of California Chancellors, "Guidelines for Implementation of University Policy on Undergraduate Admissions and for Fall 1990 Term," July 5, 1988 (UCA).

46. Minutes, University of California Board of Regents, Regents adopt resolution "Policy Ensuring Equal Treatment—Admissions," July 12, 1995 (UCA).

47. Ken Chavez, "Jackson Marchers Protest 'Mockery'," *Sacramento Bee*, July 21, 1995.

48. Quoted in Chavez, *The Color Bind*, p. 67.

49. Ibid., p. 76.

50. See John Aubrey Douglass, "Shared Governance at the University of California," CSHE Research and Occasional Papers, CSHE1.98 (March 1998).

51. State Senator John Vasconcellos to the University of California Board of Regents, July 21, 1995 (UCA).

Chapter 8

1. Andrew Hacker, "Goodbye to Affirmative Action?" *New York Review of Books*, July 11, 1996, pp. 21–29.

2. "A Noble Warrior's Next Fight," *New York Post*, June 29, 1998.

3. Jesse Douglas Allen-Taylor, "Conscious of Color," *Color Lines*, 6, no. 1 (Spring 2003).

4. Louis Freedberg, "After 20 Years, *Bakke* Ruling Back in the Spotlight: Foes of College Affirmative Action Want High Court to Overturn It," *San Francisco Chronicle*, June 27, 1998.

5. *Adarand Constructors, Inc. v. Peña*, 515 U. S., at 227.

6. For example, the U.S. Court of Appeals rejected an appeal against California's Proposition 209.

7. Ronald Dworkin, "Is Affirmative Action Doomed?" *New York Review of Books*, November 5, 1998, pp. 56–60.

8. Richard Atkinson, University of California Office of the President, media advisory, March 16, 1998 (University of California Archives, henceforth UCA).

9. Adam Cohen, "In California and Texas, Two Attempts to Maintain Campus Diversity Falter on Race," *The Nation*, 151, no. 15 (April 20 1998).

10. W. S. Swail and L. W. Perna, "Pre-college Outreach Programs: A National Perspective," in W. Tierney and L. Hagedorn (ed.), *Increasing Access to College: Extending Possibilities for All Students* (Albany: State University of New York Press, 2002).

11. University of California Office of the President, *The Schools and UC: A Guide to the University of California's Pre-Collegiate Programs* (Oakland: University of California, 1995) (UCA).

12. Ibid.

13. See John Aubrey Douglass, "A Reflection and Prospectus on California Higher Education: The Beginning of a New History," *California Policy Issues Annual*, March 2002.

14. Richard J. Coley, *Dreams Deferred: High School Dropouts in the United States* (Princeton, NJ: Educational Testing Service, 1995): 13.

15. Pat McDonough, J. Korn, and E. Yamasaki, "Access, Equity, and the Privatization of College Counseling," *The Review of Higher Education*, 20, no. 3 (1997): 297–317; National Center for Education Statistics, *Digest of Education Statistics* (Washington, DC: Department of Education, Office of Educational Research and Improvement, 1992).

16. California Department of Education, Educational Demographics Unit—CBEDS (October collection), 1998–1999.

17. See College Entrance Examination Board, *Access to Excellence: A Report on the Future of the Advanced Placement Program* (New York: CEEB, 2001).

18. Bob Laird, "Two Faces of the College Board: The Drive for Financial Success Now Dominates Its Current Direction," *CrossTalk*, 12, no. 2 (Spring 2004).

19. Saul Geiser and Veronica Santelcies, "The Role of Advanced Placement and Honors Courses in College Admissions," Center for Studies in Higher Education, University of California, Research and Occasional Papers, CSHE 3.04, June 2004.

20. California State University Institute for Education Reform, "The Advanced Placement Program: California's 1997–98 Experience," (Sacramento: California State University, 1999).

21. Ben Wildavsky, "Achievement Testing Gets Its Day in Court," *U.S. News and World Report*, September 27, 1999.

22. Report of the University of California Outreach Task Force for the Board of Regents of the University of California, *New Directions for Outreach*, University of California Office of the President, July 1997 (UCA); Kenneth R. Weiss, "UC Proposes Push to Ready Disadvantaged for College," *Los Angeles Times*, May 21, 1997.

23. See John Aubrey Douglass, *The California Idea and American Higher Education* (Stanford, CA: Stanford University Press, 2000): 216–19.

24. William Trombley, "California's Improved Financial Aid Program," *CrossTalk*, 8, no. 4 (Fall 2000).

25. Kellogg Commission on the Future of State and Land-Grant Universities, "Returning to Our Roots: Student Access," May 1998.

26. See David A. Hawkins and Jessica Lautz, *State of College Admissions*, National Association for College Admissions Counseling, March 2005.

27. Report of the University of California Outreach Task Force, *New Directions for Outreach*; see also California Postsecondary Education Commission, *Progress Report on the Effectiveness of Collaborative Student Academic Development Programs*. Sacramento: CPEC, Commission Report 96-11, December 1996.

28. Interview with author, May 22, 2001.

29. Strategic Review Panel on UC Educational Outreach to the President of the University of California, *Redefining Educational Outreach*, University of California Office of the President, February 2003 (UCA).

30. Board of Admissions and Relations with Schools, "First-Year Implementation of Comprehensive Review in Freshman Admissions," University of California, Office of the President, November 2002 (UCA).

31. Mary Ann Roser, "Groups Call UT's Efforts Lacking: Civil Rights Groups Want to Intervene in University's Appeal of *Hopwood* Case," *Austin American-Statesman*, June 9, 1998.

32. For a review of percentage plans, see U.S. Commission on Civil Rights, "Beyond Percentage Plans: Challenges of Equal Opportunity in Higher Education," Office of Civil Rights Evaluation, staff report, November 2002.

33. Ken Herman and Ralph K. M. Haurwitz, "Perry Wants Top 10 Percent Law Revised," *Austin American-Statesman*, May 26, 2004.

34. See John Aubrey Douglass, "Setting the Conditions of Admissions: The Role of University of California Faculty in Policymaking," University of California Academic Senate, February 1997 (UCA).

35. Richard Flacks and Rodolfo Alvarez, "Towards Fairness in UC Admissions," Center for Research on Chicano Studies, UCLA, November 1996.

36. Ibid.

37. "Eligibility of California's 1996 High School Graduates for Admission to the State's Public Universities: A Report of the California Postsecondary Education Commission," December 1997; Academic Assembly, University of California, "Report of the Board of Admissions and Relations with Schools," October 29, 1998.

38. Academic Assembly, University of California, "Report of the Board of Admissions and Relations with Schools," February 24, 1998.

39. Ibid.

40. Ibid.

41. Keith Widaman, testimony before the hearing of the California State Senate Select Subcommittee on Higher Education Admissions and Outreach, Sacramento, California, May 5, 1998.

42. Kenneth R. Weiss, "UC System Tries to Mask Applicants' Racial Identity," *Los Angeles Times*, November 18, 1998.

43. "Reject Proposition 54," *Sacramento Bee*, September 29, 2003.

44. Minutes, University of California Board of Regents, May 15, 1998 (UCA).

45. Report of the Task Force on Undergraduate Admissions Criteria, University of California Office of the President, December 1995 (UCA).

46. University of California Board of Regents, Policy Ensuring Equal Treatment—Admissions (SP-1), sect. 5, approved July 12, 1995 (UCA).

47. Rebecca Trounson, "UC Berkeley Urges Changes in Admissions," *Los Angeles Times*, May 24, 2001.

48. University of California Board of Regents, "Future Admissions, Employment, and Contracting Policies—Resolution Rescinding SP-1 and SP-2," May 16, 2001 (UCA).

49. Terri Hardy, "UC Ends Race Ban Under Pressure: Regents Also Say Students Won't Get in Solely on Academics," *Sacramento Bee*, May 17, 2001.

50. Ibid.

51. Michelle Locke, "UC Regents Repeal Affirmative Action Ban," Associated Press, May 16, 2001.

52. Hardy, "UC Ends Race Ban Under Pressure."

53. Locke, "UC Regents Repeal Affirmative Action Ban."

54. The regents' new resolution rescinding SP-1 stated, "In keeping with longstanding Regents policy, The Regents reaffirm that the Academic Senate shall determine the conditions for admission to the University, subject to the approval of The Regents, as provided in Standing Order 105.2."

55. Hardy, "UC Ends Race Ban Under Pressure."

56. "First-Year Implementation of Comprehensive Review in Freshman Admissions: A Progress Report from the Board of Admissions and Relations with Schools," November 2002.

57. *Undergraduate Access to the University of California After the Elimination of Race-Conscious Policies*, University of California Office of the President, Student Academic Services, March 2003, pp. 35–39 (UCA).

58. Ibid., p. 10.

Chapter 9

1. Patricia Gandara and Julie Maxwell-Jolly, *Priming the Pump: Strategies for Increasing the Achievement of Underrepresented Minority Undergraduates* (Princeton, NJ: The College Board, December 1999): 9.

2. Latino Eligibility Task Force, *Latino Student Eligibility and Participation in the University of California: "Ya Basta!"* University of California, Chicano/ Latino Policy Project, Institute for the Study of Social Change, July 1997.

3. Ibid.

4. Keith F. Widaman, "Proposed Changes in UC Eligibility Criteria to Increase Educational Access for Students Across California," Assembly of the Academic Senate, Notice of Meeting, University of California, May 21, 1998 (University of California Archives, henceforth UCA).

5. J. Kowarsky, D. Clatfelter, and K. Widaman, "Predicting University Grade-Point Average in a Class of University of California Freshmen: An Assessment of the Validity of A–F GPA and Test Scores as Indicators of Future Academic Performance," University of California, Office of the President, 1998 (UCA); Keith Widaman, testimony before the Hearing of the California

State Senate Select Subcommittee on Higher Education Admissions and Out-reach, May 5, 1998 (UCA).

6. Minutes, University of California Board of Regents, May 15, 1998 (UCA).

7. Widaman, "Proposed Changes in UC Eligibility Criteria," p. 26.

8. See Saul Geiser and Roger Studley, "UC and the SAT: Predictive Validity and Differential Impact of the SAT I and the SAT II at the University of California," University of California, Office of the President, October 24, 2001 (UCA).

9. Richard Atkinson, "A California Perspective on the SAT," Conference on the Future of Standardized Testing in University Admissions, University of California Santa Barbara, November 16, 2001 (UCA).

10. Ibid.

11. Richard Atkinson, "Standardized Tests and Access to American Universities," Robert H. Atwell Distinguished Lecture, eighty-third annual meeting of the American Council on Education, February 2001.

12. Richard C. Atkinson, "Rethinking the SAT," *The Presidency*, Spring 2001, pp. 21–27.

13. Kurt M. Landgraf, "Let's Focus on the Real Issue," *The Presidency*, Spring 2001.

14. Diana Jean Schemo, "Head of U. of California Seeks to End SAT Use in Admissions," *The New York Times*, February 17, 2001.

15. Jeffrey Brainard, "U. of California's President Proposes Dropping the SAT Requirement," *Academe Today*, February 19, 2001.

16. Robert Laird, "Two Faces of the College Board: The Drive for Financial Success Now Dominates Its Current Direction," *CrossTalk*, Spring 2004.

17. Ward Connerly, "Sensitivity vs. Standards," California Association of Scholars, Op-Ed, February 25, 2001.

18. Ibid.

19. Jack Citrin, "For True Diversity, Universities Should Consider a Lottery," *Sacramento Bee*, July 22, 2001.

20. John Cloud, "Should the SAT Matter?" *Time Magazine*, March 4, 2001.

21. Peter Sacks, "SAT—A Failing Test," *Nation*, 272, no. 13 (April 2, 2001): 7.

22. Atkinson, "A California Perspective on the SAT."

23. Brainard, "U. of California's President Proposes Dropping the SAT Requirement."

24. Geiser and Studley, "UC and the SAT," p. 16.

25. W. Camara and G. Echternacht, *The SAT and High School Grades: Utility in Predicting Success in College* (Princeton, NJ: College Entrance Examination Board, 2001).

26. Geiser and Studley, "UC and the SAT," pp. 2, 8.

27. See Rebecca Zwick, Terran Brown, and Jeffrey C. Sklar, "California and the SAT: A Reanalysis of University of California Admissions Data," Center for Studies in Higher Education, Research and Occasional Papers, June 2004; see also Rebecca Zwick, *Rethinking the SAT: The Future of Standardized Testing in University Admissions* (New York: RoutledgeFalmer, 2004).

28. California Postsecondary Education Commission, "Examining Standardized Testing in the Context of University Admissions: A Panel Discussion," Sacramento: California Postsecondary Education Commission, August 2001.

29. Ibid.

30. Author's interview with Warren Fox, Former Director, California Postsecondary Education Commission, October 2004.

31. Peter Schrag, "Atkinson's New-Model UC Reforms and Innovations," *Sacramento Bee*, April 10, 2002.

32. John Cloud, "Inside the New SAT," *Time Magazine*, October 27, 2003.

33. College Entrance Examination Board, *The New SAT and Your School* (Princeton, NJ: College Board, 2002).

34. The College Board, "The College Board Announces a New SAT—World's Most Widely Used Admissions Test Will Emphasize College Success Skills, Writing Test to Be Introduced," press release, June 27, 2002.

35. "The Week," *National Review*, 54, no. 7 (April 22, 2002).

36. Lawrence H. Summers, "Every Child Getting Ahead: The Role of Education," speech before the College Board Forum, Chicago, November 1, 2004.

37. Juan E. Mestas, "We Can't Reduce Reality to a 1,600-Point Scale," *The Presidency*, Spring 2001, p. 23.

38. "Kids Are Taking the SAT Earlier and Earlier, but Is It a Good Thing?" CBS News Sacramento, http://cbs13.com/, May 27, 2002.

Chapter 10

1. U.S. Supreme Court, *Grutter v. Bolinger*, June 2003.

2. Ibid., p. 17.

3. Ibid.; Court cases sited by O'Connor include *Wieman v. Updegraff*, 344 U.S. 183, 195 (1952) (Frankfurter, J., concurring); *Sweezy v. New Hampshire*, 354 U.S. 234, 250 (1957); *Shelton v. Tucker*, 364 U.S. 479, 487 (1960); *Keyishian v. Board of Regents of the University of the State of New York*, 385 U.S., at 603.

4. *Sweezy v. New Hampshire*.

5. *Grutter v. Bolinger*, p. 16.

6. "The Law School's educational judgment," stated Justice O'Connor in the majority opinion, "that such diversity is essential to its educational mission is one to which we defer. The Law School's assessment that diversity will, in

fact, yield educational benefits is substantiated by respondents and their *amici*." *Grutter v. Bolinger*, p. 17.

7. "Another Swing at Affirmative Action," *Inside Higher Ed*, June 6, 2006.

8. John Henry Newman, *The Idea of a University* (Notre Dame, IN: University of Notre Dame Press, 1852).

9. Anthony Lising Antonio, "When Does Race Matter in College Friendships? Exploring Men's Diverse and Homogeneous Friendship Groups," *Review of Higher Education*, 27, no. 4 (2003): 553–75; University Committee on Minority Issues, "Building a Multiracial, Multicultural University Community: Final Report of the University Committee on Minority Issues," Stanford University, 1989.

10. See Mitchell J. Chang, D. Witt, J. Jones, and K. Hakuta (ed.), *Compelling Interest: Examining the Evidence on Racial Dynamics in Colleges and Universities* (Stanford, CA: Stanford University Press, 2003); "Supplemental Expert Report of Patricia Y. Gurin." *Grutter, et al. v. Bolinger, et al.* (11 January 2001); Sylvia Hurtado, J. F. Milem, A. Clayton-Pederson, and W. A. Allen, "Enhancing Campus Climates for Racial/Ethnic Diversity: Educational Policy and Practice," *The Review of Higher Education*, 21, no. 3 (1998): 279–302.

11. Hans P. Johnson, Laura Hill, and Mary Helm, *New Trends in Newborns: Fertility Rates and Patterns in California*, Public Policy Institute of California, August 2001.

12. See U.S. Department of Education, National Center for Education Statistics, Higher Education General Information Survey (HEGIS), "Fall Enrollment in Colleges and Universities," Surveys, 2000.

13. *Grutter v. Bolinger.*

14. Martin Trow, "The Public and Private Lives of Higher Education," *Daedalus*, 104, no. 1 (Winter 1975): 113–27.

15. Richard Flacks, Gregg Thomson, John Douglass, and Kyra Caspary, *Learning and Academic Engagement in the Multiversity: Results of the First University of California Undergraduate Experience Survey* (Berkeley, CA: Center for Studies in Higher Education, 2004).

16. Ibid.

17. See Alexander W. Astin and Leticia Oseguera, "The Declining 'Equity' of American Higher Education," *The Review of Higher Education*, 27, no. 3 (Spring 2004): 321–41; see also Michael McPherson and M. O. Schapiro, *An Overview of Trends and Patterns in Participation and Financing in US Higher Education* (Paris: OECD, 1998).

18. State Higher Education Executive Officers (SHEEO), *State Higher Education Finance: FY 2005* (Boulder, CO: SHEEO, 2006).

19. For a useful discussion on why rising costs at higher education institutions have outpaced inflation, see Frank H. T. Rhodes, *The Creation of the Future: The Role of the American University* (Ithaca, NY: Cornell University Press, 2001): 136–61.

20. John Aubrey Douglass, "How All Globalization Is Local: Countervailing Forces and Their Influence on Higher Education Markets," *Higher Education Policy*, 18, no. 4 (December 2005): 445–73.

21. See Watson Scott Swail and Donald E. Heller, *Changes in Tuition Policies: Natural Policy Experiments in Five Countries*, Canada Millennium Scholarship Foundation, August 2004.

22. Michael S. McPherson and Morton O. Schapiro, *Reinforcing Stratification in American Higher Education: Some Disturbing Trends*, National Center for Postsecondary Improvement, Stanford University, 1999.

23. Linda A. Bell, "Uncertain Times: The Annual Report on the Economic Status of the Profession, 2000–2001," *Academe*, April–May, 2001, 26–35.

24. Steven Brint, "Can Public Research Universities Compete?" unpublished paper, Pennsylvania State University Sesquicentennial Celebration, February 25–26, 2005, p. 4.

25. David Ward, "That Old Familiar Feeling—With an Important Difference," *The Presidency*, Winter 2004.

26. Katharine C. Lyall and Kathleen R. Sell, *The True Genius of America at Risk: Are We Losing Our Public Universities to de Facto Privatization?* (Portsmouth, NH: Praeger/Greenwood Press, 2006).

27. Norton Grubb, "The Anglo-American Approach to Vocationalism," Research Paper 51, Centre on Skills, Knowledge and Organizational Performance, Oxford and Warwick Universities, October 2004; see also W. Norton Grubb and Marvin Lazerson, *The Education Gospel: The Economic Power of Schooling* (Cambridge, MA: Harvard University Press, 2004).

28. Mark Yudof, "Is the Public Research University Dead?" *Chronicle of Higher Education*, January 11, 2002, sect. B24.

29. See Roger L. Geiger, *Knowledge & Money: Research Universities and the Paradox of the Marketplace* (Stanford, CA: Stanford University Press, 2004): 28–36.

30. See American Council on Education, *Overview of Higher Education in the United States: Diversity, Access, and the Role of the Marketplace* (Washington, D.C.: American Council on Education, 2004).

31. Publics include Cornell (state colleges), Michigan State, Ohio State, Penn State (College Station), SUNY Albany, University of Texas (Austin), University of Alabama, University of California (Berkeley), University of Illinois (Urbana-Champaign), University of Michigan (Ann Arbor), University of Minnesota (Twin Cities), University of Missouri (Columbia), University of Wisconsin (Madison), and the University of Virginia; privates include Cornell (endowed professional colleges), Baylor University, Brown University, Harvard, MIT, NYU, Stanford, University of Chicago, University of Pennsylvania, University of Southern California, and Yale. This analysis was first presented in David Ward and John Douglass, "The Perils and Promise of Variable

Fees: Institutional and Public Policy Responses in the UK and US," *Perspectives: Policy and Practice in Higher Education* (UK), 9, no. 1 (2005): 29–35.

32. Ward and Douglass, "The Perils and Promise of Variable Fees."

33. David Ward and John Douglass, "Higher Education and the Specter of Variable Fees: Public Policy and Institutional Responses in the United States and United Kingdom," *Higher Education Management and Policy* (OECD), 18, no. 1 (2006): 1–28.

34. For a study of the Curry School at the University of Virginia, see David L. Kirp, *Shakespeare, Einstein, and the Bottom Line: The Marketing of Higher Education* (Cambridge, MA: Harvard University Press, 2003).

35. See Thomas J. Kane, "Assessing the American Financial Aid System: What We Know, What We Need to Know," in Maureen Devlin (ed.), *Forum Futures 2001: Exploring the Future of Higher Education* (Cambridge, MA: Forum for the Future of Higher Education, 2001): 63–66; Bruce Johnstone and P. Shroff-Mehta, "Higher Education Finance and Accessibility: An International Comparative Examination of Tuition and Financial Assistance Policies," International Comparative Higher Education Finance and Accessibility Project (New York: University of Buffalo, 2001).

36. Michael Mumper, "The Paradox of College Prices: Five Stories with No Clear Lesson," in Donald E. Heller (ed.), *The States and Public Higher Education Policy: Affordability, Access, and Accountability* (Baltimore, MD: Johns Hopkins University Press, 2001): 39–62.

37. Kirp, *Shakespeare, Einstein, and the Bottom Line*, p. 3.

38. Clark Kerr, *The Uses of the University* (Cambridge, MA: Harvard University Press, 1964): 49.

39. Robert Berdahl, "How Public Are Public Universities in the United States?" Speech before the American Association of Universities, University of California, Berkeley, January 26, 2004.

40. Morton Keller and Phyllis Keller, *Making Harvard Modern: The Rise of America's University* (Cambridge: Oxford University Press, 2001).

41. Keith Widaman and John Douglass, "VIP Admissions at the University of California: A Brief on Four Possible Options," Universitywide Academic Senate Office, October 23, 1997; "Policy Statement on Admissions Beyond the Scope of Established Admissions Criteria," University of California Academic Council Meeting, January 14, 1998.

42. Peter Schmidt, "Affirmative Action, Relatively Speaking at Many Selective Colleges, the Children of Employees Get an Edge in the Admissions Office," *Chronicle of Higher Education*, January 14, 2005.

43. American Council on Education, *Shifting Ground: Autonomy, Accountability, and Privatization of Public Higher Education* (Washington, DC: American Council on Education, 2004): 9.

Chapter 11

1. Alexis de Tocqueville, *Democracy in America*, vol. 2 (New York: Vintage Books, 1945): 108.

2. A. H. Halsey, "The Changing Functions of Universities in Advanced Industrial Societies," *Harvard Educational Review*, 30, no. 2 (1960): 118–27.

3. Sir Eric Ashby, *Any Person, Any Study: An Essay on Higher Education in the United States* (New York: McGraw-Hill, 1971): 3.

4. Ibid., p. 5.

5. Organisation for Economic Co-operation and Development, *Education at a Glance: Briefing Notes United States* (Paris: OECD, September 16, 2003).

6. Sandra Ruppert, *Closing the College Participation Gap*, Education Commission of the States, 2003; William G. Tierney, *State of College Admissions*, National Association for College Admissions Counseling, January 2005.

7. The Organisation for Economic Co-operation and Development, *Education at a Glance 2006* (Paris: OECD, 2006), p. 42, 50.

8. ECD, *Education at a Glance 2006*, p. 32.

9. Clifford Adelman, *Principal Indicators of Student Academic Histories in Postsecondary Education: 1972–2000* (Washington, DC: Institute of Education Sciences, U.S. Department of Education, 2004): 20.

10. John Aubrey Douglass, "Investment Patterns in California Higher Education and Policy Options for a Possible Future," CSHE Research and Occasional Papers Series, CSHE 5.02, April 2002.

11. Robert Fountain, Marcia Cosgrove, and Petra Abraham, "Keeping California's Edge: The Growing Demand for Highly Educated Workers" Campaign for College Opportunity, Oakland, California, April 2006.

12. OECD, *Education at a Glance 2005*, Indicator C6, p. 50.

13. European Higher Education Area: Joint Declaration of the European Ministers of Education, Bologna on June 19, 1999.

14. For a comparative look at European mass higher education and the influence of the American model, see Ted Tapper and David Palfreyman (ed.), *Understanding Mass Higher Education: Comparative Perspectives on Access* (London: RoutledgeFalmer, 2005).

15. Organisation for Economic Co-operation and Development, *Education at a Glance* (Paris: OECD, August 2001).

16. Quoted in Jack Cassidy, "Winners and Losers: The Truth About Free Trade," *The New Yorker*, August 2, 2004.

17. Committee on Prospering in the Global Economy of the 21st Century, National Academies, *Rising Above the Gathering Storm: Energizing and Employing America for a Brighter Economic Future* (Washington, DC: National Academics Press, 2006); original estimates in this publication were revised; see "The Disappearing Chinese Engineers," *Inside Higher Education*, June 13, 2006.

18. National Academies, "Broad Federal Effort Urgently Needed to Create New, High-Quality Jobs for All Americans in the 21st Century," press release, October 12, 2005.

19. See National Academies, *Rising Above the Gathering Storm*.

20. Cassidy, "Winners and Losers."

21. National Sciences Foundation, *Science and Engineering Indicators 2006* (Washington DC: National Science Foundation, 2006).

22. Barry McGaw and Andreas Schleichler, "OECD Briefing Notes for the United States," *Education at a Glance 2005*.

23. Paul E. Barton, *One-Third of a Nation: Rising Dropout Rates and Declining Opportunities* (Princeton, NJ: Educational Testing Service, 2005).

24. U.S. Department of Education, National Center for Education Statistics, *Dropout Rates in the United States: 2001*; see also NCES, *Digest of Educational Statistics*: 2003, Table 102.

25. Barton, *One-Third of a Nation*, p. 4.

26. Achieve, Inc., *The Expectations Gap: A 50-State Review of High School Graduation Requirements* (Washington, DC: Achieve, Inc., December 2004): 4.

27. Microsoft Chairman Bill Gates Before the National Governors' Educational Summit, March 1, 2005.

28. Robert A. Jones, "Where the Boys Aren't: for Young Males, the Drift Away from Academic Achievement Is a Trend," *CrossTalk*, 13, no. 3 (Spring 2005): 6–8.

29. Claudia Goldin and Lawrence Katz, "The Returns to Skill in the United States Across the Twentieth Century," National Bureau of Economic Research, April 11, 1999.

30. Ruppert, *Closing the College Participation Gap*, p. 16.

31. David Ward, "That Old Familiar Feeling—With an Important Difference," *The Presidency*, Winter 2004.

32. U.S. Department of Education, *A Test of Leadership: Charting the Future of U.S. Higher Education*, Report of the Secretary of Education's Commission on the Future of Higher Education (Washington, DC: U.S. Department of Education, pre-publication September 2006).

33. Donald E. Heller, "Trends in Public Colleges and Universities," in Donald E. Heller (ed.), *The States and Public Higher Education Policy* (Baltimore, MD: Johns Hopkins University Press, 2001): 11–38.

34. Ibid.

35. See Alexander W. Astin and Leticia Oseguera, "The Declining 'Equity' of American Higher Education," *The Review of Higher Education*, 27, no. 3 (Spring 2004): 321–41.

36. Rupert Wilkinson, *Aiding Students, Buying Students: Financial Aid in America* (Nashville, TN: Vanderbilt University Press, 2005).

37. L. L. Leslie and P. T. Brinkman, "Student Price Response in Higher Education," *Journal of Higher Education*, 58, 181–204.

38. Tom J. Kane, "Rising Public College Tuition and College Entry: How Well Do Public Subsidies Promote Access to College?" Working Paper Series No. 5164 (Cambridge, MA: National Bureau of Economic Research, 1995).

39. Richard B. Freeman, *The Over-Educated American* (New York: Academic Press, 1976).

40. Ibid., p. 184.

41. Ibid., p. 188.

42. Ibid.

43. For an example of this broadly excepted projection, see Lyman A. Glenny, John R. Shea, Janet H. Ruyle, and Kathryn H. Freschi, *Presidents Confront Reality: From Edifice Complex to University Without Walls* (San Francisco: Jossey-Bass, 1977).

44. Richard Flacks, Greg Thomson, John Aubrey Douglass, and Kyra Caspary, *Learning and Academic Engagement in the Multiversity: Results of the First University of California Undergraduate Experience Survey* (Berkeley, CA: Center for Studies in Higher Education, July 2004).

45. John Bishop, *Is an Oversupply of College Graduates Coming?* National Center for Postsecondary Improvement, School of Education, Stanford University, 1997.

46. Gary Becker, *Investment in Human Capital* (New York: Columbia University Press, 1964); T. W. Schultz, *Investment in Human Capital* (New York: Free Press, 1971).

47. Alan Ryan, "New Labour and Higher Education," *Oxford Review of Education*, 31, no. 1 (March 2005): 87–100.

48. David Brooks, "Psst! 'Human Capital'" *The New York Times*, Op-Ed, November 13, 2005, p. 12.

49. For an impressive synthesis of these and other studies, see Elhanan Helpman, *The Mystery of Economic Growth* (Cambridge, MA: Belknap Press, 2004): 42.

50. David Mitch, "The Rise of Mass Education and Its Contribution to Economic Growth in Europe, 1800–2000," fourth European Historical Economics Society Conference, Merton College, Oxford.

51. Ibid.

52. Ibid.

53. Golden and Katz, "The Returns to Skill in the United States Across the Twentieth Century."

54. OECD, *Education at a Glance 2005*, "OECD Briefing Notes for the United States."

55. *The Investment Payoff: A 50-State Analysis of the Public and Private Benefits of Higher Education* (Washington, DC: Institute for Higher Education Policy, 2005).

56. Sandy Baum and Kathleen Payea, *Education Pays 2004: The Benefits of Higher Education for Individuals and Society*, rev. ed. (Princeton, NJ: College Entrance Examination Board, 2005).

57. This chart is in part adopted from various sources, including Howard Bowen, *Investment in Learning: The Individual and Social Value of American Higher Education* (San Francisco: Jossey-Bass, 1977); and *The Investment Payoff: A 50-State Analysis of the Public and Private Benefits of Higher Education*.

58. *Higher Education for American Democracy*, A Report of the President's Commission on Higher Education, Washington, DC., December 1947, vol. 1: 34.

59. Alison Wolf, "Education and Economic Performance: Simplistic Theories and Their Consequences," *Oxford Review of Economic Policy*, 20, no. 2 (2004): 315–33.

60. Alison Wolf, *Does Education Matter: Myths About Education and Economic Growth* (London: Penguin, 2002); see also Ewart Keep and Ken Mayhew, "The Economic and Distributional Implications of Current Policies on Higher Education," *Oxford Review of Economic Policy*, 20, no. 2 (Summer 2004); Ryan, "New Labour and Higher Education."

61. Wolf, "Education and Economic Performance," p. 316.

62. Ibid.

63. Joseph Kahn, "Rioting in China over Label on College Diplomas," *The New York Times*, June 22, 2006.

64. In his book *The American College and the Culture of Aspiration* (Ithaca, NY: Cornell University Press, 1986), David O. Lavine discusses this theme.

65. Department of Education and Skills, England, *The Future of Higher Education* (Norwich: HMSO, 2003): 68.

66. Organisation for Economic Co-operation and Development, *Education at a Glance, August 2004* (Paris: OECD, 2004).

67. For an analysis of how the Bureau of Labor Statistics and others have estimated the need for college graduates, see Bishop, *Is An Oversupply of College Graduates Coming?*: 6–10.

68. Ibid.

69. National Center for Education Statistics, *Education Indicator: An International Perspective* (Washington, DC: U.S. Department of Education, 2004).

70. John W. Gardner, *Excellence: Can We Be Equal and Excellent Too?* (New York: Harper & Row, 1961).

71. Among the growing body of literature on this topic, see G. Glaeser, R. La Porta, F. Lopez-de-Silanes, and A. Schleiger, "Do Institutions Cause Growth," National Bureau of Economic Research Working Paper No. W10568, 2004; D. Acemoglou, S. Johnson, and J. A. Robinson, "The Colonial Origins of Comparative Development: An Empirical Investigation," *American Economic Review*, 2001, 91: 1369–1401.

72. John Aubrey Douglass, "How All Globalization is Local: Countervailing Forces and their Influence on Higher Education Markets," *Higher Education Policy*, vol. 18, no. 4, Dec 2005: 445–73.

73. Ruppert, *Closing the College Participation Gap.*

74. John Aubrey Douglass, "Higher Education as a National Resource," *Change Magazine*, vol. 37, no. 5, Sep/Oct 2005; 30–38.

Note: Throughout the index, UC stands for University of California; page numbers in *italics* indicate figures or tables.